Economic Theory and the Cities

STUDIES IN URBAN ECONOMICS

Under the Editorship of

Edwin S. Mills

Princeton University

Norman J. Glickman. ECONOMETRIC ANALYSIS OF REGIONAL SYSTEMS: Exploratons in Model Building and Policy Analysis

J. Vernon Henderson. ECONOMIC THEORY AND THE CITIES

Norman J. Glick. THE GROWTH AND MANAGEMENT OF THE JAPANESE URBAN SYSTEM

George S. Tolley, Philip E. Graves, and John L. Gardner, URBAN GROWTH POLICY IN A MARKET ECONOMY

David Segal (Ed.). THE ECONOMICS OF NEIGHBORHOOD

R. D. Norton. CITY LIFE-CYCLES AND AMERICAN URBAN POLICY

John F. McDonald. ECONOMIC ANALYSIS OF AN URBAN HOUSING MARKET

Daniel Feenberg and Edwin S. Mills. MEASURING THE BENEFITS OF WATER POLLUTION ABATEMENT

Michael J. Greenwood. MIGRATION AND ECONOMIC GROWTH IN THE UNITED STATES: National, Regional, and Metropolitan Perspectives

Takahiro Miyao. DYNAMIC ANALYSIS OF THE URBAN ECONOMY

Katherine L. Bradbury, Anthony Downs, and Kenneth A. Small. FUTURES FOR A DECLINING CITY: Simulations for the Cleveland Area

Charles F. Mueller. THE ECONOMICS OF LABOR MIGRATION: A Behavioral Analysis

Douglas B. Diamond, Jr. and George S. Tolley (Eds.). THE ECONOMICS OF URBAN AMENITIES

Alex Anas. RESIDENTIAL LOCATION MARKETS AND URBAN TRANSPORTATION: Economic Theory, Econometrics, and Policy Analysis with Discrete Choice Models

Joseph Friedman and Daniel H. Weinberg. THE ECONOMICS OF HOUSING VOUCHERS

George R. Zodrow (Ed.). LOCAL PROVISION OF PUBLIC SERVICES: The Tiebout Model after Twenty-Five Years

Economic Theory and the Cities

J. VERNON HENDERSON
Department of Economics
Brown University
Providence, Rhode Island

Second Edition
1985

ACADEMIC PRESS, INC.
(Harcourt Brace Jovanovich, Publishers)

Orlando   San Diego   New York   London
Toronto   Montreal   Sydney   Tokyo

ACADEMIC PRESS, INC.
Orlando, Florida 32887

United Kingdom Edition published by
ACADEMIC PRESS INC. (LONDON) LTD.
24–28 Oval Road, London NW1 7DX

Library of Congress Cataloging in Publication Data

Henderson, J. Vernon.
    Economic theory and the cities.

    (Studies in urban economics)
    Bibliography: p.
    Includes index.
    1. Urban economics. I. Title. II. Series.
HT321.H397   1985   330.9173'2   84-24353
ISBN 0-12-340352-9 (alk. paper)

PRINTED IN THE UNITED STATES OF AMERICA

85 86 87 88   9 8 7 6 5 4 3 2 1

Contents

6
Other Housing Topics   117

7
Transportation and Modal Choice   134

8
Transportation and the Peak-Load Problem   153

Preface

In this book I present what I believe to be the most important theoretical topics in urban economics. Since urban economics is a rather diffuse field, any presentation is necessarily selective, reflecting personal tastes and opinions. Given that, I note on what basis I chose the material that is presented and developed.

First, the basic spatial model of a monocentric city is presented, since it lays the foundation for thinking about many of the topics in urban economics. The consideration of space and spatial proximity is one central feature of urban economics that distinguishes it from other branches of economics. The positive and negative externalities generated by activities locating in close spatial proximity are central to analysis of urban phenomena. However, in writing this book I have tried to maintain strong links between urban economics and recent developments in mainstream economic theory. This is reflected in the chapters that follow, which present models of aspects of the most important topics in urban economics—externalities, housing, transportation, local public finance, suburbanization, and community development. In these chapters, concepts from developments in economics over the last decade or so are woven into the traditional approaches to modeling these topics. Examples are the role of contracts in housing markets and community development; portfolio analysis in analyzing housing tenure choice and investment decisions; the time-inconsistency problem in formulating long-term economic relationships between communities, developers, and local governments; search in housing markets; and dynamic analysis in housing markets and traffic scheduling. The book ends with chapters on general equilibrium models of systems of cities, demonstrating how individual cities fit into an economy and interact with each other.

This book is written both as a reference book for people in the profession and for use as a graduate text. In this edition, a strong effort has been made to present the material at a level and in a style suitable for graduate students. The edition has greatly expanded the sections on housing and local public finance so these sections could be studied profitably by a broad range of graduate students. Recommended prerequisites are an undergraduate urban economics course and a year of graduate-level microeconomic theory. It is possible that the book can be used in very advanced undergraduate courses if the students are well versed in microeconomics and are quantitatively oriented.

Acknowledgments

I developed much of the material in this book in journal articles and for graduate urban economics courses at Queen's University, The University of Chicago, and Brown University. Most of the material in the first edition had been presented at some stage in its development in the Urban Economics Workshop at The University of Chicago. The comments of George Tolley as well as Charles Upton and the students in that workshop were instrumental in shaping my view of what is relevant and important in urban economics. I also benefited from many discussions with Peter Mieszkowski on a variety of issues in urban public economics.

The new material in this edition has been developed in my graduate courses at Brown University. The stimulating interaction with the students both in class and as they have worked on dissertations has helped refine much of the material. Parts of the material have also been presented in workshops at a variety of universities around the country and have benefited from those presentations.

I thank Marion Wathey for her skillful typing and my family for their support.

1

Spatial Equilibrium and the Spatial Characteristics of a Simple City

In this chapter a simple model of a city is developed, with the following guidelines in mind. In specifying the model, we want to incorporate the basic features of the economic structure of cities. Thus the model should capture the essence of spatial interaction between producers and consumers in a city, and it should yield theoretical results that correspond to the basic empirical facts about cities. For example, the model should show that land rents, population density, and building heights decline with distance from the city center, as demonstrated in empirical work (e.g., Muth, 1969). It should be able to explain why higher-income people tend to live farther from city centers than lower-income people and why wages vary spatially within a city. When different cities with similar transportation technologies are compared, the level of rents, population density, and building heights should increase with city size. We also want a model of a city that can be adapted to enable us to analyze a system of cities and to describe equilibrium city sizes, factor movements, and trade patterns among the cities of an economy. Finally, the model should be consistent with the models and analyses of later chapters on housing, transportation, and public finance, which detail different aspects of urban living and are useful in analyzing specific urban problems.

In specifying the nature of cities in the model, the following assumptions are made. The economy consists of a flat featureless plain. Instead of the population spreading evenly over the plain, concentrations of population, or cities, form because it is assumed there are scale economies in production. Exploitation of these scale economies requires that there be concentrations of employment in production activities. These scale economies result from scale efficiencies in input markets, marketing, communications, transportation, and/or public service provision. Concentration of employment results in concentration of residences occupied by people who commute to the employment centers.

In cities most or all commerical activity occurs in the central business district (CBD), which is located in the central part of the city. This central location of all commerical activity results from businesses outbidding residents for this central land. The desire for businesses to be located together at the city center follows from several assumptions. First, if firms are located together, the advantages of scale economies may be more fully realized. Second, it is assumed that all goods produced in the city are shipped to a retailing and transport node at the very center of the city where they are sold to city residents and exported to other cities. This node could be a railway station, trucking terminal, or harbor (in a semicircular city). Firms minimize the costs of shipping goods to the node by locating around the node. Finally, we note that, because the business district is at the center of the city, the total costs of commuting to work for all residents are minimized relative to the business district's being at a noncentral location.[1]

Surrounding the CBD is the residential sector where all city residents live. From their home sites residents commute to the city center and then disperse to their work sites. It is this feature of most or all residents commuting to work in the CBD that distinguishes a simple city from more complicated cities, where only part of the city's labor force commutes to the CBD. At various points in the book the impact of non-CBD employment on the basic results of the model will be considered.

Finally, in a stable equilibrium solution, both the CBD and the total city will be symmetric circles. As shown later, this result follows when there is only one business district because the plain on which cities are located is featureless.

In the first section of this chapter the residential sector of the city is examined. Equilibrium of a household in space is analyzed. Then, building

---

[1] Being at the center of a circle minimizes the distance involved in traveling to all points in the circle. Since our city will be a circle, the central location of the CBD minimizes total commuting costs, given there can be only one business district. With two or more business districts, this proposition is no longer correct.

upon the properties of a household's equilibrium, we study long-run equilibrium in the housing and land markets. Finally, aggregate demand and supply relationships in the residential sector are derived. Throughout, the general concepts developed are illustrated with a simple example using specific functional forms. In the second section of the chapter, the commercial sector of the city is examined. Building upon the individual producer's profit maximization problem, aggregate relationships describing the commercial sector's use of labor, capital, and land are developed. These aggregate relationships will be used to determine equilibrium levels of employment and prices in Chapter 2.

1. THE RESIDENTIAL SECTOR

1.1 Consumer Residential Choice and Equilibrium in the Residential Sector

Residents in the city maximize utility defined over market goods and amenities subject to a budget constraint and the amenity choices facing them. Market goods are the city's own traded good x produced in the CBD, the city's import good z, and housing services h, which are rented from housing producers. The prices of the traded goods, p_x and p_z, do not vary within the city since these goods are all purchased from the same market at the center of the city. The rental price of housing may vary spatially; and, in fact, housing and housing prices are distinct items in the model.

Housing represents both a consumer good and a particular spatial location in the city. Associated with each spatial location in the residential sector is a level of amenities consumed by residents. The only amenity I consider in this chapter is leisure consumption, which is directly related, through commuting times, to access to the CBD. The rental on housing implicitly prices both housing services and access, or leisure consumption; and thus the unit price of housing $p(u)$ will vary spatially as leisure varies. This amenity formulation is perfectly general and can be expanded to include a vector of goods such as park and recreational services and clean air (see Chapter 4).[2]

With respect to leisure, we assume that residents work a fixed number of hours. Leisure is the fixed number of nonworking hours T less time spent commuting. We assume that the time it takes to commute a *unit* distance (there and back) to work is t; and t is the same everywhere in the city. (This

---

[2] I first came across the general formulation in Hartwick (1971). Diamond (1976) also used a similar formulation.

assumption implies there is no congestion; or as the number of commuters accumulates as we approach the CBD, travel speeds are unchanged.) Therefore, a consumer at distance u from the city center has leisure consumption $e(u)$ equal to

$$e(u) = T - tu.$$

Note that time costs are the only form of commuting costs in this chapter.[3] It is a straightforward exercise to add out-of-pocket commuting costs (e.g., automobile operating costs) to the model through the budget constraint. Situations where several amenities or costs vary with distance from the CBD are analyzed in Chapter 3.

Given these assumptions, I can now formally state the consumer optimization problem. Where $V(u)$ is utility at location u and y is income, the consumer

$$\max_{\text{w.r.t. } x,z,h,e,u} V(u) = V'(x(u), z(u), h(u), e(u)) \tag{1.1}$$

subject to

$$y - p_x x(u) - p_z z(u) - p(u)h(u) = 0,$$

$$T - e(u) - tu = 0.$$

For consumers this is essentially a simultaneous two-stage maximization problem. They must pick an optimal location in space, given the spatial set of amenities and housing prices; and at the optimal location, they must choose an optimal consumption bundle. For consumers *at location u*, their optimal consumption bundle is chosen according to the budget constraint and the usual first-order conditions equating price ratios with marginal rates of substitution in consumption. Given these conditions and assuming that V' is a regular utility function,[4] we can then specify individual consumer demand equations for all market goods as a function of income, all output prices, and leisure. For example, for housing

$$h(u) = h(y, p(u), p_x, p_z, e(u)), \tag{1.2}$$

where h is increasing in y and decreasing in $p(u)$.

The question we are primarily concerned with is how consumers come to choose a particular u or distance from the city center. Maximizing Equation (1.1) with respect to $e(u)$ and u yields the first-order conditions that

---

[3] I first came across this formulation in Beckmann (1974).
[4] The utility function V' should be a continuous, nondecreasing, and strictly quasi-concave function.

$\partial V'/\partial e(u) - \gamma = 0$ and $-\lambda h(u)[\partial p(u)/\partial u] - \gamma t = 0$ where γ and λ are Lagrange multipliers and are, respectively, the marginal utility of leisure and that of income. Combining to solve out γ yields the condition that holds when consumers are at their optimal locations

$$h(u)\frac{\partial p(u)}{\partial u} = -\frac{\partial V'/\partial e(u)}{\lambda}t \equiv -p_e(u)t. \qquad (1.3)$$

The term $p_e(u)$ is the monetized value of the marginal utility of leisure, where we have defined

$$p_e(u) = [\partial V'/\partial e(u)]/\lambda.$$

This term measures the marginal evaluation of leisure, which is the opportunity cost of travel time.

At their optimal locations, if consumers move an infinitesimal distance farther from the city center, they experience a loss in leisure. The value of this lost leisure is the marginal evaluation of leisure $p_e(u)$ multiplied by the reduction in leisure $-t$. Equation (1.3) states that they are exactly compensated for this lost leisure by reduced housing costs $h(u)[\partial p(u)/\partial u]$, such that utility is unchanged.[5] That is, at an optimal location they cannot improve their welfare by moving. This implies that $\partial p(u)/\partial u < 0$, where this decline in housing rents is necessary to compensate consumers for lost leisure time as they move farther from the city center. Otherwise, consumers could not be induced to live farther from the center and we could not have an equilibrium set of locations. If housing rents rose or stayed constant as consumers moved away from the city center, a consumer would always be better off moving inward since leisure would be increased with unchanged or lower housing costs.

Equation (1.3) describes a relationship between equilibrium housing rents and distance that must hold for an individual household to be in equilibrium. The next step is to derive the properties of the set of equilibrium housing prices that occurs along a ray from the city center. This set of prices is called the rent gradient. The rent gradient is defined by its height and slope, or by the level of prices at each distance from the CBD and the change in these prices as distance changes. In the next section are derived these properties and in the following section I show how the rent gradient must be consistent with equilibrium in the residential housing and land markets.

---

[5] That is, at the optimal location we are at a stationary point where infinitesimal changes in location bring no utility changes, or $dV\,du = 0$, given the constraints of the problem. This formulation involves certain continuity and smoothness assumptions about how utility varies over space, as will become clearer later.

The Rent Gradient with Identical Consumers

If all residents in a city have identical incomes and tastes, then deriving the properties of the residential rent gradient is straightforward. If consumers are identical, in a stable spatial equilibrium all residents must have the same utility level at their different locations. Otherwise residents in locations with lower utility levels will bid for locations with higher utility levels, driving up prices at those locations and/or causing spatial movements. The situation is only stable when all identical residents are equally well off.

To derive the properties of the rent gradient, we introduce the concept of an indirect utility function. As indicated earlier, for a consumer at location u, there exists a set of demand equations for market goods where demand is a function of income, prices, and leisure. When these demand equations for market goods are substituted into the direct utility function, utility indirectly becomes a function of income, prices, and leisure. We may then define the indirect utility function, or

$$V = V(y, p(u), p_x, p_z, e(u)), \tag{1.4}$$

where V is increasing in y and e, decreasing in prices, and homogeneous of degree zero in income and prices. One interesting property of the indirect utility function utilized at various points in the book is that the demand for housing (and similarly for other goods) may be represented as[6]

$$h(u) = -\frac{\partial V/\partial p(u)}{\partial V/\partial y}. \tag{1.5}$$

Equation (1.5) follows from Roy's identity.

With identical residents the rent gradient must be such that utility in Equation (1.4) is the same everywhere in the city. Therefore, housing prices must vary such that $dV/du = 0$. Accordingly I could differentiate Equation (1.4) and do appropriate substitutions to find the slope of the rent gradient.[7] Alternatively note that since Equation (1.3) specifies a relationship between actual housing prices and distance that must hold for individuals to be in

---

[6] An intuitive explanation why Equation (1.5) holds is simple. The term $-\partial V/\partial p(u)$ is the marginal utility obtained from a dollar decline in housing prices. This equals the marginal utility of a dollar ($\partial V/\partial y$) multiplied by the change in dollars available to the consumer, which equals the number of housing units $h(u)$ multiplied by the dollar change in price (or 1). Rearranging terms yields (1.5).

[7] We differentiate Equation (1.4), set $dV = 0$, divide by $\partial V/\partial y$, and substitute in Equation (1.5) and the expression for $p_e(u)$. Rearranging terms yields Equation (1.6). Equation (1.4) can also be used to derive the consumer's spatial equilibrium condition where, at a utility-maximizing location, $\partial V/\partial u = 0$ and $\partial^2 V/\partial u^2 \leq 0$.

equilibrium, it must also define the slope of the rent gradient that holds in a stable-market equilibrium. Rearranging Equation (1.3) yields the slope of the rent gradient

$$\partial p(u)/\partial u = -h(u)^{-1}p_e(u)t < 0. \tag{1.6}$$

We can solve for the height of the rent gradient at any point using the indirect utility function. To demonstrate this examine Figure 1.1a, in which a residential rent gradient between u_0 and u_1 is illustrated. The CBD and city radii are represented by u_0 and u_1, respectively; thus the residential area lies between u_0 and u_1. The basic reference point on the gradient is at the city edge u_1. Consumers at the city edge have utility $V(u_1)$ defined in Equation (1.4) by leisure $e(u_1)$ given commuting time tu_1, by income and traded good prices, and by the known price of housing at u_1. The price of housing at u_1, or $p(u_1)$, equals the known price received from producing housing on land at u_1, which borders on agricultural land. [As we shall see later, $p(u_1)$ is determined by known agricultural rents and the price of capital.] Given that all consumers have identical tastes, $V(u_1)$ defines utility throughout the city. Then from Equation (1.4), for any u_i, given the known values of V and $e(u_i)$, we should be able to solve for $p(u_i)$, the height of the rent gradient at that point.

To do so we invert Equation (1.4) to get

$$p(u) = p(y, p_x, p_z, e(u), V). \tag{1.7}$$

Substituting in for $V = V(u_1) = V(y, p_x, p_z, e(u_1), p(u_1))$ and rearranging, we get

$$p(u) = \tilde{p}(y, p_x, p_z, p(u_1), u_1, u; t, T). \tag{1.7a}$$

While this discussion demonstrates a method for deriving the equilibrium rent gradient, we still need to know how u_1 and hence $V(u_1)$ are determined. I turn

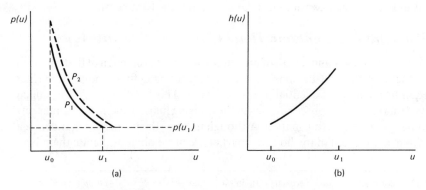

FIGURE 1.1 Rent gradients: identical consumers.

to that topic in the next section where I examine equilibrium in the housing and land markets, but first I comment on several other properties associated with the equilibrium rent gradient.

So far I have described the equilibrium change in rents for consumers moving along a ray from the city center. To determine the equilibrium pattern of rents throughout the city, circumferential movements by consumers must also be considered. Equilibrium with respect to circumferential movements occurs when along all rays from the CBD the rent gradient is the same as P_1 in Figure 1.1a, so that at a given radius from the city center all rents on that circumference are equalized. Since commuting costs to the CBD are the same from any point on that circumference, consumers will then have no incentive to switch locations circumferentially. For this reason cities on a flat featureless plain must be circular or else people will bid to fill out a circle.

Finally we note that, because $p(u)$ declines, for discrete spatial moves the consumer's housing consumption will change in response to the changing price. Since, with identical consumers, utility remains constant as locations and prices change, the housing demand response is described by the Hicks pure substitution effect where $\partial h(u)/\partial p(u) < 0$. Therefore housing consumption increases with distance as price declines. This relation is illustrated in Figure 1.1b.

This increase in housing consumption is also the reason the rent gradient is pictured as convex.[8] Convexity implies that $\partial p(u)/\partial u$ in Equation (1.6) declines with distance, or $\partial^2 p(u)/\partial u^2 > 0$. This decline in $\partial p(u)/\partial u$ in Equation (1.6) occurs because h is increasing as u increases, which causes the right-hand side of Equation (1.6) to decline, providing $p_e(u)$ does not vary much with discrete spatial moves. Alternatively stated, with convexity, as we move out the rent gradient and leisure declines, the approximately equal compensating decline in housing expenditures at each point, which is $h(u)$ $\partial p(u)/\partial u$, is achieved with smaller and smaller changes in unit prices, $\partial p(u)/\partial u$, given that housing consumption $h(u)$ is continuously increasing.

The Rent Gradient and Housing Market Equilibrium

The height and length of an equilibrium rent gradient like that pictured in Figure 1.1a must be consistent with conditions defining housing market equilibrium in the residential sector of the city. This equilibrium is determined by demand and supply conditions in the housing market and in factor markets underlying the housing market. Although most of the properties that define a stable equilibrium in the housing market are quite obvious, I state them here

---

[8] This convexity is not necessary. It implies that $\partial^2 p(u)/\partial u^2 = (-\partial h/\partial p)(\partial p/\partial u)^2 h^{-1} +$ $(\partial p_e(u)/\partial e)t^2 h^{-1} > 0$. If $\partial p_e(u)/\partial e$ is small (or positive), this condition is met.

for emphasis because it is important to have them firmly in mind for the discussion that follows and when we analyze more sophisticated situations in the housing and land markets in Chapter 4.[9] Since the housing market equilibrium cannot be entirely isolated from conditions in factor markets, I also briefly describe the supply of housing here. It is analyzed in Section 1.2.

Consumers rent housing from housing producers.[10] Housing producers produce housing according to the usual profit-maximization conditions with rented capital and land. Capital is perfectly malleable and mobile and is rented by housing producers at a fixed price in local or national capital markets. Land is owned either by a class of people called rentiers or collectively by city residents through the operation and management of the city government (see Chapter 2). I have distinguished four groups of people— consumers, producers, capital owners, and rentiers. However, the specification is general and we can collapse these people into three, two, or even one group. Consumers could produce their own housing by renting inputs; rentiers or capital owners could produce the housing; consumers could be the rentiers and own their own land; and so on.

Given this situation, four conditions define a stable equilibrium in the housing market. Although the conditions are specific to the housing market, with the land market being discussed separately in Section 1.2, since the two markets are not independent, in some of the conditions the land market is referred to.

1. In equilibrium, on the supply side, suppliers of housing rent to the consumer who is willing to pay the most for that housing; and thus housing producers have no incentive to switch customers or tenants. In Figure 1.1a, since all consumers have equal utility along the rent gradient P_1, at any location no other consumer would be willing to pay more for that housing than the current resident.

2. On the demand side, each consumer rents the housing and location that maximizes utility, given the equilibrium set of prices; and thus no renter has an incentive to move. In Figure 1.1a, since all residents have equal utility, given P_1, consumers cannot improve their welfare by bidding away, and thus raising, the price of the housing of another resident.

3. The boundaries of the residential area are the CBD radius u_0 and the city radius u_1. At these boundaries the price of residential housing equals its

---

[9] For an analysis of the attainment of residential spatial equilibrium, the reader should consult Alonso (1964), Chapters 4 and 5 and Appendix A).
[10] We assume consumers rent rather than purchase since that fits in with the structure of a single-period model and comparative statics. If consumers own housing, we would have to employ a multiperiod model, use a wealth constraint, and consider capital gains and losses.

opportunity cost, or the cost of producing housing on land in the alternative competing use at the boundary. If the residential price exceeds [is less than] that cost, housing producers and land owners have an incentive to increase [decrease] the residential area. Since the price of capital is everywhere the same, we will show that higher [lower] housing prices directly reflect higher [lower] land prices. Then, for example, if the cost of producing housing on land in the alternative use at u_1 is lower than the current price of housing there, this means the price of land in the alternative use is lower than the residential price. Landowners will individually profit by increasing the allocation of land to urban use, until land prices and hence housing costs and prices are equalized at the border of competing uses. Then the city's spatial area will be stable.

4. All housing and locations supplied are rented; and given u_0, u_1, and the rent gradient, all residents consume their desired level of housing. That is, demand equals supply and there are no holes in the city or misplaced residents. If the city population were to increase, in aggregate more housing and hence more land would be demanded. The outer bound of the city u_1 would increase, and to accommodate the new population for the same $p(u_1)$, the rent gradient would shift up to, say, P_2 in Figure 1.1a for the same income and prices. The fact that the rent gradient shifts up is proved formally in Section 1.3. The degree to which P_2 shifts up depends on both the increase in population and the partially offsetting decline in per person housing and derived land demands at each point as housing prices rise. Note that with the increase in population and rise in P_2, consumers will all be worse off if their incomes are unchanged. For example, in the indirect utility function, for the person on the new city edge (which is our reference point for defining utility levels in the city), leisure, or $e(u_1)$, declines while all other variables are unchanged.

The Rent Gradient and Nonidentical Consumers

To derive the equilibrium rent gradient when consumers are not identical is more complicated. We assume that consumers differ only by income. To solve for the gradient, the concept of a bid rent function is utilized. A bid rent function describes what unit rents a particular consumer would be willing to pay for housing services in different locations, such that he is indifferent among these locations.

To define a bid rent function we use Equation (1.7), where $p(u)$ is replaced by $p^0(u)$ so

$$p^0(u) = p(y, p_x, p_z, e(u), V). \qquad (1.7b)$$

Equations (1.7) and (1.7b) are both bid rent functions. However, $p^0(u)$ is a hypothetical bid price in a Walrasian auctioneering process, while $p(u)$ is the equilibrium price bid at which transactions occur. Bids vary with u and V in Equation (1.7b).

To determine the properties of Equation (1.7b), we differentiate the indirect utility function, holding income and other prices fixed. If we set $dV = 0$, divide by the marginal utility of income, and substitute in Equation (1.5) and the expression for $p_e(u)$, the result is

$$\partial p^0(u)/\partial u = -h(u)^{-1}p_e(u)t. \tag{1.8}$$

Equation (1.8) defines the slope of a bid rent curve, and it indicates how a person's bid rent will vary along a ray from the city center. A set of bid rent curves is pictured in Figure 1.2a. The height of the bid rent curves is defined by the utility level in (1.7b), where along any curve utility is fixed and the curves shift up [down] as utility falls [rises]. This property is expressed by the negative relationship in the indirect utility function between V and $p^0(u)$ for $e(u)$ fixed. Bid rent curves for the same individual do not cross, just as indifference curves do not cross.

In general, bid rent curves and in particular the slope of bid rent curves vary as income varies among individuals. As income changes, $h(u)$ and $p_e(u)$ will vary; hence, at each location u, from Equation (1.8), the slope of the bid curves should either increase or decrease. I choose to illustrate an equilibrium where the slope decreases as income increases. In Equation (1.8) this means that the quantity of housing consumed $h(u)$ increases *relative* to the marginal evaluation of leisure $p_e(u)$ as income increases. This assumption is discussed in detail after I illustrate the nature of an equilibrium rent gradient.

For the illustration, I first rank *groups* of equal-income consumers by the steepness of their bid rent curves. The steepest is placed near the CBD and the least steep near the city edge. Figure 1.2b shows four bid rent curves labeled a, b, c, and d, one for each of the four different groups of consumers. As just

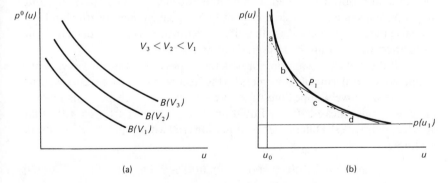

FIGURE 1.2   Bid rents and gradients for nonidentical consumers.

assumed, the steepest bid rent curve belongs to the lowest-income consumers. The equilibrium rent gradient P_1 is an *envelope* of bid rent curves and is composed of a segment for each income group where within each segment the bid rent curve and rent gradient are coincident. Each point on the gradient represents how much people have to pay to bid their house and location away from other users in their or other income groups. At the points of junction of the rent gradient segments, the dashed extensions of the bid rent curves that do not lie on the rent gradient represent what people in a particular income group would be willing to pay to live in another part of the city such that their utility is unchanged. The properties of the equilibrium rent gradient are as follows.

From Equation (1.8), the slope of a bid rent function, which is also the slope of the rent gradient, specifies the same price–distance relationship as Equation (1.3). This implies that along the equilibrium rent gradient consumers are at their utility-maximizing location.

The ordering of people by the steepness of their bid rent curves is necessary for stability and satisfies the two market equilibrium conditions. (1) Producers are renting to the highest bidders. For example, we can see by comparing the rent gradient and the dashed extensions of the bid rent curves that type b consumers would not outbid type a consumers interior to the point of junction of their equilibrium bid rent curves and rent gradient segments. (2) Consumers are at their utility-maximizing location. For example, type b consumers would be worse off, or on a higher bid rent curve, if they paid the prices type a people paid. Any other spatial configuration, such as b people living interior to type a people, would be unstable, since then type a people would be willing to pay higher prices than b people to live in b's segment of the city. (We can see this by redrawing Figure 1.2b with less steep bid rent curves nearest the city center.)

In Figure 1.2b the height of the rent gradient, the size of the residential area, and the size of the segments within which each income group lives are such that all people are housed, all land and housing is rented in the city, and all people consume their desired level of housing given their location and the prices on the rent gradient. As with a city of identical consumers, an increase in population will shift up the rent gradient and extend u_1.

If the underlying reasons for how the slopes of bid rent curves vary are examined, the ordering of consumers by the steepness of their bid curves turns out to be intuitively appealing. If slopes decrease at each point as income increases, this means, from Equation (1.8) where $\partial p^0(u)/\partial u < 0$, that $d(\partial p^0(u)/\partial u)/dy > 0$. Differentiating Equation (1.8) with respect to y for u fixed, we know

$$d(\partial p^0(u)/\partial u)/dy = h(u)^{-1}y^{-1}p_e(u)t[\eta_{h,y} - \eta_{p_e,y}] \gtreqless 0, \qquad (1.9)$$

where $\eta_{p_e,y}$ is the income elasticity of the marginal evaluation of leisure and

$\eta_{h,y}$ is the income elasticity of demand for housing. Whether Equation (1.9) is positive or negative depends on whether the expression in brackets is positive or negative, and hence it depends on whether $\eta_{h,y} \gtrless \eta_{p_e,y}$. For the assumption made earlier that the slopes of rent curves decrease as income increases, or $d(\partial p^0(u)/\partial u)/dy > 0, \eta_{h,y} > \eta_{p_e,y}$. From the definition of elasticities, this means that for a 1% increase in income, the percentage increase in housing is greater than the percentage increase (if any) in the marginal evaluation of leisure. In these circumstances lower-income people live closest to the CBD and have the most leisure.

This makes sense since lower-income people who end up nearest the CBD are those people who value leisure the most *relative* to housing. Thus they are the people who are willing to pay the highest price per unit of housing near the CBD to housing producers. A simple numerical example can be used to illustrate this point. Suppose higher- and lower-income people would consume 10 and 5 units, respectively, of housing given current prices at a location u. At that location lower-income people would be willing to pay $5 per week more (indirectly through higher housing prices and hence payments) to move slightly closer to the CBD and have a unit increase in leisure. Suppose higher-income people are only willing to pay $9 a week more (through larger housing payments) for a unit increase in leisure. Then the percentage by which higher-income people's housing consumption is larger than lower-income people's is greater than the percentage by which higher-income people's marginal evaluation of leisure is larger (i.e., 100% > 80%). This means that the increase in price bid per unit of housing to move closer to the CBD for higher-income people is less than for lower-income people (i.e., $9/10 < $5/5) and housing producers will accept the higher bids of lower-income people for high-access land. On the other hand, if higher-income people are willing to pay $11 for a unit increase in leisure, they will outbid lower-income people for high-access land (i.e., $11/10 > $5/5). The problem for higher-income people trying to live next to the CBD is that, even if they are willing to pay more than lower-income people in absolute terms for increased leisure, their percentage difference in housing consumption relative to lower-income people cannot be greater than their percentage difference in leisure evaluation or the effect of their greater leisure evaluation on unit housing prices is dissipated through their higher housing consumption. This type of argument can also be used to explain why high- or low-income people tend to live in more polluted or higher-crime areas.

The assumption that $d(\partial p^0(u)/\partial u) \, \partial y > 0$ is a rather arbitrary theoretical assumption. This assumption was made in the foregoing discussion and is made in the literature since it yields results consistent with the empirical observation that higher-income people tend to live farther from the city center in the United States. However, that empirical phenomenon could be explained on other grounds and in more sophisticated models not considered until later in the book. For example, in the housing filtering-down models in Chapter 6, higher-income people tend to live in the newest housing, which, given the age and development of American cities, generally is built on the outskirts of cities. In Chapter 10, we note that higher-income people have a fiscal incentive to suburbanize and hence to move farther away from the city center than lower-income people.

Non-CBD Local Employment   In deriving these rent gradients it has been assumed that all people commute to the CBD. This need not be so. Suppose in Figure 1.2b that on the segment of the P_1 rent gradient where type a people live, some of the type a people work in a grocery store in that area. Providing that most people still work in the CBD, the shape of the rent gradient is still determined by the same equilibrium conditions for CBD commuters and is unchanged. That is, their bidding determines the competitive price of land. Identical type a people who work locally pay the same market rents as commuters but have more leisure. To maintain equilibrium in labor markets and choice of occupation, the local wages of noncommuters will be lower than those of commuters by the value of their increased leisure. If, however, the ratio of local to CBD workers becomes too large, then the gradient will change. For example, if beyond a certain point no one commutes to the CBD, the rent gradient would be radically different.

An Illustration of Housing Rent Gradients in a Simple City

It is useful to illustrate the foregoing discussion with a simple example using specific functional forms. This example and the specific functional forms will also be used later to derive explicit aggregate relationships for a city. Consumers maximize a logarithmic linear utility function subject to a budget constraint and a leisure constraint.

Therefore, the consumer maximization problem is to

$$\max_{\text{w.r.t.} x,z,h,e,u} \quad V = A'x(u)^a z(u)^b h(u)^c e(u)^d, \qquad a + b + c = f \qquad (1.1a)$$

subject to

$$y - p_x x(u) - p_z z(u) - p(u)h(u) = 0,$$

$$T - e(u) - tu = 0.$$

The first-order conditions are $aV/x(u) - \lambda p_x = 0$, $bV/z(u) - \lambda p_z = 0$, $cV/h(u) - \lambda p(u) = 0$, $dV/e - \gamma = 0$, and $-\lambda h \, (\partial p(u)/\partial u) - \gamma t = 0$ where λ is the marginal utility of income and γ is the marginal utility of leisure time.

Substituting the first-order conditions with respect to the consumption of market goods into the budget constraint, we can get demand equations. For example, from the first-order conditions we know that $p_x x(u) = (a/c)p(u)h(u)$ and $p_z z(u) = (b/c)p(u)h(u)$. Substituting these in the budget constraint and solving, we find

$$h(u) = (c/f)yp(u)^{-1}. \tag{1.2a}$$

The other demand equations are $x(u) = (a/f)yp_x^{-1}$ and $z(u) = (b/f)yp_z^{-1}$.

By combining and arranging the first-order conditions for e and u we find

$$h(u)\frac{\partial p(u)}{\partial u} = -t\frac{Vd/e(u)}{\lambda} = -tp_e(u). \tag{1.3a}$$

As a consumer moves farther away from the city center, the value of lost leisure is compensated by reduced housing costs. By substituting $e(u) = T - tu$ and $\lambda = cV/[p(u)h(u)]$ from the first-order conditions into Equation (1.3a), we can rewrite this equation to get the slope of bid rent curves and rent gradients.

$$\partial p(u)/\partial u = -(td/c)p(u)(T - tu)^{-1}. \tag{1.6a}$$

The alternative way to derive Equation (1.6a) is to use the indirect utility function. To derive the indirect utility function we substitute the consumer demand equations and $e = T - tu$ into the direct utility function to get

$$V = Ay^f p_x^{-a} p_z^{-b} p(u)^{-c}(T - tu)^d, \tag{1.4a}$$

where $A = A'(a/f)^a(b/f)^b(c/f)^c$. Maximizing V in (1.5a) with respect to u yields Equation (1.6a).

In this illustrative example, the slope of the bid rent curve and rent gradient in Equation (1.6a) is independent of income and hence holds for all income levels. Therefore, Equation (1.6a) also describes the slope of the rent gradient in a city where people have either equal incomes or differing incomes. To find the height of the rent gradient we write Equation (1.6a) in logarithmic form, integrate, and then take antilogarithms to get

$$p(u) = C_0(T - tu)^{d/c},$$

where C_0 is the constant of integration.

The most general way to evaluate C_0 for a particular city is the following. We know the opportunity cost of land in agriculture (which can be zero) that the city must pay to get land at the border of the city. Therefore, we can determine urban housing prices at the city edge (see Section 1.2), or $p(u_1)$ in Figure 1.1b. Evaluating at the city edge, we have $p(u_1) = C_0(T - tu_1)^{d/c}$.

Solving for C_0 and substituting into the rent gradient expression, we get

$$p(u) = p(u_1)(T - tu_1)^{-d/c}(T - tu)^{d/c}. \tag{1.10}$$

This is the residential rent gradient for a city of either identical or multi-income people. The height of this gradient at any location is determined by the housing rent at the city edge, the endogenous spatial size of the city as measured by u_1 (which is solved for later in the chapter), and the parameters of the model. A rent gradient is illustrated in Figure 1.1b or 1.2b by P_1.

Another common way to evaluate C_0 is to assume that (1) all people have identical tastes and income and hence in equilibrium have identical utility levels, and (2) the utility level in the city is fixed at a level $\dot{V}$, which is given by an infinitely elastic supply curve of labor to the city at utility level $\dot{V}$ (see Chapter 2). If we know V, then by rearranging Equation (1.4a) we know

$$p(u) = (\dot{V})^{-1/c} A^{1/c} y^{f/c} p_x^{-a/c} p_z^{-b/c} (T - tu)^{d/c}$$

or

$$C_0 = (\dot{V})^{-1/c} A^{1/c} y^{f/c} p_x^{-a/c} p_z^{-b/c}.$$

1.2   Production of Housing

So far, we have investigated and illustrated consumer spatial equilibrium, housing rent gradients, and equilibrium in the housing market. We still have to investigate fully the supply side of housing, land rent gradients, and equilibrium in the land and capital markets.

Housing is produced under constant returns to scale with land l and capital k where

$$h(u) = h(k(u), l(u)). \tag{1.11}$$

Producers seek to maximize profits $\pi(u) = p(u)h(u) - p_k k(u) - p_l(u)l(u)$ where p_k is the spatially invariant price of captial and $p_l(u)$ is the price of land at location u. At a given location, inputs are employed according to the usual first-order conditions describing marginal productivity conditions, or $p_l = p(u)(\partial h/\partial l)$ and $p_k = p(u)(\partial h/\partial k)$. It often is convenient to alternatively describe production technology by the unit cost function where the unit cost of production $c = p(p_k, p_l)$. The function p is linear homogeneous, increasing in input prices and subsumes efficient factor usage by the firm.[11] If there is perfect

---

[11] In general, for the existence of unit cost functions with or without scale as an argument, h should be nondecreasing in its arguments, a right-continuous function, and quasi-concave.

competition, so that retail price equals unit production costs, the unit cost relationship can be expressed as

$$p(u) = p(p_k, p_l).$$ (1.12)

In the previous section we saw that housing prices must vary spatially to maintain consumer equilibrium. This means the gross revenue from producing a unit of housing will vary spatially. Hence, in addition to choosing optimal input combinations at any location, producers are concerned with choosing a profit-maximizing location. A producer's profit-maximizing location is one where $\partial\pi/\partial u = 0$ or

$$h(u)[\partial p(u)/\partial u] = l(u)[\partial p_l(u)/\partial u].$$ (1.13)

Equation (1.13) states that when producers move an infinitesimal distance from their optimal location, their change in land costs exactly equal their change in housing revenue. That is, given that their original location is optimal, they cannot be made better off by moving.

The next step in the analysis is to derive the characteristics of the set of equilibrium land prices, which is the land rent gradient. First, note that, if producers are identical in terms of their technology and entrepreneurial ability, profits from building housing must be everywhere equal. If housing is a competitive industry, profits are zero. Zero profits are realized by housing producers bidding up [down] the rent paid on land in locations where nonequilibrium profits are positive [negative] until profits are zero. Zero profits also imply that unit costs in Equation (1.12) must always vary through land costs to equal output prices. Given these assumptions, the slope of the land rent gradient may be found in several ways. We can differentiate the profit function and rearrange terms, given $d\pi/du = 0$; or we can differentiate the unit cost function and, after appropriate substitutions, rearrange terms to get the slope.[12] Alternatively, since Equation (1.13) specifies a land rent–distance relationship that must hold for individual producers to be in equilibrium, it must also indicate the slope of the land rent gradient that must hold in a stable-market equilibrium. Rearranging Equation (1.13) yields the slope

$$\partial p_l(u)/\partial u = h(u)l(u)^{-1}[\partial p(u)/\partial u].$$ (1.14)

---

[12] Differentiating the unit cost function yields $\partial p(u)/\partial u = \partial p/\partial p_l(u) \, \partial p_l(u)/\partial u$. To interpret this condition we note a useful property of unit cost functions. From Shephard's lemma (Diewert, 1974) $k(u)/h(u) = \partial p/\partial p_k$ and $l(u)/h(u) = \partial p/\partial p_l(u)$; or the derivative of the unit cost function equals the per unit demand for the respective factor. This may be explained intuitively as follows. The term $\partial p/\partial p_k$ is the increase in unit costs if the price of capital rises by \$1. This increase in unit costs equals the number of units of capital employed multiplied by \$1 divided by the number of housing units, or it equals $k(u)/h(u)$. Substituting the equation for $\partial p/\partial p_l(u)$ into the spatial equilibrium condition on unit costs yields Equation (1.14).

The unit cost function can be used to solve for the height of the rent gradient at each point, because given $p(u_i)$ and p_k, Equation (1.12) can be solved for $p_l(u_i)$. Inverting Equation (1.12), substituting in Equation (1.7a), and rearranging we get

$$p_l(u) = p_l(y, p_x, p_z, p(u_1), p_k, u_1, u; t, T). \qquad (1.15)$$

A land rent gradient is pictured in Figure 1.3 and is consistent with equilibrium in land markets. Equilibrium in land markets satisfies the four types of conditions listed for housing. All land supplied will be rented at a nonnegative price, or there are no holes or vacant areas in the city; and all housing producers will rent their desired quantity of land given prices (condition 4). Land rents at the borders of competing uses, such as agricultural or commercial uses, will be equalized (condition 3). Landowners in equilibrium receive the maximum rent anyone is willing to pay for their land (condition 1). Demanders of land, such as housing producers, receive their maximum possible profits (zero) at their equilibrium land site, relative to other sites that they could rent and build housing on (condition 2).

Spatial Characteristics Implied by the Equilibrium Rent Gradient

Several important results follow directly from Equation (1.14). In Equation (1.3) I showed that changes in housing costs, $[\partial p(u)/\partial u]h(u)$, due to infinitesimal spatial moves exactly equal the change in leisure multiplied by the marginal evaluation of leisure, $-tp_e(u)$. From Equation (1.14) we can see that changes in land rents paid by housing producers exactly equal changes in housing costs, and hence they also equal the value of marginal leisure losses.

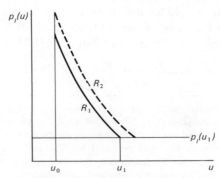

FIGURE 1.3   Land rent gradients.

That is,[13]

$$l(u)\frac{\partial p_l(u)}{\partial u} = h(u)\frac{\partial p(u)}{\partial u} = -p_e(u)t.$$

Second, Equation (1.14) may be written as

$$\frac{\partial p_l(u)/\partial u}{p_l(u)} = \rho_l^{-1}\frac{\partial p(u)/\partial u}{p(u)}, \tag{1.16}$$

where ρ_l is land's factor share in output revenue, or $\rho_l = p_l l/(ph)$. Equation (1.16) states that the percentage change in unit rents equals the percentage change in housing prices *magnified* by the inverse of land's factor share. Since land prices alone (i.e., not capital rentals) reflect housing price changes, their percentage change will always magnify those of housing prices. Thus as we approach the city center, land rents should rise much more quickly than housing rents. The term ρ_l is usually estimated to be around 0.1 and therefore a 1% rise in housing rents should induce about a 10% rise in residential land rents.

From the information on price changes in Equation (1.14) we can demonstrate how the intensity of land use varies in a city and how population density varies. There are two measures of the intensity of land use in a city. The first is the ratio of captial to land in producing a unit of housing. We define the direct elasticity of substitution as $\sigma = d\log(k/l)/d\log(p_l/p_k)$. In the city only p_l varies with distance, so we may state, using the definition of σ and Equation (1.16),

$$\frac{\partial\log[k(u)/l(u)]}{\partial u} = \sigma\,\partial\log p_l(u)/\partial u = \frac{\sigma}{\rho_l}\partial\log p(u)/\partial u. \tag{1.17}$$

Equation (1.17) indicates that a 1% increase in housing prices as we approach the city center leads to a σ/ρ_l percent increase in the use of capital relative to land per unit of housing. Typically σ is estimated to be about 0.7 and, from above, $\rho_l = 0.1$. Therefore, a 1% change in $p(u)$ will lead to about a 7% increase in the capital-to-land ratio. This strong increase in the captial/land ratio as we approach the city center will be reflected in higher buildings. This change in the k/l ratio is illustrated in Figure 1.4a. If the rent gradient shifts up because, say,

---

[13] Note that this statement is only true for infinitesimal spatial moves. For discrete spatial moves, as the price of housing changes, housing and land consumption also change. In that case, changes in housing costs holding utility constant reflect not just amenity differences but also housing consumption differences. This suggests that changes in land or housing rents can only be used to directly value amenity differences, such as the value of differential access, for infinitesimal changes in these amenities. For discrete changes one can use differences in rent expenditures to measure the value of amentity differences only if lot size is fixed.

population increases, for the same rent on capital the k/l ratio will shift up, as illustrated in Figure 1.4a. Buildings at the same location will be higher in larger cities. The increase in the k/l ratio also implies that the physical marginal product of capital is declining as we approach the CBD. Given that housing producers everywhere use capital according to the marginal productivity condition $p_k = p(u)MP_k$, this decline in MP_k matches the rise in $p(u)$, so in net the *value* of the marginal product of capital is unchanged.

The second measure of how land use intensity changes is the value of housing per unit of land. If housing production is competitive, $p(u)h(u) = p_l(u)l(u) + p_k k(u)$ or $p(u)h(u)/l(u) = p_l(u) + p_k k(u)/l(u)$. Differentiating, we get

$$\partial(p(u)h(u)/l(u))/\partial u = \partial p_l(u)/\partial u + p_k \partial[k(u)/l(u)]/\partial u.$$

Substituting in from Equations (1.14) and (1.17) we obtain

$$\frac{\partial \log[p(u)h(u)/l(u)]}{\partial u} = \left(1 + \frac{\rho_k}{\rho_l}\sigma\right)\partial \log p(u)/\partial u, \tag{1.18}$$

where $\rho_k = p_k k(u)/[p(u)h(u)]$ is capital's factor share in production revenue. Equation (1.18) states that a 1% rise in housing prices as we approach the city center will lead to a $1 + (\rho_k/\rho_l)\sigma$ percent rise in the value of housing per unit of land. For $\rho_k = 0.9$, $\rho_l = 0.1$, and $\sigma = 0.7$, a 1% rise in housing prices would lead to a 7.3% rise in the value of housing per unit of land. This is clearly a significant rise in the intensity of land use.

In terms of population density, there are two reasons why the number of people per square unit, or population density, rises as we approach the city center. First, housing consumption for equal-income people declines with higher housing prices as we approach the city center. Second, corresponding to the increasing housing prices are increasing land rents, which means, as seen in

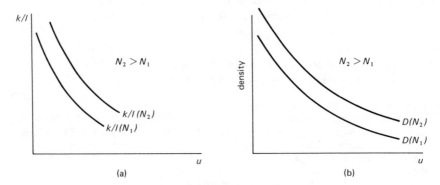

(a)   (b)

FIGURE 1.4   Capital-to-land ratios and population density.

Figure 1.4a, that less land relative to capital will be used in housing production. Both these facts indicate that per person use of land will decline as we approach the city center. Hence, population density will increase as we approach the city center. This is pictured in Figure 1.4b. Note that the density gradient will shift up if the rent gradient shifts up.

An Illustration of Land Rent Gradients

By specifying a particular production function for housing and using the results on consumption relationships from the specific utility function used in the previous section, we can illustrate a land rent gradient as well as spatial variations in density and the per person use of land. We use the production function

$$h(u) = B'l(u)^{\alpha}k(u)^{1-\alpha}. \tag{1.11a}$$

The first-order conditions for profit maximization are

$$p_l(u) = p(u)\alpha h(u)/l(u) \quad \text{and} \quad p_k = p(u)(1-\alpha)h(u)/k(u).$$

Rearranging the first condition, we get the demand for land and capital functions, or

$$l(u) = \alpha h(u)p(u)p_l(u)^{-1} \quad \text{and} \quad k(u) = (1-\alpha)h(u)p(u)p_k^{-1}.$$

Substituting in the demand equation for housing from Equation (1.2a), where $h(u) = (c/f)yp(u)^{-1}$, we can write the demand for land and capital as

$$l(u) = (\alpha c/f)yp_l(u)^{-1} \quad \text{and} \quad k(u) = (1-\alpha)(c/f)yp_k^{-1} \tag{1.19}$$

Thus the derived demand for factors is a function of income and own prices. In Equation (1.18), as we approach the CBD and land rents rise, the use of land declines and density rises. Substituting into the production function for $l(u)$ and $k(u)$ from the first-order conditions, we obtain the unit cost function

$$p(u) = Bp_l(u)^{\alpha}p_k^{(1-\alpha)}, \tag{1.12a}$$

where $B = B'\alpha^{-\alpha}(1-\alpha)^{\alpha-1}$.

The land rent gradient may be found by differentiating profits with respect to u, setting $d\pi = 0$, substituting in demand equations for $l(u)$ and $k(u)$, integrating, and then substituting in Equation (1.10) for $p(u)$. Alternatively, the land rent gradient may be found by substituting the cost function (1.12a) into the housing rent gradient (1.10) to obtain

$$p_l(u) = p_l(u_1)(T - tu_1)^{-d/c\alpha}(T - tu)^{d/c\alpha}, \tag{1.15a}$$

where $p_l(u_1)$ is the land rent at the city edge in agriculture. The slope of the land rent gradient is $-td/c\alpha$ and is steeper than the housing rent gradient of slope $-td/c$, as was indicated would be the case in Equation (1.16). The height of this gradient is a function of city spatial size and $p_l(u_1)$.

1.3 Aggregate Relationships in the Residential Sector

In the previous two sections, using basic consumer utility and producer profit maximization models, I examined the spatial variation in housing and land prices, housing consumption, the capital/land ratio, and density. With this information I can derive aggregate market relationships for the residential sector. These relationships are the usual ones describing aggregate demand for land and capital in the residential sector as a function of prices, income, and other variables. It is assumed that housing is a normal good with a positive income effect and a negative own-price effect; that capital and land are normal inputs with positive output effects and negative own-price effects; and that equilibrium rent gradients satisfy the four properties of market equilibrium discussed earlier. After examining general aggregate demand relationships, I illustrate these demand functions and market equilibrium using the specific functional forms for utility and production functions from Sections 1.1 and 1.2. I also use these functional forms to illustrate calculations of residential population, rents, and use of factor inputs.

The aggregate demand for residential land, given the area of the CBD, is measured by the radius of the city u_1. If we can solve for u_1 as a function of income, prices, and population, then we have solved for the urban demand for agricultural land. We start by assuming all people in the city are identical.

To solve for u_1, we calculate the residential population of the city. At each distance from the city center, the population $N(u)$ equals the total amount of land at that distance, $2\pi u_1$, divided by per person consumption of land, $l(u)$. Total population N is the sum of populations at all locations or

$$N = \int_{u_0}^{u_1} N(u)\,du = \int_{u_0}^{u_1} 2\pi u\, l(u)^{-1}\,du \qquad (1.20)$$

To derive an expression for $l(u)$, note that given the production function for housing in (1.11) and the associated profit maximization problem there is a derived demand for land where $l(u) = \tilde{l}(h(u),\ p_k,\ p_l(u))$. From Equation (1.2) we substitute in $h = h(y, p(u),\ p_x, p_z,\ e(u))$ and then we substitute for $p(u)$ and $p_l(u)$ from Equations (1.7a) and (1.15), respectively, to get $l(u) = l(y, p_x, p_z, p_k, p_l(u_1), u_1, u; t, T)$. Substituting this in (1.20) we have an equation in price and income variables as well as u that is integrated over. Thus

Equation (1.20) becomes

$$N = N(y, p_x, p_z, p_k, p_l(u_1), u_0; t, T) \qquad (1.20a)$$

Inverting this

$$u_1 = u(N, y, p_x, p_z, p_k, p_l(u_1), u_0; t, T) \qquad (1.21)$$

Equation (1.21) is in essence the city's (or at least its residential sector's) demand for agricultural land. I next argue the comparative statics properties of this function. In doing so I also investigate the comparative statics properties of residential rent gradients.

1. $\partial u_1 / \partial N > 0$. If population rises, more agricultural land is demanded at the same price. This will occur if the urban land rent gradient shifts up at the initial edge of the city and the city expands farther into agriculture to take advantage of the relatively lower rents. At the new expanded city edge, land rents will again be equalized. Such a shift is depicted by the shift from R_1 to R_2 in Figure 1.3. If the rent gradient shifts up at the initial u_1 (or at any point), it must shift up at all points so as to maintain equal utility for all people. Note the alternatives to a shift up can be ruled out. A shift down with increased population would mean that the original residents with lower prices are demanding less land, contradicting the properties of the demand function for land. If the curve rotates crossing the original, relative to the initial equilibrium, some people would be worse (above the original) and others better off (below the original), which contradicts the equal utility condition.

Then to show that, as population rises, more agricultural land is demanded, it is sufficient to show that the land rent gradient must shift up as population increases. That the rent gradient shifts up can be demonstrated by showing that the contrary cannot be true. Suppose population rises and the rent gradient and spatial area of the city remain unchanged. This implies either that new people consume no land and demand no housing, or that initial residents were not maximizing utility before and are now satisfied with less land (so that new people are able to get some) at the same price. This contradicts either or both the assumptions that utility and profits are always maximized in equilibrium and that land and housing are normal economic goods. If we suppose that the rent gradient falls, the foregoing inconsistencies are even more pronounced. Therefore, the rent gradient must shift up with population and hence the city area will expand.

2. Using the same type of argument, it is possible to show the following: $\partial u_1 / \partial p_l(u_1) < 0$, the normal own-price effect on factor demand; $\partial u_1 / \partial y > 0$, the normal income effect on derived demand for a factor; $\partial u_1 / \partial u_0 > 0$, or, ceteris paribus, the whole urban area expands if the CBD expands.

3. $\partial u_1 / \partial p_k \gtrless 0$. If the price of capital rises, it is unclear what happens to the

demand for land. While the demand for land relative to capital rises, the relative consumer demand for housing and both factors falls, since housing is now more costly to produce and purchase.

4. $\partial u_1/\partial t < 0$. This indicates that increased cost of access to the CBD causes people to crowd closer to the CBD. If t rises, people farthest from the CBD, say at u_1, have a greater absolute increase in commuting time than people nearer the CBD because they travel greater distances. Therefore people nearer the CBD relative to those farther away must experience an increase in land rents to offset their increased relative access advantage. This maintains a stable spatial equilibrium between those near the CBD and those farther away. This upward rotation in the rent gradient will reduce demand for land everywhere.[14] Hence u_1 will decline.

The urban demand curve for argricultural land is illustrated in Figure 1.5. The supply curve of agricultural land is also pictured and an equilibrium illustrated. Although the supply of land is drawn as infinitely elastic at $p_l(u_1)$, it could be upward sloping. For example, if the city buys agricultural produce from its hinterland and there are costs to the farmers of shipping to the city market, then agricultural land rents will vary with relative market access or distance to the city center. In certain circumstances, if the radius of agricultural production rises with city size, so will the level of agricultural land rents.[15] Then the opportunity cost of land to the city will rise.

The aggregate demand for capital can be specified in the same fashion and shown to have regular properties. The analysis can be expanded to include

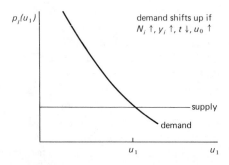

FIGURE 1.5   Urban demand for agricultural land.

---

[14] To actually rule out the alternative of an anticlockwise rotation with u_1 shifting out, it is sufficient to assume utility is separable in leisure, so housing demand depends only on income and prices.

[15] As the city expands, if in the agricultural area the *difference* in access between the farmers closest and those farthest from the CBD increases, then agricultural rents should increase.

different income groups, where we would then hypothesize a demand for agricultural land function.

$$u_1 = \tilde{u}(p_l(u_1), N_1, N_2, N_3, \ldots, y_1, y_2, y_3, \ldots, u_0, p_k, p_x, p_z; t, T),$$

where N_i is the number of people earning income y_i. The comparative static properties of this function are argued in the same way as when there is only one type of person. For example, in arguing $\partial u_1/\partial N > 0$, I use the same method, except now I must also show if the rent gradient rises in one income segment, it rises in all segments. If land rents rise in one segment, either they rise in other segments to equalize land rents at the border of competing uses or the area of this segment will expand into other segments, reducing their size. This reduction in size in itself will drive up prices in these other segments to equate demand with the reduced supply.

Specific Functional Forms

These aggregative relationships are illustrated using the logarithmic linear production and utility functions specified earlier. These illustrations will be used later in presenting an aggregate model of a city. For the illustration it is assumed that *all* consumers have *identical tastes and incomes*. To illustrate aggregate relationships is very complicated when incomes and/or tastes vary (see Montesano, 1972). The basic problem is in integrating over space when there are different types of consumers whose location is endogenous. Since the objective here is to illustrate an aggregative model, I choose to simplify and assume that consumers are identical.

We start by calculating the residential population of a city. At each distance from the city center the population $N(u)$ equals the total amount of land at that location, $2\pi u$, divided by per person consumption of land. Total population N is the sum of populations at all locations or

$$N = \int_{u_0}^{u_1} N(u)\,du = \int_{u_0}^{u_1} 2\pi u l(u)^{-1}\,du.$$

Using our logarithmic linear utility and production functions, we substitute into this equation for $l(u)$ from the demand-for-land equation (1.20) where $l(u) = (\alpha c/f)\, y p_l(u)^{-1}$, and then we substitute for $p_l(u)$ from the rent gradient equation (1.19) where $p_l(u) = p_l(u_1)(T - tu_1)^{-d/c\alpha}(T - tu)^{d/c\alpha}$. This yields

$$N = \int_{u_0}^{u_1} 2\pi u (\alpha c/fy)^{-1} p_l(u_1)(T - tu_1)^{-d/c\alpha}(T - tu)^{d/c\alpha}\,du.$$

Integrating, we get

$$N = C_1 p_l(u_1) y^{-1} t^{-2} s(t, u_0, u_1) \tag{1.22}$$

where

$$C_1 = 2\pi\left(\frac{f}{c\alpha}\right)\left(\frac{d}{c\alpha} + 2\right)^{-1}\left(\frac{d}{c\alpha} + 1\right)^{-1}$$

and

$$s(t, u_0, u_1) = (T - tu_1)^{-d/c\alpha}(T - tu_0)^{1+d/c\alpha}\left[T + tu_0\left(\frac{d}{c\alpha} + 1\right)\right]$$

$$-(T - tu_1)\left[T + tu_1\left(\frac{d}{c\alpha} + 1\right)\right] > 0.^{16}$$

An inverse of Equation (1.22) is an equation for u_1, the urban demand for agricultural land, where $u_1 = u(p_l(u_1), N, y, t, u_0, p_k)$. The properties of this function may be illustrated by differentiating (1.22) and rearranging terms to get

$$e_1\, du_1 = (dN/N) + (dy/y) - [dp_l(u_1)/p_l(u_1)] - e_2\, dt + e_3\, du_0 \quad (1.23)$$

where $e_1, e_2, e_3 > 0.^{17}$ Equation (1.23) illustrates the properties of the urban demand function for agricultural land that were discussed earlier. There is the own-price relationship, $\partial u_1/\partial p_l(u_1) < 0$. There are the aggregate demand

---

[16] Clearly, for $N > 0$, $s > 0$. If $u_0 = u_1$, $s = N = 0$, since there is no residential area. For $u_1 > u_0$ we assume that parametric values are such that $s > 0$. For any reasonable parametric values, $s > 0$.

[17]
$$e_1 = \frac{td}{c\alpha}s(t, u_0, u_1)^{-1}\left\{(T - tu_1)^{-(d/c\alpha)-1}(T - tu_0)^{(d/c\alpha)+1}\left[T + tu_0\left(\frac{d}{c\alpha} + 1\right)\right] - T\right.$$

$$\left. + 2tu_1\left(1 + \frac{c\alpha}{d}\right)\right\} > 0,$$

$$e_2 = e_1 t^{-1}u_1 - 2t^{-1} - t^{-1}u_0 e_3 > 0,$$

$$e_3 = u_0 t^2 s(t, u_0, u_1)^{-1}(T - tu_1)^{-(d/c\alpha)}(T - tu_0)^{(d/c\alpha)}\left(\frac{d}{c\alpha} + 1\right)\left(\frac{d}{c\alpha} + 2\right) > 0.$$

These variables are unambiguously positive, except for e_2, providing $s > 0$. As for s, $e_2 > 0$ for reasonable parametric values. For future reference, note that it is possible to show that $(T - tu_1)e_1 c\alpha/(td) > 1$ or that $(T - tu_1)$ multiplied by the bracketed part of e_1 and $s(t, u_0, u_1)^{-1}$ is greater than one. This latter expression reduces to

$$\frac{g(u_1) + (T - tu_1)2tu_1(1 + c\alpha/d)}{g(u_1) - (T - tu_1)tu_1(d/c\alpha + 1)},$$

where $g(u_1)$ is some positive expression and both numerator and denominator are positive. As long as $T > tu_1$ or leisure is positive, this expression is greater than one.

relationships for population and income, $\partial u_1/\partial N$, $\partial u_1/\partial y < 0$. Finally, $\partial u_1/\partial t < 0$ and $\partial u_1/\partial u_0 > 0$.

The aggregate demand for capital is the demand for capital per house summed over all households. The amount of capital per house is $k(u)$ and the population at each distance from the CBD is $2\pi u l(u)^{-1}$. Therefore at each radius the demand for capital is $k(u)2\pi u l(u)^{-1}$. From Equation (1.19) we can substitute into this relationship $k(u) = (1 - \alpha)c/fyp^{-1}$ and $l(u) = \alpha c/fyp_l(u)^{-1}$. Therefore the aggregate demand for capital is[18]

$$K = \int_{u_1}^{u_0} 2\pi u k(u)/l(u)\, du = \int_{u_1}^{u_0} 2\pi u \alpha/(1 - \alpha)p_k^{-1}p_l(u)\, du.$$

To evaluate this, we can substitute in Equation (1.20) for $p_l(u)$ and integrate. Alternatively, we can employ other information to solve for K. Given logarithmic linear utility functions, consumers spend a fixed fraction of their income on housing, or from (1.2a), $p(u)h(u) = (c/f)y$. From equation (1.19) we also know that the share of any factor is a fixed proportion of housing costs. Specifically, $p_k k(u) = (1 - \alpha)p(u)h(u)$. Combining these relationships, we see that each consumer buys $k(u) = (1 - \alpha)(c/f)yp_k^{-1}$. This expression contains no spatial variables and, therefore, aggregate demand is simply

$$K = (1 - \alpha)(c/f)yp_k^{-1}N. \tag{1.24}$$

As before, this aggregate demand function has the normal properties that $\partial K/\partial p_k < 0$ for the own-price effect and $\partial K/\partial y, \partial K/\partial N > 0$ for the income and population effects.

Finally, note that total rents at each location are the unit rent $p_l(u)$ multiplied by the amount of land at each location $2\pi u$. Therefore total residential rents are

$$\text{Rents}_{\text{res}} = \int_{u_0}^{u_1} 2\pi u p_l(u)\, du.$$

We can substitute in Equation (1.20) for $p_l(u)$ and integrate. Alternatively note that per person land rents are a fixed proportion α of housing costs, which in turn are a fixed proportion of income c/f. Therefore, per person rents are $(\alpha c/f)y$, and total residential rents are

$$\text{Rents}_{\text{res}} = (\alpha c/f)yN. \tag{1.25}$$

---

[18] Alternatively the aggregate demand for capital equals the demand for capital per unit of land summed over all units of land. From footnote 12 the amount of capital and land per unit of housing are, respectively, $\partial p/\partial p_k$ and $\partial p/\partial p_l$. Therefore $K = \int_{u_0}^{u_1} 2\pi u(\partial p/\partial p_k)/[\partial p/\partial p_l(u)]\, du$. To solve this we substitute in from Equation (1.12a), which then gives us the equation in the text.

2. THE BUSINESS SECTOR

2.1 Firms and Spatial Equilibrium in the Central Business District

Firms in the CBD produce the city's traded, or export good. As noted earlier, for cities to exist there must be some type of scale effects in production. I use a simple specification consistent with maintaining perfect competition (Chipman, 1970). Second, to have a CBD with centrally located production, in this chapter we assume firms want access to a transport-retailing node at the center of the city, from which to export or sell their products locally. In return for its exports the city imports z from other places, through the transport node.

The firm production function is

$$x(u) = G(N)x(k(u), n(u), l(u)). \qquad (1.26)$$

A Hicks neutral shift factor $G(N)$ indicates economies of scale that are dependent on city employment in x activity (the only employment source in the city); $\partial G/\partial N \geq 0$. These scale economies are the basis for agglomeration of population in the city. They are at the industry level and may be experienced by any entering firm. Each firm behaves as though $G(N)$ were exogenous. The x function denotes the firm's own technology, where output, given $G(N)$, is a function of capital $k(u)$, labor $n(u)$, and land $l(u)$. The x function is linear homogeneous and hence $G(N)x$ is homothetic.

In the shipping of products to the marketing–transport node at the city center, transport services are produced with units of x, which corresponds to the evaporation formulation of transport costs in international trade. It costs firms t_x of a unit of x to ship one unit of x one unit distance. The quantity of x actually sold in the city center is $x(u)(1 - t_x u)$ or the revenue received for each unit of x produced is $p_x(1 - t_x u)$.

These assumptions about production have a number of implications. First, in maximizing profits, the firm pays factors the value of their perceived marginal product or, for wages, $p_n = p_x(1 - t_x u)G(N)\partial x/\partial n$. Total factor payments then are $p_x(1 - t_x u)G(N)[(\partial x/\partial n)n + (\partial x/\partial k)k + (\partial x/\partial l)l]$, which, from Euler's theorem, equals $p_x(1 - t_x u)G(N)x$ if the x function is linear homogeneous. Therefore firm factor payments exhaust firm revenue. This fact plus the fact that $G(N)$ is an external scale effect that affects all firms equally ensures that perfect competition is stable and feasible.

Second, production technology may be alternatively described by the unit cost function $p(N, p_n, p_k, p_l(u))$. This function is nonincreasing in N, increasing and linear homogeneous in prices, and subsumes efficient usage of factor inputs. With perfect competition, the firm's net price should equal unit costs or[19]

$$p_x(1 - t_x u) = p(N, p_n, p_k, p_l(u)). \tag{1.27}$$

Finally, as long as $G(N)$ increases with N, for the same factor ratios the marginal products of factors increase continuously. Moreover, because $G(N)$ is a Hicks neutral shifter, the marginal products of factors increase by the same proportion for the same factor ratios. If, on the other hand, the scale effect were relatively labor saving compared to capital, this would imply that the marginal product of capital would be more beneficially affected than the marginal product of labor as a city grows. Then, for example, either capital rentals would rise relative to wages if city factor supplies are fixed (and factor prices variable) or the city's relative demand for labor would fall if factor prices are fixed (and factor supplies are variable). Clearly, assuming $G(N)$ is a Hicks neutral or nonneutral shift factor has important implications for the relative use of capital and labor in various size cities. Normally, scale efficiencies are assumed to be neutral in aggregate.

A firms spatial equilibrium is described as follows. Firm profits are $\pi = p_x(1 - t_x u)x(u) - p_l(u)l(u) - p_k k(u) - p_n n(u)$. At the firm's profit-maximizing location, $\partial \pi / \partial u = 0$ or

$$l(u)\partial p_l(u)/\partial u = -x(u)p_x t_x < 0. \tag{1.28}$$

Unit land rents decline with distance from the city center, as transport costs increase. The change in total rents exactly equals the increase in transport costs $[x(u)p_x t_x]$ of moving a unit distance. Therefore firm profits are unchanged and the firm does not benefit by moving.

To find the slope and height of the commercial land rent gradient, we first note that if all producers are identical in technology and ability, profits from producing x must be everywhere equal. If the x industry is competitive, profits will be everywhere zero and net price will always equal unit production costs. Therefore, to find the slope of the rent gradient, we can differentiate the unit cost function and do appropriate substitutions, or we can differentiate the profit function and set $d\pi = 0$.[20] Alternatively we observe that, since Equation (1.28) specifies a relationship that must hold for individual producers to be in equilibrium, it also gives the slope of the equilibrium rent gradient. The height of the rent gradient at any u can be solved directly from Equation (1.27), given p_x, t_x, and other variables.

---

[19] See footnote 11 on the existence of unit cost functions.

[20] Differentiating the unit cost function gives us $-p_x t_x du = \partial p/\partial p_l(u) \, \partial p_l(u)/\partial u \, du$. From Shephard's lemma (footnote 13) $l(u)/x(u) = \partial p/\partial p_l(u)$. Substituting this in yields Equation (1.28).

In long-run equilibrium in the urban land market, land rents in the residential sector at u_0, the boundary of the CBD, equal land rents at u_0 in the business sector, or

$$p_l(u_0)_\text{res} = p_l(u_0)_\text{bus}. \tag{1.29}$$

For this equilibrium to be stable, as indicated in the discussion of residential equilibrium with different types of consumers (p. 12), businesses must be able to outbid residences for land interior to u_0. (This is the stability condition implicit in the rent gradients in Figure 1.2.) Therefore, the slope of the bid rent curve for businesses must exceed that for residences at u_0, or

$$|\partial p_l(u_0)_\text{res}/\partial u| \leq |\partial p_l(u_0)_\text{bus}/\partial u|,$$

or, using (1.14) and (1.28), with one firm at u_0

$$N(u_0)tp_e(u) \leq x(u_0)p_x t_x. \tag{1.30}$$

Specific Functional Forms

The foregoing points are illustrated with a logarithmic linear production function of the form

$$x(u) = G(N)C'l(u)^\gamma k(u)^\beta n(u)^\delta, \qquad \gamma + \beta + \delta = 1. \tag{1.26a}$$

From the first-order conditions for profit maximization, we get the marginal productivity conditions, which may be rewritten as factor demand equations, where, for $\tilde{p}_x = p_x(1 - t_x u)$,

$$l(u) = \gamma\tilde{p}_x x(u)/p_l(u), \qquad n(u) = \delta\tilde{p}_x x(u)/p_n, \qquad k(u) = \beta\tilde{p}_x x(u)/p_k. \tag{1.31}$$

The unit cost function corresponding to this production function is obtained by substituting into the production function for $l(u)$, $k(u)$, and $n(u)$ from Equation (1.31) to get

$$p_x(1 - t_x u) = G(N)^{-1}Cp_n{}^\delta p_k{}^\beta p_l(u)^\gamma, \tag{1.27a}$$

where $C = (C')^{-1}\delta^{-\delta}\beta^{-\beta}\gamma^{-\gamma}$. Rearranging Equation (1.27a) yields a rent gradient of

$$p_l(u) = p_x^{1/\gamma}(1 - t_x u)^{1/\gamma}C^{-1/\gamma}G(N)^{1/\gamma}p_n^{-\delta/\gamma}p_k^{-\beta/\gamma}. \tag{1.32}$$

If we employ the condition that $p_l(u_0)_\text{res} = p_l(u_0)_\text{bus}$, we may write business rents as a function of $p_l(u_0)$ and distance from the city center. Substituting u_0 for u in (1.32), dividing the result by (1.32), and rearranging terms yields

$$p_l(u) = p_l(u_0)(1 - t_x u_0)^{-1/\gamma}(1 - t_x u)^{1/\gamma}. \tag{1.33}$$

The height of the business rent gradient is determined by the rent at the edge of the residential sector $p_l(u_0)$, the size of the CBD u_0, and transport costs t_x.

2.2 Aggregate Relationships in the Central Business District

Having examined equilibrium conditions for the individual producer and in the general land market, we can now determine aggregate employment of capital and labor, total output, and income from the rent of land in the CBD. Because of scale economies, general aggregate relationships for factor inputs cannot be proved by contradiction proofs. Therefore, we proceed directly to illustrating the problem with a logarithmic linear production function.

At each location from the city center the aggregate employment of labor is the employment of labor per unit of land, $n(u)/l(u)$, summed over all units of land, $2\pi u$. From the factor demand Equations (1.31), $n(u)/l(u) = \delta/\alpha p_l(u)/p_n$. Therefore total employment in the CBD is[21]

$$N = \int_0^{u_0} 2\pi u \left(\frac{\delta}{\gamma}\right)\left(\frac{p_l(u)}{p_n}\right) dN.$$

Substituting in (1.32) for $p_l(u)$ and integrating, we get

$$N = C_2 p_x^{1/\gamma} G(N)^{1/\gamma} p_n^{-1-\delta/\gamma} p_k^{-\beta/\gamma} t_x^{-2} f(t_x, u_0), \qquad (1.34)$$

where

$$C_2 = C^{1/\gamma} 2\pi \left(\frac{\delta}{\gamma}\right)\left(\frac{1}{\gamma} + 2\right)^{-1}\left(\frac{1}{\gamma} + 1\right)^{-1}$$

and

$$f(t_x, u_0) = \left\{1 - (1 - t_x u_0)^{1/\gamma + 1}\left[1 + t_x u_0\left(\frac{1}{\gamma} + 1\right)\right]\right\}.$$

Equation (1.34) describes total employment of labor in the x industry. It is sometimes interpreted as an aggregate demand function for labor in the x industry. Interpreting it as a demand function must be done with care since it

---

[21] Note that from the formulation of the production function, firm size is indeterminate, so that production activity is summed over locations rather than firms. The aggregate demand for labor may also be derived as follows. From footnote 20 the demand for labor per unit of output is $\partial p/\partial p_n$ and the unit demand for land is $\partial p/\partial p_l(u)$. Hence total employment at location u is $2\pi u(\partial p/\partial p_n)/[\partial p/\partial p_l(u)]$. Evaluating these derivatives using the unit cost function in Equation (1.27a) yields the expression above for N.

characterizes neither the demand of individual producers nor the city's demand for labor (even though the x industry is the only employer in the city). As we shall see in Chapter 2, to find the *city's* demand for labor, we have to incorporate information from the residential sector of the city to obtain a city demand function for population.

To examine the x industry's employment of labor, we differentiate (1.34) to obtain

$$\frac{dN}{N} = \frac{1}{\gamma - \varepsilon}\frac{dp_x}{p_x} - \frac{\gamma + \delta}{\gamma - \varepsilon}\frac{dp_n}{p_n} - \frac{\beta}{\gamma - \varepsilon}\frac{dp_k}{p_k}$$

$$+ \frac{e_4}{1 - \varepsilon/\gamma}du_0 - \frac{e_5}{1 - \varepsilon/\gamma}dt_x \tag{1.35}$$

where $\varepsilon = [dG(N)/dN]N/G(N)$ is the elasticity of the scale economy shift factor with respect to N and $e_4 > 0$, $e_5 \lessgtr 0$.[22] A term we shall use frequently in the next chapter, ε indicates the extent of scale economies at the *margin* of additional employment. In general, we shall assume that ε is declining with city size, or $\partial\varepsilon/\partial N < 0$, indicating that scale economies are larger at the margin when cities are small.

In examining Equation (1.34), we see that if $\varepsilon < \gamma$ or ε is relatively small, this equation will possess normally expected properties. An increase in employment is associated with a rise in output price, a decline in own input price, an increase in CBD area, and in some cases a decline in transport costs.[23] A rise in p_k, for p_x fixed, is associated with a decline in both capital and labor employment, although labor employment can be shown to increase relative to capital employment [compare the dp_k/p_k coefficients in Equations (1.35) and (1.37) for $\gamma > \varepsilon$].

If marginal scale effects are large, such that $\varepsilon > \gamma$, Equation (1.35) has seemingly unusual properties. For example, a rise in wages is associated with an increase in labor employed. However, if one interprets Equation (1.35) as stating that when scale effects are large, wages can rise as employment increases (for the same size CBD), then that makes sense.

At each location from the city center the aggregate employment of capital is $k(u)$, which can also be stated as the employment of capital per unit

---

[22]
$$e_4 = f(t_x, u_0)^{-1}(1 - t_x u_0)^{1/\gamma}\left(\frac{1}{\gamma} + 1\right)\left(\frac{1}{\gamma} + 2\right)t_x^2 u_0 > 0,$$

$$e_5 = 2t_x - t_x^{-1}u_0 e_4 > 0.$$

[23] For the same u_0, if t_x increases, rents should rise nearer the city center relative to farther away due to increased premiums on access to the transport node. This increase in rents will lead to a greater use of N relative to land but a potentially offsetting reduction in demand for all factors.

of land, $k(u)/l(u)$, summed over all units of land $2\pi u$. From the factor demand Equation (1.31), $k(u)/l(u) = \beta/\gamma)p_l(u)/p_k$. Therefore total employment in the CBD is

$$K = \int_0^{u_0} k(u)\,du = \int_0^{u_0} 2\pi u k(u)/l(u)\,du = \int_0^{u_0} 2\pi u (\beta/\gamma)p_l(u)/p_k\,du.$$

To evaluate this we can substitute in Equation (1.32) for $p_l(u)$ and integrate. Alternatively, from Equation (1.31) two first-order conditions are $p_n = \delta\tilde{p}_x x(u)/n(u)$ and $p_k = \beta\tilde{p}_x x(u)/k(u)$. Combining and solving out $p_x x$, we get $k(u) = (\beta/\delta)p_k^{-1}p_n n(u)$. Since $N = \int_0^{u_0} n(u)\,du$, we may then state

$$K_{\text{bus}} = \int_0^{u_0} k(u)\,du = (\beta/\delta)p_n p_k^{-1} N. \tag{1.36}$$

Differentiating (1.36) yields the properties of the employment function for capital.

$$\frac{dK}{K} = \frac{dp_n}{p_n} - \frac{dp_k}{p_k} + \frac{dN}{N}.$$

To make this comparable with the function for labor, we substitute in Equation (1.35) for dN/N to get

$$\frac{dK}{K} = \frac{1}{\gamma - \varepsilon}\frac{dp_x}{p_x} - \frac{\delta + \varepsilon}{\gamma - \varepsilon}\frac{dp_n}{p_n} - \frac{\beta + \gamma - \varepsilon}{\gamma - \varepsilon}\frac{dp_k}{p_k}$$

$$+ \frac{e_4}{1 - \varepsilon/\gamma}du_0 - \frac{e_5}{1 - \varepsilon/\gamma}dt_x. \tag{1.37}$$

When scale effects are small, the properties of this employment of capital equation will be similar to those of the properties of the labor equation. Increases in capital usage are associated with increases in output price and CBD area and declines in own price. An increase in the price of labor is associated with an absolute decline in capital usage, but a rise relative to labor usage [compare the coefficients of dp_n/p_n in (1.35) and (1.37) if $\gamma > \varepsilon$]. As before, if scale effects are large, the properties of Equation (1.37) may seem unusual but are plausible.

For future reference we define expressions for total CBD rents and total output actually retailed at the transport–marketing node.

$$\text{Rents}_{\text{bus}} = \int_0^{u_0} 2\pi u p_l(u)\,du,$$

$$X = \int_0^{u_0} x(u)(1 - t_x u)\,du$$

To solve these equations we can do appropriate substitutions and integrate. Alternatively, we note from the labor marginal productivity condition that $x(u) = p_n n(u) \delta^{-1} \tilde{p}_x^{-1}$ and therefore using Equation (1.34), where

$$N = \int_0^{u_0} n(u)\, du = \int_0^{u_0} 2\pi u\, \delta/\gamma p_l(u)/p_n\, du,$$

it is possible to evaluate both equations directly in terms of labor employment. Doing this, we find

$$\text{Rents}_{\text{bus}} = (\gamma/\delta) p_n N, \tag{1.38}$$

$$X = \delta^{-1} p_x^{-1} p_n N. \tag{1.39}$$

These expressions for CBD rents and output plus the expressions for CBD employment of capital and labor define the primary aggregate relationships in the CBD.

2

An Aggregative Model of a Simple City

In this chapter an aggregative model of a city is presented and analyzed. The purpose of developing an aggregative model is to solve for the city's total demand for population, factor incomes, and equilibrium city size, and to show how various economic characteristics of the city vary with city size. Given this analysis, we can solve for equilibrium city size by postulating a supply function of people to the city and then analyzing the behavior of economic agents in limiting city sizes. In addition to being used to solve for equilibrium city size, the model that is developed can be used to do comparative static analyses of the long-run effect on city size and other economic characteristics of changes in commuting costs, property taxes, and other variables.

In the previous chapter I developed a model of the residential and business sectors of a city and derived functions describing aggregate demands for labor, capital, and land in those sectors. The aggregative model combines these two sectors to find the city's total demand for factors, factor income, and city size given the supply functions of factors available to the city. The model is solved using the specific functional forms introduced in Chapter 1. In doing this it is assumed that city residents have identical incomes and tastes. In a sense a partial equilibrium framework is assumed since the city is treated as a small entity relative to the rest of the economy and world. As such, the city borrows capital at a fixed rental rate in national or international markets; it buys and sells traded goods at fixed prices or at least faces a given demand function for its exports; and it has an exogenous supply function of labor.

Given that the basic objective is to solve for city size, the initial goal is to express variables such as rents, wages, and spatial area of the city in terms of city size. With this information, since the indirect utility function is a function of income, rents, and commuting distance, utility can then be solved for as a function of city size. Reflected in the indirect utility function are the facts that a city is both a place to work (earn wages) and live (pay rents and commuting costs). For example, I show under certain conditions that as city size increases, initially utility rises as wages rise due to scale economies in production. Eventually, however, as city size continues to grow, increasing commuting costs and declining leisure offset the benefits of higher wages and people's welfare starts to decline with increasing city size. Given this analysis, we can determine what utility levels a city can offer and thus we shall have a city demand function for population. Combining this demand function with a supply function, we shall be able to solve for city size.

In solving for city size, it is essential to identify economic actors in the model and their sources of income. Laborers receive wages and incur urban costs of living by working in the city. City land rents are collected by the city government or by a city land bank company in which all city residents own equal shares. Collected land rents are then divided up equally among city residents and are a second source of income. This method avoids introducing a separate class of people, or rentiers, although we shall see in Section 2.2 the impact of their introduction. For capital, there is a separate group of people, or capital owners, who we assume in this chapter do not live in the city. The city borrows all of its capital in national or international markets.

In this chapter the final group of actors are city governments. Their activities may be to restrict city size through various zoning or land-use regulations so as to maximize their particular objective functions, and second, to act as a collector and distributor of urban land rents. In the partial equilibrium model in this chapter the existence of city governments that are able to limit city sizes may produce conflicts between the city size that is best for initial residents, any excluded residents, and possibly the economy as a whole.

In Chapter 11, which examines a general equilibrium model of a system of cities, I consider alternative and sometimes more sophisticated specifications of the nature of our actors. In particular, I detail more precisely the nature of capital owners, land developers, and land bank companies.

Those readers who are not interested in the technical derivation of city size equations may turn directly to Section 2.2 for an analysis of the solution. Until that section, I shall be demonstrating how to arrive at equations showing the relationship between city size and utility.

1. THE AGGREGATIVE MODEL

In Chapter 1, I specified logarithmic linear utility and production functions of the form $V = A'x(u)^a z(u)^b h(u)^c e(u)^d$ and $x = G(N)B'l(u)^\gamma k(u)^\beta n(u)^\delta$, where $a + b + c = f$ and $\gamma + \beta + \delta = 1$. Residents consume $x(u)$, the city's produced good; $z(u)$, its import good; $h(u)$, housing; and $e(u)$, leisure. The terms $l(u)$, $k(u)$, and $n(u)$ are firm employment of land, capital, and labor; and $G(N)$ is a Hicks neutral production function shifter where N is city population. Given these functional forms and the analysis of spatial equilibrium, we developed expressions describing city population, business employment of labor, and residential and business employment of capital and land. We use these aggregate relationships here to develop and solve a model of city size. The basic equations of the model describe full employment in the labor, capital, and land markets, demand and supply of the city's output, and income in the city.

1.1   Basic Aggregative Equations

From Equation (1.34) there is the business employment of labor

$$N = t_x^{-2} C_2 p_x^{1/\gamma} G(N)^{1/\gamma} p_n^{-1-\delta/\gamma} p_k^{-\beta/\gamma} f(t_x, u_0), \qquad (2.1)$$

where p_x, p_n, and p_k are the prices of x, n, and k; t_x is the cost of shipping x a unit distance; and u_0 is the radius of the CBD. Labor is fully employed, so business employment equals residential population, or from Equation (1.22)

$$N = C_1 p_l(u_1) y^{-1} t^{-2} s(t, u_0, u_1), \qquad (2.2)$$

where $p_l(u_1)$ is land rent at the edge, y is income, t is unit distance commuting costs, and u_1 is city radius.

The city's total usage of capital K equals the sum of its residential and business uses or, summing Equations (1.24) and (1.36),

$$K = (1 - \alpha)(c/f)yp_k^{-1}N + (\beta/\delta)p_n p_k^{-1}N$$

or

$$K/N = p_k^{-1}[(1 - \alpha)(c/f)y + (\beta/\delta)p_n]. \qquad (2.3)$$

A supply function of capital is not separately specified because the supply of capital to the city will be infinitely elastic at the current capital rental rate determined in national and international markets.

In terms of the urban land market, there are two aggregative relationships. When the market is in equilibrium, residential rents at the city edge will equal farm rents and residential rents at the edge of the CBD will equal business rents at that point. For the latter condition, from Equations (1.15c) and (1.32)

$$p_l(u_0) = p_l(u_1)(T - tu_1)^{-d/(c\alpha)}(T - tu_0)^{d/(c\alpha)}$$
$$= p_x^{1/\gamma}C^{-1/\gamma}G(N)^{1/\gamma}(1 - t_x u_0)^{1/\gamma}p_n^{-\delta/\gamma}p_k^{-\beta/\gamma}. \qquad (2.4)$$

If p_x and p_z are assumed fixed or set in national markets, we do not need to separately specify demand functions for city output. However, if p_x is variable to the city and is determined by, say, the potential export market area of the city, then we could write p_x as

$$p_x = p(X). \qquad (2.5)$$

Then it would be necessary to introduce the expression for total city output from Equation (1.39), or

$$X = \delta^{-1}p_x^{-1}p_nN. \qquad (2.6)$$

The final relationship needed to determine equilibrium in a city of a given size is the income equation for people living in the city. Laborers are the only city residents and, for now, we assume that they are paid their wage income plus their share of income from urban land use. Essentially each resident holds an equal share in a city land bank company. From Equation (1.25) total residential rents are $(\alpha c/f)yN$ and from Equation (1.38) total business rents are $(\gamma/\delta)p_nN$. However, the city pays out to the federal government (or farmers) the opportunity cost of the urban land, which is the rental value of land removed from agricultural production or the urban land area πu_1^2 multiplied by the opportunity cost of agricultural land $p_l(u_1)$. For algebraic simplicity we assume that these rental payments to the federal government are transferred back to the city, so the net loss of rental income is zero.[1] Therefore, per person labor income is

$$y = p_n + \left(\frac{\alpha c}{f}\right)y + \left(\frac{\gamma}{\delta}\right)p_n$$

or, rearranging terms,

$$y = \left(1 - \frac{\alpha c}{f}\right)^{-1}\left(1 + \frac{\gamma}{\delta}\right)p_n. \qquad (2.7)$$

---

[1] This implies there is an inefficiency in the urban land market, since people at the city edge are still charged $p_l(u_1)$, even though the effective cost of agricultural land to the city is zero. We are faced with an algebraic dilemma. If we subtract average agricultural rents from Equation (2.7), our model becomes an algebraic and expositional nightmare (although it can be solved). On the other hand, we cannot let $p_l(u_1) = 0$, given the form of our utility function and rent gradient. [If $p_l(u_1) = 0$, at the city edge the demand and use of land is infinite, or u_1 is indeterminate, and the rent gradient $p_l(u) = p_l(u_1)(T - tu_1)^{-d/c\alpha}(T - tu)^{d/c\alpha}$ has no useful interpretation in our model.]

Equations (2.1)–(2.7) provide sufficient information to enable us to solve for wages, incomes, rents, capital employment, and spatial dimensions of the city as a function of city size or population. In terms of equation counting, holding $t, t_x, p_l(u_1)$, and p_k fixed, we have seven equations; seven unknowns, p_n, y, u_0, u_1, K, p_x, and X; and one variable, N. From the way in which the aggregative equations are derived, any solutions subsume perfect competition, equalization of factor prices and private marginal products, equalization of price ratios and consumer marginal rates of substitution, and efficient land use by consumers and producers within the city.

Unfortunately, Equations (2.1)–(2.7) are sufficiently complicated that they cannot be solved directly through substitution. However, we can develop the properties of the solution by showing how the variables in the system change with city size.

1.2 Demand and Supply Relationships for City Population

Although we can show how the variables in the system vary with city size, what we really want is to determine equilibrium city size. To do this we must derive the city demand function for labor, which describes the utility levels the city can offer as its size varies, and combine it with a supply function of labor. Since, by the nature of spatial equilibrium, all identical residents of the city have equal utility levels, we examine how the utility of a representative individual changes as city size changes to determine the demand function. We choose the person at the city edge. Using the indirect utility function, or Equation (1.4a), after substituting in the unit cost function, or Equation (1.12a), for the price of housing, we have

$$V(u_1) = [A_1 p_x^{-a} p_z^{-b} p_l(u_1)^{-c\alpha}] y^f p_k^{-c(1-\alpha)} (T - tu_1)^d \qquad (2.8)$$

where $A_1 = AB^{-c}$. Since all these variables can be solved for in terms of city size or population, V, or utility, can be expressed as a function of city size; this then is the demand function.

The supply function of labor in a partial equilibrium model is exogenously given and is of the form

$$N^s = N(V), \qquad \infty \geq \partial N / \partial V \geq 0. \qquad (2.9)$$

The supply curve is presumed to be upward sloping. Potential residents may incur moving and information costs if they decide they want to leave their location in other cities. To attract more people from farther away, having higher information and moving costs, the city may have to offer higher benefits or utility levels. Of course the city may be modeled as being completely open in a long-run setting, so that the supply curve is horizontal. For the basic results presented below, which assumption is made is not critical.

To determine solutions for city size, we differentiate the equations of the model to see how key variables vary with city size. This differentiation is the key to solving for city size and for doing any comparative statics, as well as for developing the properties of a simple growth model of a city. In developing our solutions, to simplify the exposition, we make two assumptions in the textual presentation of the model, both of which are relaxed for interested readers in footnotes to the text. We first assume that the relative prices of traded goods are fixed, or that the city faces an infinitely elastic demand curve for its export. This assumption is in line with the partial equilibrium view of the city in this chapter.

The second assumption is that the area of the CBD is fixed or zoned with the result that u_0 becomes an exogenous variable. This has the effect of eliminating Equation (2.4) for equilibrium in the land market, which equates residential and business rents at u_0. Since u_0 is fixed, there is no reason to expect rents to be equalized at the border. This assumption greatly simplifies the algebra and interpretation of results.

2. PARTIAL EQUILIBRIUM CITY SIZE

To proceed to solve for city size, we differentiate the equations of the model and investigate how wages, city spatial area, the K/N ratio, and utility levels vary as city size increases, given the parameters of the model. Besides the terms of trade and borrowing rate, variables held fixed are the rent in agriculture, those describing transportation technology, and, in the textual presentation, the size of the CBD, u_0.

2.1 Wage, Capital Intensity, and Utility Rates

To find out how wages vary, I differentiate the labor employment Equation (2 1) where $N = C_2 p_x^{1/\gamma} G(N)^{1/\gamma} p_n^{-1-\delta/\gamma} p_k^{-\beta/\gamma} t_x^{-2} f(t_x, u_0)$. Differentiating and rearranging terms yields[2]

$$\frac{dp_n}{p_n} = \frac{\varepsilon - \gamma}{\gamma + \delta} \frac{dN}{N}.$$

(2.10)

The elasticity of the scale effects with respect to city population equals $(dG/dN)/(N/G)$. In general it is assumed that

$$d\varepsilon/dN < 0,$$

(2.11)

or that the elasticity of scale effects declines monotonically with city size. Equation (2.11) is consistent with empirical evidence that scale effects peter out as city size increases (Henderson 1985a).

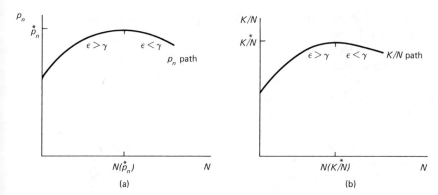

FIGURE 2.1   Wage and capital demand paths.

In Equation (2.10) if $\varepsilon > \gamma$, the coefficient of dN/N is positive and p_n increases with city size; if $\varepsilon < \gamma$, p_n decreases with city size. We assume that ε *starts out larger than* γ *and declines strictly monotonically*, so that p_n has a unique maximum, or $dp_n/p_n = 0$ when $\varepsilon = \gamma$. This is graphed in Figure 2.1a. If ε

---

[2] If u_0 is endogenous we must differentiate both the population and labor employment equations to get

$$\frac{dN}{N} = -\frac{\gamma + \delta}{\gamma - \varepsilon}\frac{dp_n}{p_n} + \frac{\gamma e_4}{\gamma - \varepsilon}du_0, \qquad (2.10a)$$

$$\frac{dN}{N} = -\frac{dy}{y} + e_1\,du_1 - e_3\,du_0, \qquad (2.12a)$$

where e_4, $e_3 > 0$ are as defined in Chapter 1. There is also an additional equation for equilibrium in the urban land market. Differentiating Equation (2.4), we get

$$\frac{td}{\alpha c}(T - tu_1)^{-1}\,du_1 - \frac{td}{c\alpha}(T - tu_0)^{-1}\,du_0 = -\frac{t_x}{\gamma}(1 - t_x u_0)^{-1}du_0 - \frac{\delta}{\gamma}\frac{dp_n}{p_n} + \frac{\varepsilon}{\gamma}\frac{dN}{N}. \qquad (a)$$

We solve (2.10a) for du_0 and substitute into (2.12a) to get

$$du_1 = (e_1\gamma e_4)^{-1}\left\{[e_3(\gamma - \varepsilon + \gamma e_4]\frac{dN}{N} + [e_3(\gamma + \delta) + \gamma e_4]\frac{dp_n}{p_n}\right\}.$$

Substituting for du_1 and du_0 in Equation (a), we get

$$\frac{dp_n}{p_n} = \frac{\varepsilon(1 + e_6) - \gamma e_6 - e_7}{e_6(\gamma + \delta) + \delta + e_7}\frac{dN}{N}, \qquad (b)$$

where

$$e_6 = e_4^{-1}\left[\frac{t_x}{\gamma}(1 - t_x u_0)^{-1} - \frac{td}{c\alpha}(T - tu_0)^{-1} + \frac{e_3 e_7}{\gamma}\right] > 0$$

$$e_7 = \gamma e_1^{-1}\frac{td}{c\alpha}(T - tu_1)^{-1} > 0.$$

does not decline monotonically but jumps up and down, there may be several local maxima to the p_n path. Second, if ε does not decline past γ for a finite N, p_n will not have a local maximum and it will either rise or fall continuously. We choose to concentrate on the situation in Figure 2.1a.

Intuitively, the following forces are at work on p_n. As long as scale economies ε is relatively large, given a fixed p_x, with increasing efficiency firms can afford to pay higher wages.[3] However, as city size increases, so do CBD rents. With u_0 fixed, more firms and labor and capital employment are competing for the fixed amount of land, thus driving up land rents. If u_0 is variable and market determined, as city size grows, residential commuting distances and u_1 rise, driving up rents in the residential area and at u_0.[4] This forces up the level of land rents businesses have to pay to bid CBD land away from residences. In Equation (2.10) these land rent effects are represented by the share of land in x production, γ. Once $\gamma > \varepsilon$, to meet their rising unit land rent obligations, firms must offer lower p_n. Thus a firm's ability to pay both higher land rents and wages out of the fixed p_x as city size increases is limited by efficiency increases or the size of ε.

To find how the spatial area of the city changes as N increases, we first differentiate the residential population equation (2.2), where

$$N = C_1 p_l(u_1) y^{-1} t^{-2} s(t, u_0, u_1),$$

to get, from Equation (1.23),

$$dN/N = -dy/y + e_1 \, du_1. \tag{2.12}$$

By differentiating the income equation (2.7), where

$$y = (1 - c\alpha/f)^{-1}(1 + \gamma/\delta)p_n,$$

we see that

$$dy/y = dp_n/p_n. \tag{2.13}$$

---

[3] If p_x is variable, substituting the differential form of Equations (2.5) and (2.6) into the differentiated form of (2.5) for dp_x/p_x, we obtain for Equation (2.10)

$$\frac{dp_n}{p_n} = \frac{\varepsilon - \gamma + \eta/(\eta + 1)}{\gamma + \delta - \eta/(\eta + 1)} \frac{dN}{N},$$

where the elasticity of demand $\eta < 0$. If $|\eta| < 1$, or demand is inelastic, this reduces city size where p_n is maximized. If $|\eta| > 1$, it increases it. These are intuitively appealing results.

[4] From footnote 2, the condition for a maximum with u_0 endogenous from Equation (b) is $\varepsilon(1 + e_6) - \gamma[e_1^{-1}(td/c\alpha)(T - tu_1)^{-1} + e_6] = 0$. From the definition of e_1 in Chapter 1 it can be shown that $e_1^{-1}(td/c\alpha)(T - tu_1)^{-1} < 1$. Therefore, as long as ε is initially greater than γ, p_n will initially rise. As ε declines, at some point where $\varepsilon < \gamma$ (given that the coefficient of ε is greater than that of γ), p_n will reach a maximum at $N(\overset{*}{p}_n)$. This implies that $N(\overset{*}{p}_n)$ for u_0 variable is greater than for u_0 fixed. This makes sense given the inefficiencies implied in fixing u_0.

Substituting Equation (2.13) into (2.12) and then substituting in Equation (2.10), where wage changes are a function of population changes, we can solve for u_1, where

$$du_1 = e_1^{-1} \frac{\varepsilon + \delta}{\gamma + \delta} \frac{dN}{N}. \tag{2.14}$$

Therefore the spatial area of the city increases continously as population grows.

To find out how the demand for capital varies with city size, we differentiate the capital employment Equation (2.3), where

$$K/N = p_k^{-1}[(1 - \alpha)(c/f)y + (\beta/\delta)p_n],$$

to get

$$\frac{dK}{K} - \frac{dN}{N} = \frac{dp_n}{p_n}. \tag{2.15}$$

Substituting in Equation (2.10) for wage changes and rearranging terms yields

$$\frac{dK}{K} = \frac{\delta + \varepsilon}{\delta + \gamma} \frac{dN}{N}. \tag{2.16}$$

Capital employment rises with city population, but the K/N ratio varies as the city grows. It is interesting to note how and why.

The K/N ratio rises as long as the coefficient of dN/N in Equation (2.16) is greater than one and hence as long as $\varepsilon > \gamma$. However, once $\varepsilon < \gamma$, K/N must decline. The explanation underlying these conditions is as follows. The price of capital p_k is fixed in this partial equilibrium situation; therefore, as city size grows, firms at the various locations will employ factors such that their marginal products of capital (MP_k) remain constant. From the assumptions of Chapter 1, for any firm, MP_k can be defined as being an increasing function of the scale effect N and, by diminishing return arguments, a decreasing function of $k(u)/n(u)$ and $k(u)/l(u)$. Here as long as $\varepsilon > \gamma$ firms can pay a constant MP_k, even with the individual $k(u)/n(u)$ and hence K/N rising, which has a negative effect on MP_k, because of the relatively large scale effect. The rising K/N also makes possible the payment of higher wages when $\varepsilon > \gamma$ as city size increases. However, once $\varepsilon < \gamma$, to meet escalating land rental and marginal product of land conditions given a reduced degree of marginal scale economies, for all firms the use of $k(u)$ and $n(u)$ to $l(u)$ must increase Then to maintain a given p_k and MP_k with the adverse effects of a rising $k(u)/l(u)$ and of a declining degree of marginal scale economies, in addition to N rising, the individual $k(u)/n(u)$ and hence K/N must decline. These changing factor ratios also result in wages declining [i.e., both $k(u)/n(u)$ and $l(u)/n(u)$ are declining].

This variation in K/N is graphed in Figure 2.1b. Note that as a city grows, the usual notion is that it uses more and more capital relative to other factors. However, beyond the point where wages that firms can offer are at a maximum, the city cannot maintain this growth in capital usage.

Having determined how wages, spatial area, and the K/N ratio vary with city size, we can now determine city size by deriving a city demand for population function. If we differentiate Equation (2.8) for the utility of a representative individual, where

$$V(u_1) = [A_1 p_x^{-a} p_z^{-b} p_l(u_1)^{-c\alpha}] y^f p_k^{-c(1-\alpha)} (T - tu_1)^d,$$

we get

$$dV/V = f(dy/y) - td/(T - tu_1) du_1. \tag{2.17}$$

Substituting in Equation (2.13), where $dy/y = dp_n/p_n$, and then in Equations (2.10) and (2.14) for dp_n/p_n and du_1, respectively, we get[5]

$$\frac{dV}{V} = (\gamma + \delta)^{-1} \left\{ \varepsilon [f - td(T - tu_1)^{-1} e_1^{-1}] \right.$$

$$\left. - \gamma \left[f + \left(\frac{\delta}{\gamma}\right) td(T - tu_1)^{-1} e_1^{-1} \right] \right\} \frac{dN}{N}. \tag{2.18}$$

Given the definition of e_1 in Chapter 1, it can be shown that $c\alpha > tde_1^{-1}(T - tu_1)^{-1}$, and therefore the coefficient of ε is positive, given that $f = a + b + c > c$ and $\alpha < 1$. If ε is sufficiently larger than γ, the bracketed expression will be positive and V will increase with population. What happens as population continues to increase from a point where $dV/dN > 0$? Although u_1 and e_1 also change value, the basic impact is through ε declining as N increases. As ε declines toward γ with increasing city size, utility will reach a maximum, or $dV = 0$ when ε is still greater than γ, given that the coefficient of ε in Equation (2.18) is less than that of γ. Then with further growth, utility will start

---

[5] For u_0 varying dV/V may be obtained by substituting into Equation (2.17) the expressions for du_1 and dp_n/p_n from footnote 2. This yields

$$\frac{dV}{V} = \left(\varepsilon \left[f(1 + e_6) - \frac{td}{(T - tu_1)e_1} \left(1 + e_6 + \frac{\gamma e_3 - e_7 e_3}{e_4 \gamma}\right) \right] \right.$$

$$\left. - \gamma \left\{ fe_6 + \frac{td}{(T - tu_1)e_1} \left[f + \frac{\delta}{\gamma} \left(1 + e_6 + \frac{e_3}{e_4} - \frac{e_7 e_3}{e_4 \gamma}\right) \right] \right\} \right) [e_6(\gamma + \delta) + \delta + e_7]^{-1} \frac{dN}{N}.$$

Comparing this equation when u_0 is variable with Equation (2.17) for u_0 fixed, we see that the coefficient of ε increases, while the change in the coefficient of γ is unclear. Thus it seems likely that $dV = 0$ at a larger N (lower ε) for u_0 variable than for u_0 fixed.

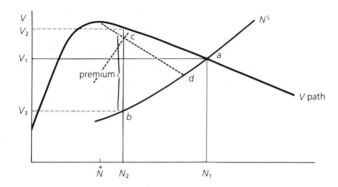

FIGURE 2.2   Utility path and city size.

to decline. Thus, comparing Equation (2.18) for dV/V with Equation (2.10) for dp_n/p_n, we find that utility reaches a maximum before p_n does (at $\varepsilon = \gamma$). Since, as city size grows, utility changes are the value of wage changes *deflated* by leisure losses from increased commuting time, this result is intuitively appealing. This city size that maximizes utility is smaller than that which maximizes wages. Of course, if ε is always less than γ, the V path declines over all ranges of N; and if ε is always sufficiently greater than γ, the V path rises over all ranges of N. A utility path with a unique maximum is graphed in Figure 2.2.

This situation where ε starts out larger than γ and then declines past γ is meant to capture the notion that, as a unit, cities have declining efficiency as their sizes becomes larger and larger. Instead of assuming that the degree of marginal scale economies declines with city growth, one can simulate this effect of declining efficiency in a simple model of a city by assuming that congestion and the average unit costs of commuting increase with city size. Dixit (1973) used this assumption.

2.2   Solving for City Size

The Competitive Solution

In discussing equilibrium city size, Figure 2.2 is used to illustrate the problem. The utility path derived from Equation (2.18), which reflects the trade-off between production scale benefits of increasing city size versus consumption scale costs, is interpreted as a city "demand" function for population. It shows the various utility levels a city can offer, under the market equilibrium constraint of equal utility for all residents. The supply function of population is given by Equation (2.9).

The competitive solution is the traditional one, where equilibrium size is determined by the intersection of demand and supply curves. For supply curve N^s equilibrium is at point a, with city size N_1 and utility V_1. People enter the city until utility falls to the level of the opportunity utility (along N^s) for the marginal entrant. Note if supply intersected the V path to the left of its maximum, stability would require that the slope of N^s exceed that of the V path.

Alternate Solutions

For any supply curve of people to the city, particularly those to the right of the maximum point of the V path, there exists the possibility that restrictions on city size will benefit certain of the economic agents in the model. For example, given N^s in Figure 2.2, suppose city size is restricted to N_2. This has the impact of raising *potential* utility for people in the city to V_2. Those excluded from the city will have much lower utility, given by their place on the N^s curve, and hence they will be willing to pay a premium to enter the city so as to get V_2. To see who in fact would benefit from such restrictions and what city size would result, we must first consider how city size can be restricted in an economy with freedom of migration.

To restrict entry into the city in the context of existing institutional mechanisms, zoning is required. Given the optimal spatial area (u_1^*) of the city, optimal lot size $l^*(u)$, and optimal land-use intensities $(k/l)^*$ at the desired equilibrium solution, zoning would prohibit the conversion of farm to residential land beyond u_1^*, fix lot sizes $l^*(u)$, and regulate land-use intensities $(k/l)^*$ (to control population density). Taken together, these would fix the number of dwelling units in the city and hence regulate city population. Then the key to entering the city for excluded residents is acquiring a dwelling unit. If city size is restricted to N_2 and hence excluded people experience utility less than the potential level V_2 in the city, excluded residents would be willing to pay a premium to live in the city. This premium is equal at most to the monetized value of the difference between V_2 and their current utility on the N^s curve. What will be the impact of this, and how will N_2 be chosen? The analysis follows Henderson (1982a).

To answer that, for reasons that will become apparent, we first consider a situation in which all land in the city is owned by a group of absentee landlords, or rentiers. Within our framework, we assume they, not the residents, own the shares in the city land bank company so that they collect the usual rents implied by the city's equilibrium rent gradient. But with restricted city size and excluded residents willing to pay premiums to enter the city, rentiers can collect premiums above the rents implied by the equilibrium rent gradient that reflects only a schedule of premiums for access to the CBD. That is, if city size is restricted and excluded residents are willing to pay premiums to enter the city, residents in the city are going to have to pay premiums to retain their dwelling units. In general terms, the rentiers thus face the following problem.[6]

We retain the definition of *potential* utility in Equation (2.8) for convenience and assume that the land bank company imposes a (non-discriminatory) *lump-sum* charge of F on each dwelling unit. By retaining Equation (2.8), F will include the shares in land rents, which in the previous section were paid to city residents, plus the premiums on entry to the city. The land bank company seeks to maximize profits, FN, subject to the constraint that *realized* utility of city residents, $V = V(y - F, ...)$ from (2.8) does not fall below utility along N^s, which is $V^s = V^s(N)$ from inversion of Equation (2.9).

Thus the land bank company seeks too maximize

$$FN + \alpha[V^s(N) - V(y - F, ...)], \tag{2.19}$$

where y and other arguments of $V(y - F, ...)$ are a function of N. Maximizing Equation (2.19) with respect to N and F and combining the two first-order conditions to eliminate $\alpha[= -N/(\partial V/\partial y)]$, we get

$$F = \left(\frac{-\partial V/\partial N}{\partial V/\partial y}\right)N + \left(\frac{\partial V^s/\partial N}{\partial V/\partial y}\right)N. \tag{2.20}$$

In Equation (2.20) city size is set such that the marginal benefit of increasing city size, or the additional fee F paid by the last entrant, just equals the marginal cost. On the right-hand side of (2.20) marginal cost is the reduction in revenue paid by existing residents, where is N times the monetized $[1/(\partial V/\partial y)]$ value of the reduction in per resident potential utility the city can pay out (the V path when $\partial V/\partial N < 0$), plus N times the monetized value of the increase in the alternative utility level, $V^s(N)$, the land bank company must meet. The lump-sum fees are heuristically the monetized value of distance (denoted "premium") at N_2 between the V path and the N^s curve in Figure 2.2. As N increases, this distance declines both because the V path is downward sloping and the N^s curve is upward sloping. Alternatively stated, for a monopoly land bank company, the V path and N^s curves are "average" utility curves, which have corresponding total $[NV$ and $NV^s(N^s)]$ curves and corresponding marginal curves $[V - (-\partial V/\partial N)N$ and $V^s(N) + (-\partial V^s/\partial N)N]$, respectively, below the V path and above N^s. A profit-maximizing monopolist heuristically (given Figure 2.2 is in V, N space not \$, N space) sets city size where the two marginal curves intersect, implying that

---

[6] We discuss the problem in general terms because imposing a fee itself affects the calculation of $V(\cdot)$ in Equation (2.8) and the precise nature of the fee (lump-sum, income tax, property tax, etc.) affects the solution to (2.20).

$V - V^s(N) = (-\partial V/\partial N)N + (\partial V^s/\partial N)N$, or $F \approx [V - V^s(N)]/(\partial V/\partial y) =$ $[(-\partial V/\partial N)N + (\partial V^s/\partial N)N]/(\partial V/\partial y)$ as in Equation (2.20). These marginal curves are graphed by the dotted lines in Figure 2.2, which intersect at point c.

Given rentiers own the land, restricting city size is not a desirable solution for city residents whose realized utility level is V_3, as opposed to the potential V_2, nor is it desirable for excluded residents. Excluded residents (up to point a) are those along N^s to the right of point b, whose alternative utility levels exceed V_3. Excluded and existing residents would be better off with an unrestricted city size of N_1, yielding potential *and* realized utility of V_1. If institutional structures are such that city residents through the city government set zoning laws, they will favor unrestrictive policies. However, if the rentier-owned city land bank company, or development corporation, can set zoning regulations, then restrictive policies will result. These institutional structures are discussed in Chapter 10.

Now we are ready to return to the normal assumption of this chapter that existing city residents own the land bank company. The only rigorous solution to this problem in a *static* situation is one were the city residents get their shares in the land bank company by purchasing them from the rentiers. That is, to get potential utility level V_2, each city resident must first pay the capitalized value of F (paid indefinitely under renting) to *purchase* a share in the land bank company, thus reducing effective utility to V_3 (after accounting for the purchase cost). (Note this is not precluded by the analysis to date in this chapter). Thus the solution is unchanged whether residents rent or purchase shares in a land bank company.

I have three comments on this solution. First, there is no way the residents can acquire ownership such as free homesteading that allows owner-residents to realize higher utility levels along V by *restricting city size*. While it would benefit included residents to restrict city size so as to realize high utility levels along the V path, there is no ready mechanism in a static model to determine who would restrict who, nor who (along N^s) would be included versus excluded. The only way to achieve a solution where some residents can claim the benefits of city size restrictions (without introducing rentiers) is to introduce dynamic considerations. Such a model is presented in Chapter 10.

Second, city size at N_2 in Figure 2.2 is not a Pareto-efficient size, given it is a monopoly solution. A perfectly discriminating monopolist would achieve a Pareto-efficient solution. In that case the solution in Figure 2.2 would be at point d where the marginal utility path intersects the opportunity cost curve (N^s) of migrants (i.e., the utility path and its marginal curve correspond to the average revenue and marginal revenue product curves in the standard perfectly discriminating monopsonist diagram of the demand for labor in production of widgets, while the N^s curve corresponds to the supply of labor curve). The monopolist's profits would be the area between the utility level associated with point d and the N^s curve. The implication is also that the competitive solution at point a is not Pareto-efficient. That fact will be analyzed in the welfare analysis of a system of cities later in the book. Third, this partial equilibrium situation where the rentiers of this city have monopoly power implies that this urban site has special features, which other sites do not have. Otherwise developers in uninhabited sites would compete for the residents.

3. COMPARATIVE STATICS

Suppose a city is initially in equilibrium in Figure 2.2 at the traditional market solution, given by the intersection of demand and supply curves. Comparative static analyses are used to find out what happens to this equilibrium in terms of city sizes, wages, utility levels, etc., if the value of exogenous variables or parameters change by small amounts. There are many examples of comparative statics exercises in the urban literature. Almost all concentrate exclusively on the residential sector of the city, ignoring the production sector and the city's interaction with the rest of the economy. A good summary of these residentially focused analyses is Wheaton (1979).

In presenting an example of comparative static analysis, we allow for changes in all sectors of the city. A parametric change that directly affects the residential sector so as to potentially alter equilibrium city size will thus indirectly affect the production sector by altering scale levels and wage levels the city can pay out. The ultimate solution depends on the interaction and outcome of all effects on all sectors.

Second, while the urban literature generally assumes that the supply curve of people to the city in Figure 2.2 is infinitely elastic, we make a more traditional "partial" equilibrium assumption (partial to the rest of the economy) that the supply curve is upward sloping so that changes in exogenous variables or parameters will affect utility levels as well as city sizes in Figure 2.2, as the point of intersection of N^s with the shifting V path changes. If N^s was infinitely elastic, as the V path shifted while city size would change, utility would not (given an infinitely elastic supply of people). Thus any good or bad policy of the city would only affect city size and not the welfare of its residents. We allow the welfare of residents to be affected, which is the only assumption consistent with general equilibrium in the economy.

One comparative statics exercise in urban models is to vary the commuting cost variable t to determine the effect on city size. We examine the effect of a change in t on city size here briefly. Suppose we are currently at equilibrium as determined by the intersection of a demand and supply function as at point a in Figure 2.2. Then, commuting costs t exogenously increase. What happens to city size?

To see this we differentiate the equations in our model, allowing both city size and t to vary, where the change in t is given exogenously. Differentiating the employment and income equations, we still get $dp_n/p_n = (\varepsilon - \gamma)/(\gamma + \delta)\,dN/N$ and $dy/y = dp_n/p_n$, respectively. Differentiating the residential population equation, we have $dN/N = -dy/y + e_1\,du_1 + e_2\,dt$. Substituting into this for dy/y and then dp_n/p_n, we find

$$du_1 = e_1^{-1}(\varepsilon + \delta)/(\gamma + \delta)\,dN/N - e_2/e_1\,dt.$$

Differentiating the utility equation, we now have

$$dV/V = f(dy/y) - td/(T - tu_1)\,du_1 - u_1 d/(T - tu_1)\,dt.$$

Substituting into this for dy/y and then dp_n/p_n and du_1, we obtain

$$dV/V = e_8\frac{dN}{N} + \left[\left(\frac{e_2}{e_1}\right)td - u_1 d\right](T - tu_1)^{-1}\,dt, \qquad (2.21)$$

where

$$e_8 = f\left(\frac{\varepsilon - \gamma}{\gamma + \delta}\right) - e_1^{-1}\left(\frac{\varepsilon + \delta}{\gamma + \delta}\right)td(T - tu_1)^{-1}.$$

From the definitions of e_1 and e_2 in footnote 17, Chapter 1, we can show that $e_2 < t^{-1}u_1 e_1$ and hence that the coefficient of dt is negative. From the labor supply equation (2.9) we know by differentiation that $dN/N = \xi\,dV/V$. Combining the demand and supply equations yields

$$\frac{dN}{N} = \frac{e_1^{-1}(T - tu_1)^{-1}(e_1 u_1 d - e_2 td)}{1/\xi - e_8}\,dt.$$

The numerator of this expression is negative. If city size is beyond $N(\dot{V})$, from Equation (2.18) we can shown that $e_8 < 0$ and hence the denominator is always positive. In that case, for $dt > 0$, $dN/N < 0$; or city size declines as t increases. [For city sizes less than $N(\dot{V})$, we can show that for a stable equilibrium $1/\varepsilon - e_8 > 0$, or dN/N is also negative for $dt > 0$.]

In summary, an increase in t leads to a decline in population and, from Equation (2.21), a decline in utility levels. The declines occur not just because of the adverse effect on consumers of the increase in commuting times, but also because of the wage declines that result as city size and scale start to decline. The decline in population is limited, however, by the upward sloping supply curve of people to the city, and the decline in alternative utility levels facing marginal potential emigrants.

3

Extensions of the Basic Spatial Model

In this chapter I consider two separate extensions of the spatial model in Chapter 1, both dealing with externalities that distort spatial equilibria. As discussed in Chapter 1, people crowd into urban areas to exploit external economies of scale in production that arise because of spillover benefits among firms in terms of labor and other input market efficiencies. But this phenomenon of people crowding into a limited spatial area so as to have access to common work sites or other facilities is itself the cause of many disamenities and externalities.

This close proximity of residents results in social externalities such as noise pollution, neighborhood externalities such as the benefits to a resident of nearby residents maintaining their houses and gardens, and congestion externalities in the use of parks, roads, and outdoor recreation sites. General externality relationships and detailed ways of dealing with them are discussed in Chapters 4–8 for housing, neighborhoods, and auto transportation. In this chapter I deal with the primary spatial dimensions of two sets of urban problems—racial prejudice and air pollution. I focus on the spatial aspects of these problems, which also provides opportunities to apply the model developed in Chapter 1. The more general aspects of racial prejudice are dealt with in later chapters.

1. RACIAL PREJUDICE

There is an extensive literature on the impact of racial prejudice on spatial equilibrium (e.g., Bailey, 1957; Rose-Ackerman, 1975; Yinger, 1976; and Courant and Yinger, 1977). I present one characterization of the situation that captures the basic points in the literature and then comment on the characterization.

Assume there are two income groups in the city: high-income whites and low-income blacks. We start by assuming both groups have identical preferences and initially there is no racial prejudice. Utilizing the indirect utility function from Chapter 1 where $V = V(y, p_x, p_z, p(u), e(u))$, the equilibrium slope of the rent gradient for either group is determined by evaluating Equation (1.6): $-p_e(u)t/h(u)$. We assume the lower-income group, blacks, have steeper slopes so that they live closer to the CBD (see Section 1.1 of Chapter 1). The initial equilibrium is pictured in Figure 3.1. Blacks live between u_0 and u_b and whites between u_b and u_1. The opportunity cost of housing just beyond the city edge is p_a. The spatial separation of whites and blacks is a natural market phenomenon, based on income differences.

Now we introduce a common characterization of racial prejudice, a characterization I comment on later. Blacks are assumed to still have no tastes concerning the race of their neighbors, but whites are prejudiced and do not want to live next to blacks. In particular, it is assumed that a white's discomfort is a decreasing function of distance from the nearest black. In this characterization the level of discomfort at any distance is independent of the actual *number* of blacks nearby, something I comment on later. To formally prove the propositions in the literature, it is assumed the discomfort part of the utility function is separable from the rest of the utility function, so for whites, indirect

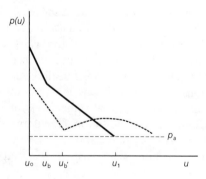

FIGURE 3.1   Racial prejudice.

utility is now

$$V(y, p_x, p_z, p(u), e(u)) + D(u - u_b),$$ (3.1)

where

$$D(\cdot) < 0, \qquad D' > 0 \qquad \text{for} \quad u - u_b < \tilde{u},$$

$$D(\cdot) = 0, \qquad D' = 0 \qquad \text{for} \quad u - u_b \geq \tilde{u}.$$

The distance of a white away from (toward u_1) the nearest black at u_b is $u - u_b$, presuming whites still live in an outer ring around blacks. The critical distance separating a white from a black where discomfort disappears is $\tilde{u}$. Note since $D(\cdot) \leq 0, D' \geq 0$ indicates that declining distance up to $\tilde{u}$ reduces discomfort. It is common to assume $D'' \leq 0$ so that discomfort declines at a decreasing rate—the initial movements away from blacks reduce discomfort the most. The invention of prejudice in some sense (see later) means blacks impose externalities on whites if they live close by.

Separability of the utility function in (3.1) has two conveniences. First, the first component of (3.1) represents the preference structure of the unprejudiced blacks, as well as the preferences of whites apart from racial discomfort. Second, the demand for housing and marginal evaluation of leisure functions for whites are the same as before prejudice, so there is no interaction between prejudice and demand for market goods. We shall use this property in proving the basic propositions.

Maximizing Equation (3.1) with respect to distance, whites now have equilibrium rent gradient slopes

$$\frac{\partial p(u)}{\partial u} = -\frac{p_e(u)t}{h(u)} + \frac{D'}{\lambda} \lessgtr 0.$$ (3.2)

The marginal utility of income is λ, and we have substituted in Roy's identity $\{h(u) = -[\partial V/\partial p(u)]/(\partial V/\partial y)\}$. In the white area, as distance from the black border increases, there are opposing effects on land rents. Declining access works to lower bid rents; but increasing distance from blacks and hence declining discomfort works to raise bid rents. The rent gradient for whites no longer need be downward sloping at all points.

A new equilibrium is pictured in Figure 3.1 by the dashed rent gradient. For any u, $p(u)$ combination for whites, the $-p_e(u)t/h(u)$ component of the slope of the rent gradient in Equation (3.2) has the same value as before prejudice (the separability assumption). Thus, as long as we are interior to $\tilde{u}$ where discomfort disappears (which is not shown in Figure 3.1), the slope of the new rent gradient for whites for any u and $p(u)$ combination must be less steep than the unprejudiced rent gradient. After $\tilde{u}$, for any u, $p(u)$ combination, the slopes would be the same.

The characteristics of the new equilibrium and the reasons for them are as follows.

1. The new gradient crosses the old from below (i.e., rotates anticlockwise). We can see this by ruling out the alternatives. First, the new rent gradient cannot be the old given the change in slopes for whites. However, the demand for housing for both groups, given separability in (3.1), is still characterized by the same function. Thus the rent gradient cannot either rise or fall at all points, since relative to the initial equilibrium that would imply, respectively, an excess supply or excess demand for housing. Finally, the new rent gradient cannot cross the old from above since that would violate relative slope conditions: The slope of the new gradient in the white sector must be less negative (or equal to) than the initial gradient.

2. The size of the black area expands in the new equilibrium. Since the new rent gradient crosses the old from below, prices in the black area must be lower (for all blacks) and hence their consumption of housing and land increases. Intuitively, at the old border, upon introduction of prejudice, prices in the white area near the old border drop as whites seek to move away from blacks. Blacks then move into these border areas to take advantage of the lower prices. The reduction in prices and increase in consumption implies a larger black area with lower population density.

3. The size of the city expands. In Figure 3.1 the only way we could get a smaller city would be if the new rent gradient recrossed the old before u_1. However, this violates the relative slope conditions that the new gradient not be steeper than the old.

In summary, prejudiced cities are spatially larger than unprejudiced ones of the same population. Intuitively, spatial dispersion of whites from blacks helps alleviate whites' discomfort. Blacks are benefited in terms of the housing market from the prejudice of whites—a white-flight result. Finally, whites pay for their prejudices with generally higher housing prices and longer commutes, over and above their basic discomfort.

There are various implications and peculiarities of the characterization of prejudice and these resulting spatial impacts that we must note. First, if white prejudices are strong enough, it is possible to have a gray belt area where no one lives between the white and black areas. In Figure 3.1, if the rent gradient for blacks would descend to p_a at u'_b, then there would be an empty gray belt, followed by the start of the white area with the rent gradient for whites rising from p_a before reversing and declining as we approach the new city edge. Second, if multiple black and white income groups exist where on the basis of income there could be alternating rings of whites and blacks or mixed areas, analyzing the impact of prejudice is very difficult. Whites in a ring can be "squeezed" by blacks on both the interior and exterior of their ring perhaps causing them to try to hop beyond the exterior group of blacks. As one experiments with possible situations and configurations, it becomes clear that in some cases it is impossible to characterize a stable equilibrium.

Third, there is a question of optimality of land allocation, given that blacks impose externalities on whites, as originally analyzed by Bailey (1957). These externalities are unpriced so that when blacks move closer to whites they are not charged for the increased discomfort they impose on whites. Thus, with white-flight, blacks push whites further out from the city center and, in Bailey's analysis, occupy too large a part of the city so that the marginal product of land is too low in the new low-density black area and too high in the crowded white area. Accepting sovereignty of whites' tastes in Equation (3.1), Bailey argued in a similar framework that it is optimal to restrict the black area of the city so blacks do not expand as far as u_b' in Figure 3.1. This feature of externalities in land markets is detailed in Section 2 of this chapter on pollution. Optimal land allocation from that section would involve either externality taxation of blacks' movements or racial zoning of land so that at the optimal black–white border (interior to u_b' in Figure 3.1) there is a discontinuity in land prices with black border land prices exceeding white ones (see Figure 3.2).

There are two responses to Bailey's characterization and adaptations of it in the literature. First, rather than assuming sovereignty of consumer tastes, we could deal with the fact that aspects of tastes are endogenously determined by the cultural environment. Alternatively viewed, under reasonable characterizations of social welfare functions, we may want to penalize prejudiced people. Second, as Loury (1978) pointed out, an optimal solution accepting sovereignty of tastes probably involves a complete reshaping of the city. Blacks would be moved out of the inner ring of the city and put in an enclave on the edge of the city. The idea is to minimize the length of the border contact between whites and blacks so as to minimize the numbers of whites affected. Having blacks in a ring does not do this. Of course, taking a larger view of the whole economy with a system of cities, rather than looking at just one city, the optimal solution is to have separate sets of all-black and all-white cities. Accepting sovereignty of consumer tastes implies spatial separation of racial groups.

The final set of comments relates to the validity of our characterization of the nature of prejudice and the discomfort function. First, there is no a priori reason to assert that one group is prejudiced and the other unprejudiced. Blacks also may experience discomfort from living next to whites. Then who invades whose area and who is penalized for their prejudices is determined by which group has the greater extent and spatial rate of decline of prejudice, with the most prejudiced group [defined in rates of decline in Equation (3.2)] losing out.

Second, in the initial characterization of prejudice some whites may not be prejudiced. In that case, if $\tilde{u}$ in Equation (3.2) is sufficiently small and the number of unprejudiced whites sufficiently large, it is possible that, with the introduction of prejudice for some whites, the equilibrium rent gradient will be unchanged. With the introduction of prejudice, as prices near the border area start to drop when prejudiced whites seek to move, unprejudiced whites will move into these areas for miniscule price reductions. Thus we could have a new equilibrium with the same rent gradient as before prejudice and the same-sized black area. The white area would contain an interior ring of unprejudiced whites and an outer ring of prejudiced (and unprejudiced) whites, providing the distance between the outer and inner edges of the ring of unprejudiced whites is at least $\tilde{u}$.

Finally, the specification of the nature of discomfort is odd. In particular, the level of discomfort of, say, whites may be a function of the *number* of blacks nearby, rather than discomfort being zero for zero blacks and $D(u - u_b)$ for one to all blacks at u_b. Discomfort may not register until, for example, the proportion of blacks to whites nearby to a white rises beyond some threshold level—small proportions may even be desired by whites. In this case where discomfort is a function of proportions in discrete spatial areas and discomfort has a positive threshold level, mixed communities may be part of a stable solution. For example, blacks could be spread in thin ribbons throughout a white base city, rather like a marble cake. An analysis of more sophisticated specifications of prejudices has been attempted by Schelling (1969, 1971).

2. INDUSTRIAL AIR POLLUTION

The literature on pollution is too extensive to even briefly survey in a book on urban economics. Instead, we focus on a narrowly defined problem with a strong spatial aspect to it. The firms in the CBD of Chapter 1 are assumed to emit air pollutants that disperse into the residential sector of the city. This problem will illustrate the basic results in the pollution literature (e.g., Baumol and Oates, 1975) for a situation in which there are a large number of both polluters and pollutees. Moreover, it will extend these basic results to an explicit spatial setting and show that optimal environmental policies in a spatial setting involve not just Pigouvian taxes on pollution, but also land-use regulation. In contrast to the previous section on race, the emphasis in this section is on the optimal allocation of resources, although equilibrium allocations are also discussed. The discussion is adapted from Henderson (1977b).

As in Chapter 1, firms in the CBD produce a marketable good x according to the production function $x(u) = G(N)x(n(u),k(u),l(u))$, or Equation

(1.26). Instead of labeling $k(u)$ capital in this chapter we are going to call it natural resources, or raw materials, that are used in production and imported by the city. As before, $G(N)$ is a Hicks neutral shift factor and $n(u)$ and $l(u)$ are inputs of labor and land. Since firm size remains indeterminate in this formulation, we identify firms by distance from the city center or by rings.

The second output of firms is airborne emissions that result in pollution or a decline in air quality and an increase in fallout of particulates. Pollution enters the utility function as a disamenity but does not affect production activity. Emissions result from the employment of the resource k and may be abated by employment in antipollution activity such as scrubbing, filtering, and two-stage combustion. Pollutants are emissions that have been dispersed by air currents and acted upon chemically by the sun's radiation and moisture in the air. As distance from an emitting source increases, the volume of pollutants per cube of air declines due to horizontal and vertical spatial diffusion of emissions and fallout or environmental absorption of pollutants.

Since we only identify pollution damages from residents, we are primarily concerned with firms' contributions to pollutants at the circular residential–CBD boundary and beyond. As before, this boundary is at distance u_0 from the city center. I examine pollution dispersion in the residential sector beyond the boundary but first focus on the buildup of pollutants at the residential–CBD boundary and on how much each firm's emissions contribute to the buildup of pollutants at the boundary.

It is not obvious how a firm's total contribution to pollutants summed over all points on the residential–CBD boundary varies with its distance from the city center. As a firm moves away from the city center toward the CBD boundary, it would seem that its emissions would have less opportunity to disperse before reaching residents and would contribute more to pollution. But as it moves closer to the CBD boundary in one direction, it is simultaneously moving farther from points on the boundary on the opposite side of the CBD, allowing for greater dispersion of emissions in that direction. However, if emissions disperse rapidly with distance, then this movement farther away from points on the opposite side of the CBD will have little impact on pollution there, since the firm's emissions will have almost entirely dissipated anyway. Then the critical factor is the movement toward points on its side of the CBD. We assume pollution is a convex function of distance from the source of emissions and that as a firm moves closer to a residential boundary its contribution to pollution for a given level of emissions increases. This argument essentially implies that additional emissions of firms at the city center contribute relatively little to total pollution, whereas additional emissions of firms at or near the CBD edge contribute more to increased pollution.

We specifically model pollution production and consumption as follows. We identify all firms by distance from the city center or the ring they are in and aggregate at the ring level. This simplification is possible since all firms are assumed to have identical production processes (and are of indeterminate size), the city is perfectly symmetrical, and stochastic factors such as wind direction and speed are ignored. Then the contribution to *pollutants* at all points *on the CBD boundary* of firms in a ring at distance u is

$$f(k(u), n_a(u), u_0, u),$$

where $k(u)$ is employment of natural resources in the ring at distance u from the city center and $\partial f/\partial k(u) \geq 0$. Employment in antipollution activity is $n_a(u)$, where $\partial f/\partial n_a(u) \leq 0$. We assume that $\partial f/\partial u_0 < 0$, or that as the CBD expands, the emissions of a firm at distance u are more dispersed before they reach residences. As we move nearer the CBD edge, a given level of emissions contributes more to pollution, or $\partial f/\partial u > 0$. Also, $\partial^2 f/(\partial k\, \partial u)$ should be positive, or as a firm moves toward the nearest residential point, the marginal effect on pollutants of employing an additional unit of k increases.

Total pollutants at all points on the CBD boundary are described as a simple sum of contributions by all CBD rings, or total pollutants are[1]

$$F(u_0) = \int_0^{u_0} f(k(u), n_a(u), u_0, u)\, du. \tag{3.3}$$

These pollutants in a symmetrical circular city are evenly distributed over all points on the residential boundary.

Residential pollution is then a function of the pollution level at u_0, or $F(u_0)$, and distance from the CBD. As we move beyond u_0, pollutants continue to diffuse. For a person located at distance u, pollution or the disamenity in the preference function is $a(u)$ and

$$a(u) = a(F(u_0), u, u_0), \tag{3.4}$$

where $F(u_0)$ is as defined in (3.3) as $\partial a/\partial F(u_0) \geq 0$; $\partial a/\partial u_0 > 0$, or as the CBD boundary shifts toward residents, for the same $F(u_0)$, pollution at each u rises. Pollutants disperse with distance, or $\partial a/\partial u \leq 0$. It seems reasonable to assume that $\partial^2 a/\partial u^2 > 0$, or pollution is a convex function of distance. The radius of the city is u_1 and it is assumed that $a(u_1) > 0$. Although $a(u_1) > 0$, we assume one city's pollution does not extend to other cities. If it did, we would have a spillover situation and, in general, some form of federal intervention would be required to set optimal pollution taxes.

---

[1] To account for increasing returns to pollution creation or decreasing ability of the environment to absorb and disperse pollutants, we could write (3.3) as $F(u_0) = \int_0^{u_0} g(F(u_0)) f(u)\, du$ where $\partial g/\partial F(u_0) \geq 0$. Then in the sections that follow we would have to tax firms according to their own contributions to pollutants plus the effect of their emissions on reduced dispersion of other firms' emissions.

It should be noted that our characterization of pollution production and consumption contains a strong implicit assumption. The spatial dispersion of pollutants within the CBD and beyond the CBD in the residential area are implicitly assumed to have different functional representations. Given the discontinuity in building heights between the industrial and residential areas and given the differences in chemical reactions among pollutants in the area where they are being dispersed from smoke stacks relative to residential areas where they are just diffusing, this assumption is probably reasonable and more general than the alternative.

However, if the spatial dispersion is the same within and beyond the CBD border, our specification in Equations (3.3) and (3.4) is misleading. Our general results on Pigouvian taxes would be similar but the analysis of land-use controls would be different, as I shall point out. For the record we note the alternative specification. If spatial dispersions are the same, then firms in ring $\tilde{u}$ in the CBD contribute

$$s(k(\tilde{u}), n_a(\tilde{u}), u, \tilde{u}) \tag{3.4a}$$

to pollution for any family in ring u in the residential area. Thus $\partial s/\partial k > 0$, $\partial s/\partial n_a < 0$, $\partial s/\partial u < 0$, $\partial s/\partial \tilde{u} > 0$. Pollution to any resident in ring u of CBD firms [the equivalent of (3.4)] is thus

$$\int_0^{u_0} s(k(\tilde{u}), n_a(\tilde{u}), u, \tilde{u}) \, d\tilde{u}.$$

I footnote critical results based on this specification as we go along.

2.1   Controlling the Output of Pollution

Without environmental policies in a market economy, firms are paid for their x output but they freely dispose of their airborne wastes or emissions. Therefore they have no incentive to engage in antipollution activity or to account for marginal pollution damages in their decisions to employ additional units of natural resources. To induce firms to employ resources in a Pareto-efficient manner, it is necessary to charge them for their contributions to pollution at a price or unit tax equal to marginal damages of pollution.

To find optimal pollution taxation policies we must calculate the marginal damages to residents of pollution. The actual welfare maximization problem underlying the problem is footnoted later. We focus on an intuitive derivation here. To do this we examine the residential sector of the city. Consumers at distance u from the city center consume the city's produced good $x(u)$, its import good $z(u)$, land $l(u)$, disamenities $a(u)$ defined in Equation (3.4), and leisure $e(u)$. Leisure is the fixed amount of nonworking time less the time it takes to commute to work in the CBD. Therefore the utility function of a consumer at location u is defined for this chapter as $V = V(x(u), z(u), l(u), a(u), e(u))$, where V is decreasing in $a(u)$ and increasing in all other arguments. Note land consumption has replaced housing consumption in the utility function. To simplify exposition when we introduce national resources in production of x, we pull out capital. Housing services from capital could in fact be buried in the $x(u)$ argument in $V(\cdot)$.

The utility lost from an increase in disamenities is $\partial V/\partial a(u)$, which evaluated in units of x is $[\partial V/\partial a(u)]/[\partial V/\partial x(u)]$. From Equation (3.4) the increase in disamenities at location u with an increase in pollutants at u_0 is $\partial a(u)/\partial F(u_0)$. In the ring at each distance u from the city center there are $N(u)$ people, so that the total marginal damages at location u from additional pollutants at u_0 are

$$-\frac{\partial V/\partial a(u)}{\partial V/\partial x(u)} N(u) \frac{\partial a(u)}{\partial F(u_0)}.$$

Summing over all residential locations gives us the total marginal damages in the city from additional pollutants at u_0. This is defined as τ where

$$\tau = -\int_{u_0}^{u_1} \frac{\partial V/\partial a(u)}{\partial V/\partial x(u)} N(u) \frac{\partial a(u)}{\partial F(u_0)} du. \tag{3.5}$$

This is the price, or unit tax, firms should be charged for their contributions to pollution at u_0.

Let us examine the behavior of a firm given that such a tax can be set. The profits of a firm facing optimal pollution taxes are[2]

$$\pi(u) = G(N)x(k(u), n(u), l(u))(1 - t_x u) - p_k k(u)$$

$$- p_n(n(u) + n_a(u)) - p_l(u)l(u) - \tau f(k(u), n_a(u), u_0, u). \tag{3.6}$$

The first term is the value of the firm's output of x where the price of x is normalized at one, and all other prices are defined in units of x. The second, third, and fourth terms are factor payments of the firm where p_n and $p_l(u)$ are, respectively, the wage rate and land rental at u. The last term is the firm's pollution charges. The unit tax rate is τ, and $f(u)$ is the assessed contribution of firm emissions to pollution at u_0. The firm views τ as a fixed price or tax that it cannot influence.[3] Given that firms are identified with CBD rings, additional pollutants are symmetrically distributed in the residential sector. The unit tax

---

[2] If the specification of pollution follows that in Equation (3.4a), total pollution taxes for firms in ring $\tilde{u}$ would be

$$\int_{u_0}^{u_1} N(u)\frac{\partial V/\partial a(u)}{\partial V/\partial x(u)} s(k(\tilde{u}), n_a(\tilde{u}), u, \tilde{u}) du.$$

[3] If the firm can influence τ by its behavior, then the first-order conditions for profit maximization derived later will not be applicable, and implementing an optimal solution will be more difficult.

rate τ is the same for different rings in the CBD.[4] It is $f(u)$, the assessed level of pollutants, that varies for the same level of emissions with location throughout the CBD.

Maximizing profits with respect to various inputs, we have as the first-order conditions for profit maximization

$$p_n = G(N)[\partial x/\partial n(u)](1 - t_x u) = -\tau[\partial f/\partial n_a(u)], \qquad (3.7)$$

$$p_l(u) = G(N)[\partial x/\partial l(u)](1 - t_x u), \qquad (3.8)$$

$$p_k = G(N)[\partial x/\partial k(u)](1 - t_x u) - \tau[\partial f/\partial k(u)]. \qquad (3.9)$$

Equation (3.7) states that the marginal product of labor will be equalized (to the wage rate) in its two activities, producing x and reducing pollution. In order to reduce its tax bill, the firm employs labor in antipollution activity until its marginal cost p_n equals its marginal benefit. This benefit is the reduction in pollution taxes from employing one more laborer, or the pollution reduction multiplied by the unit tax price of pollution. If τ is correctly assessed, then Equation (3.7) satisfies conditions for the Pareto-efficient allocation of resources since the social marginal product of labor is equalized across locations and activities.[5]

---

[4] Suppose there are multiple firms in each ring. In general, for practical purposes, it will be necessary to disaggregate from rings to coordinates and sum vertically and horizontally over all coordinates to assess taxes. Unlike a ring, a firm's pollutants will not be symmetrically distributed in the residential sector and, the damages it causes different residents at the same u will vary.

[5] This can be seen by examining the welfare maximization model. The maximization problem is identical to that in Chapter 12 except for four considerations. First, we have some labor employed in antipollution activity; second, we have an additional constraint defining consumer amenities. Third, rather than dealing with capital and capital ownership, we assume that the city imports a natural resource $k(u)$ at a fixed price p_k. Finally, rather than consuming housing produced with capital and land, residents just consume land as their housing good. The planner maximizes

$$J = V^0(x(u), z(u), l(u), a(u), e(u)) + \int_{u_0}^{u_1} \lambda_1(u)[V(x(u), z(u), l(u), a(u), e(u)) - V^0] \, du$$

$$+ \lambda_2 \left[\int_0^{u_0} G(N)x(n(u), l(u), k(u))(1 - t_x u) \, du - \int_{u_0}^{u_1} x(u)N(u) \, du - \int_{u_0}^{u_1} p_z z(u)N(u) \, du \right.$$

$$- p_k \int_0^{u_0} k(u) \, du \left] + \int_{u_0}^{u_1} \lambda_3(u) \left(a(u) - a\left(\int_0^{u_0} f(u) \, du, u, u_0 \right) \right) du \right.$$

$$+ \int_{u_0}^{u_1} \lambda_4(u)[T - e(u) - tu] \, du + \lambda_5 \left\{ N - \int_0^{u_0} [n(u) + n_a(u)] \, du \right\} + \lambda_6 \left[N - \int_{u_0}^{u_1} N(u) \, du \right]$$

$$+ \int_{u_0}^{u_1} \lambda_7(u)[2\pi u - l(u)N(u)] \, du + \int_0^{u_0} \lambda_8(u)[2\pi u - l(u)] \, du.$$

Equation (3.9) states that a firm employs natural resources until the social marginal cost of k to the city, which is p_k, is equated with the social marginal product of k, which equals the private marginal product less the marginal damages of additional pollution. Alternatively stated, the marginal benefits, or $G(N)[\partial x/\partial k(u)](1 - t_x u)$, equal the marginal cost under taxation. This marginal cost is the price of k plus the firm's increase in taxes from employing additional k, or $\tau[\partial f/\partial k(u)]$. Again, Equation (3.9) satisfies the criterion describing the efficient use of k within the city as derived in footnote 5. From a conceptual point of view there are alternative taxation policies to taxing pollution per se. One alternative is a policy of a tax $[\tau(\partial f/\partial k)]$ on employment of k combined with a subsidy $[-\tau(\partial f/\partial n_a)]$ on employment of labor in antipollution activity.

Note that as marginal pollution damages rise, for a given opportunity cost of k, k should be employed such that its private marginal product rises. The positive benefits from employing k should rise to offset the increased negative pollution effects. In general, as marginal pollution damages increase, this implies less k should be used relative to other factors in x production, so that its private marginal product rises. For example, for firms located nearer the CBD boundary, $\partial f/\partial k(u)$ may be higher given the assumptions about pollution dispersion. In that case, $\partial x/\partial k(u)$ may be higher, indicating with a homothetic production function less use of k relative to other factors in x production. This implies that although marginal damages are higher for firms located nearer the CBD boundary, their total damages may not differ as much compared with firms interior to them since less k relative to other factors is used.

We must also be concerned with the firm's profit position after taxation, which has implications for the stability of the taxation equilibrium. Substituting (3.7)–(3.9) back into (3.6) yields

$$\pi(u) = \tau[(\partial f/\partial k)k(u) + (\partial f/\partial n_a)n_a(u) - f(k(u), n_a(u), u_0, u)] \gtreqless 0. \quad (3.10)$$

In a competitive industry with free costless entry, for equilibrium we require that $\pi \rightarrow 0$. For example, if $\pi < 0$, firms will exit from the industry until $\pi \rightarrow 0$, if that is possible. In (3.10) π may not equal zero, in which case there

---

If we maximize J with respect to k and then substitute in Equation (5.3) for τ and substitute in the expression for $\lambda_3(u)$ found by maximizing J with respect to $a(u)$ and $x(u)$, the result is

$$p_k = G(N)[\partial x/\partial k(u)](1 - t_x u) - \tau[\partial f/\partial k(u)].$$

Similarly, maximizing J with respect to n and n_a and performing the same substitutions, we get

$$\lambda_5 = G(N)[\partial x/\partial n(u)](1 - t_x u) = -\tau[\partial f/\partial n_a(u)].$$

These are criteria for the optimal use of $k(u)$, $n(u)$, and $n_a(u)$.

will be either exit or entry *with no opportunity for* $\pi \to 0$ in the model, providing (3.7)–(3.9) are always satisfied. Only if f is linear homogeneous in k and n_a does $\pi = 0$. This, of course, is a version of the familiar adding-up problem. If $\pi \neq 0$, this implies firms should be lump-sum taxed or subsidized so as to ensure that $\pi \to 0$. This adding-up problem may be neutralized if there is a *fixed immobile* factor of production such as land so that (3.8) is generally not satisfied.[6]

2.2 The Allocation of Land between Businesses and Residences

The normal market interpretation of conditions describing the optimal allocation of land between competing uses in situations where there are *no* externalities is that unit land rents should be equalized at the border of competing uses. In a free-market situation with or without externalities, this condition is satisfied in long-run stable equilibrium in the land market. However, when externalities are present, in general, it is not optimal for land rents to be equalized at the border of competing uses, especially where one competing use is imposing externalities on the other (see Stull, 1974). In a monocentric model of a city, we are concerned with the optimal allocation of land between businesses and residences. This is essentially a question of determining the optimal relative size of the CBD, or the location of the border of the CBD, u_0. Note a ghettoization solution, such as mentioned in Section 1, is assumed away because of firms' need for access to the transport node at the very center of the city.

If one obtains the general criterion defining the optimal location of u_0 and interprets it in a market setting, the result is[7]

$$\text{business rents at } u_0 + \tau \left(- \int_0^{u_0} \frac{\partial f(u)}{\partial u_0} \, du \right)$$

$$= \text{residential rents at } u_0 + \int_{u_0}^{u_1} \left(- \frac{\partial V / \partial a(u)}{\partial V / \partial x(u)} \right) N(u) \left(\frac{\partial a(u)}{\partial u_0} \right) du. \quad (3.11)$$

---

[6] However, it is not so helpful to have the fixed factor be the traditional entrepreneur used to give a determinate firm size, since in that case there is an optimality condition that says that shadow marginal products of the mobile entrepreneurs should be equalized across firms. If production functions are linear homogeneous and all other factors are paid the value of their marginal products, the residual return to mobile entrepreneurs should be equalized (to their shadow marginal product) across firms. However, with pollution entrepreneurs earn their shadow private marginal product plus/minus the residual in (3.10). With $\pi(u) \neq 0$ differing by location and with entry or exit, the return to entrepreneurs will exceed or fall short of their shadow private marginal product by varying amounts in these firms, indicating a suboptimal allocation of entrepreneurs within the city and economy (see Meade, 1952).

This criterion has a straightforward explanation. The first line of (3.11) is the marginal benefits of extending the business district one more unit, which includes two factors. First, there is the productivity of land in production of x as represented by rents businesses are willing to pay at location u_0. Second, there is the effect of extending the area of the CBD on increased dispersion of the firms' emissions. This increased dispersion or reduction in pollution is measured as $\int_0^{u_0} [-\partial f(u)/\partial u_0] \, du > 0$, and the value throughout the city of this reduction is τ.

The marginal cost of extending the CBD boundary one unit includes two factors. First, there is the lost value of land in consumption as measured by rents residents are willing to pay for this land. Second, there is increased residential pollution $[\partial a(u)/\partial u_0]$ caused by moving the CBD boundary closer to residents and hence raising the level of pollution throughout the residential sector of the city.[8]

An efficient division of land occurs when the marginal benefits of increasing commercial land use equal the marginal cost. In the literature that

---

[7] To find the optimal location of the CBD boundary u_0, we maximize J in footnote 5 with respect to u_0 and then $n(u)$, $n_a(u)$, $a(u)$, $x(u)$, $N(u)$, $l(u)$, and $k(u)$ to solve out the multipliers. The result is

$$G(N)(1 - t_x u_0)\left[x(u_0) - \frac{\partial x}{\partial n(u_0)} n(u_0) - \frac{\partial x}{\partial k(u_0)} k(u_0) \right]$$

$$+ \int_{u_0}^{u_1} \frac{\partial V/\partial a(u)}{\partial V/\partial x(u)} N(u) \frac{\partial a(u)}{\partial F(u_0)} \left[f(u_0) - \frac{\partial f}{\partial k(u_0)} k(u_0) - \frac{\partial f}{\partial n_a(u_0)} n_a(u_0) \right] du$$

$$+ \int_{u_0}^{u_1} \frac{\partial V/\partial a(u)}{\partial V/\partial x(u)} N(u) \left[\frac{\partial a(u)}{\partial F(u_0)} \int_0^{u_0} \frac{\partial f(u)}{\partial u_0} du + \frac{\partial a(u)}{\partial u_0} \right] du$$

$$= \frac{\partial V/\partial l}{\partial V/\partial x} l(u_0) N(u_0).$$

The market interpretation of this equation is straightforward, assuming all other pollution policies are optimally set. Using Equation (3.10) for profits π, the definition of τ, and Equations (3.7)–(3.9) for the marginal productivity of n, n_a, $l(u)$, and k, the first two lines of this equation reduce to $\pi(u_0) + p_l(u_0)l(u_0)$. From (3.10), we know $\pi(u_0) = 0$ if f is linear homogeneous in k and n_a. Alternatively, $\pi = 0$ if the government follows a policy of optimal lump-sum taxes or subsidies when f is not linear homogeneous. In either case the first two lines of the equation above reduce to business land rents actually paid out at the edge of the CBD. The right-hand side of the equation from the first-order conditions of the consumer maximization problem equals residential land rents at the interior edge of the residential area. Given these relationships, this equation reduces to Equation (3.11).

[8] Even if u_0 changes by a discrete amount, this has a negligible effect on u_1, the radius of the city, since the circumference at u_0 is a fraction of the circumference at u_1. Therefore, if u_0 increases discretely, that increase will result in a discrete increase in general residential pollution levels caused by moving firms nearer to all residences (even if u_1 expands and some residents move slightly farther away).

deals with similar situations (e.g., Stull, 1974), the effect on pollution dispersion of increasing the CBD edge either is not relevant in the model or is ignored. Such would be the case under the pollution specification in Equation (3.4a), where the dispersion of pollution within and beyond the CBD border is functionally the same.[9] In that case the only externality would be that when firms expand into the residential area they do not account for the effect of their expansion on moving pollution sources closer to residents. Equation (3.11) would then state that business land rents should equal residential rents plus a positive term, or that in a market situation business land rents should *exceed* residential land rents at the border of their competing uses. However, given our primary specification with the second externality or the effect of increasing u_0 on pollution dispersion within the CBD, it is no longer certain that business rents should exceed residential rents at the border.

These comments imply that the rent gradient in the city should, in general, be discontinuous at u_0. Figure 3.2 illustrates a possible rent gradient. The initial rising part of the residential rent gradient as we move away from u_0 is possible because, in addition to the negative effect of declining leisure on rents, there is now a positive effect of declining pollution as we move farther

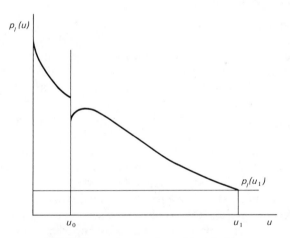

FIGURE 3.2   Rent gradient with pollution.

---

[9] In that case the corresponding version of Equation (3.11) is

$$\text{business rents at } \tilde{u}_0 = \text{residential rents at } u_0$$

$$+ \int_{u_0}^{u_1} N(u) \left[\frac{-\partial V/\partial a(u)}{\partial V/\partial x(u)} \right] s(k(\tilde{u}_0), n_a(\tilde{u}_0), \tilde{u}_0, u)\, du.$$

Note the last term is the same as total taxes paid by firms at $\tilde{u}_0$, the border.

from the CBD. From the analysis of Chapter 1, the slope of the residential rent gradient can be shown to be

$$\frac{\partial p_l(u)}{\partial u} = l(u)^{-1}\left(-\frac{\partial V/\partial e}{\partial V/\partial x}t + \frac{\partial V/\partial a\,\partial a}{\partial V/\partial x\,\partial u}\right) \lesseqgtr 0. \tag{3.12}$$

Given $\partial V/\partial a$, $\partial a/\partial u < 0$, the second term of (3.12) is positive. Thus the whole expression may take a positive value, especially when $\partial a/\partial u$ is large near the CBD.

To maintain a discontinuity in the rent gradient at u_0, it will be necessary to increase or decrease the size of the business area relative to the free-market equilibrium where land rents are equalized at u_0. This requires zoning land use and changing the area of the business district so Equation (3.10) is satisfied and land rents are no longer equalized at the border of competing uses. Alternatively, commercial areas could also be restricted in size relative to a free-market situation by discriminatorily taxing potential business land use relative to residential use, exterior to the optimal u_0.

2.3   Problems in Implementing Pollution Control Policies

A major problem facing governments wanting to implement pollution policies is to acquire sufficient information to design optimal policies. To tax pollution, the information needed is the optimal tax rate τ, which is the same for all firms, and the contribution to pollution of firms or $f(u)$. Knowledge of $f(u)$ requires monitoring firm emissions and determining how they disperse with distance. Knowledge of τ requires evaluating marginal damages to different consumers $[\partial V/\partial a(u)]/[\partial V/\partial x(u)]$. The empirical literature on this subject is not helpful since the direct estimates of pollution costs are most speculative, and for indirect estimates of perceived pollution costs (land value studies utilizing how land values vary spatially with pollution), the results are sometimes perverse. Moreover, it is not clear that consumers understand or properly evaluate the health damages of pollution. Second, there is the problem of assessing or solving for the final *optimal* tax and *optimal* marginal damages as opposed to the initial pretax equilibrium values of these variables. People have suggested an iterative procedure of initially setting taxes equal to current marginal damages and then successively lowering the tax and marginal damages to their optimal level. This still requires knowing when the optimum is reached. Finally, there is the problem that pollution is determined on a day-to-day basis by the stochastic influences of wind and weather conditions and hence fluctuates from day to day for a given level of emissions. A basic question is whether policymakers should be concerned about average annual or monthly pollution levels or about maximal pollution levels during these time intervals.

Given the foregoing types of considerations, Baumol and Oates (1975) argued persuasively in a nonspatial context that the information required for policymakers prohibits achieving optimal pollution levels. They suggest a standards approach where desired community levels of air quality are set, presumably with the idea that the optimal level of pollution is considerably less than it currently is. As they make clear, the actual choice of standards is somewhat arbitrary. Unit pollution charges are then imposed and adjusted until, given firms' reactions, community air quality approaches the standards. Since all firms face the same pollution charges but are allowed to adjust to whatever pollution is efficient (profit maximizing) for them, when the target air quality level is reached, the allocation of resources among firms will be efficient. The marginal costs of reducing pollution will be equalized (to the unit pollution charge) across firms, which minimizes the cost of achieving a given set of standards. In a spatial context, the argument (Tietenberg, 1974) is to divide up industrial areas into some type of grid or other geographic demarcation and assign a specific set of standards to each of the squares according to proximity to residential areas and possibilities for dispersion of emissions.

2.4   The Impact of Pollution Control Policies on City Size

I do not deal with city size models until later in the book. However, it is important to point out that optimally taxing pollution may not lead to a decline in city size (Henderson, 1974a; Tolley, 1974).

In a partial equilibrium model where we look at the size of one city in the economy and local authorities tax pollution and distribute the tax proceeds to residents, it is unambiguously the case (Henderson, 1974a) that city residents are made better off. In setting optimal taxes, we have by definition maximized the welfare of residents. Thus their welfare is improved relative to a case where pollution is not taxed. This increase in welfare should attract new people to the city and increase city size.

In a general equilibrium model where we look at a system of cities, this result should still hold but there are complexities. First, as I point out in Chapter 12, it may not be optimal for local authorities to retain all tax proceeds within any city. Second, pollution taxation of polluting goods will raise the cost of those goods relative to nonpolluting goods, and hence lower the national demand for those goods. Thus, while the size of any city producing a polluting good may increase, the numbers of cities specialized in production of polluting goods may decline.

4

Basic Housing Models

In this chapter, I restructure the model of housing services and the housing market presented in Chapter 1, so as to be able to consider some of the more complex situations encountered in the housing market. In Chapter 1, I treated housing as a regular good whose provision and factor proportions in production respond instantly to price changes. This implies that a city's spatial design and building heights will be costlessly and instantly adjusted in response only to current population, income, and price variables. Housing capital is thus perfectly malleable and mobile, like so many building blocks. While it may be reasonable to describe long-run spatial equilibrium in a city under the assumptions of perfect malleability and mobility of capital, for many problems it is essential to incorporate the fact that housing is a durable good. It is provided in a dynamic context, and is long-lived and immobile, adjusting in quantity through depreciation, maintenance, demolition, and reconstruction.

In Section 1 of this chapter, I outline a model of the housing market and analyze the investment and maintenance decisions of individual landowners. In doing so I isolate the time dimension of the problem from the spatial dimension and focus on the traditional model of firm investment decisions. In Section 2, I combine spatial and time dimensions and reanalyze the problem in Chapter 1, examining the elements of a spatial model of a monocentric city with durable immobile capital. Finally, in Section 3, I conclude by noting alternative ways in the literature of modeling durable housing. In the next chapter I turn to modeling a variety of housing problems building upon the concepts developed in this chapter.

1. A SIMPLE HOUSING MODEL

The durable goods model of housing that I present represents a synthesis of certain existing work on housing models, and it does not follow any one researcher's particular approach.[1] There are several critical features to the model. From a landlord's point of view, housing services available from any housing unit such as a single-family house or an apartment unit can generally only be consumed by one household. This can be viewed as an indivisibility on the supply side since the services offered can only be sold to one household and not divided among different consumers.[2] Second, from a consumer's point of view, housing consumption is also indivisible, so that each household generally only consumes the services supplied by the housing unit of one landlord. Third, in making current decisions, landlords are concerned not only with current market conditions, but also future conditions. Their objective is to maximize the present value of profits. In doing so they have an initial purchase decision, followed by depreciation of their unit over time. They must decide in each successive time period how much maintenance to do in response to depreciation and current and future market conditions. Finally, they must decide if and when to demolish the building and put up a new structure with perhaps a different land use.

Developing a model with features of both durability and indivisibilities is a challenge economists have not fully met. In this chapter we focus on the decisions of the individual agents in the housing market, placing them in a setting consistent with market equilibria. This framework will then be used in this and subsequent chapters to analyze housing problems. In this chapter, based on Rosen's (1974) work, simple characterizations of the equilibria will also be developed.

We first turn to a formal analysis of the decisions facing consumers and a single landlord. The analysis is carried out with consumers and the landlord facing market conditions that are consistent with feasible equilibria.

---

[1] It is inspired primarily by the work of Sweeney (1974a, 1974b) and Rosen (1974), although it is influenced by other work (e.g., Arnott, 1980, and Wheaton, 1982, 1983).

[2] This description should not be confused with the definition of "indivisible commodities," which focuses on nonconvexities of the consumption set (see Section 3.3)—what I refer to here really is mutual exclusivity in supply.

A city is divided into n neighborhoods, where each neighborhood, j, has an amenity vector, A_j, associated with it. Amenities could include commuting time to the CBD, pollution levels, parks, crime rates, and income and racial composition of the neighborhood (see the next chapter). Consumers pick their best neighborhood and house given the spectrum of amenity and housing cost conditions offered by the different neighborhoods. These neighborhoods could represent discrete geographic areas, derived in a Tiebout equilibrium, where similar types of residents seek to group together (see Chapter 10); or the neighborhoods could represent a circle of residents all the same distance from the CBD in a simple monocentric model of a city. We start by looking at equilibrium in one neighborhood.

1.1 Consumer and Landlord

Consumers and the Revenue Schedule

To analyze the decisions of a landlord in a particular neighborhood, we first posit the revenue schedule the landlord faces at any point in time for the services of the housing unit. Given the landlord sells the services of the unit to just one household, housing services are not sold at a constant unit price in the market but rather there is a schedule of all-or-nothing offers for different quantities of services. It is all-or-nothing because either a household buys all the landlord's currently offered services or none at all. To properly derive the revenue schedule facing a landlord, we would have to examine the set of willingness-to-pay schedules held by consumers in the city plus the offerings of all other landlords. In this section we start with consumers and then analyze the offerings of one landlord. In the next section we characterize the set of offerings of all landlords and simple market equilibria.

The willingness-to-pay schedule for housing services is derived in much the same fashion as bid rent curves and rent gradients in Chapter 1, apart from incorporating the aspect that the landlord's supply of housing to a consumer is indivisible. In terms of the *equilibrium* schedule for a consumer, any consumer who is going to live in our landlord's neighborhood, the jth neighborhood, has a best alternative equilibrium utility level, V^0, from living elsewhere in the city, given amenities and equilibrium rent schedules in other neighborhoods. The consumer's utility level in the jth neighborhood is $V(x, h, A_j)$ where x is all other goods, h is housing services, and A_j is the vector of neighborhood amenities. Substituting in the budget constraint, $y - W_j - x = 0$, where W_j is potential payments for housing in the jth neighborhood and x is the numeraire, we form the implicit function

$$V^0 - V(y - W_j(h), h, A_j) = 0. \tag{4.1}$$

In Equation (4.2), W_j is the consumer's maximum willingness-to-pay, which maintains the best alternative utility level. Inverting (4.1) we get

$$W_j = W_j(h; y, A_j, V^0), \tag{4.2}$$

where by differentiation of (4.1), (or invoking the implicit function theorem),

$$\partial W_j/\partial h = V_h/V_x > 0, \qquad \partial^2 W_j/\partial h^2 < 0,$$

where W is increasing in h according to the marginal evaluation (V_h/V_x) of additional units of housing services, but it is strictly concave in h, given diminishing marginal rates of substitution between market goods.

We plot $W_j^c(h)$ for consumer c in Figure 4.1, as an indifference curve between h and the cost of h. Apart from concavity, these curves have two basic properties. First, as consumer c's best alternative utility level rises, W^c must shift down (for h constant), representing in Equations (4.1) and (4.2) decreased willingness-to-pay for h [i.e., in Equation (4.1) for h and A_j fixed, utility can only rise by $x = y - W$ rising, or W falling]. Second, for identical tastes, as income rises across consumers, the marginal evaluation of housing, V_h/V_x, must rise, assuming housing is a normal good. That is, $d(\partial W_j/\partial h)/dy|_h = [(V_x V_{hx} - V_h V_{xx})/V_x^2]\ dx/dy$, where $dx/dy = 1$. The term in the square brackets is positive if and only if h is a normal good. If it is positive, then $\partial W_j/\partial h$ comes less negative as income rises. Thus, at any point in W, h space as income rises (hence x and V^0 must also rise for W, h fixed), the W curve rotates upward at that h, or becomes steeper. In Figure 4.1, $y^A > y^B > y^C$ for the three sets of willingness-to-pay curves, $W_j^A(\cdot)$, $W_j^B(\cdot)$, and $W^C(\cdot)$.

Given the set of equilibrium willingness-to-pay curves with a continuum of consumer types, as interacted with a continuum of offerings of other landlords (see Section 1.2), an individual landlord faces a rent schedule $R_j(h)$ for his housing unit. In Figure 4.1, the rent schedule will form an

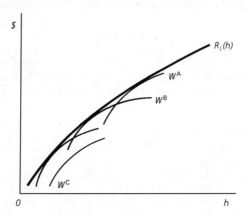

FIGURE 4.1   Revenue schedule.

envelope of the equilibrium willingness-to-pay curves facing landlords. At the points of tangency, $\partial R/\partial h \equiv R_h > 0$ and $R_h = W_k$ (by the envelope theorem), but it is not necessarily concave given the set of offerings of other landlords (see later). The rent schedule $R_j(h)$ will shift with willingness-to-pay to live in their neighborhood versus others given changes in amenities and housing supply conditions in this and other neighborhoods.

Production of Housing Services

Housing services of the landlord in time s are produced with the original lot size $l(0)$ endowed at the time of purchase, 0, and the capital stock, $K(s)$, on the lot in time s. Thus

$$h(s) = h(l(0), K(s)), \tag{4.3}$$

where $h_K \equiv \partial h/\partial K$ and by diminishing marginal product $h_{KK} \equiv \partial^2 h/\partial K^2 < 0$. The capital stock in s is the sum of depreciated previous capital inputs, $k(s)$, where $K(0) = k(0)$ is the initial structure and $k(s; s > 0)$ is the investment or maintenance in each successive period. In the simple case of expotential depreciation at a constant rate δ,

$$K(s) = \int_0^s k(v)e^{-\delta(s-v)} \, dv \tag{4.4}$$

so that

$$\dot{K} \equiv \partial K/\partial s = k(s) - \delta K(s). \tag{4.5}$$

In (4.5) the net change in the capital stock in each period is gross investment, $k(s)$, minus depreciation of the existing capital stock. Note $K(s)$ and $k(s)$ are measured in the same units but the former is a stock and the latter a flow.

The total cost of doing a given amount of maintenance k in any time period s is

$$C = C(k, s). \tag{4.6}$$

Note that $C_K > 0$ and, if $C_{KK} = 0$, C_K is simply the purchase price of a unit of capital in any period. Without loss of generality for the framework we are outlining here, we assume $C_{KK} = 0$.[3] The time derivatives of $C(\cdot)$ are noted later.

---

[3] What role could $C_{KK} \neq 0$ play? If $C_{KK} > 0$, then costs rise at an increasing rate with the amount of maintenance done in any one period. This suggests it is efficient to spread any desired permanent jump in the capital stock over several periods, so diseconomies ($C_{KK} > 0$) in any one period are reduced. Adjustment of the desired level of capital stock will then be noninstantaneous and adjustment paths will need to be analyzed. However, if $C_{KK} \leq 0$, there are no adjustment costs to scheduling permanent changes in K to occur all at once, and adjustment is instantaneous.

The Landlord's Problem

The landlord maximizes the present value of future profits, Π, where, assuming perfect foresight,

$$\Pi = \int_0^T [R(h, s) - C(k, s)]e^{-rs}\, ds - S(0) + S(T)e^{-rT}. \qquad (4.7)$$

The market revenue schedule in period s is $R(h, s)$, and r is the discount rate. The term $S(0)$ is the purchase price of land in time 0, although it can also include an existing structure $K(0)$ valued at replacement cost $C_K K(0)$ (for $C_{KK} = 0$). The term $S(T)$ is the selling price of housing and land in time T; $S(T)$ can reflect future discounted profits for the next landlord of the existing housing unit in T. Alternatively, if the building is demolished in time T, $S(T)$ includes the sales price of the lot, the proceeds from selling the existing capital $K(T)$ in time T, and the costs of demolition and restoration of land to a preconstruction condition. With perfect competition among identically skilled landlords and with perfect foresight, $\Pi \to 0$, so that the initial price of land, $S(0)$, equals the present value of all future profits, and the return on housing investment equals the discount rate.

To describe the properties of the optimal maintenance path, we substitute into Equation (4.7) $k(s) = \dot{K} + \delta K$ from Equation (4.5) and derive the Euler equation (see footnote 4),

$$R_h h_K = C_K(\delta + r), \qquad (4.8)$$

where $R_h h_K$ is the marginal revenue product of an additional unit of investment, and investment in any period proceeds until the marginal revenue product equals marginal cost. Note $R_h h_K = (V_h/V_x)h_K$. Marginal cost is the opportunity cost of holding capital one period. The purchase cost of a unit of capital is represented by C_K. The opportunity cost of holding that unit one period is foregone interest on the money invested, rC_K, plus the value of losses in the stock itself during that period due to depreciation, δC_K. We could add a second term to the right-hand side of Equation (4.8), C_{Ks}, which could represent the notion that the relative price of capital is expected to appreciate during this period, so that there are savings from doing more investment today while capital is cheap, rather than waiting until tomorrow. We assume for now $C_{Ks} = 0$.

We graph the two sides of Equation (4.8) in Figure 4.2. The marginal revenue product curve is downward sloping (assuming $R_{hh}h_K^2 + R_h h_{KK} < 0$ for second order conditions), and $C_K(\delta + r)$ is flat assuming $C_{KK} = 0$. Equilibrium is at K^*. Note $h_{K'}$ and thus $R_H h_K$ and K^* will vary as initial lot size $l(0)$ varies. This is analyzed in the next section, where we show $l(0)$ will rise with K^*.

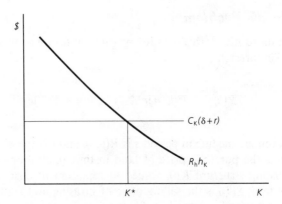

FIGURE 4.2   Equilibrium investment.

The Landlord's Maintenance Path

If the real revenue schedule for housing and the cost of maintenance are constant over time, the curves in Figure 4.2 are time invariant. This implies that K^* is constant and that $\dot{K} = 0$, or from Equation (4.5),

$$k = \delta K.$$

Maintenance in each period, k, just offsets depreciation. This is a stationary situation in which the landlord's situation and output is replicated from period to period. We will tend to assume this characterization of technology in discussing housing problems. However there is a common alternative characterization.

The alternative is that housing could age with time so that maintaining the capital stock at a given level becomes more and more expensive as the house ages. We note two ways to represent this in our model. First, in our formulation, $\partial C_K/\partial s \equiv C_{Ks}$ could be greater than zero. In this context s refers not to time per se but house age; and $C_{Ks} > 0$ represents the notion that the cost of putting a unit of capital investment in place rises with the age of the house. In this case $C_K(s)(\delta + r)$ in Figure 4.2 will rise over time [although the right-hand side of Equation (4.8) would now have a term, C_{KS}, added on], so that $\dot{K}$ declines and $\dot{K} = k - \delta K < 0$.

An alternative formulation of aging is to assume that the rate of depreciation δ changes over time so that, for example, Equation (4.4) becomes

$$K(s) = \int_0^s k(n)\exp\left[- \int_n^s \delta(v)\, dv \right] dn, \qquad (4.4a)$$

and Equation (4.5) becomes

$$\dot{K}(s) = k(s) - \delta(s)K(s). \tag{4.5a}$$

If $\dot{\delta} = d\delta/ds > 0$, so $\delta(s)$ increases over time, this means that both new additions and the existing capital stock will wear out more quickly as the house ages. Thus in Figure 4.2 $C_K(\delta(s) + r)$ will rise over time and $\dot{K}$ will decline so that $\dot{K} < 0$.

In either case, for a fixed $R_j(h)$ schedule, because of the aging nature of housing, it is natural and optimal for housing to deteriorate over time. That does leave open the question of whether $R(h)$ can remain time invariant in this situation (see later). Deterioration implies in Figure 4.1 that the landlord is moving back along the $R_j(h)$ schedule with time, so that in each succeeding period the landlord plans to rent to lower and lower housing demanders (i.e., lower and lower income groups). In the simple version of this model, this implies housing must change tenants each period as we move along $R_j(h)$, the locus of willingness-to-pay curves.

Rather than having the owner change tenants from period to period, one could incorporate moving costs into the model and optimize to show that tenants may stay longer than one period. They will also pay the owner to "overmaintain" his units relative to the housing provided along $R(h)$ if housing changed hands each period. The tenants have some desired housing $\dot{h}$ given incomes and market opportunities. They will move in when $h > \dot{h}$ and move out when $h < \dot{h}$ and pay the owner to overmaintain housing to keep it near $\dot{h}$ during their tenure so they may consume almost their desired housing without moving. Sweeney (1974b) presented an extended analysis of this.

Finally, as $\dot{K}$ declines, and either C_{Ks} or $\delta(s)$ rises over time for a fixed $R_j(h)$ schedule, this implies that eventually the landlord will tear down the house and rebuild. The date of demolition is determined by the transversality condition for Equation (4.7) where[4]

$$R_j(T) = C_K\delta(T)K(T) - \dot{S}(T) + rS(T). \tag{4.9}$$

Equation (4.9) states that, in the period in which housing is demolished, the marginal benefits from holding housing one more period, which is the rental revenue $R_j(T)$, should just equal the marginal costs. The marginal costs of holding housing one more period are further losses from depreciation of the capital stock $[C_K\delta(T)K(T)]$, less any capital gains on the land $[\dot{S}(T)]$ plus foregone interest on the sales value $[rS(T)$, including proceeds from selling

---

[4] Defining $I = [R(h,s) - C(\dot{K} + \delta K, s)]e^{-rs}$, the Euler equation is $\partial I/\partial K - d(\partial I/\partial \dot{K})/ds = 0$ and the transversality condition is $I - \dot{K}(\partial I/\partial \dot{K}) + \partial(S(T)e^{-rT})/\partial T = 0$.

structures]. We footnote an illustration of the filtering and demolition process for one landlord.[5]

This technological formulation is at the heart of some explanations of the deterioration of American inner cities. If housing ages naturally it is only inevitable that inner cities must pass through a process of deterioration and then rejuvenation. The problem with this explanation is that it is at odds with patterns observed in much of the rest of the world. The old inner-city

---

[5] It is fairly easy to illustrate this filtering process for one housing unit. Assume a time-invariant revenue function $R = h^{\eta}$, where $\eta < 1$. Housing services $h(s) = AL(0)^{\alpha}K(s)^{\beta}$, where $L(0)$ is fixed and α, $\beta < 1$. The aging process is described by $\delta(t) = \delta e^{\gamma t}$, so that $k(s) = \dot{K}(s) + \delta e^{\gamma s}K(s)$. Therefore, the present value of profits is

$$\pi = \int_0^T [A^{\eta}L(0)^{\alpha\eta}K^{\beta\eta} - p_k(\dot{K} + \delta e^{\gamma t}K(s))]e^{-rs}\,ds - s(0) + s(T)e^{-rT}.$$

The Euler equation reduces to $A^{\eta}\beta\eta L^{\alpha\eta}K^{\beta\eta-1} = p_k(r + \delta e^{\gamma s})$; or rearranging, the optimal value of capital stock in any period is

$$K(s) = [p_k(r + \delta e^{\gamma s})A^{-\eta}\beta^{-1}\eta^{-1}L^{-\alpha\eta}]^{1/(\beta\eta-1)}.$$

Given β, $\eta < 1$, $K(s)$ decreases over time or net investment declines continuously. If we differentiate the Euler equation with respect to time and substitute in the expressions for $\dot{K}$ and $K(s)$, we find

$$k(s) = [p_k(r + \delta e^{\gamma s})\beta^{-1}\eta^{-1}A^{-\eta}L^{-\alpha\eta}]^{1/(\beta\eta-1)}\delta e^{\gamma s}\left[1 - \frac{\gamma}{(r + \delta e^{\gamma s})(1 - \beta\eta)}\right].$$

Despite the decline in net capital stock, gross investment $k(s)$ is always positive if $\gamma < (r + \delta e^{\gamma s})$ $(1 - \beta\eta)$ or if the aging parameter γ is small relative to the discount or depreciation rate δ.

To solve for the length of life of a building, we assume perfect competition, or that $s(0)$ is such that $\pi = 0$. We decompose $s(T)$ into demolition costs $D(T)$, scrap value $p_kK(T)$, and land price in T. We assume the selling price of land in T is the same as in 0, or the opportunities for investment are static. Therefore, with $\pi = 0$ for our example the profit equation may be rewritten as

$$s(0)(1 - e^{-rT}) = \int_0^T [A^{\eta}L^{\alpha\eta}K(s)^{\beta\eta} - p_kk(s)]e^{-rs}\,ds + e^{-rT}[p_kK(T) - D(T)].$$

If we substitute in for $k(s)$ and $K(s)$ and integrate, we get an equation containing parameters and the variables T and $s(0)$. (The purchase price of the land $s(0)$ is a dependent variable since it must be consistent with the arbitrary revenue and production functions.) To solve for $s(0)$ and T, we need a second equation containing these variables. This is the terminal condition Equation (4.9), where now

$$A^{\eta}L^{\alpha\eta}K(T)^{\beta\eta} = p_kK(T)(r + \delta e^{\gamma T}) + r(s(0) - D(T)).$$

Substituting in for $K(T)$, we have an expression in parameters and unknowns T and $s(0)$. Given these two equations we can solve for T and $s(0)$ in terms of our parameters. For example, for $L(0) = p_k = A = 5$, $\beta = \frac{2}{3}$, $\eta = \frac{3}{4}$, $r = 0.05$, $\delta = 0.05$, $\gamma = 0.025$, $D(T) = \$343$, rough calculations indicate $T = 25$ and $s(0) = \$732$.

neighborhoods of many countries continue to house high-income people in well-maintained houses. For example, the neighborhoods that housed the elite in Montreal, Toronto, or Vancouver 50 or more years ago, house the elite of those cities today. This would suggest that housing does not necessarily age "naturally" and that the changes in American inner cities are due to changing social and political conditions (not relevant to Canada) that affect the demand side of the model.[6]

Irreversibility

I have implicitly assumed that housing investment is completely reversible by not imposing a constraint in Equation (4.7) that $k(s) \geq 0$. Reversibility means that a landlord can sell off unwanted capital (doors, closets, stairways, fireplaces) at full market price C_K at any time. This assumption underlies both the Euler equation (4.8) and the transversality condition (4.9) and is made to keep the technical formulation simple. In Section 2, I consider a model where investment is irreversible. For now, two comments on reversability are in order.

First, if investment is in fact irreversible, Equation (4.8), which determines the optimal $k(s)$, is only valid if the desired $k(s)$ that satisfies Equation (4.8) is nonnegative for all s [so a nonnegativity constraint on $k(s)$ in Equation (4.7) imposes no costs]. Providing economic conditions are stable, this may not be an unusual situation. Even in a model with aging and continuous filtering down so that $\dot{K} = k - \delta K < 0$, desired k may always be positive. Footnote 5 illustrates such a case.

Second, if investment is reversible and if housing ages naturally (i.e., $C_{Ks} > 0$, or $\dot{\delta} > 0$), without demolition costs, it would be efficient to tear housing down each period and completely replace it. Since $K(0)$ can be bought and then resold after one period (where $[1 - \delta(0)]K(0)$ remains) at a constant price $C_K(0)$, demolishing and reconstructing the house in each period maintains $\delta(s)$ or $C_K(s)$ at its lowest level. This points out two problems. Aging and reversibility present a conflict since there is a certain absurdity to assuming that by tearing down building each period one can stop that capital from aging. Second, demolition costs play a critical role in models with reversibility and aging of housing; they are in essence a way of sneaking a cost of reversibility into the model.

---

[6] I have two conditions in mind. One is the degree of fiscal autonomy of localities. In the United States, for example, counties are responsible for schooling. In Canada, however, localities have much less autonomy, and many services (e.g., schooling) are provided at the provincial level. The impact of this differential in autonomy will become clear in Chapters 9 and 10. The second condition is the South–North migration of blacks following World War II.

1.2   Market Equilibrium

With housing durability and costly redivision of land, the general analysis of housing market equilibrium is simply very messy. There are no simple general theoretical models dealing with general situations, although there are computer simulation models. We can however characterize some of the properties of equilibria in simple situations. To do so we first look at the supply offerings of landlords in one situation. From this we can describe the derivation of the rent schedule. At the moment we are still looking at either one neighborhood of a city, or a city composed just one neighborhood.

Supply Offering

We start by characterizing supply offerings in a stationary situation where there is no aging and all economic conditions are assumed to be time invariant over an infinite horizon. We also start by assuming that landlords have fixed lot sizes over this horizon, given costly redivision of land. As we shall see with time varying conditions simple characterizations of supply offerings are difficult. By imposing indefinite stationarity, we are essentially reverting to a neoclassical "long run" (static) model.

For any level of long-run profits Π^0, what offer must the landlord receive to be willing to supply h of housing services? From (4.7), given $L(0)$ is previously purchased, in an invariant infinite horizon situation

$$\Pi^0 = \frac{(P - C_K k)}{r} - C_K K. \tag{4.10}$$

K is the level of capital stock chosen today which will be maintained indefinitely. P is the amount the landlord must be offered each period to maintain a given level of housing services and hence K. Given K is maintained at one level, $k = \delta K$. Substituting in and rearranging

$$P = r\Pi^0 + C_K(r + \delta)K. \tag{4.11}$$

What are the properties of P? First, for any Π^0

$$\frac{\partial P}{\partial h} = \frac{C_K(r + \delta)}{h_K} > 0,$$

$$\frac{\partial^2 P}{\partial h^2} = -\frac{C_K(r + \delta)}{h_K^3} h_{KK} > 0. \tag{4.12}$$

Offer curves are upward-sloping convex curves, as illustrated in Figure 4.3. In the set for landlord C, P shifts up as Π^0 rises. As "alternative" profits rise, so does the compensation demanded by landlords. How do offer curves vary across landlords? They vary by lot size. Holding P and h fixed, offer curves

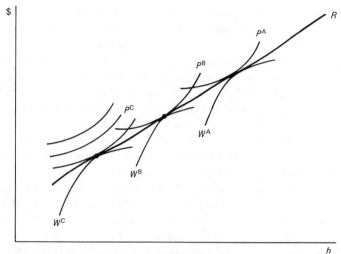

FIGURE 4.3   Landlord offer curves.

rotate so that

$$\partial\left(\frac{\partial P}{\partial h}\right)\bigg/ \partial L\bigg|_{P,h} = -\frac{(\delta + r)C_K}{h_K^2}(h_{KL} - h_{KK}h_L/h_K) < 0,$$

where we have substituted in $\partial K/\partial L = -h_L/h_K$ for h fixed. Given $h_{KL} > 0$ and $h_{KK} < 0$, we know offer curves rotate clockwise or become less steep, as illustrated by curves P^B and P^A, where $L^C < L^B < L^A$ in Figure 4.3.

Market Equilibria without Aging

Market equilibrium is informally characterized by the tangency points of willingness-to-pay and offer curves, where the locus of these tangency points forms the revenue schedule, R, facing any landlord. At the points of tangency from (4.12) and (4.2), $V_h/V_x = C_K(r + \delta)/h_K$, which is Equation (4.8). What are the properties of the schedule, not already cited? What is its shape? How does the market match-up the precise number of consumers with W^C functions against the precise number of landlords with P^C functions? What happens if economic conditions are not time invariant? What happens if there is aging? How do neighborhoods fit into this framework? The remainder of this section of the chapter is devoted to answering these questions.

We first focus on the general shape of $R(h)$ in Figure 4.3. In general the market does not guarantee that there will be a continuum of W and P functions, with a continuum of tangencies of differing W and P curves. We illustrate one extreme. Suppose there are a continuum of consumers by income so there is a continuum of W curves but only a few types of available lot sizes and hence P curves. We could also assume the reverse. Then simple experimentation with graphing reveals that $R(h)$ will generally have a scalloped shape, with convex sections as we move along each P curve and concave sections for ("border") consumers who are indifferent between two P curves. In the border sections as we traverse from one P curve to another, no housing will actually be supplied, although the concave section of the $R(h)$ function defines the prices offered. If neither producers nor consumers form a continuum, then R will not be continuous. In summary, the only general restriction on $R(h)$ is that it be non-decreasing in h.

To see the impact of time variant economic conditions on a specific $R(h)$ function, we examine a particular example. We start by looking at an even simpler time invariant situation. Suppose in addition to our previous assumptions, that at the time K is being chosen in Equations (4.10) and (4.11), $L(0)$ is also being chosen and that there is a continuum of consumers by income. In this case, $R(h)$ will be a straight line if housing is produced with constant returns to scale and input prices and demand conditions are assumed to be the same forever. K will be the same, always governed by the same Equations (4.8) and (4.12) and $l(0)$ will be chosen according to $R_h h_l/r = \partial S(0)/\partial l(0)$, in Equation (4.7), where $\partial^2 S(0)/\partial l(0)^2 = 0$. In that case there is a constant unit cost at time zero to expanding h and, given demand and desired factor proportions are time invariant, the future is always a replica of the present. Then expanding h in R, h space is governed by constant unit costs of providing additional h, and $R(h)$ is a straight line.

Suppose starting with this straight line $R(h)$, it turns out developers were wrong, and in the future the tiny group of people at the highest end of the income spectrum experience a small increase in income. In a static model of costless lot size adjustment and reversibility of investment, the whole area would be altered spatially with new lot sizes (for all people) and altered factor proportions. However, with costly lot size adjustment, for small enough income changes, only K will be adjusted maintaining the original lot-size divisions and housing units in the area. Then, the end of the $R(h)$ function will have to be stretched out and up into a convex shape, following the offer curves of landlords with the largest lot size. Thus $K(s)/l(0)$ on high-income lots will rise relative to other lots as housing services for high-income people are increased in response to their income increases. It would take significant income or relative price changes to make it profitable to redesign the entire area or even part of it, incurring demolition, redivision, and reconstruction costs, to again equalize factor proportions.

As an aside note that, starting from time zero with lot-size division, $R(h)$ will in general not be a straight line if demand or supply conditions are expected to change over time. Lot sizes will then be governed by the first-order condition $\int_0^\infty R_h h_l e^{-rs} ds = \partial S(0)/\partial l(0)$. If, for example, we expect incomes of high-income people to rise over time, requiring housing services and capital to expand over time on their fixed lot sizes, while we expect incomes of low-income people to decline over time, requiring capital to contract over time on low-income lots, we would expect $[K(0)/l(0)]^H$ for high-income people to start off lower than $[K(0)/l(0)]^L$ for low-income people. Then for the same factor purchase costs in period 0, factor proportions will vary across the income and housing service spectrum and the competitive costs of supplying housing in period 0 will thus also vary across the housing spectrum, so $R(h)$ has a nonconstant slope.

In summary, the shapes of $R(h)$ functions, the division of land, and the age of structures in a city depend on the history and future of income, population, and price movements in the city and the costs of demolition, redivision, and reconstruction. Tracking this process of historical development and equilibrium prices and quantities at each point in time is very difficult analytically and in fact has not generally been done. There are two types of models in the literature that start to do so under simple conditions. First, there are growth models of a monocentric city as described in Section 2. Second, there are tightly structured filtering-down models, which I review next.

Equilibrium with Aging

Filtering down provides some order in the historical structure of a city because houses are continually being demolished and reconstructed, due to the aging process alone. Thus any disturbance to a stationary situation does not, for example, necessarily result in permanent variations in factor proportions for the same underlying-factor market conditions because adjustment occurs automatically over time with filtering down. However, characterizing a filtering-down equilibrium is still difficult.

A filtering-down equilibrium has only been modeled under a critical assumption. The assumption is to strictly limit the types of housing available, as in Sweeney's (1974a,b) fundamental work. Sweeney assumed a universally accepted hierarchy of discrete quality levels of housing units, where the number of potential levels is fixed. Construction occurs at various upper levels and filters down until demolished at various lower levels. Filtering occurs because the cost of maintaining a house at a given quality level escalates with the length of stay at that level. However, in filtering, housing cannot skip quality levels. Thus, for any original unit, a plot of quality against time is a declining step function with the level (but not length) of the steps exogenously given. Under these assumptions Sweeney could prove the existence of a stationary state equilibrium and could do comparative analyses of stationary states. To prove existence, Sweeney had to respecify the theory of consumer behavior to deal rigorously with the fact that a consumer's choice set has holes in it (quality levels vary discretely—see Section 3.3).

In a stationary state, the rate of filtering, the stock of housing at each quality level, the rates of construction and demolition and prices are all time invariant. With continuous housing types in a filtering down model, we would expect the $R(h)$ schedule to be thus stationary in a stationary state, an issue raised earlier.

Neighborhoods

To incorporate neighborhoods into the derivation of the rent schedule, we simply extend the analysis to a multidimensional framework as in Rosen (1974). Rosen was concerned with modeling housing and certain other goods as being packages or bundles of attributes. Each housing unit is a specific bundle of attributes such as floor space, fireplaces, plumbing fixtures, yard space, and so on, plus locational features such as access, crime rates, parks, and air quality. Since the bundle is sold as a whole at a one price, we do not observe prices of attributes. However the prices of attributes may be inferred, or are implicit.

In terms of neighborhoods, keeping the assumption that there is a good produced called h, the attributes we are concerned with are neighborhood amenities A. The R schedule is now a function $R(h, A)$. Each neighborhood has its own R function in \$, h space, based on the producer offer curves specific to that neighborhood given its stock of lot sizes and based on the willingness-to-pay curves of all consumers to live in that neighborhood given amenities in that neighborhood relative to other neighborhoods. That is, we have equilibrium willingness-to-pay curves of $W(h, A)$. In Figures 4.1 and 4.3 what is illustrated is a slice of $R(\cdot)$ as we vary one attribute h, holding all others A fixed. Thus it is the R schedule for one neighborhood. As amenities improve (vs. decline) relative to other neighborhoods, we would expect the R schedule to shift or rotate up (vs. down). The implicit price of the attribute h is R_h. Implicit prices of the amenity attributes are R_A, the infinitesimal shifts in R as amenities shift infinitesimally (by neighborhood comparisons). These implicit prices are estimated in the hedonic price literature (e.g., Brown and Rosen, 1982; Murray, 1983; Rosen, 1974).

Formally analyzing equilibrium in this multidimensional case is difficult. There is the issue of what are the supply functions of attributes such as crime rates across neighborhoods. That is, some attributes may depend on population composition and income levels. Second, people may not face continuous offerings of attributes in a city so that the consumption set may not be continuous and convex (see Section 3). Third, when some economic change makes it feasible to reshuffle lot sizes and structures in a few neighborhoods of the city, we will have whole new sets of producer-offer curves in those neighborhoods and new willingness-to-pay curves throughout the city. Comparative static or dynamic analyses then become complex and in fact have not been done. Finally, there is the issue of what is a neighborhood, in terms of defining amenity vectors.

With filtering down or aging, the issues are also complex. Housing in any particular neighborhood is often constructed all at the same time, designed to house a relatively homogeneous group of neighbors (see next chapter). Thus, filtering involves a turnover of neighborhood population composition. This presents a problem in solving for neighborhood size, because the number of similar income people varies by income level, so that the eligible number of residents of a neighborhood will vary over its age cycle. No such model has been solved.

2. DYNAMIC DEVELOPMENT OF A MONOCENTRIC CITY WITH DURABLE CAPITAL

There is now a substantial literature analyzing the dynamic development of a monocentric city when capital is durable and immobile (see Anas, 1978; Arnott, 1980; Brueckner, 1981a; Fujita, 1982; and Wheaton, 1982, 1983). The articles and their results differ according to their assumptions about whether people have perfect foresight or are myopic, whether capital depreciates and redevelopment is permitted or not, whether utility levels and/or incomes vary over time or not, whether housing is divisible in consumption or not, and whether time is continuous or discrete. It is not possible in a few pages to synthesize all the types of analyses and results in these papers. Here I attempt to state the problem and give a flavor of the analyses. The underlying problem is most vividly stated for the situation analyzed in Anas (1978) in which people are myopic, so that they expect today's prices and income to persist indefinitely. I state that problem informally and then analyze the more general problem.

2.1 A Myopic World

Assume a city growing in population, with real incomes growing or held constant. Capital is perfectly durable (i.e., does not depreciate) and is immobile. In period 1, development occurs according to the period 1 rent gradient R_1 from Chapter 1 (see Figure 4.4a), where this gradient is expected to

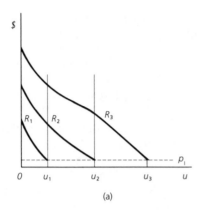

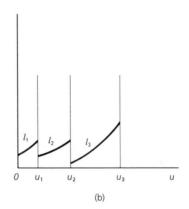

(a)   (b)

FIGURE 4.4   Myopic development.

persist indefinitely. The city edge is u_1. The endogenous lot size gradient is l_1 in Figure 4.4b whose positive slope reflects the negative slope of R_1. In period 2, with population and perhaps income growth, the housing gradient shifts up to R_2, following the Chapter 1 analyses. Unfortunately, u_1 of the city is already developed. New development occurs between u_1 and u_2 in Figure 4.4a according to the heavier part of R_2, where R_2 is expected to persist indefinitely. Lot sizes from u_1 to u_2 are given by l_2 in Figure 4.4b. In period 3, the new rent gradient is R_3, and new development occurs between u_2 and u_3 with lot sizes l_3; and so on, from period to period. In terms of population densities (inverse of lot sizes), we have period-to-period discontinuities where lot sizes at the outer edge of yesterday's development fall in moving to the inner edge of today's development. Given the low population densities near the city center (between, say, 0 and u_1 in Figure 4.4b) and the rising rent gradient over time, we might expect the inner areas of the city to be demolished and redeveloped in later periods, to conserve on the then high opportunity cost level, with a resulting shift down in the l gradient in inner areas.

    Apart from the problem that developers are repeatedly fooled, Figure 4.4a does serve to illustrate the general problem. It also helps illustrate the problem as perceived by developers who are not repeatedly fooled. Knowledgeable developers want to determine lot sizes, intensity of development, and timing of development given that they know the rent gradient in the city will be shifting up over time. Given the rising time path of rents, we might expect them to initially "overdevelop" relative to the current rent gradient, and then later to "underdevelop," in a type of time averaging strategy. We now turn to a more general statement of that problem. While it is not possible in a few pages to derive detailed development patterns, basic principles can be illustrated. In doing so I draw upon the work of Arnott (1980), Fujita (1982), Mills (1983), and Wheaton (1983).

2.2 Development with Perfect Foresight

In describing the problem, we make the following fairly typical assumptions. The city population is assumed to grow at an exogenous rate, initial incomes and any income growth are also exogenously given, and the discount rate r is constant. Services from a housing unit are indivisible, and consumers only rent at one location. There is no technological change in the housing sector. The development market is characterized by perfect foresight and competition. Capital is perfectly durable and immobile, so that the level of housing services per housing unit once constructed is time invariant. Finally, redevelopment is not permitted, so the horizon for a developer's unit is infinite. Relaxing any of these assumptions alters some of the results. In particular, the last assumption of no redevelopment is very strict, and relaxing it allows for much more flexible development patterns.

I start by looking at the developer's maximization problem given investment is *irreversible*. To do so I first describe developer's rent schedules and then the conditions defining optimal strategies. I then examine conditions in the housing market over time.

Irreversible Investment

Consumers who only rent face a succession of static maximization problems. Given that, we can use the willingness-to-pay formulation at the beginning of the chapter to derive each period's rent schedule for a housing unit, replacing neighborhood amenities by distance from the CBD, u. Thus each developer faces a rent schedule for each housing unit of

$$R(h, u; s),$$

where s is time. For this function, $\partial R/\partial h = V_h/V_x$ and $\partial R/\partial u = -(V_e/V_x)t < 0$, where h is housing services, x is all other goods, e is leisure (after commuting time of $T - tu$), and T is the time to commute a unit distance to and from work.

Developers with land at any location u must choose capital K, lot size l, and time of development τ for their land holdings at that location. Assuming atomistic competition, developers maximize the present value of profits defined at time zero *per unit of land holdings*. Denoting these profits by B, for any developer

$$\max_{K,l,\tau} B = \int_{\tau}^{\infty} \frac{R(h, u; s)e^{-rs} \, ds}{l} - \frac{C(K)e^{-r\tau}}{l}. \tag{4.12}$$

First-order conditions are

$$\partial B/\partial K = \frac{\int_\tau^\infty R_h(s)h_K e^{-rs}\,ds - C_K e^{-r\tau}}{l} = 0, \tag{4.13a}$$

$$\partial B/\partial l = -\int_\tau^\infty \frac{R(s)e^{-rs}\,ds}{l^2} + \frac{\int_\tau^\infty R_h(s)h_l e^{-rs}\,ds}{l} + \frac{C(K)e^{-r\tau}}{l^2} = 0, \tag{4.13b}$$

$$\partial B/\partial \tau = -\frac{R(\tau)e^{-r\tau}}{l} + \frac{rC(K)e^{-r\tau}}{l} = 0. \tag{4.13c}$$

Rearranging these in order we get the following economic conditions that are of interest.

$$\left(\int_\tau^\infty R_h e^{-r(s-\tau)}\,ds\right)h_K = C_K \tag{4.14}$$

$$\left(\int_\tau^\infty R_h e^{-rs}\,ds\right)h_l = B \tag{4.15}$$

$$R(\tau) = rC(K). \tag{4.16}$$

In (4.14), with irreversible investment, capital is invested until the marginal purchase cost in τ, C_K, equals the marginal benefits—the physical marginal product, h_K, times the present value to τ of all future marginal revenues. In (4.16), development occurs when the revenue losses, $R(\tau)$, from waiting one more period equal the opportunity costs of investing capital now, $rC(K)$. Finally in (4.15), land is chosen such that the present value in time zero of all future marginal revenue products equals the marginal cost B. By specifying B as marginal cost we mean that in perfect competition the price per unit of land in time zero will equal the profits per unit of land in time zero.[7] Thus the value of land reflects its future productivities, even if its use is frozen.

For (4.13a) and (4.13b), second-order conditions require the usual declining marginal revenue products for land and capital. For (4.13c) it is required that $\partial^2 B/\partial \tau^2 = -R_\tau e^{-r\tau}/l \geq 0$, or $R_\tau \geq 0$. That is, spot (or current period) revenue on a housing unit must rise following development (otherwise it would pay the developer to either wait or to have developed earlier).

---

[7] Alternatively, a developer with existing fixed holdings of land will allocate land to this particular project until its profitability per unit of land B equals profitabilities in the other allocations of land. Of course, we would expect developers to adjust their land holdings until profitability per unit (at the margin) equals the price of land.

Other common relationships describing property and land values can also be defined from Equations (4.12)–(4.16). We note them for their interest. Given B is the value of a unit of land at time zero, if $V(\tau)$ is the value of the lot at τ the time of construction, then from (4.12) and (4.16).

$$V \equiv Be^{r\tau}l = \int_{\tau}^{\infty} R(s)e^{-r(s-\tau)}\,ds - R(\tau)/r$$

$$= \int_{\tau}^{\infty} [R(s) - R(\tau)]e^{-r(s-\tau)}\,ds. \qquad (4.17)$$

The value of a lot at the time of development is the surplus of the present value of actual further rents over the rent level at τ, given $R(\tau)$ just covers the opportunity cost of capital [Equation (4.16)]. Second, the property value at τ, $P(\tau)$ of land plus structures following irreversible investment is simply the present value of all future rents (what you could sell the building for), or

$$P(\tau) = \int_{\tau}^{\infty} R(s)e^{-r(s-\tau)}\,ds$$

Dividing through by (4.16) and inverting,

$$\frac{C(K)}{P(\tau)} = \frac{R(\tau)/r}{\displaystyle\int_{\tau}^{\infty} R(s)e^{-r(s-\tau)}\,ds}. \qquad (4.18)$$

Thus the ratio of the cost of structures to property value equals the ratio of the present value of rents unchanged from the current level to actual present value. The more quickly rents rise in the future, the greater will be land values, or the ratio of property value to structure costs.

The Housing Market over Time

In this section I discuss a general framework for analyzing the development process, focusing on where development occurs in each period. Does development occur from the city center moving out continuously, thus requiring the most intensively used land to be committed to use first, or are inner rings of land left temporarily vacant (for speculation) while some outer rings are developed first? I pose the question in an Alonso bid rent framework used by Wheaton (1983) and then indicate the methodology for determining a complete answer (Fujita, 1982).

Developers at each u from the city center choose the τ that yields them the highest B, the present value of profits at a common time zero. The question is whether as u increases τ will increase or decrease. If it increases, development occurs "regularly," from the center moving out. The problem is illustrated in

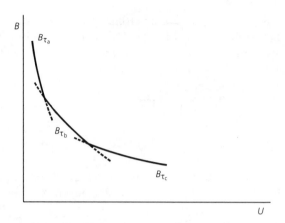

FIGURE 4.5   Timing of development.

Figure 4.5. First, for any τ_i, B declines with distance from the city center, since from Equation (4.10)

$$\left.\frac{\partial B}{\partial u}\right|_{\tau} = \int_{\tau}^{\infty} \frac{\partial R/\partial u}{l} e^{-rs}\,ds < 0.$$

Thus for each τ in Figure 4.5 there is a downward sloping $B(u; \tau)$ function in B, u space. However, the slope of the function changes with τ according to the sign of

$$d\left(\frac{\partial B}{\partial u}\right)\Big/\partial\tau \gtrless 0. \tag{4.19}$$

For the set of B curves for each τ, development occurs along the outer envelope of these curves since, for developers at each u, that maximizes the B they receive.

Thus, in Figure 4.5, development proceeds from the center moving out if $\tau_a < \tau_b < \tau_c < \cdots$ but the reverse if $\tau_a > \tau_b > \tau_c > \cdots$. A formal determination of what occurs requires differentiating a carefully respecified set of first-order conditions for each developer (Fujita, 1982) accounting for changes in income and utility levels as well as commuting costs over time. In (4.19) not only must we account for the pure impact of time $[-(\partial R/\partial u)e^{-rt}/l]$ on $\partial B/\partial u$, which favors development occurring from the center out (so $|\partial B/\partial u|$ falls with time) but also for the impact of income and utility changes on the shape of the $\partial R/\partial u$ terms. In general, it is difficult to make definitive statements. Of course, if the distance shapes of the R functions are time invariant or if access premiums decline over time, then $d(\partial B/\partial u)/dt > 0$, and in Figure 4.5

development occurs from the center out. Declining access premiums appear to be an empirical feature Mills (1972) of twentieth-century U.S. cities.

3. OTHER MODELS OF THE NATURE OF HOUSING AND THE HOUSING MARKET

There are two other models of housing in the literature that I will mention. A third is Rosen's (1974) extension to considering housing services h to be a vector of attributes. The analysis of that follows directly from the discussion of neighborhood amenities at the end of Section 1.2.

3.1 Housing as Peanuts

In traditional empirical work, where researchers are trying to explain total family housing expenditures as a function of incomes, effective prices, and family composition, housing services are treated like peanuts, as being perfectly divisible in supply and consumption and sold in the housing market at a constant unit price. Figure 4.3 and its analysis are replaced by regular demand and supply curves for the neighborhood housing market, where supply is upward sloping given a diminishing marginal product of capital applied to the fixed neighborhood land area. One can distinguish between short- and long-run supply, to account for noninstantaneous adjustment of capital investment to changing market conditions. While the special indivisibility and durability features of housing are ignored and thus the model has limited usefulness in analyzing certain aspects of the housing market, it may be a reasonable assumption to make when trying to explain differences in total housing expenditures of families using either aggregate or panel data where spatial detail and price variation is largely ignored (i.e., market segmentation into neighborhoods is ignored so variations in R_j functions cannot be accounted for).

3.2 Housing Indivisibilities on the Consumption Side

The heterogeneity notion of housing being a bundle of attributes as modeled by Rosen (1974) can be taken one step further (Ellickson, 1983). One can postulate that each house is unique or virtually so; and the fixed housing stock of a city will not generally be such that effectively the offerings of desired attribute bundles are continuous (i.e., there are holes in the relevant consumption space). Assuming both indivisibilities for consumers in occupying units and discontinuities in the bundles available, we have a problem of indivisible commodities (Mas-Colell, 1977) where continuity and convexity of consumption sets are absent. If one views that it is critical to account for this problem, it is necessary to employ Mas-Colell's framework and notions of approximate equilibria to analyze market outcomes. Unfortunately, the framework does not readily lend itself to comparative static analyses because of the complexity of both the nature of the problem and the specialized (for economists) formal apparatus required to solve the problem.

Nor generally has the problem of indivisible commodities been placed in a dynamic context, which asks how these holes in consumption space in the short run arise in the context of dynamic optimization. The exception is Sweeney's hierarchy model noted in Section 1.2, where the discrete types of housing available are defined exogenously. [As an interesting aside, Sweeney dealt with the nonconvexity of consumption sets problem by utilizing the concept of "relative convexity" (in the context of exact equilibria), rather than Mas-Colell's concept of "approximate equilibria" (in the context of regular notions of convexity).]

5

Housing Topics:
Utilizing the Basic Model

In this chapter I discuss common topics in the housing literature that deal with certain housing policies, utilizing the model presented in Chapter 4. The coverage is not intended to be comprehensive but simply to look at policies that present interesting theoretical problems and issues. Part of the discussion concerns normative issues dealing with externalities in the housing market, and part concerns positive issues dealing with the impacts of actual types of government policies. In Section 1 of the chapter, I examine housing market externalities, land use regulation, home improvement loans, and urban renewal. In Section 2, I look at the impact of rent control on housing markets, under various institutional regimes. In the final section I look at the economic impacts of zoning policies that attempt to regulate housing inputs and quality such as minimum lot-size zoning.

1. HOUSING MARKET EXTERNALITIES

In this section I examine two types of housing market externalities: social and neighborhood quality.

1.1 Social Externalities

Social externalities arise because the characteristics of people's neighbors enter their utility functions as separate arguments. The presence of different types of neighbors and their characteristics may increase, decrease, or leave neutral one's level of satisfaction. For example, one may have preferences defined over whether one's neighbors are noisy, friendly, generous, secretive, religious, white or black, childless, young or old, rich or poor, etc. In a city of N people, each person has preferences with respect to having each of the other $N - 1$ people as neighbors, so that whoever moves in next door to a person affects his utility and vice versa. Since these social preferences or externalities are unpriced in the market, in general the equilibrium spatial arrangement of people will be nonoptimal. Davis and Winston (1964) demonstrated this in the context of a housing assignment problem. I footnote a simple example to illustrate the point.[1]

---

[1] Suppose we have three people bidding in an auction for contiguous locations numbered 1, 2, 3 along a straight line. The locations are owned by different landowners who behave atomistically and passively, in the sense that they are willing to simply accept the highest nonnegative bid offered to them during the auction process. The opportunity rent on the locations is zero. In the table is a matrix of preferences defining how much our three antisocial people are willing to pay not to have others as neighbors. The three are constrained, however, to live side by side along a line. The only stable configuration is the arrangement A, B, C (or C, B, A). An equilibrium set of prices for this arrangement is 3, 0, 3. The base price, 0, prices the middle spot. Person C pays $3 for location 3 because he is willing to pay $3 not to live at location 2 and have A as his neighbor, and because he must pay $3 or B will bid away location 3 to avoid living next to A. Person A pays $3 for location 1 so that C does not bid it away. The price of spot 1 must always equal the price of spot 3 in any stable equilibrium since both locations offer the same neighbor. The social loss from this arrangement is $1 for A, $4 for B, and $8 for C—a total of $13. The spatial arrangement B, A, C (or C, A, B) has a smaller social loss of $10. Without bribing, however, this spatial arrangement is not sustainable because starting from this arrangement A will always outbid B for spot 1. The assignment is only stable if C is willing to do one of the following—bribe B to bid more for spot 1, bribe A to locate in spot 2 or bribe the landowner of spot 1 to rent it to B. Although with only three people along a line it may seem naive to rule out explicit bribes of this type, once the problem is expanded to n people arranged in a spatial area, the number of bribes required to reach an optimal arrangement becomes prohibitive. Moreover, the government certainly does not have this information about residents' preferences and thus cannot implement an optimal solution.

Loss from Having Various
Neighbors ($)

	Possible neighbors		
	A	B	C
A	0	−1	−3
B	−3	0	−1
C	−3	−8	0

In this context, a Pareto-efficient spatial arrangement of people can occur only if there exists a bribing mechanism that allows the possibility of people bribing other people in the city to live or not live next to them or others and if the tatonnement process is costless. Since in our economy widespread explicit bribing among residents is not an acceptable social custom and the type of agreements reached among neighbors and potential neighbors may not be legally enforceable, people will generally only alter their residential situation by moving themselves. They will not bribe various people to live next to them or to switch places with others. Consequently, social externalities are not priced, and the equilibrium spatial arrangement will thus be nonoptimal.

Although the market cannot solve the generalized social externality problem, it may be able to solve the most obvious problems of this sort. In particular, people's preferences about neighbors might be primarily determined by one or two discernible characteristics, such as race, income, or land use. For example, suppose there are two land use groups in a city: retail and residential. These groups may generally prefer to locate next to others with similar land uses. For example, retail users want to utilize common parking and mall facilities and attract each others' customers, while residents prefer not to locate next to commercial activity because of noise pollution and other disamenities. Therefore, people within each group may always be willing to bid more for a spot next to a similar type land user. As a result, the tatonnement process should lead to a solution where renters in each group are clustered together. In Chapter 3, I illustrated two equilibria where this spatial separation of groups occurred, one on the basis of race and the other of the basis of residential versus polluting industrial use. However, even with this type of situation where large groups of users prefer to separate themselves from others, the configuration of groups and division of land may still be suboptimal for several reasons.

First, there are many different groups of land users in a city such as industrial, retail, residential single-family, residential multifamily, and highrise. While members of each group may cluster together, there is no general mechanism to ensure an optimal spatial configuration of the groups, where which groups border what other groups is designed to minimize negative externalities at the borders. An example of this is illustrated in footnote 1, when we replace individuals A, B, and C by groups A, B, and C. The whole idea of city planning from an economist's point of view is based on this notion. City planning through both the allocation of public lands and land-use zoning to regulate the use of private lands in theory is trying to achieve an optimal spatial configuration of groups of land users. Apart from trying to quantify the magnitude of some of the externalities, economists have had little to say about the details of city planning.

Instead, economists have focused on two other problems connected with various land users clustering into homogeneous groups: conflicting preferences and land-use encroachment. In analyzing these problems, the overall question of city planning is bypassed, and these two narrower issues are focused on. Both issues present alternative bases for the need for land-use regulation, and their starting point assumes homogeneous clusters have already occurred. We turn to these now.

Conflicting Preferences

Although various land users may generally cluster into homogeneous groups, there is a problem if A people want to live next to B people but B people would prefer to live separate from A people. A common example is the gas station owner who wants to locate in a residential neighborhood. The residents surrounding the gas station suffer from noise and odor pollution, although other nonimmediate but nearby residents may benefit in net from the shopping convenience offered by the proximity of a gas station. Let us assume for the moment that the losses of residents immediate to the gas station exceed gains to nearby but not contiguous residents. Land-use zoning precludes the gas station owner from moving in, by zoning all land use to be residential. This protects residents from suffering unexpected losses in utility, capitalized into lower land values. However, there is the problem that, if nonimmediate residents benefit more from the shopping convenience of a nearby gas station than contiguous residents suffer, a potential Pareto-efficient solution that would allow the gas station to move in is ruled out. Such a solution, however, would require compensation to the losing residents (and how are they identified?).

For this reason, some economists argue against the use of zoning to regulate land use and in favor of the bribing solutions we previously ruled out as being socially unacceptable and legally difficult to enforce. However, in this case, bribing may be workable if the obnoxious user has to bribe residents to get permission to move in. In fact, a solution involving both land-use regulation and users bribing residents may be similar to what happens in land markets in certain situations. First, land-use zoning is enacted, protecting groups of land users from the invasion of obnoxious users (i.e., their property rights to not just their land but also to nonobnoxious neighboring users are protected). However, zoning boards are established to grant variances (exemptions) to land-use zoning, *providing* the affected contiguous neighbors do not object. If indeed it is optimal for an obnoxious user to move in, that single user can bribe contiguous residents not to object, in which case a variance will be granted, the contiguous residents will be compensated for their losses (via bribes), and the nearby noncontiguous residents and the gas station owner will gain. The notion of bribing in this context can be quite broad. Rather than money it might involve payment-in-kind such as the building of a park, paying for cable TV lines, building additional convenience stores, etc. These types of arrangements are not uncommon when large developments are involved. In summary, land-use zoning laws generally protect one set of land users from other obnoxious users, by carving up the city into different spatially distinct land uses. Variances may permit reasonable deviations from this strict pattern of spatially separated uses.

Land-Use Encroachment

The second problem in land-use allocation that occurs in the market grouping of land users is that people in different groups may be willing to pay different amounts to live next to or separate from each other. An example of this problem was analyzed formally in Chapter 3, Section 2 for the case of residential versus commercial land users. The basic problem is briefly reviewed to make the analysis of this section complete. In that example, commercial users are indifferent as to the nature of their neighbors whereas residents want to live away from polluting commercial users, in a situation where the air quality losses to residents decline with distance from commercial users.

In that example, the land-use problem is that, in an optimal configuration, land values of residents near commercial users fall below the opportunity value of land (in commercial use), because the discomfort of residents near commercial users (relative to those further away) is capitalized into lower land values. From this optimal configuration, if zoning does not prohibit it, commercial users will move into the residential area to take advantage of the low land prices. Land-use zoning can prohibit this nonoptimal encroachment.

Alternatives to Land-Use Zoning

Although zoning has been the land-use regulating tool referred to in this section because of its widespread use, there are two alternative tools that I should mention. A private-market alternative to zoning is contracts. When, say, a residential neighborhood is initially developed, the initial sales contracts and all subsequent sales contracts prohibit the redevelopment and resale of land for nonconforming uses (see also Chapter 10 on contracts). The initial pattern of development planned by a developer can be very flexible, allowing for a perceived best mix of residential and retail users. Although the contracts freeze this initial pattern, the contracts may be restructured explicitly through neighborhood consent (voting of current residents) or implicitly through lapses in enforcement. Siegan (1970) discussed this type of arrangement focusing on Houston, the only large U.S. city where contractual arrangement rather than zoning have traditionally governed land use.

A public policy alternative to zoning is taxation, which when properly designed can duplicate any zoning solution. Initially a city's land use is carved up. Then encroachment or nonconforming uses in a neighborhood are permitted providing (only) the nonconforming users pay a tax when they enter an area designed for uses other than theirs. The taxes paid would vary with the externalities the nonconforming users impose. An example of taxes under encroachment is discussed in Section 2 of Chapter 3. Taxation as a replacement for zoning is advocated by many economists because it is an explicit but impersonal mechanism (the payment of preset taxes) permitting land-use change in response to changing market conditions, in contrast to the slow and very personal methods of granting variances or of rezoning (which from an economists's point of view can involve bribes of both a proper and improper nature).

1.2 Neighborhood Quality

The second general type of externality concerns the maintenance decisions of people's neighbors, rather than the characteristics of their neighbors per se. The outside quality of neighbors' houses affects residents' locational satisfactions by affecting their view and the pleasure and pride they take in inviting friends to their houses and hence neighborhood. Second, neighbors' maintenance policies affect residents' safety and the safety of their children, in terms of lighting at night; repairs of stairways, railings, and roofs; snow removal; and garbage disposal. As we saw in the profit maximization expressions in Chapter 4, for a landowner (who may be the occupant), only the private benefits of maintenance are captured. In addition to the private benefits, there are these external social benefits or neighborhood externalities from upkeep. Since the landowners are not compensated for these externalities, they do not account for them in maintenance decisions and hence the level of upkeep is too low.

There is a particular twist to this problem and potential solutions to it that makes it useful to formally state a simple version of it. This statement is based on the work of Schall (1976) and Stahl (1980). Consider a neighborhood where there are n housing units each owned by a different landlord. The ith person in the neighborhood maximizes utility, $V = V(x_i, h_i, Q_i)$, subject to the budget constraint $y - R(h_i, Q_i) - x = 0$. Neighborhood quality Q for simplicity is defined for the ith person as

$$Q = \sum_{\substack{j=1 \\ j \neq i}}^{n} h_j/(n - 1). \tag{5.1}$$

For the ith person, neighborhood housing quality is simply defined as the average level of services per housing unit in the rest $(1, 2, \ldots, i - 1, i + 1, \ldots, n)$ of the neighborhood. As in Chapter 4, Equation (4), $R(h_i, Q_i)$ is the rent schedule for the ith dwelling unit based on willingness-to-pay and supply offer curves where in equilibrium along the schedule

$$R_h = V_h/V_x, \qquad R_Q = V_Q/V_x. \tag{5.2}$$

Equation (5.2) reflects the slopes of the tangent, underlying willingness-to-pay curves.

Each landlord maximizes the present value of profits corresponding to Equation (4.7), noting the addition of Q_i in the $R(\cdot)$ function. As before, the equilibrium condition for investment, or maintenance k_i, is

$$R_h h_K = C_K(r + \delta). \tag{5.3}$$

This standard equilibrium is illustrated in Figure 5.1. However, this equilibrium is no longer optimal. The easiest way to see this is to jointly maximize profits of all neighborhood landlords, holding the utility of all consumers fixed [at the levels defining the $R(\cdot)$ schedules] so as to acheive a Pareto-efficient solution.

From Equation (4.7), joint profit maximization involves maximizing

$$\sum_{j=1}^{n} \int_0^T [R(h_j, Q_j; s) - C(k_j(s))] e^{-rs} \, ds - \sum_{j=1}^{n} S_j(0) + \sum_{j=1}^{n} S_j(T) e^{-rT}, \tag{5.4}$$

where for simplicity we have assumed a common horizon T that could be infinity. As before, $S_j(0)$ and $S_j(T)$ are initial and final selling prices and $k_j(s) = \dot{K}_j + \delta K_j$. The condition for optimal investment in any period is

$$R_h h_K + \frac{h_K^i}{n-1} \sum_{\substack{j=1 \\ j \neq i}}^{n} R_Q^j = C_K(r + \delta). \tag{5.5}$$

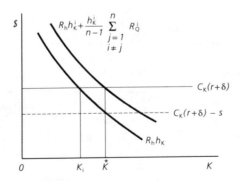

FIGURE 5.1   Investment with externalities.

The new term on the left-hand side of (5.5) is the externality involved. The external benefit of increasing k_i is the increase in i's housing, h_K^i, times the increase in neighborhood quality from h increasing, $1/(n-1)$, times the sum of increases in willingness-to-pay for increased Q by all other residents. The optimal level of investment for any landlord is given by K^* in Figure 5.1, indicating that the optimal level of housing services for the i unit exceeds the equilibrium level.

Neighborhood Equilibrium

For simple situations it is possible to compare the free market equilibrium in the whole neighborhood with the optimal neighborhood solution. To do this comparison, we must deal with the fact that as K and h move from equilibrium to optimal levels for all residents, Q is simultaneously changing for all residents altering both arguments in the $R(h, Q)$ schedules, causing $R(h, Q)$ to shift in R, h space. To do the comparison we assume all residents, landlords, and plots of land in the neighborhood are *identical*. Landlords will all have the same set of supply offer curves. The observed R, h in equilibrium will be a point. However, if we fix alternative utility levels ($V°$ in Equation 4.2) for the problem, given residents are identical, the potential $R(\cdot)$ schedules facing landlords are coincident with willingness-to-pay schedules, and we can define for later reference two alternative characteristics of these schedules.[2]

    (i)   Complements: h_i and Q_i are complements if and only if $\partial^2 W/\partial h\,\partial Q = \partial^2 R/\partial h\partial Q \equiv R_{hQ} > 0$.

   (ii)   Substitutes: h_i and Q_i are substitutes if $R_{hQ} < 0$.

Substitutability is defined as a decline in willingness-to-pay for more housing as neighborhood quality increases, indicating that, holding utility fixed, the two goods are substitutes for each other.

Given these definitions we turn to the analysis of equilibria. Given identical residents and plots of land, in equilibrium it must be the case that $h_1 = h_2 = \cdots = h_n = Q_1 = Q_2 = \cdots = Q_n$, and thus the uniform housing quality per housing unit by definition in Equation (5.1) equals neighborhood housing quality. Thus in Figures 5.2a and 5.2b equilibrium must lie along the 45° line where $h = Q$. We plot the h_i, Q_i combinations satisfying the investment equilibrium condition [Equation (5.3)]. To derive these combinations we differentiate (5.3) to get $R_{hh}h_K^2\,dK + R_h h_{KK}\,dK + R_{hQ}\,dQh_K = 0$.

---

[2] This criterion does not solely depend on the cross partial second derivative of the utility function.

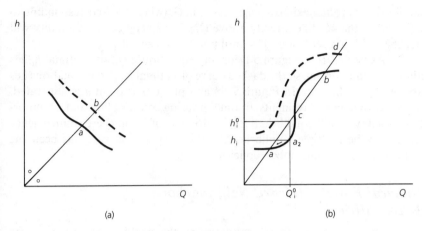

FIGURE 5.2   Neighborhood equilibrium.

Thus

$$\frac{dK}{dQ} = \frac{R_{hQ}h_K}{-(R_{hh}h_K^2 + R_h h_{KK})}\Bigg|_<^> 0 \quad \text{as} \quad R_{hQ}\Bigg|_<^> 0. \tag{5.6}$$

By diminishing marginal rates of substitution and productivity ($h_{KK} < 0$ and $R_{hh} \equiv W_{hh} < 0$ for identical residents), the denominator of (5.6) is positive, so the sign of dK/dQ is the sign of R_{hQ}. Given h_i is a monotonically increasing function of K_i, the sign of the slope of the line $(dH/dQ = h_K\,dK/dQ)$ plotting equilibrium h_i, Q_i is given by (5.6).

Substitutes   In Figure 5.2a we assume h and Q are substitutes so the line of equilibrium h_i, Q_i combinations is downward sloping. Equilibrium is at point a. In comparison, for the optimum *for any* Q_i, the optimal h_i must be higher from Figure 5.1, given we have added a positive term to the left-hand side of Equation (5.5). This is illustrated by the dashed line in Figure 5.2a where holding Q_i fixed, the optimal h_i level exceeds the equilibrium. The optimal solution is at point b.

Complements   In Figure 5.2b we assume h and Q are complements and illustrate one possible equilibrium-optimum scenario. In Figure 5.2b, the solid line of equilibrium combinations must be upward sloping. For later reference for public policy analysis I depict a situation with multiple equilibria. In Figure 5.2b, a and b are "stable" equilibria, while c is unstable. [For example, suppose we are out of equilibrium at point a_2 *where* Q_i^0 at a_2 is in excess of the Q_i where for the same h_i, $Q_i = h_i$. Then for that Q_i^0 for any landlord, the profit maximizing h_i is less than Q_i^o (where the h corresponding to Q_i^o is h_i^o on the 45° line directly above Q_i^o). Thus neighborhood quality will decline as h_i's are set below Q_i^o's until point a is reached.]

As before from Figure 5.1, for any equilibrium Q_i, the optimal h_i lies above the equilibrium, so the dashed curve of optimal h_i, Q_i combinations lies above the equilibrium. In Figure 5.2b, an optimum at point d is illustrated. Again, with identical residents, optimal housing consumption and neighborhood quality exceed equilibrium levels. However, if h and Q are complements, there may be multiple equilibria, and this very special case has been the implicit basis for some public policies.

General Policies toward Neighborhood Externalities

We note four general solutions to the problem of moving from equilibrium investment decisions depicted by Equation (5.3) to optimal decisions depicted by Equation (5.5). First, we could subsidize maintenance, to lower the marginal costs of maintenance to $C_K(r + \delta) - S$ in Figure 5.1, where subsidized marginal costs intersect the private benefit schedule $(R_h h_K)$ at the optimal level of capital. The optimal subsidy is the value (at the optimum) of the externality term in Equation (5.5), which is subtracted from the right-hand side of Equation (5.3), or equivalently added to its left-hand side, to yield, in effect, Equation (5.5) as the guide to maintenance decisions. One could argue that federal programs subsidizing home improvement loans constitute an effort to implement this solution.

A second possible solution is through zoning ordinances and building codes that require landowners to light outdoor entrances, have adequate garbage disposal, and repair external structures. However, such ordinances are unlikely to deal with problems of gardening, landscaping, and painting. Of course, the residents may not be so concerned with the latter items but rather with maintenance of features that promote safety.

Third, we could concentrate ownership of housing in the neighborhood. At the extreme, a single owner of all neighborhood land faces the maximization problem in Equation (5.4), with the potentially optimal solution in Equation (5.5). However, any concentration of ownership, say, toward the owner of the i plot, adds terms to the left-hand side of (5.3) equal to $h_K^i(n - 1)$ times the sum of any R_Q^j terms for other houses (in the set $1, 2, \ldots, i - 1$, $i + 1, \ldots, n$) the landlord owns in the neighborhood. This assumed benefit of moving toward the optimum by concentrating ownership must be weighed against the costs of potentially introducing monopolistic behavior in the housing market.

There is also the question of why, since a landlord could profit [see Equation (5.4)] from buying up the neighborhood and internalizing the externality, concentration would not occur naturally in the market. To the extent it does not occur naturally, it must be because individual housing holdings of this magnitude are generally inconsistent with optimal portfolio holdings (Chapter 6) for an individual. Moreover, at the same time, residents may have a strong preference for owning their individual houses.

The final and perhaps most relevant solution is that informal neighborhood mechanisms may arise to virtually eliminate the problem. The critical factor is that the externality is reciprocal, where, while a resident's maintenance affects his neighbors' well-being, their maintenance affects his well-being. If people with similar tastes for housing are grouped together, the magnitude of the total and marginal external benefits will be approximately the same in each Equation (5.5). Then the neighbors involved will all benefit from voluntarily agreeing to increase maintenance and housing services to the optimal level without bribing taking place. Essentially each resident will "bribe" his neighbors to increase their upkeep by increasing his own upkeep. Such a solution may well be realized in most stable home-owner neighborhoods where people know each other. Various forms of social pressure can be applied to induce neighbors to maintain their houses and implicitly agree to internalize this externality. Of course, in transient neighborhoods where neighbors may not know each other, such solutions are less likely. But in this case, the problem may be solved to some extent by concentrated ownership (e.g., apartment buildings and complexes).

Urban Renewal and Neighborhood Externalities

The notion of the neighborhood externality has often been the intellectual basis of public policies involving reconstruction of neighborhoods. This is particularly true of the urban renewal policies in the United States of the 1950s and 1960s, which involved partial or complete demolition of neighborhoods followed by massive redevelopment and reconstruction. There seemed to be two bases for the presumed need for massive redevelopment.

First, there was a "big push" argument. Somehow, some neighborhoods are stuck at low-quality levels, but a big shot of capital housing will move the neighborhoods permanently to a higher-quality level (even though the externality problem per se is not thus solved—i.e., Equation (5.3) still governs maintenance decisions). The only situation in which this argument has validity is the one of multiple equilibria in Figure 5.2b. If a neighborhood somehow starts off at point a in Figure 5.2b, a big push past point c would move the neighborhood to point b, nearer the optimum. Since market participants, given atomistic behavior, cannot recognize that they are stuck (nor could they do much about it individually), government intervention is required to administer the big shot. In applying this very special argument, it is completely unclear how we should determine if we are in situation with multiple equilibria and, if so, whether we are stuck at a point like a or whether we are already at b.

The second basis seems to involve notions of filtering down. Suppose housing filters down naturally and that people are concerned with neighborhood quality and perhaps homogeneity. Then we would expect housing in a neighborhood to generally be built at about the same time, ensuring all residents of some uniformity to quality and allowing developers and the city to exploit economies of scale in development (housing plus neighborhood infrastructure). Then, for neighborhoods where housing is built at the same time, the housing should filter down together. At some point demolition and reconstruction becomes optimal. It is at this time that people have asserted that we need public policy intervention.

The argument is that, because of neighborhood externalities, redevelopment or reconstruction of housing must be done on a large scale and requires a large package of land. A developer is unlikely to build one or two new houses on a block of old and decaying houses because the externalities imposed by the decaying structures will lower the selling price of the new buildings relative to a situation where the whole block is redeveloped. If the whole block is redeveloped, then *initially* these externalities are internalized and the problem of having decaying buildings on the block is eradicated. However, redeveloping the whole block requires assembling a large quantity of land and buying up *all* the existing structures. This introduces the traditional holdout problem, where the last seller(s) of old structures on the block holds out for a tremendous price. At the limit the developer will have to pay all his potential profits from the redevelopment to the holdout and this discourages potential developers from undertaking the project. This then requires public intervention in the form of eminent domain, where the initial residents are forced to sell for the public "good" at "fair" market prices (which may be contested) to the developer by way of the city government.

There are two general objections to this argument. The first argument is an empirical one. The political misuse of eminent domain in the United States to effectively transfer resources from low-income residents of urban renewed areas to developers and future high-income residents is well documented (Wilson, 1966). There are few, if any, examples of urban renewal projects that were (ex post) justified on cost–benefit grounds (Rothenberg, 1967). Urban renewal appears to have generally demolished *stable* (not filtering-down) low-income neighborhoods, displacing these residents, with inadequate compensation. The true basis for these actions appears often to be either to rightly or wrongly transfer benefits (the land) to a few people or institutions or to eliminate the eyesore of slums. In the latter case, of course, these displaced people must move somewhere, and hence create new low-income housing areas.

The second general argument is that the holdout problem necessitating public intervention initially through eminent domain is not a serious one. It may only be a problem when developers have inadequate purchase strategies or are inadequate bargainers. It may be that if the buying is done carefully and secretively, most if not all houses and buildings on a block can be bought up by a single party before other owners find out, especially if the buildings are initially owned by a variety of absentee landowners who have little or no contract with each other. Even if holdouts arise, their bargaining power is limited, because if development proceeds without them they may incur substantial losses (as in the case of a single-family house about to be surrounded by high-rises or commercial development).

Free Enterprise Zones

It should be recognized that proposals for free enterprise zones in the United States are similar in spirit and potential impact to urban renewal. Under free enterprise zone proposals in the United States, certain distressed areas of a city would be designated free-enterprise zones, and businesses located and locating in those areas would receive certain valuable tax or safety regulation exemptions. Of course, businesses already in those areas may generally not face high effective tax liabilities nor extensive regulation. The tax exemptions or safety regulation exemptions are of most value to businesses with either high tax liabilities or hazardous activities. To get exemptions, these businesses must move into the free enterprise zones; they then are the ones willing to pay the most for the land there. The exemptions make the land in the zone valuable to those outside, but it may not make the original residents or businesses valuable.

The implication is that existing land users will be driven out over the long term and displaced by higher-quality users. That will improve the area, but the general problem is unsolved. First, the original land users have to move to another part of the city and continue their low level of consumption of business and residential structures, so a new distressed area may be created. Second, offering tax exemptions in one part of the city but not others creates a spatial misallocation of resources. With original uniform tax policies, the original allocation will have been the correct one, ceteris paribus. Tax policies that spatially discriminate will cause people to move from their best locations to nonoptimal ones.

2. AN APPLICATION OF THE BASIC MODEL: RENT CONTROL

Suppose rent control is imposed in only one neighborhood of a metropolitan area, a typical rent control situation in the United States. Rent control specifies a permanent maximum rent that may be charged for a particular housing unit. We assume the imposition of rent controls is unanticipated. First, I examine the impact of rent controls, where the intent of the law is met, meaning payments between tenants and landlords consist only of the legal rent controlled rents and rental units are not converted to owner-occupied units. Then I examine market mechanisms that alleviate the impact of rent control.

In Figure 5.3a, $R(h)$ is the revenue schedule facing a landlord prior to rent control, and we assume the landlord is providing h_A housing services to person A for rent R_A. With rent control, the rent the landlord can charge is lowered to R_C. However, since rent control affects only a tiny portion of the city and opportunities elsewhere in the city are unchanged, we assume willingness-to-pay curves and market equilibrium conditions are imperceptibly changed and $R(h)$ remains the potential rent schedule. The landlord's actual schedule with rent control is $R(h)$ up to point c and $\bar{R}_C$ beyond. Similarly in Figure 5.3b, the marginal revenue schedule is $R_h MP_K$ up to point c and then zero beyond there.

With rent control the landlord's long-run equilibrium position is at h_c in Figure 5.3a an K_c in Figure 5.3b, presuming it is not efficient because of demolition and land redivision costs to demolish and reconstruct the units in

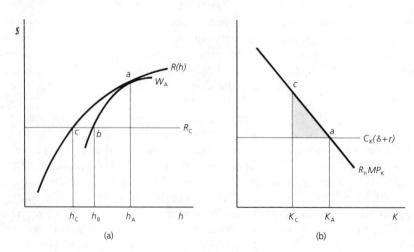

FIGURE 5.3   Rent control.

the neighborhood. At point c in Figure 5.3a the landlord provides housing such that the maximal willingness-to-pay just equals the allowable rent. The landlord of course no longer operates at tangency points of his supply offer curves to the revenue schedule, given the restriction of rent control. In Figure 5.3b at c, as $K \longrightarrow K_c$ but $K < K_c$, marginal revenue exceeds marginal cost; while as $K \longrightarrow K_c$ but $K > K_c$, marginal cost exceeds marginal revenue. The latter figure indicates the shadow marginal revenue product of capital is far in excess of marginal costs at c and that factor proportions are "distorted" in the sense that, if land redivision was not costly, given allowable rents, lot sizes would be reduced shifting $R_h MP_K$ down (of course, then allowable rents might be reassessed). Figure 5.3b also indicates in each period the loss in current profits (excess of marginal revenue product over marginal costs from point c to point a) from rent control, once point c is reached. We shall discuss the landlord's total losses more fully below.

The movement from point a to point c is also of interest. We assume investment is irreversible, to make the adjustment process realistic. With irreversibility, the landlord cannot immediately sell off the now excess capital and go directly to point c. The landlord ceases maintenance temporarily, and net disinvestment takes place through depreciation at a rate δ. Initially as h declines, the original tenant A stays in the unit since the tenant's willingness-to-pay W_A exceeds the allowable payment $\bar{R}_c$ until point b. In a free market, of course, the tenant would move out when housing moved below h_A; but here the reduced rent may increase the tenant's length of tenure because he is *locked in* by the rent savings from controls. Beyond point b tenant A leaves. The owner continues disinvestment until point c is reached. At point c net disinvestment ceases, and tenants with willingness-to-pay tangent to $R(h)$ at c become the permanent type of tenants.

For the neighborhood as a whole and for each individual unit, there is the implication that the income level of residents declines under rent control, as we move from points like a with high housing demanders down to points like c with low housing demanders in Figure 5.3a. Thus, once units deteriorate past points corresponding to b in Figure 5.3b, higher-income people leave the neighborhood and go to other parts of the city, and lower-income people move in. Thus the imposition of rent control in the absence of mitigating factors leads to a decline in neighborhood quality.

The cost of this decline in this situation where rent control affects only one tiny neighborhood or community of a (large) city or metropolitan area is borne entirely by landlords. The framework presumes, because residents (vast) alternatives are unaffected by rent control, that, to retain its residents, the rent-controlled neighborhood must continue to offer the same utility levels to potential residents that they could get before rent control. The negative impacts of rent control are fully capitalized into property values. The decline in property values at the time rent control (time 0) is initiated is the value of the landlord's lost profits. We evaluate this assuming a situation where demand and supply conditions remain the same forever, Without rent control, the landlord's profits would have been

$$\Pi \text{ (free market)} = \int_0^\infty [R_A - C(k_A)]e^{-rs} ds = \frac{R_A - C(k_A)}{r} \quad (5.7)$$

where k_A is the maintenance required to maintain housing at h_A. With rent control the landlord's profits become

$$\Pi \text{ (rent control)} = \int_0^{s_c} R_c e^{-rs} ds + \int_{s_c}^\infty [R_c - C(k_c)]e^{-rs} ds$$

$$= \frac{R_c}{r} - \frac{C(k_c)e^{-rs_c}}{r} \quad (5.8)$$

where k_c is the maintenance required to maintain housing at h_c. From 0 to time s_c housing is depreciating from h_A to h_c, so that $K_c = K_A e^{-\delta s_c}$ or $s_c = [\log(K_A/K_c)]/\delta$. Subtracting (5.8) from (5.7) we get the value of lost profits and the decline in property values P

$$\Delta P = \frac{R_A - C(k_A) - R_c}{r} + C(k_c)\frac{e^{-rs_c}}{r}. \quad (5.9)$$

Where $k_A = \delta K_A$ and $k_c = \delta K_c$ and the cost of a unit of capital is C_K we may rewrite this as

$$\Delta P = \frac{R_A - R_c}{r} - \frac{\delta}{r} C_K K_A \left[1 - \left(\frac{K_c}{K_A}\right)^{1+r/\delta} \right]. \quad (5.9a)$$

Property values decline by the present value of lost rents less the savings in maintenance. Maintenance is saved both because there is no maintenance from time 0 to s_c and because after s_c, $k_c < k_A$. (Note if the pre–rent control solution was a unique profit-maximizing solution, $\Delta P > 0$, so rent control imposes a loss.)

While landlords lose, the initial tenant has temporary gains. The tenant's gains are the excess of willingness-to-pay over R_c for the time in the dwelling unit. These are (ignoring the problem that these gains themselves will affect willingness-to-pay)

$$\int_0^{s_b} [W(h(K_A e^{-\delta s})) - R_c]e^{-rs} ds, \quad (5.10)$$

where at s_b K has declined to the level $K_b (= K_A e^{-\delta s_b})$ that just produces housing serivces h_b in Figure (5.3a). Person A's successors will also experience excesses of willingness-to-pay over rents until point c is reached.

If rent control were imposed on the whole city, the analysis would be very different. The best alternatives of potential residents of this neighborhood would all be affected. If only this city in the economy experienced rent control, then following Chapter 2 analyses, presumably city size, utility levels, and land rents would all eventually decline with the introduction of this distortion.

2.1 Market Mechanisms Mitigating the Impact of Rent Control

When rent control is imposed, two phenomena arise to mitigate and perhaps even eliminate the impact of rent control. In general, we would expect the market to generate forces to alleviate the impact of rent control, given its distortionary nature. This analysis of how this happens draws upon the work of Skelley (1985). First, there can be side payments between the landlord and tenants; and, second, rental units can be converted to condominiums. Since I do not analyze tenure choice until the next chapter, I tend to focus on the former phenomenon, but can draw the obvious parallels with the latter. While economists recognize that side payments can alleviate the impact of government price controls, in the case of rent control, exactly how the payments can or will occur in the context of rent control laws is not obvious. At the time of rent control, both the existing tenant and landlord have a variety of legal rights from which they can bluff and bargain with each other. We will derive the features of the optimal contract between them, which will eliminate the distortionary impacts of rent control. In that case the primary impact of rent control will be to transfer wealth between landlords and tenants, not a change in the level of housing services. The magnitude and direction of flow of transfers will depend upon the structure of legal rights and the level at which R_c is set.

New Tenant

To derive the features of the optimal contract, we start with the simplest case, where at the time of rent control there is no existing tenant in the landlord's unit. Either the unit by chance is temporarily vacant, or it is a newly constructed unit subject to rent control. Although the landlord faces an official rent of R_c, unofficially his *potential* from the willingness-to-pay of new tenants remains $R(h)$ as determined by the free housing market in the rest of the city. For that potential rent schedule his optimal output of services is, say, h_A in Figure 5.3. Rent control is effectively avoided if the landlord can rent h_A to the new tenant at official rent of R_c, but a total payment of effectively R_A. The method by which the gap between R_A and R_c is filled must be carefully structured.

The gap cannot be filled with a period-by-period side payment of $R_A - R_c$. Once in the dwelling unit, the tenant will generally have occupancy rights and cannot be evicted without cause. Hence, once in the unit, the tenant could cease to make the side payment and only pay the official rent R_c. Since the side payment is at least in theory illegal, the landlord has no legal recourse to collect the side payments. Thus the landlord would demand a "key money" payment of, say for now, the present value of side payments for the length of time the tenant is in the dwelling unit. Then the tenant would have no opportunity to default.

However, such a key money payment presents two problems. First, once the tenant is in the dwelling unit and has made the large lump-sum payment, the landlord could cease maintenance, eventually drive the tenant out, restore the building, and try to collect another large key money payment. The only way to avoid this type of problem is to have the tenant take over responsibility for maintenance (ignoring the problem that it may be more costly [less efficient $C(\cdot)$ functions] for tenants to do maintenance). In that case the tenant's key money payment would be reduced by maintenance costs and would become the present value of $R_A - R_c - C(k_A)$.

The second problem in structuring the key money payment concerns the length of stay of tenants and rights of succession. First, the length of stay may be uncertain; and second, the tenant has an incentive to try to signal a small length of stay to reduce the key money payment—the present value over the length of stay of potential side payments. Moreover, once the tenant takes over maintenance, as the end of his length of stay approaches the tenant will be doing maintenance which benefits will persist into the future for future tenants. Since the tenant could not collect under this contractural structure for these benefits, he will underinvest in maintenance (which would then also affect the key money payment). These problems are entirely avoided if the landlord contracturally grants the tenant the rights to choose a successor and to also collect a key money payment from his successor.

We can now state the structure of the optimal contract between a landlord and new tenant. The landlord explicitly grants (in a lease) the tenant the rights to do maintenance and to choose a successor and gives the tenant's successors the same rights. In a sense all future tenancies will be a succession of sublets, where the sublet has full rights of occupancy. Assuming an infinite horizon and a stationary situation, the initial tenant will make a key money payment to the landlord of

$$\frac{R_A - R_c - C(k^A)}{r}. \tag{5.11}$$

The initial tenant will collect a key money payment equal to (5.11) as evaluated at the time he leaves, from the successor. This process will continue as the apartment is passed from tenant to tenant. These types of contractural arrangements are observed in the marketplace (e.g., see Hardman, 1983, on Cairo).

Several comments on this contract are in order. With an infinite horizon, from Chapter 4 $(R_A - C(k_A))/r$ is the property value of the building. Thus the tenant is in essence purchasing the building at a price reduced by the fixed stream of R_c obligations. R_c acts as an infinite life mortgage payment. In practice, of course, the landlord retains effective redevelopment rights, in a less than infinite horizon world for tenancy.

Second, for the key money to flow from tenant to landlord, (5.11) must be positive and sufficiently large. It must be large enough to compensate the tenant at the margin for undepreciated maintenance the tenant has done at the time he vacants the unit. However, there is no guarantee (especially if $R_c \rightarrow R_A$) that (5.11) is even positive. For low values of (5.11) the contract must be restructured so that the *contract* rent is set permanently below R_c at a level R_0 such that $R_A - R_0 - C(k^A)/r$ exceeds a minimum bound (Shelley, 1985), such as the value of the capital stock of the unit. In theory this presents no problems to either party since as R_0 declines, key money payments rise by the exact value of the reduction in the value of the stream of future rental payments. In indicating that, in fact, contract rents could be set below control rents, we note that the primary reason is that the tenants are now assuming the costs of maintenance.

Third, whatever the specifics of the contracts are, there are no overall equity or efficiency impacts of rent control. The landlord makes the same profits as before rent control, and the tenant gets the same benefits as dictated by his willingness-to-pay curve given alternatives in other neighborhoods. However, in practice it should be recognized that it may be more costly for tenants to do maintenance than for landlords due to differentials in economies of scale and experience. Given this, in practice if rent control is relatively mild, a contract that turns over maintenance to the tenant (in return for reduced contract rents and a key money payment) may not in fact be beneficial.

Finally, this case where rent control has no impacts represents the polar set of institutional arrangements to that where rent control is completely binding. There are a variety of intermediate alternatives such as the legal inability to grant succession rights, which are discussed in Skelley (1985).

Existing Tenants

The above contractual arrangement deals with new tenants. The contracts are structured such that there are no equity or efficiency effects of rent control. However, the equity but not efficiency implications will generally be dramatically different if there is an existing tenant in the unit. At a minimum, the existing tenant has the right of occupancy and to a low rent payment R_c. The tenant may also have the right to take over maintenance if the landlord stops maintenance, especially since it might be hard to stop the tenant from doing so. The tenant probably will not officially have the right to choose the successor, although subletting might be hard to monitor and prohibit.

If the tenant is granted by rent control laws the right to do maintenance and to choose (contractually) the successor, then the tenant in essence is granted a benefit equal to Equation (5.11)—the present value of the reduction in rents less the increase in maintenance costs. The lower R_c is set the greater the benefit to the existing tenant and the loss to the landlord.

If rent control laws do not grant the tenant these rights, he will be willing to purchase them, because the tenant's gain in benefits will be positive. If the tenant does not purchase the rights, the unit will deteriorate until time s_b when his willingness-to-pay falls below R_c. Then the tenant's gain from rent control is $\int_0^{s_b} [W(h) - R_c]e^{-rs} ds$, from Equation (5.10). This is the minimum benefit he can receive under rent control. If the tenant does not purchase the rights and does not vacant at time 0, the landlord's lost profits are

$$\int_0^{s_b} [R_A - R_c - C(k_A)]e^{-rs} ds + C_K(K_A - K_B)e^{-rs_b}, \qquad (5.12)$$

where the second term is the cost of restoring the deteriorated unit at time s_b back to K_A. At time s_b the landlord would then be facing a new tenant situation.

Providing the initial equilibrium is a dynamic optimum, (5.12) must exceed (5.10) since

$$\int_0^{s_b} [R_A - C(k_A)]e^{-rs} ds > \int_0^{s_b} W(h)e^{-rs} ds - C_K(K_A - K_B)e^{-rs_b}. \qquad (5.13)$$

The left-hand side is the original profits at the optimal solution, while the right-hand side are profits in a situation where the landlord does maintenance only periodically (once every s_b periods), which is inefficient.

What does (5.13) imply? It implies [depending on the magnitude of (5.11)] either that the tenant will be willing to purchase the rights of maintenance and choosing successors or that the landlord will be willing to grant the tenant these rights and pay him (through reductions in the contract rent below R_c) to take over maintenance. For example, with large magnitudes in (5.11) by purchasing the rights the tenant then has a claim on these "lost profits" in the form of better housing (higher consumption levels while in the unit) plus a key money payment from his successor.

In summary, there is always a set of contractual arrangements that will eliminate the efficiency effects of rent control. What rent control can do is effect a wealth transfer between tenant and landlord with the magnitude of that transfer depending on the rights granted existing tenants and the level R_c is set at.

3. ZONING REGULATIONS GOVERNING HOUSING INPUTS

In Section 1 we discussed zoning as a land-use tool, regulating the allocation of land among uses such as for residential single-family dwellings, residential multiple-family dwellings, commercial development, and so on. However, zoning regulations can also cover much more specific aspects of land use within these broad categories. Of particular interest here are zoning regulations within residential neighborhoods that attempt to regulate the minimum quantity or quality of housing services provided by any housing unit. Such zoning may be designed to ensure some degree of homogeneity and provide residents with a guarantee of a minimum level of neighborhood quality. The zoning may have a related purpose of trying to exclude lower-income people from higher-income neighborhoods or communities for reasons discussed in Chapter 10, by setting a high minimum level of consumption. These types of regulations are widespread.

In this section I investigate the economic nature of zoning that attempts to regulate housing qualities or quantities. Due to legal constraints, it is not possible to simply set minimum housing levels (e.g., minimum property values). Instead *inputs* into the production of housing services must be zoned, such as minimum lot size or floor space requirements. This constraint results in outcomes very different from what would occur with the simple regulation of housing consumption levels. In essence, a primary impact is to distort the housing production process, with sometimes ambiguous effects on housing quantities produced and consumed. To see this we formally investigate an example where minimum lot sizes are zoned (see Grieson and White, 1981; Henderson 1985c).

We analyze the impact of the zoning law in the typical simplest context, neoclassical static equilibrium. To do that, following section 1.2 of Chapter 4, we assume relative input opportunity costs and per family housing demand h are time invariant over an infinite horizon. This implies that in designing new housing (where zoning laws are effective) the developer faces a straightline revenue schedule for housing services. Defining p_l and $p_k [= C_k(r + \delta)]$ as the unit opportunity costs of land and capital, we then may specify a unit cost function (in rental terms) for housing services and a demand function for land of the forms

$$R_h \equiv p = p(p_l, p_K) \tag{5.14}$$

$$l = l(p_l, p_k, h) \tag{5.15}$$

The function $p(\cdot)$ is the average (equals marginal) cost of an additional unit of housing services in rental terms.

Now suppose that minimum lot-size zoning is imposed so that minimum lot sizes are set at l^z. The minimum lot size zoning affects factor proportions in housing up to h^z, where h^z is the output level in Equation (5.15), where the l demanded in the absence of zoning just equals l^z. Beyond h^z, the zoning restriction is thus ineffective. Below h^z, zoning is effective, and we have a fixed (l^z) variable (K) input situation that can be analyzed using the traditional U-shaped short-run average and marginal cost curve framework.

For $h < h^z$, defining C as total costs we have for total, average, and marginal costs respectively

$$C = p_l l^z + p_K K \tag{5.16}$$

$$\frac{C}{h} = (p_l l^z + p_K K)/h > p \tag{5.17}$$

$$dC/dh|_{l^z} \equiv C' = p_K/h_K < p \tag{5.18}$$

As is usual we can show that up to h^z, average costs lie above p and are declining as h increases, while marginal costs lie below p and are rising. For later reference it is also useful to note what happens to factor proportions. At h^z and beyond, we have optimal factor usage where $p_l = ph_l$ and $p_K = ph_K$. Below h^z

$$p_l/p_K > h_l/h_K, \tag{5.19a}$$

$$p_K/h_K < p. \tag{5.19b}$$

Equation (5.19a) can be seen by differentiating h_l/h_K, where $d(h_l/h_K) = (h_{lK}/h_K - h_l h_{KK}/h_K^2) dK = (h_{lK}/h_K - h_l h_{KK}/h_K^2)h_K^{-1} dh > 0$, given with CRS (constant returns to scale) $h_{lK} \geq 0$ and $h_{KK} \leq 0$. Thus for $dh < 0$, $d(h_l/h_K) < 0$. Equation (5.19b) can be seen by differentiating p_K/h_K to get $d(p_K/h_K) = -(p_K h_{KK}/h_K^2) dK > 0$.

In summary, the impact of zoning on the production side is to distort factor proportions below h^z and raise average costs C/h above p, the undistorted unit cost of production. However, marginal cost C' falls below p because the abnormally large land input (l^z) enhances the marginal productivity of capital. The question now is how these cost impacts interact with the demand side to affect the quantity of housing services supplied and consumed.

As with rent control we must distinguish between two cases. In one case, zoning only affects a small portion of a city of perfectly mobile residents, so that potential residents of the zoned area have fixed, best-alternative utility levels, and any negative impacts of zoning are fully capitalized into lower land values. In the second case, effects are not fully capitalized into lower land values, and utility levels are allowed to vary. We start with the second case.

3.1 No Capitalization

There are two contexts in which there is little or no capitalization. First, corresponding to the rent control analysis, zoning is widespread throughout the entire housing market (e.g., a city) so that overall utility levels are affected. This of course is the most general zoning situation. Second is a very particular situation where zoning is imposed only in a small neighborhood of the city but the price of land is fixed so that effects cannot be capitalized. For example, suppose in the neighborhood only a small portion of the undeveloped land is going to be developed and all undeveloped land is owned by atomistic competitive developers. Since there is much more undeveloped land than will be developed, with competition, land is assumed to be available at a fixed opportunity cost reflecting the value of land in alternative uses such as farming or recreation. Note however for no capitalization to occur, it must also be the case that potential residents' best alternatives are inferior to this neighborhood (given its competitive price of land) so there is room for their utility levels to be reduced. For example, this community could be the exclusive highest-income community of a metropolitan area.

We now turn to analyzing the combined demand and supply impacts of zoning. We can illustrate the demand side in Figure 5.3 with an indifference curve diagram. Prior to zoning the consumer maximizes utility $V = V(x, h)$ subject to $y - x - ph = 0$. In Figure 5.3, prior to zoning, the consumer's budget line is B^0, and he consumes at point a where $V_h/V_x = p$.

With zoning, l is raised above the desired level to l^z. Then, the consumer's budget constraint becomes $y - x - C = 0$, and his optimal consumption condition becomes $V_h/V_x = C'$. In Figure 5.3, the zoning budget line is B^z where $x = y - C$. For $h \longrightarrow 0$, the intercept of B^z is shifted down on the x axis reflecting the high C/h for low levels of h; and B^z is concave reflecting the rising C'. After h^z, B^z and B^0 are coincident. Suppose with B^z optimal consumption is at point b with housing equal to h_1. We can break the move from a to b into two parts: a negative income and a positive substitution part. To see this we redefine income as "virtual income," $y - C + C'h$. Then the equilibrium in Figure 5.3 can also be defined as one where "price" is constant at C_1' (the slope of B^z at x_1, h_1) on the dashed straight lines and the intercept on the x axis is shifted to $y - C_1 + C_1'h_1$. Then, in equilibrium, x is this intercept minus $C_1'h_1$, or $x_1 = y - C_1$.

Relative to no zoning the shift down in the intercept represents the negative income effect and the lower price (C_1'), the positive price effect.

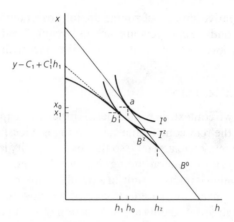

FIGURE 5.4   Impact of zoning.

Whether the income or the price effect dominates is unclear in general and depends on the specific forms of the functions used. This ambiguity can be demonstrated formally[3] or illustrated. We know h_1 can be less than h_0 for all l^z. An example is right angle indifference curves in Figure 5.3, which would always lead to a fall in h because in the relevant range B^z is interior to B^0 (i.e., there is no price effect with these indifference curves). We also know h_1 can be greater than h_0 for all l^z. An example is (almost) straight line indifference curves (where the price effect is extreme).

In summary, the primary impact of minimum lot size zoning is not to raise housing consumption above what it would have been. Assuming both x and h are normal goods, the basic impact is to raise housing expenditures (i.e., $C^z > ph_0$ from the x axis of Figure 5.4) and lower utility levels. Providing the

---

[3] We can examine the consumer's utility maximization problem to show that as l^z is raised above the desired level, h may rise or fall. With zoning the consumer has a constrained utility maximization problem, where we maximize $V(x, h)$ subject to $h = h(l^z, K)$ and $y - x - C = y - x - p_K K - p_l l^z = 0$. Differentiating the resulting first-order condition for K, $V_h/V_x = p_K/h_K$, and substituting in $dK = (dh - h_l dl)/h_K$ and $dX = -p_l dl^z - p_K(dh - h_l dl)/h_K$ we get

$$\frac{dh}{dl^z} = \frac{\left(p_l - p_K\dfrac{h_l}{h_K}\right)h_K\left(V_{xx}\dfrac{V_h}{V_x} - V_{hx}\right) + V_h\left(h_{Kl} - h_{KK}\dfrac{h_l}{h_K}\right)}{-\left\{h_K\left[V_{xx}\left(\dfrac{V_h}{V_x}\right)^2 - 2V_{xh}\dfrac{V_h}{V_x} + V_{hh}\right] + V_h h_{KK}/h_K\right\}} \gtrless 0.$$

Given CRS (constant returns to scale) in h production and strict quasi-concavity of $V(\cdot)$, the denominator is positive. In the numerator the second term represents the positive price effect. The first term represents the negative income effect, where $V_{xx}V_h/V_x - V_{hx} < 0$ for a normal good, and $p_l - p_K h_l/h_K > 0$ from (2.19a).

zoning regulations persist into the future, this also means property values may rise above what they would have been without zoning. For example, any future similar new residents will be prepared to pay for h_1, the cost of constructing that h_1 in the future. Then property values of current h_1's will reflect construction costs (C_1), or expenditures. This also means the value of existing unzoned property will rise, so, say, future residents will get equal utility (I^z in Figure 5.4) from purchasing new zoned and old unzoned housing.

Benefits of Zoning for Existing Community

What are rationales for a community imposing minimum lot-size zoning with these impacts? It depends on the community's objective. One objective might be to raise housing consumption above the no-zoning level. This fails if $h_1 < h_0$. However, for functions where h_1 can exceed h_0, it is then possible for the community to set l^z to maximize h—that is, to maximize housing quality and property values. However, a potential limit to maximizing h is lowering utility below the level acceptable to new residents, which would drive them to other communities. Of course, minimum lot-size zoning is not an efficient way to raise h, in the sense that h could be raised more (for any alternative utility level) if, for example, all inputs into the production process could be zoned and raised by the same percentage.

A second objective might be to simply lower utility to exclude certain undesired potential residents. For example, suppose h^z where zoning becomes ineffective represents the typical situation for an existing resident, whereas potential new residents have lower desired housing quality and tax bases. By imposing zoning and raising housing costs to potential new lower-income residents, their utility can be lowered sufficiently to drive them into other communities.

A final objective might be to raise the average community tax base. If tax assessments are effectively based on housing expenditures (initial purchase price at construction) even if consumption falls with zoning, the tax base will rise. Second, if property values reflect expenditures, and tax assessments are based on property values, then the tax base will also rise. If the issue then is not housing quality of new residents but tax base, zoning can be effective (but not efficient) in achieving its objective.

3.2 Impacts with Capitalization

We now alter the community context in which zoning is enacted to go back to the case where capitalization occurs. Suppose the undeveloped section of the community is small relative to the number of potential residents so that some of these people will spill over into the rest of the metropolitan area. In that case, without zoning, these residents will compete for new properties in

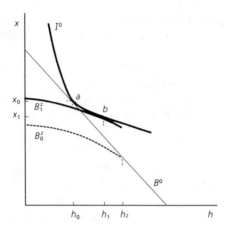

FIGURE 5.5   Impact of zoning with full capitalization.

this community, bidding around the price of land until in equilibrium their utility level is equated to the alternative utility level available to people like them moving into the rest of the metropolitan area. This is a condition for spatial equilibrium.

Suppose that without zoning, their x, h consumption is depicted by x_0, h_0 at point a in Figure 5.5, where I^0 represents the indifference curve given their alternative utility level elsewhere and B^0 their budget line given equilibrium housing and land prices. With the imposition of minimum lot-size zoning, their budget curve would become the dashed B_0^z if land prices remained constant. However, for them to move into the community rather than going to the alternative, they must get back to I^0. This occurs with land prices falling until B^z shifts up to B_1^z, where they consume x_1, h_1 at point b. In this case h_1 always exceeds h_0, by inspection of the diagram.[4] Given h rises, property values are higher than they otherwise would be. As before expenditures rise, although generally by much less for any h. In this case, in essence any "income" effect of zoning is fully capitalized into lower land costs and the "price" effect (lower marginal cost) on housing induces greater consumption.

The point is that if a community is competing for scarce residents it cannot impose welfare costs of distortionary zoning on them. Those are capitalized into lower land values received by speculators. However, the community objectives of raising housing quality and tax bases above what they would otherwise be is achieved.

---

[4] Algebraically, we can show $dh/dl^z > 0$ by differentiating the first-order condition $V_h/V_x = p_K/h_K$ and substituting in from $dV = V_x dx + V_h dh = 0$ (as well as $dK = (dh - h_l dL)/h_K$).

6

Other Housing Topics

In this chapter I examine some other important aspects of the housing market. In Section 1, I present a model of tenure choice and identify the considerations that determine whether an individual will rent or own. The considerations of interest are people's wealth, time path of income, and institutional factors. In Section 2, we examine search in the housing market. There appears to be no one model that contains enough of the critical aspects of the housing market to present on its own, so I focus on identifying the critical aspects. In the final section, I outline some considerations for analyzing racially separated housing markets.

1. TENURE CHOICE

Durable goods such as housing generally serve a dual purpose for consumers, purposes that so far I have kept separate. Housing serves as a consumption good (shelter) and as an investment good (portfolio holdings of housing). While it is typical in writing about the housing market to designate separate groups of people—renters and landlords—in fact in the United States most people are both. As such we need to analyze the determinants of people's demands for housing as a consumption versus an investment good, where in general these demands by a family will be unequal. Given such an analysis, we can then discuss tenure choice, which is the question, not of whether you own any housing per se, but of whether you *owner-occupy* your own *consumption*, or shelter demand.

If people's consumption demand is less than their portfolio demand, for reasons discussed in Section 1.2 of this chapter, we would expect people to satisfy their consumption demand by owner-occupying part of their portfolio demand and then purchasing and renting out the balance of their portfolio demand. Such people are net lenders of housing, as well as an owner-occupiers. On the other hand, if their consumption demand exceeds their portfolio demand, they will rent their entire consumption and will purchase and rent out their entire investment demand. Such people are gross and net renters of housing. We assume net renters are constrained, so that their tenure in shelter cannot be split, ruling out a situation where they own part of their house and someone else owns the other part. (As we shall see, this is quite separate from the question of mortgaging a house. Ownership refers to holding the title and bearing the entire risk of capital gains and losses, which is separate from the issue of when you borrow in your portfolio using your house as collateral.)

In Section 1.1, I analyze shelter versus portfolio demands, to see what types of people in terms of wealth levels and time paths of income are likely to be net lenders versus net renters of housing. In Section 1.2, I explore three institutional aspects of the housing market, which in the context of the Section 1.1 analysis determine tenure choice—whether you owner-occupy or rent your shelter demand. Sections 1.1 and 1.2 draw heavily upon Henderson and Ioannides (1983).

1.1   Shelter versus Portfolio Demands

To analyze portfolio demand for a good, we must introduce uncertainty and considerations of risk. Adopting a conventional framework, we assume people have a two-period utility function

$$U(x, h_c) + E[V(W(\theta))],   \tag{6.1}$$

where $U(\cdot)$ is direct utility in period 1, with arguments housing consumption h_c and other goods x. Wealth in period 2, $W(\theta)$, is affected (see below) by the unknown (in period 1) state of nature in period 2. Ex-post indirect utility in period 2, $V(W(\theta))$, is a function of wealth, and unspecified arguments that can embed a multiperiod future and corresponding future price distributions. The expected value of period 2 utility, $E[V(\cdot)]$, is the sum over all possible states of nature of potential ex-post utility times the probability of the corresponding state of nature occurring.

Equation (6.1) is maximized subject to period 1 and 2 budget constraints, incorporating the notion that people will want to borrow and lend against future and current incomes to smooth out their consumption levels across periods. That is, they will want to hold a portfolio. In specifying the budget contraints, for now, we keep consumption and investment demands separate. In period 1, for consumption purposes, income y will be spent on the numeraire x and housing h_c rented at price R; and for investment purposes it will be spent on fixed interest rate savings S and on housing investments h_1 purchased at price P and rented out at R. Note for simplicity in specifying portfolio holdings we have reverted to the housing production model of Chapter 1, where the unit cost of housing is constant. Thus

$$y_1 = x + Rh_c + S + (P - R)h_1. \tag{6.2}$$

Period 2 wealth, $W(\theta)$, is period 2 income, y_2, plus principal and interest on the fixed return savings (at rate r) plus uncertain sales revenue from housing. That is, housing is specified as the risky (relative to S) asset in the portfolio. Thus

$$W(\theta) = y_2 + S(1 + r) + Ph_1(1 + \theta), \tag{6.3}$$

where for notational convenience the state of nature and the uncertain return on housing investment are both denoted by θ (i.e., the state of nature defines only return on housing).

Individual Holdings

Maximizing (6.1) subject to (6.2) and (6.3) with respect to h_c, x, h_1, and S yields after rearrangement (where $V' \equiv \partial V / \partial W$)

$$U_h/U_x = R, \tag{6.4a}$$

$$\frac{rP}{1 + r} = R + \frac{P}{1 + r} \cdot \frac{E[V'\theta]}{E[V']}. \tag{6.4b}$$

Equation (6.4a) is the usual optimal consumption for h_c and x. Equation (6.4b) is the optimal portfolio condition for S and h_1. In (6.4b), $rP/(1 + r)$ is the present value of the opportunity cost of a unit of housing investment, or the money P spent purchasing the unit (rather than S) times the foregone interest on S that would have been collected in the next period, discounted [at $1/(1 + r)$] to today. The other side of (6.4b) is the marginal benefit of a unit of housing investment, or the revenue R collected from rent of a unit of housing plus or minus the value of the capital gains or losses on housing. In a world of perfect certainly without capital gains, for optimal investment the known housing return, R, should equal its opportunity cost $rP/(1 + r)$.

With uncertainty, both capital gains and losses and risk aversion must be accounted for, and this is done by the second opportunity cost term in

(6.4b). Following convention, where $V'' \equiv \partial^2 V/\partial W^2$, we assume $V'' < 0$, implying that people are risk averse. If people were risk neutral so $V'' = 0$, then the second term on the right-hand side would be $PE[\theta]/(1 + r)$, or the discounted value of the expected capital gain or loss. If this was zero, or $E[\theta] = 0$, then the term would vanish. With $V'' \neq 0$, we can rewrite this term as $PE[\theta]/(1 + r) + P \operatorname{cov}(V', \theta)/\{(1 + r)E[V']\}$, where $\operatorname{cov}(V', \theta) < 0$ given $V'' < 0$ so as θ rises V' falls. Thus with risk aversion and the negative covariance term, an optimal portfolio has an expected return on housing investment $R + PE[\theta]/(1 + r)$ greater than monetary opportunity cost $rP/(1 + r)$, to compensate for the bearing of risk.

Net Lenders and Net Renters

Given Equations (6.4a) and (6.4b), we can differentiate these equations and do "comparative statics" to see how consumption versus portfolio demands vary as incomes vary. The results of these analyses are straightforward, but require some definitions to present. Period 1 wealth, W_1, is $y_1 + y_2/(1 + r)$, and we state that period 1 wealth increases if and only if

$$dW_1 = dy_1 + dy_2/(1 + r) > 0.$$

Second, the tilt of wealth changes if and only if

$$dy_1 - dy_2/(1 + r) \neq 0.$$

If $dy_1 - dy_2/(1 + r) > 0$, the time path is tilted to the present since current income increases more (decreases less) than the present value of the increase in future income. Similarly, if $dy_1 - dy_2/(1 + r) < 0$, the time path is tilted to the future. Finally, we define

$$A \equiv -V''/V'$$

as the coefficient of absolute risk aversion, where in the literature it is argued that it is most "reasonable" to assume that A decreases as period 2 resources increase.

We now turn to the results. The derivation based on differentiating Equations (6.4a) and (6.4b) is detailed in Henderson and Ioannides (1983); fortunately, explanations of the results are straightforward.

1. Consumption demand for housing is unaffected by tilt of the income stream if there is a perfect capital market and depends only on the level of period 1 wealth. Thus, in Figure 6.1, we can draw iso-consumption lines with slope $-(1 + r)$, along which wealth is constant but tilt is changing with no impact on h_c demand. With a positive wealth demand for housing, as these iso-consumption lines shift out, h_c demand rises so $h_c^1 < h_c^2 < h_c^3$.

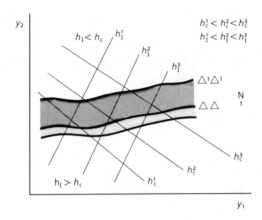

FIGURE 6.1 Consumption–portfolio equilibrium.

2. If wealth rises, for the same tilt to income, the portfolio demand for housing is unchanged. That is, portfolios are used to transfer income between periods so as to smooth out consumption. If incomes in both periods rise (or fall) by the same present value amount, there is no need to change the amount of money transferred between periods, or the portfolio in general. Thus we can draw in iso-investment lines with slope $(1 + r)$ along which $dy_1 - dy_2/(1 + r) = 0$, but wealth increases. The question remains as to what happens to investment demand as tilt changes.

3. The demand for housing investment increases as income is tilted toward period 1, assuming $V(\cdot)$ exhibits decreasing absolute risk aversion [A declines as $W(\theta)$ rises]. Thus, for $dy_1 - dy_2/(1 + r) > 0$ (for $dW_1 = 0$), it is optimal to save more of the risky asset to transfer some of today's increased income to tomorrow. Thus, assuming $dA/dW(\theta) < 0$, in Figure 6.1. $h_I^1 < h_I^2 < h_I^3$.

To combine these results, in Figure 6.1 we draw in a hypothetical locus $\Delta\Delta$ of points for which, as y_1 and y_2 vary, $h_I = h_c$ (with both increasing as we move to the east in Figure 6.1). The locus $\Delta\Delta$ must have slope greater than $-(1 + r)$ and less than $(1 + r)$, so that as we move along it, h_c and h_I both rise. As we move north of $\Delta\Delta$, h_c rises and h_I falls, so $h_I < h_c$ and people are net renters of housing. Thus, *net renters* of housing are *high*-wealth people and those with incomes tilted toward tomorrow (e.g., those acquiring human capital). The wealth result is independent of the assumption about the degree of risk aversion A. In contrast, net *lenders* (owners) are *low*-wealth people and those with incomes tilted toward today. The wealth result is surprising, at least on the surface. Note it does not require low-wealth people to be the direct landlords of high-wealth people. Net lenders can pool their money through stock in real estate corporations, and these corporations can be the direct landlords.

I now introduce institutional considerations for two purposes. First, we shall see whether the net-lender–low-wealth result is robust. Second, we can discuss tenure choice per se. At the moment there is no reason to owner-occupy per se. Even for net lenders, it is equivalent to owner-occupy that part of portfolio holdings equal to one's consumption demand, or to rent out the entire investment and rent one's own consumption from some other person.

1.2 Institutional Factors

I consider the impact of three factors on the net renter–net lender analysis and on tenure choice.

The Rental Externality

Henderson and Ioannides (1983) identified a fundamental externality connected with the rental of a durable that, ceteris paribus, makes it cheaper to own than to rent. The externality requires more detail in the model to show that consumption services h from occupying h_c units of housing depend on the rate of utilization u. Thus, for example, in Equation (6.1)

$$h = h_c f(u) \qquad f' > 0, \qquad f'' < 0. \tag{6.5}$$

In (6.5) for the same u, services double if we double capacity, but less than double for the same h_c if we double u.

The externality comes on the cost side. The true costs of utilization, besides time costs, include maintenance and repairs connected with obvious damages and breakdowns but also wear and tear (chipped and dirtied paint, scratched and stained floors, etc.). As an owner-occupier, the owner bears all these costs, which are specified to be

$$h_c T(u), \qquad T' > 0, \qquad T'' > 0. \tag{6.6}$$

$T(\cdot)$ is the utilization cost function per unit of housing. However, a renter only *directly* bears part of these costs, denoted as

$$h_c \tau(u), \qquad \tau' > 0, \qquad \tau'' > 0, \tag{6.7}$$

where $\tau(\cdot)$ is the function representing costs directly incurred. We assume

$$\tau(u) < T(u)\,\forall u, \qquad \tau'(u) < T'(u)\,\forall u.$$

That is, the landlord cannot collect in total and at the margin completely from the tenant for damages caused by utilization, such as, for example, wear and tear. The landlord cannot collect in full because it is too costly to write and enforce a contract that covers all forms of costs of utilization.

The fact that the landlord is *directly* incompletely reimbursed for utilization costs has two implications. First, the *private marginal costs of* utilization, for renters, τ', are lower than for owner-occupiers, T', for any u, so that renters' equilibrium rates of utilization are higher than for owner-occupiers and thus higher than is optimal. Owner-occupiers pick optimal rates because they face the true costs of utilization. However, although landlords do not directly collect for costs of utilization, to stay in business, they must indirectly cover all costs. That is, their net return on housing must still cover opportunity costs, or ignoring capital gains

$$\frac{rP}{1+r} = R - \frac{T(\bar{u}) - \tau(\bar{u})}{1+r}.$$

The term $[T(\bar{u}) - \tau(\bar{u})]/(1 + r)$ is the costs of utilization ($\bar{u}$ chosen by the tenant) not directly recovered from the tenant. To recover opportunity costs of investment $rP/(1 + r)$, and hence to be willing to hold housing in a portfolio, a landlord's gross rent R must rise to cover any losses from utilization costs.

This is a classic externality, which, ceteris paribus, means renting is inferior to owning. Renters are induced to overutilize their dwelling units relative to what is optimal, but they must (on average) bear in fact the entire costs of their excessive utilization through increased rents. Owner-occupiers have lower costs of occupancy based on optimal utilization rates.

What is the impact of this externality that makes owner-occupancy potentially cheaper on the housing market? First, it gives a basis for net lenders (owners) in Section 1.1 to owner-occupy that part of their portfolio demand that equals their consumption demand. Thus in Figure 6.1 all people for whom $h_I \geq h_c$ will be owner-occupiers. Second, it suggests that potential net renters (where $h_I < h_c$ in Figure 6.1) for whom $h_I \rightarrow h_c$ should distort their consumption and investment choices to bring h_c and h_I into equality so as to owner-occupy their investment and consumption and avoid the costs of the rental externality.

Thus, in Figure 6.1, the locus $\Delta\Delta$ at which $h_c = h_I$ must be adjusted. First, it shifts north to, say, $\Delta'\Delta'$ into that part of the original rental region where $h_I < h_c$ but $h_I \rightarrow h_c$. Second, rather than a locus we now have a fat strip of people depicted by the shaded region in Figure 6.1, for whom $h_I = h_c$. This region contains all people (income combinations) who find it optimal to distort their choices and bring h_I and h_c into equality so as to avoid the rental externality.

This impact of the rental externality does not affect the result that high-wealth people, controlling for income tilt, will be net renters (unless renting is entirely eliminated). The rental region north of $\Delta'\Delta'$ still contains the higher-wealth people. We turn to two other institutional factors that might affect the analysis of wealth and tenure choice.

Taxes

Suppose individuals face income taxes. Imputed rents to owner-occupiers are tax exempt while rental income of landlords is taxable. The remaining tax treatment of housing (e.g., deductibility of mortgage interest payments) is the same for rental and owner-occupied units. In short, the tax system makes owner-occupying cheaper than renting. Assume momentarily that the income tax rate is constant so that individual tax burdens are proportional. In this case, the impact of the tax system on tenure choice is identical to that of the rental externality. Owner-occupancy per unit of housing is cheaper than renting by some constant proportion. In Figure 6.1 this simply stretches out the region of wealth in which people owner-occupy. As with the rental externality, unless the tax advantage is so great as to eliminate renting entirely, we would still find a region, where controlling for the tilt of the income path, high-wealth people rent their consumption.

An effectively progressive tax system, however, could eliminate the region of high-wealth renters, implying everyone would owner-occupy their consumption. The reason is that, although the discrepancy between desired consumption and investment increases with wealth, so does the per unit subsidy to owner-occupied consumption. There will be a set of pairs of average tax rates and marginal tax rates (degree of progessivity) above which renting would be eliminated.

Capital Market Imperfections

Capital market imperfections can be introduced by imposing the constraint in maximizing Equation (6.1), subject to (6.2) and (6.3), that $S \geq 0$, so that consumers cannot borrow against future income, for current consumption. If we are going to impose this restriction, to be realistic, we should also allow borrowing against durables offered as collateral. Thus, while $S \geq 0$, housing investment can in Equation (6.2) be purchased with a downpayment $P(1 - L)h_1$, where L is that percent of the purchase price that is mortgaged (i.e., the mortgage is PLh_1). In period 2, Equation (6.3) must be adjusted to account for repayment of the mortgage $(1 + r)LPh_1$ at fixed rate r. Note in Equation (6.3) the owner still bears the risk of *all* capital gains and losses.

The constraint $S \geq 0$ and the existence of mortgage loans only affects people who would like $S < 0$. For these constrained people under *relevant mortgage loan terms*, the principal impact of the constraint is to make it less attractive to own. Owning requires risky investment, when, in fact, either total dissavings is desired to increase current consumption or dissavings in the safe asset is desired (but prohibited) in order to finance purchases of the risky asset. A relevant mortgage loan term is $P(1 - L) - R > 0$; or $P(1 - L) > R$ so that an owner-occupier requires a greater gross cash outlay to consume a unit of housing than a renter. Thus for constrained people renting is attractive since current consumption of all other goods is higher than under owning. Why the constraint that $P(1 - L) - R > 0$? If $P(1 - L) - R < 0$, for any potential landlord, the net outlays on housing investments are negative, indicating that everyone will have an infinite demand for housing investments unless default is costly. Collateral has no meaning if negative net outlays are allowed.

What is the impact on tenure choice of capital market imperfections? The basic wealth effects on tenure choice are unchanged by capital market imperfections. For high-wealth people, if the tilt of their income is such that $S \geq 0$ is a binding constraint, then raising their investment toward their consumption demand to owner-occupy is even more costly than it was before. Capital market imperfections would only increase the size of the region in Figure 6.1 where high-wealth people rent. It would also enlarge the region of lower-wealth people with incomes tilted to the future who rent. But, in summary, this *standard specification of capital market imperfections* is not sufficient to alter our basic types of findings.

Capital market imperfections can only alter the predicted tendency of low-wealth people to be landlords if the capital market restriction is re-specified so that a minimum wealth level was required to obtain a loan, or there is a minimum size requirement on a mortgage (eliminating mortgages for cheaper homes). If there are sufficient fixed costs to making loans (irrespective of loan size), then a rational banker could impose such restrictions.

Transactions Costs

The final consideration is outside the model, but it is most relevant. Owner-occupancy and housing purchase, in general, involve transactions costs—finance charges (points) on mortgages, title searchers, search to minimize the risk of buying a bad house, and compensation for real estate agents. If some people move frequently thereby altering the location of their housing consumption because, for example, of job search and relocation or changes in family composition, the fact that owner-occupancy involves additional high transactions costs relative to renting becomes important. The standard real estate literature indicates on the basis of all monetary considerations (tax, maintenance and transactions costs) that it is cheaper to rent than own, if a person plans to move within 3 to 5 years (Shelton, 1968). If wealth level and frequency of moving are negatively correlated, then that could help explain the existence of low-wealth renters.

In summary, standard economic considerations suggest that controlling for income tilt, low-wealth people will be landlords of higher-wealth tenants. To the extent that this predicted relationship is not observed, it must be because of the following considerations: progressivity of the income tax system, where the tax advantages in the United States (tax exemption of imputed rents) of owner-occupancy increase with income; capital market imperfections applied "discriminatorily" to low-wealth people; and a positive correlation between low wealth and frequency of moving. In short, in analyzing tenure choice, institutional considerations are critical.

2. SEARCH

For most people, owner-occupancy involves the commitment of a considerable portion of their wealth and portfolio to housing. What makes the process of purchasing particularly risky and costly is that housing is a heterogeneous good. A house's true quality can only be partially discerned at the time of purchase and only completely known after some period of occupancy. Prices vary with the quality and characteristics of a house, and consumers must inspect houses to discover their basic characteristics and thus determine if quoted prices are high or low given their assessment of quality. In summary, given the commitment of resources involved to an infrequent purchase and given the nature of the commodity, search is an important aspect of the housing market; and we turn to a brief discussion of it. Unfortunately, the literature on search in the housing market is very limited.

For a consumer, searching for a house is an expensive (i.e., time-intensive) process; and people presumably search with a strategy, involving trade-offs between price and quality. Search involves a sequential process of looking at one house after another, and, at each step, deciding whether to continue searching or purchase the best price–quality prospect at hand. In addition, potential buyers may temporarily drop out of the market, especially in a situation where they first enter the market to discover current market conditions in order to decide whether to search seriously for a purchase. Although most of the search literature assumes people search from a known distribution of prices, for infrequent purchases such as housing, it would seem desirable to consider situations where people search from an unknown distribution and thus learn about the properties of the distribution as part of their strategy.

On the other side of the market, sellers must have a strategy. As people troop through their house they must decide at what point to sell, considering the trade-offs of the possibility of increased profits from future offers against the opportunity cost of delaying acceptance of a current offer.

Given the strategies of buyers and sellers, a market equilibrium results, hopefully depicted in a dynamic setting describing the distribution of offered and accepted (i.e., matches) price–quality combinations at each point in time. In a sophisticated setting, we would expect at a point in time that accepted prices for the same quality house would actually vary across matches according to the varying search and selling costs of people in the market and the length of time they have already spent searching. Moreover, this problem of the market matching heterogeneous buyers with heterogeneous housing that is purchased infrequently suggests that there is a role for intermediaries who aid the search process. In the housing market we should account for the behavior of brokers, or real estate agents, who exploit scale economies in the search process by providing listings and house descriptions and facilitating matches.

Unfortunately, there is no search model that incorporates all these critical elements and very few models that attempt to even incorporate more than one. The problem is a very difficult one, and it has resulted in two main lines of thinking in the literature relevant to housing. We now examine these.

2.1 Buyers' Search Strategies

Most search work focuses on the buyer's optimal strategy when searching in a market to buy one unit of a homogeneous good. Searching sequentially, if the present minimum price quoted so far is S, the expected benefits from searching one more time are the gain from any lower price times the probability of that lower price integrated over prices lower than S, or

$$\int_0^S (s - x)\, dF(x)$$

The known probability distribution of sellers' prices x is $F(x)$. Integrating by parts, the expected benefits are

$$\int_0^S F(x)\, dx \equiv g(S). \tag{6.8}$$

If the time cost of each search is c, it pays to search one more time providing $c < g(S)$. The optimal search strategy is to search until any price R is obtained such that

$$g(R) \leq c, \tag{6.9}$$

so that it no longer pays to search again. This R is the *reservation price*.

This model of buyers' strategies can be generalized to some extent. First, it does not matter whether recall is permitted—whether a buyer can go back and claim any offer received so far or whether the buyer can only claim the most recent offer. In both cases, the buyer simply searches until the price R defined by Equation (6.9) is found; previous quotations (above R) are irrelevant. Second, this search process assumes an infinite horizon—that is, people can search indefinitely at a cost c per period, with no opportunity costs to delaying purchasing per se. If the horizon is limited, the basic ideas are unchanged. In that case, R in Equation (6.9) generally rises with the length of search. As the terminal time *by which a purchase must be made* approaches, buyers become more desperate and raise their reservation price. Finally, the assumption that $F(x)$ is known can be relaxed to allow for learning about the distribution of prices, although relaxing the assumption makes the analysis much more complex (Rothschild, 1973).

In terms of the literature specific to housing, Courant (1978) applied the analysis of buyers' strategies to help explain the persistence of racially segregated neighborhoods (see Section 1 of Chapter 3 and Section 3 of this chapter). Consider a situation in which blacks and whites currently live in separate neighborhoods and in which housing prices in the black neighborhood are somewhat higher than in the white neighborhood. What could explain a situation where blacks do not move into the white neighborhood to take advantage of currently lower prices? Courant suggested that blacks have different search costs in the two neighborhoods, where in the white neighborhood they face higher search costs because of prejudice, reflected in either harassment or lower probabilities that white sellers (relative to black sellers in the black neighborhood) will accept reasonable price offers from them. For any differential in expected search costs, there is a maximum price differential between the two neighborhoods below which blacks will decide not to search in the white neighborhood. Thus the neighborhoods could remain segregated.

The general analysis of buyers' strategies in searching to purcase a homogeneous good has a critical shortcoming that should be mentioned. It ignores the strategies of sellers and the process of generating the $F(x)$ distribution, consistent with a market equilibrium. This turns out to be a critical problem (Rothschild, 1973). If sellers know the distribution of reservation prices R generated by Equation (6.9) for all buyers, then each seller will maximize *expected* profits by choosing one price to sell at. If all stores have identical cost structures in producing the homogeneous good, then all sellers will choose the same selling price. In short, the whole problem collapses, and we return to a market clearing at one price. The question is how to characterize a market setting incorporating the strategies of both buyers and sellers, where in equilibrium a homogeneous good is sold at different prices at the same point in time. Pratt, Wise, and Zeckhauser (1979) showed that such equilibria can be constructed (not necessarily will generally result) if buyers have different search costs, so some high-price stores cater to buyers with high search costs, and others to those with low search costs.

2.2 Quality Variations

The literature just analyzed in Section 2.1 deals with search for a homogeneous good. Housing is distinctly heterogeneous. Heterogeneity is in general dealt with in the signaling (Spence, 1974) literature, not search literature. In the signaling literature there is no uncertainty explicitly incorporated, and price differences in the market can serve to signal quality differences for a heterogeneous good.

In an unusual application to the housing market, Yinger (1981) modeled a "search" process where price is an unambiguous indicator of quality (and prices for each quality level are uniform in the market). Search arises because people must search to find the quality level they want, which is not immediately visible (i.e., they must search through the neighborhood to find "their" house). Yinger implicitly assumed a static situation where search is *completely* costless, so people search indefinitely until they find their dream house (i.e., there is no quality-search cost trade-off), and all houses identical to their dream house sell at the same price.

What is innovative about Yinger's article is that it is the first attempt to introduce the role of brokers. In the process of buyers searching for their dream house and sellers searching for a corresponding buyer, brokers act as matchmakers. Brokers maximize profits with respect to advertising expenditures spent on attracting both listings (sellers) and buyers; or equivalently they maximize profits with respect to their expected number of matches given the advertising costs of raising the expected number of matches. Brokers presumably offer economies of scale in search by providing advice and listings from which buyers can select likely candidates. Unfortunately Yinger implicitly had no costs to search, so it is unclear why people use brokers in the first place.

3. RACIAL SEPARATION AND SEGREGATION

In this section we examine various explanations for residential separation and/or segregation of blacks from whites. For our purposes separation is a free-market, or voluntary, phenomenon, whereas segregation involves market discrimination, or is separation that is involuntary and perhaps forced by collusive actions of various economic agents. The basic facts in the United States that researchers attempt to explain are that (1) blacks live separate from whites, (2) blacks often pay higher rents than whites for comparable units in comparable neighborhoods, although sometimes the reverse is the case, and (3) controlling for income, blacks have a lower incidence of homeownership than whites but the same statement might not hold if wealth (rather than income) was controlled for. A good review of the empirical evidence and problems with interpreting it is contained in Smith (1981). What model of race and the housing market explains the racial separation and price differentials? So far in this book we have examined two models of atomistic behavior in the housing market that start to explain some of the facts.

3.1 Atomistic Behavior

A Preference for Separation

In Section 1 of Chapter 3, we examined a model of racial separation, based upon simple specifications of preferences. The basic point was that if large groups of people, such as whites, have negative preferences about living next to other large groups of people, such as blacks, the market will work to allocate land such that these groups live separate. In Chapter 3 we assumed blacks are indifferent about living next to whites but whites do not want to live next to blacks. The result was an allocation of land separating the two groups. In that case, we have voluntary separation in that not only does neither party object to the arrangement but the solution can be achieved in an atomistic competition framework.

However, these voluntary separation models fail to explain the differences in housing prices paid by blacks and whites. In fact, following the analysis in Chapter 3 and Figure 3.1, with the specification of preferences in the preceding paragraph, we would expect blacks to pay lower housing prices than whites. This pattern of housing prices is not generally consistent with observed patterns. In this type of model the only hypothesis that is consistent with blacks paying higher prices is that blacks have a greater aversion to living next to whites than whites to blacks. This explanation for housing prices is never cited in the literature.

Finally, we note that there has been some attempt to analyze a more sophisticated specification of preferences, where preferences are, say, defined over neighborhood racial composition. Whites might be indifferent about or even desire (a preference for diversity) the presence of relatively small number of blacks in the neighborhood. However, beyond some critical small percentage of black families, whites start to experience utility losses from further increases in the percentage of blacks. If that percentage grows, the neighborhood may "tip," and most whites will attempt to move out of the neighborhood into ones with small percentages of blacks. The notions of "tipping" and blacks driving whites first from the inner city out to suburbs (and now from some suburbs to either others or back into the inner city) are in the popular literature, but have not been seriously modeled.

3.2 Prejudice and Search

The second model with atomistic behavior where blacks live separate from whites was outlined in the previous section on search. The model is very much a partial explanation. First, it starts with the presumption (say, relevant to the northern United States) that whites arrived first in the urban area and that blacks came later and faced limited opportunities in terms of locational choice. In essence, we postulate a presumption of a historical pattern of ghettoization, where blacks are separated from whites and restricted to a relatively small area of the city and hence pay higher prices (due to the restriction on the total supply of land to blacks). The question is how this situation persists.

An obvious answer is that there is segregation, where because of prejudice some whites are prepared to resist blacks moving into white areas. This can take the form of social pressure on whites who are selling houses not to sell to blacks. If a sale of a white to a black actually occurs, resistance means trying to persuade the black not to move into the house or, failing that, trying to persuade the black to move out soon after occupancy and resell the house. These latter forms of resistance involve burning crosses, stones thrown through windows, arson, physical violence, harassment of children, and social ostracism. All this activity is summarized in Section 2.1 by Courant's (1978) model of different search costs for a black of searching for a house in black versus white neighborhoods. Given an existing pattern of segregation, this is a viable explanation of its persistence.

3.3 Collusion Models

There is another class of models generally proposed by noneconomists that attempts to explain the observed patterns of prices and racial separation. Because this class of models is so prevalent, it is essential to review it. The models are all based on the notion that some key group of economic agents in the housing market bands together and conspires to exclude blacks from entering white areas. These collusion models are based on the premise that it is profitable to discriminate against blacks so that they are spatially separated from whites into an area of restricted size such that they pay higher rents than whites. How does this ghettoization come about?

The first explanation is that real estate agents conspire implicitly or explicitly to ghettoize blacks. The implication is that it maximizes profits to ghettoize blacks. However, one must consider whether in fact profits are maximized by ghettoizing blacks, as opposed to, say, ghettoizing whites. If we consider a fixed area to be split among a fixed number of blacks and whites, it pays to restrict the land allocation to blacks if and only if the price elasticity of land demand of blacks is less than that of whites.

However, the basic notion of a conspiracy in and of itself seems implausible. Real estate brokerage is a highly competitive industry whose firms are loosely connected. Even in smaller urban areas there are hundreds of real estate agents (even excluding those people whose private transactions do not go through a broker). They are too large and disorganized a group to band together. Therefore, discrimination must occur either because of the personal prejudices of agents or because it is individually profit maximizing for these agents to discriminate and ghettoize blacks.

In general it will not be profit maximizing to discriminate. The commission-based income of real estate sales agents is an increasing function of volume, or the turnover of housing units, and of the level of sales prices. If blacks in the ghetto are paying higher housing prices than whites, real estate agents could sell blacks homes in the white area at higher prices than to whites and thus increase their profits (as blockbusters have done in many areas). Only if agents perceive (which is not credible in an atomistic competition situation) that their own actions will later lower market prices in the urban area and hence possibly incomes from future sales *might* this selling policy not maximize the present value of the agents' commission-based income.

Therefore a more likely explanation for those who allege the implicit collusion of real estate agents is that, because brokers are individually prejudiced, the search costs of finding homes and unprejudiced agents and owners is raised for blacks relative to whites. This increase in search costs lowers the rate of black homeownership and raises the prices paid by blacks.

A second possible conspiratorial group are mortgage lenders. Again, even in small urban areas there are dozens of mortgage lenders, including banks, savings and loan institutions, and private individuals. However, if a neighborhood bank or group of banks decides not to make mortgages to blacks in a white area, that in itself may be sufficient to reduce the supply and raise the cost of mortgage funds to blacks and discourage most attempts at integration. However, the case that it is unprofitable for a bank to lend to blacks, especially if they are willing to pay more for housing, rests on special presumptions (apart from considerations of differential perceived risk between blacks and whites, which in itself may or may not constitute prejudice). Only if the bank fears an ensuing mass exodus of whites caused by its own policies might it refuse to make mortgages to blacks. Any expected decline in housing prices due to this exodus is in itself not a problem for the bank, since the value of already-held white mortgages is essentially unchanged and the black mortgages would offer additional opportunities for profitable investments. The problem concerns deposits; the bank may fear that incoming blacks will have lower wealth and savings than whites. This would reduce the local supply of funds to the bank and the volume of bank business as whites withdraw their deposits, causing a capital loss.

In summary, models of collusion are not persuasive when collusion involves large numbers of agents. First, it is costly to organize large numbers of agents; second, it always pays each individual to break any collusive agreement. However, racial prejudice of whites against blacks, as well as vice versa, is sufficient to explain racial segregation and, under certain conditions, price differentials. Since spatial separation of whites and blacks is almost universal in the United States, it is difficult to ignore explanations based on widespread prejudices. Causes of racial segregation, of course, are critical to policy making. If we wish to encourage integration, the way is then not through housing policies per se, but to focus on the causes of prejudice.

7

Transportation and Modal Choice

In the next two chapters I analyze pricing and investment policies in urban transportation. Since most trips in urban areas are made by automobiles, I tend to focus on policies affecting road travel. Travel patterns on roads are characterized by peak periods of heavy use when people are going to or returning from work and by nonpeak periods of lighter use when people are going to or returning from shopping and recreation.[1] During peak periods, roads are very congested and travel speeds are slow, resulting in large losses in potential leisure time for travelers. The choice of pricing and investment policies for congested roads may radically affect these congestion costs and travel patterns during the day. These policies will also affect the consumer's choice of travel modes and the use and potential of alternatives to road travel in peak periods, such as rapid transit or buses. Finally, I note that, since commuting costs are a major determinant of city spatial characteristics, as demonstrated in Chapters 1 and 2, transportation policies will have a strong impact on city sizes and characteristics.

---

[1] Approximately 40–45% of all trips in North American cities are between home and work sites or business-connected activities; 15–25% are between home and social and recreation sites, and 10–20% are between home and shopping sites. About 90% of all trips are made by auto. References on this include the 1980 Population Census and Meyer, Kain, and Wohl (1965, pp. 90, 91).

134

As a starting point in this chapter I examine the nature of road travel and congestion and analyze optimal investment and pricing policies for a congested system such as a road or for a system such as rapid transit. Using the concepts and model developed, I turn to situations where there are constraints prohibiting the implementation of optimal policies. For example, in general, it may not be feasible to impose congestion tolls on road users, or there may be a nonoptimal budgetary limit on public financing of capital facilities. Of particular interest in this chapter are policies concerning the operation and use of alternative modes, such as roads and rapid transit, in circumstances where pricing and investment options for road travel are constrained. Finally, I review the question how much land should be devoted to roads at various distances from the CBD in a monocentric model of a city.

In the next chapter I examine the nature of peak-period travel, such as the morning or evening rush hours. Topics analyzed are the commuter's decision when to travel on a particular facility and the effect of congestion tolls on this decision, the cost of travel, the optimal provision of transportation facilities, and the peak-period regulation of traffic.

1. CONGESTED SYSTEMS

To understand the nature of congested systems such as roads and the nature of the congestion externality, it is helpful to specify fully the various ways of modeling the situation. Congestion occurs when the users of a system interfere with each other as they use the system, resulting in losses to all users. On a congested road, over normal ranges of road usage, the vehicular speed of travel is a decreasing function of density, or the number of cars per unit road length, and an increasing function of road capacity or width. The more tightly packed together cars are, the more they interfere with or impede each other, reducing the travel speed of all users. An increase in capacity relieves this packing together and mutual interference, increasing the travel speed of users.

Consider a congested road system where all vehicles enter the system at one point, travel through the system, and then exit at another point. For a flow of cars entering the road in a given time interval, their speed of travel is initially just a function of the number of entrants, or how tightly packed together the entering cars are. Once in the system, the density of traffic for initial entrants changes as the initial entrants draw apart, overtake traffic already in the system, or are overtaken by later entrants. For cars traveling through the system, this process of changing densities, and hence speeds, and the general ebb and flow of traffic is very complex and difficult to model.

Three ways to model congested systems are discussed here, all involving different naive assumptions but all useful for analyzing different aspects of the economics of transportation.

1. *Current demand dependent on past and future travel conditions.* In the next chapter I consider a situation where demand to travel at time t is a function of speed and travel costs at times before and after t, as well as at t. Analyzing this type of situation provides a basis for understanding how consumers substitute on the demand side among alternative times of travel and for understanding the nature of peak-period travel patterns and problems. To carry out the analysis, however, we must assume on the supply side that current travel conditions are not influenced by past or future travel conditions. This means that for a given road capacity, the speed of travel of an entrant is solely a function of the number or flow of cars entering the road at the same time as the entrant does. This speed of travel remains constant throughout the journey, implying that entering groups do not draw apart and are not overtaken by or do not overtake later or earlier entrants. At different points on the road, people will be traveling at different speeds, according to the number of people who entered the system at the same time they did. This simplification on the technical side of specifying speed–flow relationships allows us to work with the sophisticated demand specification.

2. *Current travel speeds dependent on past and future conditions.* The second way to model a congested system is entirely different and treats the system as a black box problem (Agnew, 1976, 1977). Although the model probably best depicts computer operations, it is helpful in analyzing road travel. At any instant travel conditions and speeds are the same for all users in the system regardless of where they are in the system or when they entered. Speed of travel is a function of road capacity and system load or the total number of cars on the road at a point in time. The load on the road changes according to the difference between entrants and exits in any time period, and speed adjusts throughout the road uniformly and instantaneously to the new load. This model is useful for illustrating how the speed of travel for an entrant will be influenced by the number of later and earlier entrants; and it yields interesting steady-state solutions. It also provides for an understanding of movements to and away from steady-state solutions and an understanding of the role that congestion tolls play in such movements (see Agnew, 1976, 1977). However, the model is sufficiently complex that, so far, no one has been able to utilize it in situations where the demand to travel at time t is a function of travel times and costs at times before and after t. Therefore, it is assumed that demand to travel at time t is only a function of the travel cost associated with that time.

3. *The traditional model.* The traditional way to model congested systems is a "static" version of the first and second ways. Traffic flows and density are assumed to be uniform in the single period of analysis, without regard to how these densities and flows start up or dissipate at the beginning and end of the single period or without regard to why consumer demand should be uniform throughout the period. Essentially, the traditional model examines possible steady-state solutions, without considering the movement to the steady state (as from the startup point of zero flows) and without considering how to move and how to price movements between different steady-state solutions with different densities and flows. Thus this model cannot adequately analyze peak-period and varying traffic patterns. However, it is quite adequate for analyzing modal choice and the steady-state allocation of traffic between different roads or between roads and transit in a given time period.

Having summarized various ways of modeling traffic situations, we are now ready to examine steady-state travel relationships and the externality nature of congestion. We denote D as density, or cars per mile on the road; S as speed, or miles per hour; and R as a measure of road capacity. Then in the steady state, where density is uniform throughout the system, speed is a nonincreasing function of density, or

$$S = S(D, R), \qquad \partial S/\partial D \leq 0, \qquad \partial S/\partial R \geq 0. \qquad (7.1)$$

The steady-state uniform flow of cars per hour entering, exiting, and/or passing any given point in the road is F. F measures the rate at which cars are passing through the system; hence F equals cars per mile multiplied by miles per hour, or

$$F = SD. \qquad (7.2)$$

Comparing different steady states, as density on the road increases, flow will initially increase, but eventually may start to decline, or

$$\frac{\partial F}{\partial D} = S(1 - \varepsilon), \qquad \varepsilon = -\frac{\partial S}{\partial D}\frac{D}{S} \geq 0. \qquad (7.3)$$

When density is very low and speed is correspondingly high, $\varepsilon < 1$ or $\partial F/\partial D > 0$. However, as density increases, because of the tighter packing of cars on the road, or increased congestion, speeds start to decline radically and eventually $\varepsilon > 1$ and $\partial F/\partial D < 0$.

These relationships are graphed in Figure 7.1. Each steady-state flow of cars is associated with two different possible steady-state densities, starting from an infinitesimal density where $F \longrightarrow 0$ and going to the case where there

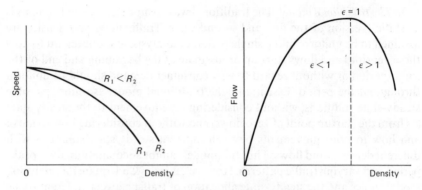

FIGURE 7.1   Speed-density-flow relationships.

are so many cars packed on the road that $S \longrightarrow 0$ and $F \longrightarrow 0$. A system operating beyond the point of maximal flow is clearly inefficient, since any flow beyond the maximal flow could be achieved with a lower density or less cars on the road, higher speeds, and hence with lower travel times and costs.

The congestion externality arises because, when an additional car enters the road and causes cars to be slightly more tightly packed together, that additional car lowers the speed and raises the travel times of all other cars traveling at that time. The additional traveler does not account for the costs that he imposes on other users when making his decision to travel on this road as opposed to other roads or modes or when making his decision to travel at this time as opposed to other times. Because he does not account for the full social costs of his trip on this road at this time, his choice of this road and this time as opposed to other roads, times, or goods may be socially inefficient. It is this problem that we examine in much of the material to follow.

Finally, we note that often when discussing single-period situations, it is assumed ε in Equation (7.3) is always less than 1; hence we are never operating on the back-bending part of the flow curve in Figure 7.1b. Since there is then a strictly monotonic relationship between flow and density, as well as between density and speed for a given R, there is a strictly monotonic relationship between flow and speed. Given this, it is convenient to describe speed as directly being a decreasing function of flow and to relate the congestion externality to traffic flows. Moreover, given that we are examining only a single period, flow equals total trips in each period; hence the term *trips* rather than *flows* is commonly used. Speed is then a decreasing function of total trips. Although Agnew (1976) pointed out that this specification leads to problems and errors in analysis in some dynamic contents, for expositional simplicity, we adopt this convenience in the next section.

2. MODAL CHOICE

In this section I first examine optimal pricing and investment policies for congested systems such as roads, using the traditional single-period model. I allow there to be two modes of travel, such as roads and rapid transit, between which consumers can substitute, so as to highlight problems in consumer choice of different transport modes. Then pricing and investment policies in situations where road travel cannot be optimally priced or there are constraints on the financing of road or transit capacity are examined. In order to examine optimal and second-best pricing and investment policies, I use a simple welfare maximization model, adapted from Mohring's (1970) peak-load model.

Consumers maximize utility, which is a function of a composite good g and two different transportation services, x and z. Different types of services might be travel on different roads by car or travel by car versus transit. Given the different types of services or amenities these goods offer and the different costs of the goods, the consumer has to decide how much of each to buy. Although for a particular trip, the consumer usually buys either x or z but not both, over the period of a week or year the individual or his family buys some of both services.

The I consumers in a city maximize $V(x, z, g)$ subject to a budget constraint $p_x x + p_z z + p_g g = y^i - h^i$. The term y^i is income measured in dollars of fixed resources available to consumer i; and h^i is the head tax imposed on consumer i where head taxes [subsidies] are designed to cover deficits [surpluses] in the government financing of transportation facilities. We use head taxes, rather than other more realistic types of taxes, to abstract from problems associated with the welfare costs of more realistic types of taxes.

The per unit cost of producing g is a constant and, given perfect competition in the private sector, equals price p_g. The per unit variable costs of supplying x and z are $C(X, K_x)$ and $C'(Z, K_z)$, where $X = \sum_i x^i$ or total trips of all users, $Z = \sum_i z^i$, and K_x and K_z are expenditures on transportation facilities. Unit variable costs are a decreasing function of capacity, or $\partial C/\partial K_x < 0$; and they are an increasing function of total trips X, or $\partial C/\partial X > 0$. These variable costs may be interpreted as the time costs of travel and/or the physcial (out-of-pocket) costs of operating cars, both of which utilize resources available to the consumer and society. Total variable costs for X are $XC(X, K_x)$ and hence the marginal cost of X is $C(X, K_x) + X[\partial C(X, K_x)/\partial X]$. The marginal cost consists of the average variable cost of producing the additional trip, $C(X, K_x)$, plus the amount by which the variable costs of all other trips are increased, $X[\partial C(X, K_x)/\partial X]$. This second term is the congestion factor.

Society's resources are spent on G, X, Z, K_x, and K_z where G is provided in the private sector and K_x and K_z are measured in dollars of resources spent on transport facilities. To find conditions for any Pareto-optimal solution we maximize the utility of one individual, holding utility levels of all others fixed. Maximization is carried out with respect to policy variables, which are head taxes, prices of transportation services p_x and p_z, and capital expenditures on transportation K_x and K_z. Policymakers are constrained by the social resource constraint

$$\sum_{i=1}^{I} y_i \equiv Y = XC(K, K_x) + ZC'(Z, K_z) + p_g G + K_x + K_z.$$

The total resources available to the society, Y, is simply the sum of individual resources. The other side of the equation is the cost of producing all goods in the system.

2.1 A First-Best World: No Institutional Constraints or Costs

Suppose policymakers face no pricing or financing constraints and the costs of implementing congestion tolls are zero. Then we may achieve an optimal solution by maximizing one person's utility level while holding other utility levels fixed at $\bar{V}^i$ subject to the resource constraint. We first examine optimal investment policies by maximizing

$$L = V^1 + \sum_{i=2}^{I} \alpha_i(V^i - \bar{V}^i) + \lambda[Y - C(X, K_x)X$$

$$- C'(Z, K_z)Z - K_x - K_z - p_g G] \tag{7.4}$$

with respect to K_x and K_z. Doing this and rearranging the first-order conditions, we get

$$-\frac{\partial C(X, K_x)}{\partial K_x}X = 1, \qquad -\frac{\partial C'(Z, K_z)}{\partial K_z}Z = 1. \tag{7.5}$$

Equation (7.5) says that capital facilities should be expanded until the last dollar spent on facilities brings forth one dollar in marginal benefits, or reduction in variable travel costs. This reduction in variable travel costs equals the reduction in unit costs or $\partial C(X, K_x)/\partial K_x$ multiplied by the units produced, or total trips on each facility.

To get the optimal pricing policy we differentiate (7.4) with respect to head taxes, p_x, and p_z. After various substitutions of well-known demand relationships, the result is[2]

$$\begin{bmatrix} S_{xx} & S_{zx} \\ S_{xz} & S_{zz} \end{bmatrix} \begin{bmatrix} p_x - \text{SMC}_x \\ p_z - \text{SMC}_z \end{bmatrix} = \begin{bmatrix} 0 \\ 0 \end{bmatrix}. \tag{7.6}$$

The terms SMC_x and SMC_z equal the social marginal costs of an additional unit of x and y. They are defined to be

$$C(X, K_x) + \frac{\partial C(X, K_x)}{\partial X} X \quad \text{and} \quad C'(Z, K_z) + \frac{\partial C'(Z, K_z)}{\partial Z} Z.$$

Then, for example, $C(X, K_x)$ is the average or private travel cost incurred on each trip; and $[\partial C(X, K_x)/\partial X]X$ is the increase in travel costs for all other travelers caused by the additional trip and the resulting increase in congestion.

---

[2] This may be shown as follows. In the maximization problem we use indirect utility functions, define ϕ^i as the marginal utility of income for individual i, and recall from Roy's identity that $x^i = -(\partial V^i/\partial p_x)/\phi^i$ and $z^i = -(\partial V^i/\partial p_z)/\phi^i$. Then, maximizing V^1 with respect to p_x, p_z, and h^i, we get (after substitutions into the first term of these equations where $\alpha^1 = 1$)

$$-\sum_i \alpha^i \phi^i x^i - \lambda[\text{SMC}_x(\partial X/\partial p_x) + \text{SMC}_z(\partial Z/\partial p_x) + p_g(\partial G/\partial p_x)] = 0, \tag{a}$$

$$-\sum_i \alpha^i \phi^i z^i - \lambda[\text{SMC}_x(\partial X/\partial p_z) + \text{SMC}_z(\partial Z/\partial p_z) + p_g(\partial G/\partial p_z)] = 0, \tag{b}$$

$$-\alpha^i \phi^i - [\text{SMC}_x(\partial x^i/\partial h^i) + \text{SMC}_z(\partial z^i/\partial h^i) + p_g(\partial g^i/\partial h^i)] = 0, \quad \text{for } i = 1, 2, \ldots, I. \tag{c}$$

By differentiating the budget constraint of an individual with respect to p_x, p_z, and h^i, we know that

$$-x^i - p_x(\partial x^i/\partial p_x) - p_z(\partial z^i/\partial p_x) - p_g(\partial g^i/\partial p_x) = 0,$$

$$-z^i - p_x(\partial x^i/\partial p_z) - p_z(\partial z^i/\partial p_z) - p_g(\partial g^i/\partial p_z) = 0,$$

$$1 + p_x(\partial x^i/\partial h^i) + p_z(\partial z^i/\partial h^i) + p_g(\partial g^i/\partial h^i) = 0.$$

Aggregating the first two of these relationships over all individuals, we know $X + p_x(\partial X/\partial p_x) + p_z(\partial Z/\partial p_x) + p_g(\partial G/\partial p_x) = 0$ and $Z + p_z(\partial Z/\partial p_z) + p_x(\partial X/\partial p_z) + p_g(\partial G/\partial p_z) = 0$. From these relationships we substitute into Equation (a)–(c) for $p_g(\partial G/\partial p_x), p_g(\partial G/\partial p_z)$, and $p_g(\partial g^i/\partial h^i)$, where, for example, Equation (a) becomes

$$-\sum_i \alpha^i \phi^i x^i + \lambda[X + (p_x - \text{SMC}_x)(\partial X/\partial p_x) + (p_z - \text{SMC}_z)(\partial Z/\partial p_x)] = 0.$$

The new (a) and (b) equations we call Equations (a') and (b'). In the new Equation (c) we multiply each equation by x^i and sum over all individuals and repeat the process for z^i. Thus we end up with new two equations, one for X, or Equation (c^x), and one for z, or Equation (c^z), where for example, Equation (c^x) is

$$-\sum_i \alpha^i \phi^i x^i + \lambda[X + (p_x - \text{SMC}_x)\sum_i (\partial x^i/\partial h^i x^i) + (p_z - \text{SMC}_z)\sum_i (\partial z^i/\partial h^i x^i)] = 0.$$

We then subtract Equation (c^x) from Equation (a') and (c^z) from (b') to get Equation (7.6), given our definition of S_{ij}.

The S_{ij} terms are pure Hicks–Slutsky substitution terms, where, for example, for the ith individual

$$S^i_{xz} = \left.\frac{\partial x^i}{\partial p_z}\right|_{\bar{V}^i} = \frac{\partial x^i}{\partial p_z} - z^i\frac{\partial x^i}{\partial h^i},$$

where $\partial x^i/\partial h^i$ is usually negative since h^i is a tax, or negative income. The substitution term S_{xz} then is simply $\sum_i S^i_{xz}$. The pure substitution effects with a change in p_x or p_z occur because, when p_x and p_z are increased, more revenue is received from the higher prices and individuals are compensated with lowered head taxes since less revenue is needed from head taxes to pay for capital facilities.

In solving (7.6), we know that if the matrix is non-singular or its determinant $|S|$ is nonzero, then $p_x - \text{SMC}_x$ and $p_x - \text{SMC}_z$ must equal zero. The second-order conditions of utility maximization require that $|S| = S_{xx}S_{zz} - S_{xz}S_{zx} > 0$. Therefore the solution to (7.6) is $p_x = \text{SMC}_x$ and $p_z = \text{SMC}_z$, or price equals social marginal cost. For transportation where $\text{SMC}_x = C(X, K_x) + [\partial C(X, K_x)/\partial X]X$, individuals incur $C(X, K_x)$ privately when they travel but need to be charged a congestion toll equal to the external costs imposed on other travelers, or $[\partial C(X, K_x)/\partial X]X$. If there is no congestion, $\text{SMC}_x = C(X, K_x)$ and no toll is needed for price to equal social marginal cost.

One final point in this first-best world is that tolls collected cover capital costs of facilities if there are constant returns to scale. The conceptual point is rather simple. If we apply a variable factor X to a fixed factor K_x and charge marginal cost, after we pay X the value of its marginal product, rents are left over. Under constant returns to scale, these rents exactly equal the value of the marginal product and the opportunity cost of the fixed factor.

In our model, the point may be made as follows. Assuming $C(X, K_x)$ is a homogeneous function, from Euler's theorem $(\partial C/\partial K_x)K_x + (\partial C/\partial X)X = rC$, where r is the degree of homogeneity. Rearranging and multiplying through by X we get

$$X(X\partial C/\partial X) = rCX - K_x(X\partial C/\partial K_x).$$

If investment is optimally provided then $(X\partial C/\partial K_x) = -1$, so that we can rewrite the expression as

$$X(X\partial C/\partial X) = rCX + K_x.$$

The left-hand side terms are tolls collected—the individual toll $(X\partial C/\partial X)$ multiplied by the number of trips. These tolls equal capacity costs plus rCX. With constant returns to scale, $r = 0$ so that optimally set tolls exactly cover optimal capacity costs. If there are increasing [decreasing] returns to scale, r

< 0 $[r > 0]$; and then tolls fall short of [exceed] capital costs and a head tax [subsidy] is needed to cover capital costs.

The foregoing analysis is an abstract description of a first-best world where all the basic results of welfare economics apply. Marginal benefits equal marginal costs in investment, price equals social marginal costs, and optimal rents on a capital facility cover its cost if there are constant returns to scale.

The framework developed can be applied directly to the issue of public subsidization of capital facilities and the question of when revenues from marginal cost pricing are likely to cover total costs of providing a good. The framework can also be adapted to incorporate institutional constraints and phenomena faced in urban provision of transportation. Such constraints are the use of gasoline taxes for financing road capacity, budgetary limits on deficit financing of capital facilities, and the politicized issue of subsidization of transit fares.

We choose to apply the framework to examining the provision of rapid transit and the issue of whether rapid transit should be subsidized from general revenues. There are two interrelated subsidization issues. One is whether capital expenditures need be subsidized when transit fares are set equal to marginal costs of transporting passengers. The other is whether transit fares themselves should be subsidized so that private transit travel costs fall short of marginal costs.

2.2   The Case of Rapid Transit

Subsidization of Capital Expenditures

In the foregoing discussion of a first-best world we showed that if there are increasing returns or declining average costs to providing a service, then revenue from marginal cost pricing will not cover total costs. Subsidies from public tax revenues will in general be needed to make up the difference. In deciding if capital facilities for rapid transit should be subsidized we must determine whether rapid transit fits this decription of declining average costs. At the same time we must also analyze under what conditions it is desirable to provide rapid transit at all, let alone subsidize it.

Rapid transit involves the provision of heavy initial fixed levels of capital expenditures in the form of basic track and stations, which are somewhat independent of traffic volume. Over low ranges of passenger volume, marginal operating costs in terms of trains, maintenance, safety measures, conductors, time costs of travel, and policing are assumed to be low and perhaps a declining function of volume. Therefore, at least for low to medium traffic volumes, average total costs are declining and subsidization of capital facilities to cover deficits, given marginal cost pricing, is justified.

However, when passenger volume becomes high and facilities become very congested, marginal operating costs start to rise or at least level off, as breakdowns, theft, accidents and crowding become more prominent and time costs of travel increase (e.g., the length of stops increases). Then average total costs may level out or even start to rise, eradicating the need for a subsidy.

Before providing any subsidy, it is necessary for a policymaker to decide if the provision of rapid transit at all is justified. That is, in general equilibrium terms, is social welfare raised by the existence of rapid transit, given its resource costs? This question is usually examined in a partial equilibrium diagram where the criterion for providing transit is that the consumers' surplus from the existence of rapid transit should exceed the deficit incurred, under marginal cost pricing.

It should be noted that public subsidies are never really necessary, even with declining average costs. The transit authority could adopt a two-part pricing scheme. To ride the trains at all, each year consumers would be required to pay an annual fee or purchase a card that permits them to buy transit tokens or fares (essentially, this would be a private head tax). Each trip or token would then be priced at marginal operating costs. The annual fee would be set to capture sufficient consumers' surplus so as to cover the deficit but it would not interfere with the consumers' decisions to purchase marginal trips.

Subsidization of Transit Fares

So far the discussion in this chapter has dealt with a first-best world, in which it is optimal to price goods according to marginal cost. However, in a second-best world the marginal cost pricing prescription and the optimal investment criterion may not hold, given the particular constraints that impose a second-best, as opposed to first-best, world on us. I illustrate a second-best situation in which it is efficient to subsidize rapid transit fares as well as capital expenditures.

In our welfare maximization model there are two transport goods, x and z, which we now designate as being, respectively, road trips and transit trips. We assume roads and transit are reasonably close substitutes for consumers, a *critical* assumption to the case for subsidizing transit fares. Unlike a first-best world, congestion on roads is unpriced. We assume the basic reasons congestion is unpriced are political and institutional constraints. The actual costs of pricing are very small, involving an inexpensive signaling device attached to a car that identifies the car as it passes through the congested system and a sensory system in the road picking up the signals. On this computerized system each person would be charged the appropriate congestion toll at that time and billed monthly. Over a period of time the commuter would become familiar with the cost of traveling at various times on various facilities and hence would be making choices in the face of known prices. The system is probably not inherently any more expensive than other monitoring and metering systems, such as for electricity, water, or telephones. Therefore, we view the congestion pricing constraint as basically a political or social constraint.

If congestion on roads is unpriced, this means automobile travel is priced at less than marginal cost. If other goods are priced at marginal cost, this implies that automobile travel is implicitly subsidized relative to other goods and thus is overconsumed relative to other goods. There are two optimal ways to solve this problem of distortions in relative prices and consumer choices. One is to impose congestion tolls, a solution we have ruled out. The other is to subsidize all other goods by the same relative amount as road travel, so that consumers are no longer encouraged to use roads relative to other goods. This proposition follows from the general literature on optimal taxation (Baumol and Bradford, 1970). The basic idea is that Pareto efficiency requires marginal rates of substitution in consumption (which will equal price ratios in a market economy) to equal *ratios* of social marginal costs of production for any two goods. With unpriced congestion this condition will not be satisfied, since consumer price ratios will not equal ratios of social marginal costs, but by subsidizing and lowering the price of all other goods we can bring consumer price ratios into equality with ratios of social marginal costs.

Clearly, in our complex world an urban policymaker cannot subsidize all goods in the economy because of unpriced congestion. However, the policymaker may do the next best thing, which is to subsidize close substitutes for automobile travel, such as rapid transit. To the extent that subsidization induces travelers to switch from roads to transit, road congestion will be alleviated and all travelers will be made better off.

This proposition is illustrated in Figure 7.2. Equilibrium without congestion pricing and without transit subsidies is at points e, where road travel is relatively underpriced and overconsumed. The effect of a subsidy S to transit is to shift down the supply curve in the transit sector, inducing greater use of transit. At the same time, in response to lower transit fares, the demand for road travel declines. This is represented by a shift back in the demand curve in that sector, as people shift to traveling by transit. As the size of the subsidy is increased, this shift from road to transit travel should be more pronounced.

Given the possibility of subsidization, the basic questions are, What is the magnitude of the optimal subsidy? How much of a shift from road to transit travel is desirable? Are optimal investment criteria changed because of

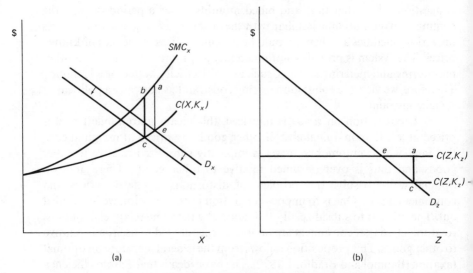

FIGURE 7.2   Subsidizing transit fares.

the pricing constraint? To rigorously answer these questions we turn to our welfare maximization model.[3]

Each consumer maximizes $V(x, z, g)$ where $x, z,$ and g are, respectively, the household consumption of auto trips, transit trips, and all other goods. The budget constraint is $y^i - h^i = C(X, K_x)x + p_z z + p_g g$ where for roads the

---

[3] A common approximation of the criterion for the optimal subsidy is pictured in Figure 7.2. Suppose the subsidy is currently S in Figure 7.2b and equilibrium is at point c in both sectors. In Figure 7.2b at point c the welfare cost from having lowered price below social marginal cost is approximated by the area eac. In Figure 7.2a the welfare gain from having reduced road congestion is approximated by the area $eabc$. The optimal subsidy is attained when the increase in social costs from lowering transit price one more unit, which is the slice ac in Figure 7.2b, just equals the corresponding increase in social benefits as the demand curve for road travel shifts back, which is the slice bc in Figure 7.2a. (Note that there is no corresponding welfare change in the g sector of the economy.) In algebraic terms the area of the marginal welfare cost slice ac equals $-S(\Delta Z/\Delta p_z)$. The area of the marginal social benefit slice bc is $X(\partial C/\partial X)(\Delta X/\Delta p_z)$. Therefore by this graphical derivation the optimal subsidy is

$$p_z - \text{SMC}_z \equiv S = -\frac{\Delta X/\Delta p_z}{\Delta Z/\Delta p_z}\left(X\frac{\partial C}{\partial X}\right).$$

As $\Delta p_z \to 0$, the expressions $\Delta Z/\Delta p_z$ and $\Delta X/\Delta p_z$ reduce to S_{zz} and S_{xz}. Therefore this expression is the same as Equation (7.8), except for the term $(\partial C/\partial K)X$, which from Equation (7.7) is a number somewhat greater than one. Therefore the subsidy derived from a diagrammatic analysis that ignores the question of a changing optimal investment criterion is somewhat larger than the optimal subsidy.

individual simply pays the average variable cost of travel or there is no toll. Since the government no longer controls p_x, or $p_x = C(x, K_x)$, it seeks to maximize utility with respect to K_x, K_z, p_z, and the h^i. The Lagrangian function that is maximized with respect to K_x, K_z, p_z, and the h^i is the one in Equation (7.4), except that an additional term $\theta[C(X, K_x) - p_x]$ is added stating the pricing constraints.

Maximizing with respect to K_x, we see that the optimal investment criterion for roads changes to

$$-\frac{\partial C}{\partial K_x} X = 1 - \frac{\theta}{\lambda} \frac{\partial C}{\partial K_x}. \qquad (7.7)$$

Since $\partial C / \partial K_x < 0$, the right-hand side of (7.7) is greater than one. This suggests that investment in roads should be restricted so that the marginal benefits of investment $[(-\partial C / \partial K_x) X]$ exceed the marginal resource costs of investment ($\$1$). By "underinvesting" in road capacity, the transport authority raises the marginal private costs of travel (nearer its shadow cost), discouraging use of roads relative to transit and encouraging a more efficient allocation of resources in consumption. In Figure 7.2a, underinvestment shifts up the average and marginal cost curves, reducing the consumption of X. The optimal investment criterion for transit is the same as in Equation (7.5).

Note that this underinvestment situation for roads when congestion is unpriced holds quite apart from the issues concerning rapid transit: Equation (7.7) applies even if rapid transit did not exist. Second, "underinvestment" means that, in this second-best situation of unpriced congestion, K_x is reduced below the level where $(\partial C / \partial K_x) X_x = 1$. It does not mean that K_x in (7.7) is less than the K_x in a first-best situation in Equation (7.5) where congestion is priced. In fact, given the higher congestion levels that prevail in a second-best situation, optimal capacity in Equation (7.7) is likely to be higher than in the very different congestion situation underlying Equation (7.5). Wilson (1983) made a presuasive case that under relevant parameters this will be the case.

Maximizing the new Lagrangian with respect to p_z and the h^i and performing appropriate substitutions, we find the pricing criterion for transit.[4]

---

[4] In footnote 2 only Equations (b) and (c) are relevant. To the left-hand side of these equations we add the terms $+\theta(\partial C / \partial X)(\partial X / \partial p_z)$ and $+\theta(\partial C / \partial X)(\partial x^i / \partial h^i)$, respectively. Performing the manipulations in footnote 2, we obtain

$$p_z - \mathrm{SMC}_z = -\frac{S_{xz}}{S_{zz}} \left(p_x - \mathrm{SMC}_x + \frac{\theta}{\lambda} \frac{\partial C}{\partial X} \right).$$

Substituting in $p_x = C$ and for θ / λ from Equation (7.7), we find that this equation reduces to Equation (7.8).

This criterion defines the magnitude of the optimal subsidy where

$$\text{SMC}_z - p_z \equiv S = \frac{S_{xz}(\partial C/\partial X)X}{S_{zz}(\partial C/\partial K_x)X} > 0. \tag{7.8}$$

Because roads and transit travel are substitutes, $S_{xz} > 0$. The magnitude of the subsidy S is (1) an increasing function of the degree of road congestion as measured by $X(\partial C/\partial X)$; (2) an increasing function of consumer willingness to switch from roads to transit, thus relieving road congestion as measured by S_{xz}; (3) a decreasing function of the general switch to z consumption (from, say, g consumption) in response to lower z prices; and (4) a decreasing function of the response of travel costs to changing capacity investment. These results are intuitively appealing. Subsidization is an attractive policy when the degree of road congestion is high and consumers can be induced through transit subsidization to switch away from road travel. It is also an attractive policy when underinvestment in roads is ineffective in raising travel costs and hence inducing people to travel by transit.

The size of the fare subsidy to rapid transit can be expressed in measurable variables. Rearranging (7.8), we obtain

$$\text{SMC} - p_z \equiv S = \frac{X(\partial C/\partial X)X\eta^s_{xz}}{X(\partial C/\partial K_x)Z\eta^s_{zz}}, \tag{7.9}$$

where η^s_{ij} are real income held constant price elasticities. The variables X and Z are observable and the actual form of the congestion relation, or $C(X, K_x)$, is well known. In applying Equation (7.9) to the real world we would be particularly concerned with peak-period travel when road congestion is heaviest. The estimates of η^s_{ij} would need to be applicable to peak-period situations. The major objection to implementing or maintaining such policies concerns the size of η^s_{xz}. Many economists believe η^s_{xz} is very small or road users cannot be induced into transit cars within the range of feasible subsidies. (We rule out $p_z < 0$ since people could then earn their living from riding transit cars!)

Finally, we note that if demand for the combined transport goods is perfectly inelastic, so that underpricing roads distorts not the choice between roads and other goods but only the choice between roads and transit, the optimal policy is to subsidize transit such that both transportation goods receive the same percentage, implicit or explicit, subsidy. Under this assumption, there is no welfare loss from not being able to price road congestion explicitly. The only distortion created by not being able to price road congestion is between the consumption of transit and roads, and this can be fully corrected by subsidizing transit. However, given the possibilities for car pooling; for transforming single-purpose into multipurpose trips; for spatial rearrangement of job, retailing, and home sites; and for foregoing marginal trips, it seems unlikely that the demand for transportation trips is very inelastic.

The foregoing analysis could be applied to a situation where x and z are two competing roads but where only congestion on the z road can be priced. For example, z could be a tollway and x a freeway. The optimal congestion toll is one where price remains less than SMC. A toll on the z road that set price equal to marginal cost would induce relatively too many people to travel on the x road, resulting in relatively too high congestion levels on the x road.

3. EXTENSIONS OF THE MODEL

A number of other constraints and situations can be investigated in our model. I mention two here.

3.1 Budgetary Limits

Suppose public budgetary considerations reduce the amount of money available for transportation to a nonoptimal level. For example, there could be a limit on the deficit a transport authority may have. This deficit constraint could be added to Equation (7.4) through the constraint $p_x X + p_z Z + D = K_x + K_z + XC + ZC'$, where D is the allowable deficit. The need for a deficit would exist even in a world of complete congestion pricing if there were nonconstant returns to scale in road services, since with nonconstant returns to scale optimal tolls do not cover capital costs. Road construction is viewed as having two components; the variable number of lanes and then components fixed in size, such as shoulders, buffer zones between roads and housing, and median strips. Therefore, the average cost curve for capacity declines as capacity increases, indicating increasing returns to scale and the fact that tolls will not cover capital costs. Then government subsidization is needed but may be limited to some inefficient level such as D in the constraint above. With this type of constraint one can work through the welfare maximization model to show that one simply raises prices above social marginal costs to make up the deficit. The optimal investment rule still is to invest until the last dollar brings forth a dollar's reduction in total variable costs.

3.2 Gasoline Tolls

Gasoline tolls are a prevalent part of transportation policy. In addition to raising revenue, they raise the price of road travel above private cost and, as such, partially price externalities, such as air pollution and congestion.

However, they are a very inadequate substitute for congestion tolls. Within a speed range of 25 to 50 mph, gasoline consumption per mile is nearly constant (Johnson, 1964), so a gas tax simply raises the cost of travel within this speed range by the same amount per mile. On the other hand, congestion levels vary considerably in this speed range, and thus desired congestion tolls also vary. Therefore, the problem for a policymaker is how to use the gasoline tax, which raises travel price on different roads by the same amount, whereas what is desired is a set of taxes that raises travel prices by different amounts according to congestion levels on different roads. In examining what the optimal gasoline toll is, we follow Mohring's discussion (1970, pp. 699–701).

In our model we let x and z be two types of road trips that are imperfect substitutes in consumption. Travel on the x road is very congested while on the z road it is relatively less congested. The gasoline toll T is effectively the same on both roads; therefore, $p_x - C = T = p_z - C'$, where gasoline tolls are the only way to raise price above average cost. This relationship may be incorporated into the maximization problem in Equation (7.4) by adding the constraint

$$\theta[(p_z - p_x) + (C(X, K_x) - C'(Z, K_z))]. \tag{7.10}$$

Redoing the maximization problem yields new investment criteria

$$-\frac{\partial C(X, K_x)}{\partial K_x} X = 1 - \frac{\theta}{\lambda} \frac{\partial C(X, K_x)}{\partial K_x} > 1,$$

$$\tag{7.11}$$

$$-\frac{\partial C'(Z, K_z)}{\partial K_z} Z = 1 + \frac{\theta}{\lambda} \frac{\partial C'(Z, K_z)}{\partial K_z} < 1.$$

Here $\theta = \partial V^1/\partial(p_z - p_x) = -\partial V^1/\partial(C - C') > 0$, or as the gap between average cost levels on the two roads declines, utility rises. Therefore, the optimal investment criteria say we should stop investing in the x road when marginal investment benefits $[(-\partial C/\partial K_x)X]$ still exceed marginal cost ($1) and vice versa for the z road. That is, we should "underinvest" in the x road and "overinvest" in the z road, which should help induce consumers to travel on the less congested road and should offset price distortions (discussed next).

The new pricing criteria are[5]

$$p_x - C_x = T - X\frac{\partial C}{\partial X} = \frac{\theta}{\lambda}\frac{S_{zz} + S_{zx} - (\partial C/\partial X)|S|]}{|S|} < 0,$$

$$\tag{7.12}$$

$$p_z - C_z = T - Z\frac{\partial C'}{\partial Z} = -\frac{\theta}{\lambda}\frac{[S_{xx} + S_{xz} - (\partial C'/\partial Z)|S|]}{|S|} > 0.$$

---

[5] In Equations (a)–(c) in footnote 2 we add terms due to the new constraint and then perform the same operations.

Providings $S_{zx}(= S_{xz})$ is relatively small, the numerators of the two equations are negative, given $S_{xx} < 0$ and $|S| > 0$. Then the optimal gasoline toll is one where the toll exceeds the congestion externality $[Z(\partial C'/\partial Z)]$ on the less congested road and falls short of the congestion externality on the more congested road. That is, the toll must necessarily be set at a compromise level, trading off the costs of overpenalizing z users against the costs of underpenalizing x users.

In summary, the optimal transport policy where gasoline tolls are the only way of pricing congestion on different roads is a two-pronged one. The toll overprices [underprices] travel on less [more] congested roads but this relative penalization is offset by a more favorable investment policy toward less congested roads. This suggests an argument for overinvestment in rural as opposed to urban roads, given that gasoline tolls probably underprice urban congestion and travel while overpricing rural travel.

4. THE ALLOCATION OF LAND TO ROADS IN AN URBAN AREA

One area of theoretical concern in the urban economics literature is the question how the amount of land devoted to roads should vary with distance from the city center. Consider a monocentric model of a city where everyone commutes to the CBD. As we approach the CBD, the number of commuters passing through each residential ring increases, because the number of commuters is an accumulation of all people who live farther from the CBD plus the people in the current ring. If travel time is a function of the number of travelers, or there is congestion, this would suggest that the absolute amount of land devoted to roads might increase as we approach the CBD, so as to relieve congestion as the number of travelers increases.

However, as we saw in Chapter 1, the opportunity cost of land rises as we approach the CBD, indicating increased marginal costs of investing in roads. Therefore, in allocating land to roads, the policymaker has to trade off the rising marginal costs of investment as one approaches the CBD against the potentially rising marginal benefits caused by additional travelers and potentially increased congestion. The general conclusion is that the relative amount of land devoted to roads in each ring increases as we approach the CBD (noting that the total amount of land in each ring is simultaneously declining). The absolute amount of land devoted to roads also probably increases as we approach the CBD, particularly in small cities. In larger cities with a higher opportunity cost of land near the CBD, the absolute amount of land devoted to roads may decline at some points as we approach the CBD, especially near the CBD. Mills (1967), Mills and de Ferranti (1971), Oron,

Pines, and Sheshinski (1973), and Solow and Vickrey (1971) all have extensive discussions of this topic.

5. CONCLUSIONS

In this chapter we first examined the nature of congested systems, such as roads, and derived the usual optimal pricing and investment rules for congested roads. We then turned to the issue of whether rapid transit should be subsidized. Transit capital facilities may need to be subsidized because with declining total average costs of provision, marginal cost pricing will not yield sufficient revenue to cover total costs. However, it was pointed out that public subsidies per se may not be needed. The transit authority could employ a two-part pricing scheme where travelers pay a fixed annual fee to use the transit facilities and then pay the marginal cost price for each trip. The annual fee is set so as to cover any deficit.

It may also be desirable to subsidize transit fares so they are less than marginal costs. This situation arises if transit is a reasonable substitute for roads, and if congestion on roads is unpriced so the private cost of road travel is less than the marginal cost. Thus road travel is implicitly subsidized and hence overused relative to other modes. Then the urban policymaker has a two-pronged policy. One prong is to underinvest in roads and the other is to subsidize rapid transit fares. Both prongs are designed to discourage road travel.

Finally, we examined the implementation of a gasoline toll that raises the per mile cost of travel by a fixed amount, essentially independent of the speed of travel. Gasoline tolls tend to overprice uncongested roads, on which no toll is needed, and underprice very congested roads, where a very high toll is needed. To offset these price effects and encourage movement to uncongested roads, it is optimal to overinvest in lightly congested roads and underinvest in heavily congested roads.

8

Transportation and the Peak-Load Problem

In this chapter I examine the phenomenon of peak-period travel, such as the morning or evening rush hour for commuters. Peak periods of travel are usually characterized by low traffic volume and low congestion at the start of the period, a steady buildup of traffic and congestion until the latter half of the period, and then a decline in traffic volume as the peak period ends. At the height of the peak period, roads are usually heavily congested and traffic moves very slowly. This is a phenomenon of popular concern because of the heavy time costs (and frustration) involved in traveling at that time.

To understand the nature of the peak period, it is essential to examine how and why individuals choose to travel at different times during the peak period. Once we understand the individual's decision of when to travel, we can derive an aggregate peak-period pattern of traffic, demonstrating the buildup of traffic flows and congestion during the peak period. We can then demonstrate the impact of capacity expansion on the buildup of traffic flows and congestion. We can also show that congestion tolls or other forms of regulation can be used to eliminate the heaviest congestion at the height of the peak period, to efficiently alter the peak-period pattern of traffic flows, and to lower travel costs for all commuters.

The individual's decision of when to travel during the peak period is based on the cost of travel at different times during the period. The cost of travel is a function of (1) road congestion, and hence travel costs, at these different times and (2) the scheduling cost of traveling at times other than a personally most desired one, based on the difficulties of coordinating family and work activities with arrival and departure schedules. The inclusion of scheduling costs is very important when a large number of people are trying to get to or leave from the same place at the same time. Road capacities are such that not only is it impossible for everyone to travel together, but some people prefer to travel late or early to avoid the traffic jams incurred by those people who travel at the most desired times. People's commuting and work schedules must be fit in with school hours of children, work hours of a spouse, daylight hours, shopping hours, and hours of various recreational activities.

This problem of picking a commuting schedule is a critical and only recently explored aspect of peak-period travel analysis. Vickrey (1969) and de Palma, Ben-Akiva, and Cyna (1983) analyzed the problem in a pure queuing or bottleneck problem, and Henderson (1974b, 1977a, 1981) in more general commuting contexts. There is also work on the optimal assignment of traffic in a queuing system with multiple outlets or multiple-access links to minimize waiting time (Filipiak, 1981). The model presented here is based primarily on Henderson (1981).

In Section 1, I start with a discussion of the scheduling and traffic flow situation. In Section 2 a simple model of commuting is presented, analyzing the basic equilibrium and then analyzing the impact of capacity expansion and congestion pricing. Section 3 introduces more complex considerations, dealing with the impact of scheduling on worker productivity.

1.   MODELING A PEAK-PERIOD SITUATION

In modeling a peak-period situation, I consider the commuting trip to work, where, in general but not always, commuters are assumed to have identical preferences and skills. Before turning to technical specifications, I give a brief overview of the scheduling problem and the road congestion model in this situation.

Until recently most firms in the CBD of a city tended to have identical work schedules. For example, the Port Authority in New York estimated for 1970 that 75% of the $\frac{1}{2}$ million workers in Lower Manhattan had 9–9:14 A.M. work starting times (O'Malley, 1974). However, given road, parking garage, and elevator capacities, it is physically impossible for almost 400,000 workers to arrive at their desks simultaneously around 9 A.M. For example, in Lower Manhattan in 1970 it appears that at most about 125,000 of these people arrived in the 8:45–9:00 A.M. interval.

In this type of traditional commuting situation, equilibrium must be characterized by a number of people consistently arriving early or perhaps late for work. Early arrivals will have high costs of waiting for work to start, but since they travel at the beginning of the peak period when roads are less congested, they will have relatively low travel costs. Commuters traveling at the height of the peak period will have low or no waiting costs, but they will face high congestion levels and have very high travel times and costs. In a stable equilibrium, given this trade-off between waiting time and travel time, an equilibrium pattern of arrivals will evolve such that commuters are all satisfied with their particular schedules.

However, this traditional commuting situation presents two sources of waste in utilization of resources. First, since substantial numbers of people arrive early for work, they must sit "idle" for significant periods of time. Second, transport facilities are heavily overburdened by the concentration of arrivals right around the single work starting time. This concentration plummets travel speeds and escalates congestion levels and capacity requirements.

An obvious solution to this problem is for firms in a business district to have differing work schedules, or staggered starting and quitting times. Then desired arrival times and arrivals will be spread out. This relieves the overburdening of transport facilities, reducing congestion and travel times, and perhaps even reducing capacity requirements. Second, with appropriate scheduling, the period of idle waiting time involved with a single starting time can be entirely eliminated. People can start work when they arrive. This shortens the amount of time people need to spend at work, without reducing time actually spent working.

In Lower Manhattan within 2 years after the partial introduction of staggered work hours in 1970, about 25% of arrivals had been shifted off the heaviest peak time. While data on productivity and reduction in idle time (total hours in the business district) were not collected, information on employee morale, absenteeism, and punctuality indicated significant improvements in those variables (O'Malley, 1974). Subway congestion was significantly reduced, although in New York no estimates of travel time savings were made. However, in a Toronto demonstration project, auto commuters, who constituted over 50% of the participants, experienced average travel time reductions of about 25% (Greenberg and Wright, 1974; Guttman, 1975).

The recognition of the benefits of staggered work hours and flexitime have led to the widespread implementation of varying starting times across firms in CBDs and even within firms. In this chapter we are going to model this more recent type of situation. However, as will be pointed out, our analytical model can also be directly applied to the traditional fixed starting time situation by appropriate redefinition of variables.

In modeling staggered work hours, two main features must be accounted for. First, people have a most desired work schedule, based on their own "biological clock" and based on the scheduling of home and family activities. Movements away from this time impose scheduling costs for the commuter. Of course, these scheduling costs will vary with family composition and employment status (O'Malley, 1974; and Guttman, 1975). Section 2 of this chapter focuses on these scheduling considerations.

Second, staggered work hours may affect production activity. Neoclassical production analysis suggests two opposing effects. Within a firm, the concept of diminishing marginal returns indicates that it would be best to uniformly distribute employee work hours over the 24-hour day. This would enhance labor marginal productivity and reduce capacity requirements. On the other hand, urban economic theory suggests that there must be external economies of scale in production in cities connected with the interaction of firms' employees in business districts. White-collar jobs involve extensive communications and interactions with corresponding people in opposing or complementary firms. The larger the mass of people at work in a business district the greater will be their individual productivity. Given the initial very negative reactions by firms to altering their starting times from the traditional schedule in their business district (O'Malley, 1974), it would appear that this latter productivity effect is perceived as being dominant. This perception, of course, would explain the persistence of traditional identical work schedules in business districts, despite the potential benefits of modifications. Section 3 of this chapter concentrates on these productivity impacts.

In analyzing peak-period traffic, we use the first model of a congested system discussed in Chapter 7. Groups or flows of cars from the start of the peak period are continuously leaving the suburb and moving onto the road, traveling the road as a group, and then exiting in the CBD. For an entrant, the speed of travel is solely a function of the number (or flow) of cars entering the system at the same time the entrant does, and this speed of travel is constant throughout the journey.[1]

---

[1] Given an equilibrium array of departure times, it must be the case that people leaving at time t will not catch up to people who left at time $t - 1$ and people who leave at time $t + 1$ will not catch up to people who left at time t. Otherwise, the speed of travel for entrants can no longer be constant throughout the journey and no longer just a function of the number of people entering at the same time they do. It must be true that if traffic departure flows onto the road are increasing continuously, people leaving at time t never encounter travelers from other departure times. Those ahead of them travel faster, those behind slower. However, if the opposite is true, we must ask if those behind catch up to those ahead. This can be determined by examining exit times, where if people who leave at time t exit after those who left at $t - 1$, then those behind do not catch up. Travel time on the road is T_r, and the exit time for people leaving at t is $t + T_r$. If $|dT_r/dt| < 1$, the reduction in travel time for those traveling later is not enough for them to catch up given the difference in departure times. In our model we will avoid this problem.

2.   A SIMPLE STAGGERED WORK-HOURS MODEL

In a staggered work hour equilibrium, commuters in the business district choose a fixed starting time from the equilibrium distribution of starting times. We assume all commuters work the same fixed number of hours, although we shall investigate the effects of relaxing this assumption. I also comment on a flexitime model, where starting times are not fixed, but are chosen anew each day by commuters. This type of situation yields the same kind of results as a staggered work hour equilibrium. In this section we assume there are no productivity effects on wages from choosing different work schedules. I incorporate that rather complex consideration in Section 3.

2.1   Commuter Decision-Making and Equilibrium

The Consumer Problem

Commuters seek to minimize the costs of commuting, defined as traveling and scheduling costs. Our representation is consistent with a simple utility maximization problem, allocating time over the day.[2] For a situation with identical preferences, a representation commuter seeks to minimize

$$T(A(s)) + C(s - \bar{s}). \tag{8.1}$$

The $T(\cdot)$ and $C(\cdot)$ functions represent travel and scheduling costs, respectively. I now define their arguments. First, s is the time this worker chooses to start work. The worker chooses s either by choosing to work in a firm with a starting time for all its employees of s or by choosing s from the range of starting times of a firm that offers its employees a choice of different work schedules. The endogenous starting and ending times of the morning commuting period in terms of arrivals in the business district are s_1 and s_2, respectively. Thus $s_1 \leq s \leq s_2$. Since all workers work the same number of hours H, the evening range of departure times are $s_1 + H$ to $s_2 + H$. The fixed work hour assumption also implies that the morning pattern of arrivals between s_1 and s_2 is identical to the evening pattern of departures between $s_1 + H$ and $s_2 + H$.

The term $A(s)$ refers to both the total equilibrium number of arrivals in the business district at time s and the number of departures at time $s + H$.

---

[2] It is sufficient to assume a utility function separable in leisure, scheduling, and market goods, so that, for example, the consumer problem is to maximize $f(T - t(s)) + g(s - \bar{s}) + U(x)$ subject to the budget constraint $y - P_x x = 0$. Nonworking time is T and $t(s)$ represents travel time so that $T - t(s)$ is leisure time.

Total daily (going and returning) travel costs for a commuter thus are

$$T(A(s)), \qquad T'(1) = 0, \qquad T'(A > 1) > 0, \qquad T'' \geq 0. \qquad (8.2)$$

People's cost of travel is related to their speed of travel, where declining speeds imply higher costs due to higher time and frustration costs for a given trip distance. Speed of travel for a commuter in turn is related to the number of people on the road at the same time as the commuter, where an increase in the flow (measured by arrivals) of traffic increases congestion and reduces travel speed. Thus T' is a measure of the congestion rate. The restriction that $T'' > 0$ is consistent with empirically estimated congestion functions (Inman, 1978). The implicit assumptions that all commuters travel on one system (or are distributed in proportion to capacity over an existing set of systems) and that they all travel the same distance can be relaxed in applying the model, but this relaxation generates no new principles.

Note that $T(\cdot)$ in Equation (8.2) is also a function of capacity levels K on the road system. In general, $\partial T(\cdot)/\partial K < 0$, or expansions in capacity for the same number of travellers will reduce travel times and costs. Sections 2.2 and 2.4 examine capacity considerations.

The $C(s - \bar{s})$ function in (8.1) is the opportunity cost of working time. This opportunity cost has its lowest value for work schedules with a starting time of $\bar{s}$, this being the schedule that is best coordinated with family activities, daylight hours, etc. As starting times move away from $\bar{s}$ in either direction, opportunity costs rise, perhaps imperceptibly at first and then more rapidly as inconveniences grow. For simplicity, we assume that all commuters have the same $C(\cdot)$ function and that it is symmetrical about $\bar{s}$.[3] Thus

$$C(t - \bar{s}; t - \bar{s} = -x < 0) = C(s - \bar{s}; s - \bar{s} = x > 0), \qquad \text{all } x$$

$$dC/ds \equiv \dot{C} \begin{Bmatrix} \leq \\ = \\ > \end{Bmatrix} 0 \qquad \text{if} \quad s \begin{Bmatrix} \leq \\ = \\ > \end{Bmatrix} \bar{s}, \qquad (8.3)$$

$$\ddot{C} > 0.$$

The $C(\cdot)$ function is graphed in Figure (8.1a).

Note that the $C(\cdot)$ function could be simply redefined as a waiting time—late arrival cost function in the traditional fixed starting time model. In that case $\bar{s}$ would be the fixed starting time. While in that case it would be desirable to make $C(\cdot)$ asymmetrical about $\bar{s}$ to deal with the presumably stiff costs of being consistently late for work, our model could be applied directly to analyzing the traditional peak-hour situation.

---

[3] Nonsymmetry of C about $\bar{s}$ is easy to introduce. Varying $\bar{s}$'s is not because it raises the messy situation of a multinodal distribution of arrivals.

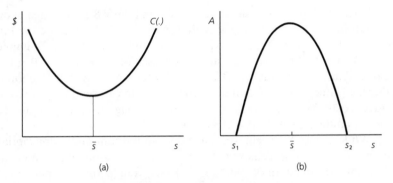

FIGURE 8.1   Cost and arrival functions.

Commuter Equilibrium

For our identical commuters to be in equilibrium two basic conditions must be met. First, in Equation (8.1) they must all have the total costs of commuting, or

$$T'\dot{A} + \dot{C} = 0$$

$$\dot{A} \equiv dA/ds \tag{8.4}$$

$$\dot{C} \equiv dC/ds$$

Second, all commuters must arrive during the peak time, s_1 to s_2; or where $\bar{N}$ is all commuters

$$\bar{N} = \int_{s_1}^{s_2} A(s)\,ds. \tag{8.5}$$

Equations (8.4) and (8.5) may be used to illustrate an equilibrium pattern of arrivals. Rearranging (8.4), given the definition of $C(\cdot)$ in (8.3),

$$\dot{A} = -\frac{\dot{C}}{T'}\begin{Bmatrix}>\\=\\<\end{Bmatrix}0 \qquad \text{if} \quad s\begin{Bmatrix}<\\=\\>\end{Bmatrix}\bar{s}. \tag{8.6}$$

Also,

$$\ddot{A} = -[\ddot{C} + (\dot{A})^2 T'']/T' < 0.$$

This concave equilibrium pattern of arrivals is depicted in Figure 8.1b. The symmetrical pattern of arrivals about $\bar{s}$ is necessary for equilibrium, given the symmetrical $C(\cdot)$ function. This can be shown by interpretation of (8.6) or by inspection of (8.1). Since $C(\cdot)$ has the same value at $\bar{s} - \delta$ and $\bar{s} + \delta$ for all δ, in equilibrium in (8.1), $T(A(\bar{s} - \delta)) = T(A(\bar{s} + \delta))$ for all δ, implying that $A(\bar{s} - \delta) = A(\bar{s} + \delta)$, or that arrivals are symmetric about $\bar{s}$.

In examining the overall arrival pattern in Figure 8.1b, the area under the equilibrium pattern must equal $\bar{N}$ in Equation (8.5). In interpreting this, symmetry also implies that $\bar{s} - s_1 = s_2 - \bar{s}$, and Equation (8.2) implies $A(s_1) = A(s_2) = 1$. Arrivals start at 1, because for $A > 1$, $T' > 0$, or T increases. Thus, if $A > 1$ at $s_1[s_2]$, one commuter could arrive a fraction of time earlier [later] and for an infinitesimal change in $C(\cdot)$ significantly reduce his travel costs. More generally, if the onset of congestion only occurs for $A > m$ commuters, then $A(s_1) = A(s_2) = m$.

While Figure 8.1b represents a stable equilibrium under appropriate assumptions once it is achieved, there is some question about how the equilibrium is attained. In postulating (8.1), (8.4), and (8.5), the implication is that commuters know the distribution of arrivals and the set of travel costs facing them, implying that this pattern is repeated day after day and people develop consistent commuting patterns. There is no Walrasian auctioneer auctioning off starting times each day at the breakfast tables, and commuters must sort themselves out by themselves. While this may be a strong requirement, it is consistent with observed traffic patterns. Moreover, a similar equilibrium would arise in a model where commuters in choosing s are maximizing expected benefits, given a perceived distribution of possible commuting costs associated with each s and ways of acquiring information about commuting costs at different times. Second, with no production effects, firms presumably are willing to stagger work hours in response to employee demands. This can involve internal staggered hours or staggering across firms. To move from a nonstaggered equilibrium to the one in Figure 8.1b, firms would have to be willing to adjust starting times in response to employee demands. The inducement to adjust would be workers' willingness to shift to firms offering better work schedules in a nonequilibrium situation.

Equilibrium with Nonidentical Preferences

We can incorporate differences in preferences into this model by, say, allowing the shape of the $C(\cdot)$ function to vary while maintaining the same best starting time $\bar{s}$ for all commuters. (We can vary $\bar{s}$'s also but this raises the messy possibility of the equilibrium involving a multinodal distribution of arrivals.) Suppose there are two groups of people B and D where $|\dot{C}_B(x)| > |\dot{C}_D(x)|$, all $x \geqslant 0$. Equilibrium is pictured in Figure 8.2.

Each group of people has an Equation (8.1) and a corresponding equilibrium condition in Equations (8.4) and (8.5). At any point of overlap of these arrivals, in Equation (8.5) both groups will have the same T' (we could, of course, allow this to differ also). Thus people B with their steeper $C(\cdot)$ function will require a higher $\dot{A}$ for equilibrium—hence the shape of the A curves in Figure 8.2. The equilibrium configuration in Figure 8.2 with D people

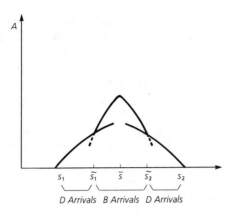

FIGURE 8.2   Nonidentical arrivals.

commuting on the tails is the only one that satisfies the necessary global equilibrium condition that, if people alter their s's, they cannot be made better off. For example, if D people move from the interval $s_1, \tilde{s}_1$ to $\tilde{s}_1, \bar{s}$ (or vice versa for B people), they are worse off. The extension of the A curve for D people as we move beyond $\tilde{s}_1$ indicates from (8.5) the level of arrivals necessary to yield D people equal benefits with an arrival time in $s_1, \tilde{s}_1$. Since equilibrium arrivals for B people are higher than this, D people would be worse off if they moved into the interval $\tilde{s}_1, \bar{s}$. No other equilibrium configuration of arrivals meets this criterion. For example, if we put B people on the tails in a redrawn Figure 8.2, they would benefit by moving from their $s_1, \tilde{s}_1$ interval to the $\tilde{s}_1, \bar{s}$ interval.

Note that, for such an equilibrium, if firms employ both B and D people they will have to offer differing starting times for their two groups of employers. There is also the empirically testable hypothesis, that, if the $C(\cdot)$ functions vary across people in some identifiable way (e.g., by number and age of family members), we should expect to see similar people having two arrival intervals—one before and one after the height of peak arrivals.

2.2   Impact of Capacity Investments on Equilibrium

A model that incorporates scheduling costs is critical to a proper evaluation of the impact of significant road capacity expansions. Most preinvestment evaluations are done in a static context, assuming a fixed pattern of arrivals and evaluating the travel time reductions for that fixed pattern. However, evaluations of capacity expansions tend to show very limited travel time reductions at the height of the peak period and dramatic changes in the patterns of traffic flows. This is predictable from our model.

A basic impact of significant capacity investments is to allow traffic to bunch up around $\bar{s}$, or to allow more people to arrive near their most desired time. This bunching up will also reduce the length of the peak period, $s_2 - s_1$. However, the extent to which travel times around the height of the peak are actually reduced may be quite limited.

The impact of increasing capacity K is illustrated in Figure 8.3, where the equilibrium pattern A_2 has the same total commuters $\bar{N}$ as A_1 but a larger capacity, or $K_2 > K_1$. To show that this is the impact of expanding K, we first note that both curves in Figure 8.3 have the same areas ($\bar{N}$) under them and both must be symmetric about $\bar{s}$. Second, by differentiation of Equation (8.4) holding s and A constant (i.e., $d\dot{C} = 0$),

$$\left.\frac{d\dot{A}}{dK}\right|_{s,A} = -\frac{\partial T'/\partial K}{T'}\dot{A}\left\{\begin{matrix}>\\=\\<\end{matrix}\right\}0 \quad \text{if} \quad \dot{A}\left\{\begin{matrix}>\\=\\<\end{matrix}\right\}0. \tag{8.7}$$

In (8.7) $\partial T'/\partial K < 0$, or we assume capacity expansion reduces the congestion level for any A. Thus in Figure 8.3 for any point of cross-over of the two equilibrium curves, because $|\dot{A}|_{K_2} > |\dot{A}|_{K_1}$, the A_2 curve must cut the A_1 curve *from below*. For this reason the curves can only cross once on each side of $\bar{s}$ and, because each curve contains the same area under it, $s_1^2 > s_1^1$ and $s_2^2 < s_2^1$.

2.3 The Impact of Congestion Pricing

The extent of staggering work hours depicted in Figure 8.1 is not optimal. When commuters, through their firms, adopt work schedules, they do not account for the effect of their decisions on other people's travel costs—

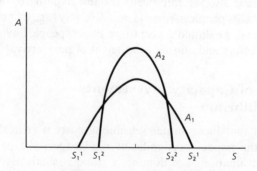

FIGURE 8.3 Investment impact.

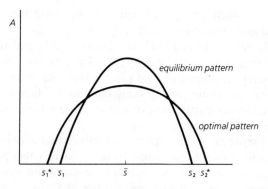

FIGURE 8.4   Optimal pattern.

raising costs for those with the same schedules and lowering costs for all other schedules. This externality, of course, is a version of the traditional congestion externality. Here the externality at any s is $T'A$, or the increase in travel costs if one more person commutes at s multiplied by the number of commuters affected.

To derive an optimal arrival pattern for any capacity level, we minimize overall commuting costs

$$\int_{s_1}^{s_2} A(s)[T(A(s)) + C(s - \bar{s})) \, ds, \tag{8.8}$$

given $\bar{N} = \int_{s_1}^{s_2} A(s) \, ds$. Rearranging the Euler equation [where the state variable is accumulated arrivals at time s, $N(s) = \int_{s_1}^{s} A(s) \, ds$ and $\dot{N} = A(s)$],

$$\dot{A} = \frac{-\dot{C}}{2T' + T''A} \left\{ \begin{matrix} > \\ = \\ < \end{matrix} \right\} 0 \quad \text{as} \quad s \left\{ \begin{matrix} < \\ = \\ > \end{matrix} \right\} \bar{s}. \tag{8.9}$$

Given $T'' \geq 0$, all other necessary conditions for an optimum are satisfied. Boundary conditions require that, at s_1 and s_2, $-[A(s_1)]^2 T'(A(s_1)) = -[A(s_2)]^2 T'(A(s_2)) = 0$. Thus $A(s_1) = A(s_2) = 1$ (minimal flows), given $T'(1) = 0$, as in an equilibrium pattern.

The optimal pattern of arrivals is depicted in Figure 8.4. Since for any A and s, $|\dot{A}_{\text{opt}}| < |\dot{A}_{\text{equil}}|$ from Equations (8.6) and (8.9), at any crossover point of the curves the A_{opt} curve *must* cut the A_{equil} curve from above as depicted. For this reason, *given the same total flows* (areas under the A curves), $s_1^* < s_1$ and $s_2^* > s_2$. Thus the impact of congestion pricing is to reduce the traffic flows around $\bar{s}$, where congestion is heaviest.

To achieve such an optimal solution, we could impose the usual congestion toll on commuters, here equal to AT', the measure of the congestion externality. Adding AT', to Equation (8.1) and differentiating yields the equilibrium flows depicted by (8.9). The tolls that are heaviest at $\bar{s}$ eliminate the heavy congestion around $\bar{s}$ and induce commuters to spread out their travel and work starting and quitting times to s's where tolls are lighter. In this case, in choosing starting times commuters are made to account for the external effects of their decisions.

In this simple model, an optimal solution could also be attained by taxing firm starting times. Firms would be taxed $A(s)T'(A(s))$ per worker for workers starting at time s. The tax would be passed onto workers through wage adjustments relative to workers starting at times s_1 and s_2, where $AT' = 0$. The institutional advantage of imposing the tax this way is that collection is easy, compared to the economic and political problems of taxing commuters directly.

The viability of this second taxation procedure depends on three assumptions. First, everyone travels on the same mode so that AT' is equal for all commuters at any time; second, car pooling does not occur. These first two assumptions are simply a statement that taxing starting times does not provide the correct incentives to adjust modes and occupants per car on roads. The final assumption is either that all workers in a firm start at the same time or else that wages may differ for similar workers in the same firm. Clearly, within a firm, for there to be an equilibrium with similar workers starting at different times, wages must vary by starting time as taxes vary. This could be institutionally difficult, although wages do vary by 8-hour shifts in a variety of industries. It is easiest to assume that all workers in a firm start at the same time, so equilibrium under taxation only requires some wage adjustment across firms. This wage difference problem will be raised again in Section 3.

2.4 Role of Toll Revenues and Capacity Considerations

The revenue raised from congestion tolls is the key to demonstrating how in practical examples the imposition of a toll improves the welfare of commuters on the tails of the arrival distribution. For example, in Figure 8.4 people at s_1^* and s_2^* relative to s_1 and s_2 have unchanged travel costs but *higher* $C(\cdot)$ costs. To show that they actually gain from imposing congestion tolls, it is necessary to bring in revenue considerations. Commuters on the tails of the distribution (and, in fact, at all starting times) gain in net once the toll revenue raised is uniformly distributed back to the commuters in a lump gift form. This is why A_{opt} in Figure 8.4 represents a welfare maximum.

Another way to view the problem is to bring in capacity cost considerations. The collection of toll revenue reduces or eliminates other levies imposed prior to the introduction of tolls that were needed to finance capital costs. If the prior levy was an annual or daily lump-sum fee on users only covering capital costs, people throughout the arrival distribution benefit in net from congestion tolls because the reduction in lump-sum fees for users exceeds any increase in day-to-day costs [additional $C(\cdot)$ costs for people on the tails and the advent of high tolls for people nearer the peak of arrivals].

Toll revenues are also intimately related to optimal capacity evaluation. Optimal capacity is that which equates the marginal benefits of *infinitesimal* capacity expansion (so the pattern of arrivals may be held fixed) with marginal costs. If capacity is denoted by K and the price per unit of capacity is $1, adding K to Equation (8.8) yields an optimal capacity condition of

$$- \int_{s_1}^{s_2} A \, \partial T / \partial K \, ds = 1. \tag{8.10}$$

If $T(\cdot)$ is homogeneous of degree zero in A and K, so that a doubling of capacity and traffic flows leaves travel speeds unchanged, just as in Chapter 7 we can show that tolls from optimal congestion pricing just cover optimal capacity costs. Capacity costs equal $K[\int_{s_1}^{s_2} A(\partial T / \partial K) \, ds]$ if (8.10) is satisfied. Tolls equal $\int_{s_1}^{s_2} A(A \, \partial T / \partial A) \, ds$. Thus tolls equal capacity costs because T being homogeneous of degree zero implies $-K \, \partial T / \partial K = A \, \partial T / \partial A$. If tolls exceed capacity costs, that implies capacity levels are too low; or, if $\int_{s_1}^{s_2} A(A \, \partial T / \partial A) \, ds > K$, then $\int_{s_1}^{s_2} A(A \, \partial A / \partial T) \, ds = \int_{s_1}^{s_2} (-A)(K \, \partial T / \partial K) \, ds > K$ and hence

$$\int_{s_1}^{s_2} A \, \partial T / \partial K < 1.$$

Note, in moving from equilibrium (zero) to optimal congestion pricing, optimal capacity levels should change, which is not accounted for in Figure 8.4. In general, if a transport planner satisfied (8.10) for the equilibrium prior to tolls, then the optimal capacity will be less than the equilibrium because the elimination of the heavy arrivals around $\bar{s}$ reduces the need for capacity. In that case the movement to optimal investment along with optimal pricing would tend to spread out arrival patterns even more in Figure 8.4.

2.5 Extensions

There are a variety of ways to extend the model. Most are not easy. In our specific model everyone travels the same distance on the same road and works the same number of hours. Having multiple roads in a deterministic model is fairly easy to introduce, since in equilibrium all that is required is that consumers spread themselves out across roads to equalize total travel costs. Having different travel distances on the *same* road is beyond our congestion formulation. Since the number of travelers and congestion will increase as we move in toward the business district, the problem must be modeled in a congestion situation where, say, the speed of travel is a function of the total system load as in Agnew (1976) (see Chapter 7, Section 1). Connecting this into our problem with *non*steady state traffic flows presents a type of problem that has yet to be solved. Introducing variable hours of work where hours of work would vary with starting time is possible but can present complications.

Finally, we note that the current model can easily be adapted to a waiting time situation where people arrive late and early around a single work starting time $(\bar{s})$. The adoption simply involves changing variable and function labels and making a decision about how to specify exit times (in terms of whether you arrived late or early). The current model also is a model of flexitime where commuters can choose from day to day their work starting time, assuming consistent behavior and ignoring the elements of uncertainty introduced.

3. PRODUCTIVITY EFFECTS AND SCHEDULING

The introduction of production effects serves two purposes: One is to illustrate the nature and characteristics of possible production equilibria under staggered work hours, and the second is to raise certain institutional problems involved in sustaining a staggered work hours equilibrium. By necessity this section is quite technical.

We assume each firm has an instantaneous production function at time t of the form

$$g(N(t))an(s).$$

The firm's own work force is given by $n(s)$, and the coefficient a represents its internal technology. Thus for simplicity we are ignoring diminishing returns within the firm—a factor viewed by firms as being unimportant in staggered work hours. An external economy of scale shift factor is represented by $g(N(t))$, where $N(t)$ is the total number of employees working in the business district at time t. The specifications $g' > 0$ and $g'' < 0$ capture the primary production problem associated by firms with staggered work hours. If a firm shifts to an early schedule where $N(t)$ is very low, productivity will be low because its employees will have fewer employees in other firms in the business district to interact and do business with.

Firm profits per employee starting work at time s are

$$\pi(s) = [H - (s_2 - s_1)]g(\bar{N})a + \int_s^{s_2} g_0(N(t))a\, dt$$

$$+ \int_{s_1+H}^{s+H} g_1(\bar{N} - N(t))a\, dt - W(s). \tag{8.11}$$

The term H is the fixed length of work day, s_1 is the beginning time of morning arrivals, and s_2 is the ending time. Given a commuting period of $s_2 - s_1$, any firm has $H - (s_2 - s_1)$ hours when all workers are present in the business district and thus production by one of its employees during this interval is $[H - (s_2 - s_1)]g(\bar{N})a$, where $\bar{N}$ is total business district work force.

Moving to the second expression on the right-hand side of (8.11), $N(t)$ is the number of employees at work in the business district at time t. Thus $N(t)$ is accumulated arrivals, or

$$N(t) = \int_{s_1}^{s_2} A(s)\, ds, \qquad \dot{N} = A(s). \tag{8.12}$$

Therefore, a worker's production from the time he or she arrives, s, until all workers have arrived is $\int_s^{s_2} g_0(N(t))a\, dt$. Turning to the third expression, in the evening, people exit from the business district in the same order that they arrived. Total employees at time $t + H$ are

$$\bar{N} - \int_{s_1+H}^{s+H} A(s)\, ds = \bar{N} - N(t). \tag{8.13}$$

Equations (8.12) and (8.13) are illustrated for an equilibrium in Figure 8.5.

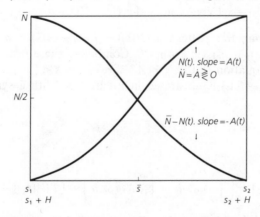

FIGURE 8.5   Arrivals and departures with production effects.

Given (8.13), a worker's production during the evening rush period before he leaves is $\int_{s_1+H}^{s+H} g_1(\bar{N} - N(t))a\,dt$. Note $g_0(x) \equiv g_1(x)$ all x, or the 0 and 1 subscripts only designate morning versus evening production, not differences in functional form.

Given how wages vary in equilibrium with starting time s, firms choose s to maximize profits. Alternatively, given identical production functions and workers, $d\pi/ds = 0$ for all s in any stable equilibrium. Otherwise, further shifting among starting times will occur. Differentiating (8.16), we see that equilibrium requires that

$$a(g_1 - g_0) = W. \tag{8.14}$$

The definition of the commuter's problem and commuter equilibrium must be adjusted to account for these wage effects. We now assume commuters seek to maximize wages net of commuting costs, or to maximize

$$W(s) - T(A(s)) - C(s - \bar{s}). \tag{8.15}$$

Differentiating (8.15) and combining with (8.14), we find for commuters to have equal net benefits from working that

$$\dot{A} = \frac{a(g_1 - g_0) - \dot{C}}{T'}, \qquad \ddot{A} < 0. \tag{8.16}$$

An equilibrium solution, such as depicted in Figure 8.1, where the arrival pattern is symmetric about $\bar{s}$ satisfies (8.16) and equilibrium conditions on boundary points, where $\pi(s_1) = \pi(s_2)$ given $W(s)$ from (8.21). If arrivals are symmetric about $\bar{s}$, then from Figure 8.1 $N(\bar{s}-\delta)=\bar{N}-N(\bar{s}+\delta)$, all δ; and thus

$$g_1(\bar{N} - N(\bar{s} - \delta)) - g_0(N(\bar{s} - \delta)) = -[g_1(\bar{N} - N(\bar{s} + \delta)) - g_0(N(\bar{s} + \delta))] > 0.$$

Note for a symmetric pattern $g_0(N(\bar{s})) = g_1(\bar{N} - N(\bar{s})) = g(\bar{N}/2)$ so that $[g_1\bar{N} - N(\bar{s} - \delta)] - g_0(N(\bar{s} - \delta)) > 0$. Combining these results with Equation (8.3), in Equation (8.16) $\dot{N} = \dot{A} > [<]0$, as $s < [>]0$. This pattern of $N(t)$ and $N - N(t)$ is illustrated in Figure 8.5. With a symmetrical arrival pattern,

$$s_2 - \bar{s} = \bar{s} - s_1,$$

where

$$\pi(s_1) - \pi(s_2) = \left(\int_{s_1}^{s_2} g_0 a\,dt - \int_{s_1+H}^{s_2+H} g_1 a\,dt \right) - [T(A(s_1)) - T(A(s_2))]$$

$$- [C(s_1 - \bar{s}) - C(s_2 - \bar{s})] = 0 \qquad \text{if} \ \ \bar{s} - s_1 = s_2 - \bar{s}.$$

Note that as before, equilibrium at s_1 and s_2 requires congestion to approach zero, which given our functional assumptions implies that $A(s_1) = A(s_2) = 1$.

The new feature of equilibrium is that wages must vary according to starting time. The instantaneous marginal product of a worker is illustrated in Figure 8.6a, where $dg_0/ds > 0$ and $dg_1/ds = [dg_1/d(\bar{N} - N(s))][-A(s)] < 0$. The curves are not necessarily concave throughout. A worker starting at $\bar{s}$ has the highest total productivity during the peak periods—operating on the $\bar{s}$ to s_2 segment of MP(s) and the $s_1 + H$ to $\bar{s} + H$ segment of MP($s + H$), where MP is instantaneous marginal product. Total productivity of a worker declines as he moves away from $\bar{s}$ in either direction to lowest productivity at s_1 and s_2. Thus total daily wages should vary qualitatively as illustrated in Figure 8.6b.

Such required wage variations for identical skill workers may present an institutional impediment to attaining and sustaining staggered work hour equilibria. This may be a partial explanation of why staggered work hours was a nonexistent or minor feature of scheduling in business districts for so long. If we assume all similar-skill workers of each firm start at the same time, that at least would eliminate the need for wage variation for identical-skill workers in the same firm and would only require wage variation across firms. If we reintroduce scheduling taste [$C(\cdot)$ function] differences for identical-skill workers, then in Figure 8.2 workers will in part sort themselves out across firms by their tastes given the firms' starting times.

If we allow skill differences among workers, we will get the same type of equilibrium as illustrated in Figure 8.2. For example, suppose there are two groups of workers with productivity ga_1 and ga_2, where $a_1 > a_2$. Then, by similar arguments as for taste differences, in equilibrium a_1 people will arrive at times near $\bar{s}$ and a_2 people on the tails. This, of course, makes sense because

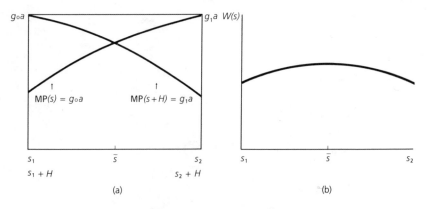

FIGURE 8.6   Productivity effects.

in general total productivity in Figure 8.4a is enhanced for starting times around $\bar{s}$, and it is most profitable to enhance (by a multiplicative term) the productivity of the most productive. If firms use both types of workers in production, then from Figure 8.2 their different types of workers must start work at different times and receive different wages on the basis of both basic productivity differences ($a_1 > a_2$) and starting time differences.

Two additional points should be noted. This requirement that wages differ across identical skill individuals according to their work schedules holds regardless of the specification of production effects (e.g., the introduction of diminishing returns) as long as production effects are present. Second, our results are consistent with the results to be obtained from flexitime models, where people must work the same number of hours but choose their starting time on a day-to-day basis. Flexitime would introduce the complication that the distribution of $T(A)$'s is uncertain on a day-to-day basis, as is the distribution of cumulated arrivals. Thus everyone operates on expected values, eliminating the deterministic nature of the model but not the basic principles.

Finally, we note that once again we can derive optimal commuting patterns. However, in this case there are now two externalities present: a congestion externality and an external scale economy externality. Thus, if a firm decides to put its starting times nearer $\bar{s}$, it has a negative external effect of increasing relative congestion but also a positive effect of increasing relative productivity in other firms. The trade-off of these external effects and the analysis of optimal arrival patterns and pricing is presented in Henderson (1981).

9

Issues in Urban Public Economics

In the next two chapters four topics of both recent and long-standing interest in the field of urban public economics are examined. Although the discussion is primarily focused on theoretical and conceptual issues, it is prompted by very practical and critical fiscal issues in cities. In this chapter I examine the incidence of the property tax, fiscal federalism, and the impact of intergovernmental grants, such as revenue sharing, on local govenment decision making, In the next chapter, I examine various aspects of the Tiebout model, especially as it relates to the process of fiscal fragmentation of metropolitan areas, or the formation of "bedroom" suburbs. Although the various topics are treated separately, they are closely linked, as will become apparent.

1. THE PROPERTY TAX

The property tax is used extensively in American cities to finance local public expenditures. As a tax on housing services, it is nominally a very heavy tax relative to taxes on other consumer goods, with tax payments effectively ranging from 10 to 30% of annual rental payments. It is also a comprehensive tax, covering not only residential land, structures, and improvements, but also commercial land and structures and often commercial capital formation,

171

inventories, and some consumer durables. In fact, excluding capital in the agricultural sector of the economy, the tax covers most of the private physical wealth of the nation. This fact plays a key role in the analysis of property tax incidence.

In analyzing the property tax I am concerned with two interrelated sets of questions and issues. The first concerns the distortions created by the property tax and the costs of these distortions. While this is not the issue I focus on in this chapter, I do comment on it at various times. What are these distortions? The property tax on residential housing may be viewed as an excise tax that raises the price of housing and lowers the return to producing housing. This distorts the consumption level of housing relative to other goods. As a tax on commercial capital and land, the property tax may raise the price of these inputs relative to other inputs, such as labor, and distort producer choices of production inputs. This tax on inputs of goods produced in urban areas should also raise the price of urban goods relative to goods not affected as much by the property tax, such as agricultural products and imports.

The second set of issues relates to the question of what is the incidence of the property tax, or who effectively (as opposed to nominally) pays the property tax and bears its burden. This is the issue I focus on. Do property taxes primarily come out of the pockets of consumers in the form of higher gross housing and retail prices (producer price plus tax), or are they passed back to owners of capital and land in the form of lowered returns to these factors? Of course, if housing is owner-occupied, this distinction between residents and owners of factors is basically eliminated. However, there remains the question in a dynamic context of under what conditions current permanent increases in property taxes are borne by past, current, or future owner-occupiers through changes in property values.

The answers to these questions determine whether the property tax is basically a progressive or regressive tax. Under one view in the literature, consumers of housing and retail goods tend to bear the burden of the part of the tax that falls on capital, and landowners tend to bear the burden of the part that falls on land. Given this analysis, the property tax is usually estimated to quite regressive. The other view in the literature inspired by Mieszkowski's (1972) work is that capital owners tend to bear the burden of the tax on capital. In this case, since lower-income people tend to rent rather than own housing, while middle- and upper-income people tend to be owner-occupiers, and since ownership of business capital is concentrated in the upper-income brackets, the property tax is estimated to be proportional or mildly regressive up through upper-middle-income ranges and then quite progressive thereafter. Aaron (1975) presented a variety of calculations illustrating these statements. Since these two views reach different conclusions, it is useful to sort out the issues involved; that is the focus of most of Section 1 of this chapter. I present a basic analysis and then discuss some of the unresolved issues in the literature.

Before proceeding with the comparisons, I should note that the incidence of the property tax is only half of the story. The other half is the incidence of benefits of government expenditures made from property tax revenue. Combining these two halves would tell us the incidence of the total fiscal system. Unfortunately, there is very little evidence on and analysis of this second incidence question.

1.1 Property Tax Incidence in the National Economy

This presentation of property tax incidence is based on the work in Mieszkowski (1972) and subsequent developments (e.g., Courant, 1977); Brueckner, 1981b; Hamilton, 1975, 1976). Mieszkowski's basic result is straightforward. Consider an economy composed of identical communities. Starting from a no-tax position, property taxes are imposed at the same rate in all communities. They are imposed on all capital (and land if it is in the model). Since the same rate is imposed nationwide and is imposed on all capital and land, the tax may be viewed as effectively a national tax on the assumed fixed supplies of capital and land. Since the factors taxed are fixed in supply, they will bear the entire burden of the tax. This means that the posttax returns to capital and landowners will fall by the full amount of tax, or the posttax costs to users of capital and land will be unchanged from the pretax level. In a supply and demand curve diagram, the tax shifts down the national demand for capital (or land) by the full amount of the tax, against a perfectly inelastic supply curve. Since then the posttax returns to capital, and landowners fall by the full amount of the tax, capital and landowners split the burden of the tax according to their relative shares in factor incomes. This result also means that there are no distortions created by the property tax since consumer and factor prices remain unchanged.

There are several criticisms of this analysis, which I note and some of which I analyze.

1. Communities may impose different tax rates, so that one might expect returns to capital to fall by the "national average" tax rate. Then, as Mieszkowski suggested, people in high-tax communities will pay [be reimbursed] through, for example, higher [lower] consumer prices for the excess [short fall] of their tax relative to the national average. Just how the national average should be computed has been the source of some debate (Courant, 1977). Second, just who will pay for local taxes in excess of the national average has also been the source of some debate, centering around the

assumption of whether residents are mobile or immobile between communities (Hamilton, 1976; Brueckner, 1981b; Wilson, 1982; Hobson, 1982). We shall explore both these issues in a simple model below.

2. Tax revenue raised is not spent on public goods. Revenue is either implicitly destroyed or returned to consumers as lump-sum grants. If revenue was spent on local public goods, Hamilton (1975) suggested that, since local public goods are valued by consumers, the tax could be viewed as a benefit tax that consumers are willing to and do pay. However, in a world of identical communities (and hence identical desired levels of public services and tax rates), Mieszkowski's result is basically unassailable. The property tax still shifts down the national demand for capital (or land) against a fixed supply curve. Only if something intervenes to stop the shifting down of these demand curves can the result be put in doubt. In Hamilton's (1975) world, in addition to the property tax, "perfect" zoning is imposed to prohibit the shifting down of the demand curves. This unusual feature is commented on in Section 1.2.

However, it is true that introducing local public goods as the raison d'être of property taxes changes the analysis. First, as explored in Henderson (1985b), introduction of local public services that are produced in the economy, introduces a property-tax-exempt sector (roads, parks, sidewalks, schools, etc.) in the national economy, into which capital (and land) can flow to escape property taxation. Just as in the analysis of corporate tax incidence (Harberger, 1974), the introduction of a tax-exempt sector alters the analysis of incidence and raises a variety of rich considerations that we do not explore here because they are beyond the scope of this presentation. Second, with explicit public goods the analysis of who pays for taxes in excess of the national average is changed. I show below that if people in high-tax communities desire the higher levels of public services they purchase, they will pay for the excess taxes. That is, at the margin (but not overall), the property tax is a benefit tax.

3. The national supplies of capital and land may not be fixed in a dynamic context. If the posttax returns to capital and landowners fall, over time these resources may be withdrawn from production (e.g., savings rates may fall). This possibility in the analysis of tax incidences is not normally explored and we only point out its existence here.

Tax Incidence in a One-Good World

I explore some of the issues raised above in the simplest model possible—a one-good world of identical individuals. I first specify the equations describing equilibrium within a community and then the equations describing equilibrium across communities. We start by assuming a two-community world, communities 1 and 2, and explore property tax incidence when the two communities impose different tax rates. The analysis of incidence is carried out in the traditional framework where all tax or tax increases are infinitesimal, so the primary results may be obtained through comparative static analyses.

Within each community the good produced and demanded is housing. Total housing demand is $N_i h(y, \hat{p}_i)$, where N_i is the population of the ith community, $h(\cdot)$ is an individual demand function, $\hat{p}$ is the gross price of housing in community i, and y is income exogenous to the model (i.e., exogenous endowments of manna, the numeraire good). Note this formulation also implies that capital and land rents are spent outside our communities by absentee owners. Housing demand equals housing supply $H(K_i, l_i)$, where l_i is the *fixed* endowment of land in community i, and K_i is the capital employed in community i (supplied from the national market). Thus the first equation for housing market equilibrium in basic and differentiated forms is

$$N_i h(y, \hat{p}_i) = H(K_i, l_i), \tag{9.1a}$$

$$\hat{N}_i - \eta_i \hat{\hat{p}}_i = \rho_{k_i} \hat{K}_i. \tag{9.1b}$$

In (9.1b) a circumflex ($\hat{\ }$) represents a rate of change; or, for example, $\hat{N}_i \equiv d \log N_i = dN_i/N_i$. The price elasticity of demand is given by $\eta_i \equiv -(\partial h/\partial \hat{p})(\hat{p}/h)$, and ρ_{ki} is capital's share in housing revenue assuming factors are paid according to marginal productivity conditions $[\rho_{ki} = (\partial H/\partial K_i)(K_i/H) = p_k K_i/pH$, for p the price of housing]. Note land employment does not change, given a fixed supply of land.

Equation (9.2) defines the gross price of housing in terms of the net price received by producers p and the tax rate t. In basic and differentiated form we have

$$\hat{p} = p(1 + t), \tag{9.2a}$$

$$\hat{\hat{p}} = \hat{p} + \tau, \quad \text{where} \quad \tau = d \log(1 + t) = dt/(1 + t). \tag{9.2b}$$

Equations (9.3a) and (9.3b) assume a perfectly competitive housing market and factors employed according to marginal productivity conditions. First, we have the price equals unit cost of production condition, where

$$p = p(p_k, p_l),$$

$$\hat{p} = \rho_{ki} \hat{p}_k + \rho_{li} \hat{p}_{li}, \tag{9.3b}$$

where in (9.3b) from Shephard's lemma $\partial p(\cdot)/\partial p_k = K_i/H_i$, so $\rho_{ki} = (K_i p_k)/(H_i p)$. The price of land in community i is p_{li}. Note p_k is not indexed by community since local prices must equal national prices, while the same is not true for p_{li}. Second, we define the elasticity of substitution in examining factor employment responses to price changes as (noting $\hat{l}_i = 0$)

$$\hat{K}_i = \sigma_i(\hat{p}_{li} - \hat{p}_k). \tag{9.4}$$

Rearranging (9.1b) and combining (9.1b)–(9.4) we get for later reference

$$\hat{p}_i = \frac{\hat{N}_i - \rho_{ki}\hat{K}_i}{\eta_i}, \tag{9.1c}$$

$$\hat{p}_{li} = \frac{\hat{p}_i - \rho_{ki}\hat{p}_k}{\rho_l}, \tag{9.3c}$$

$$\hat{p}_k = \frac{\hat{N}_i}{\eta_i} - \tau_i - \hat{K}_i\left(\frac{\rho_{li}}{\sigma_i} + \frac{\rho_{ki}}{\eta_i}\right). \tag{9.5}$$

Equations (9.1c) and (9.3c) are used to solve for internal community changes and (9.1c) and (9.5) for national changes. By taking (9.1c) and (9.5) for each community and combining with conditions in national markets, we can then solve for the national and local impacts of a set of property tax changes in all communities. With respect to national markets, we have two situations—one where population is immobile between communities and one where it is perfectly mobile.

National Markets: Immobile Local Residents

With immobile local residents the populations of the economy's two communities N_1 and N_2 are fixed. Equilibrium in national markets is defined by full employment of capital at a uniform national price, or

$$K_1 + K_2 = \bar{K}, \tag{9.6a}$$

$$\hat{K}_2 = -\alpha_K \hat{K}_1, \qquad \alpha_K \equiv K_1/K_2. \tag{9.6b}$$

To solve for the national change in p_k in response to tax changes τ_1 and τ_2, we set $\hat{N}_1 = \hat{N}_2 = 0$ in (9.5) and substitute in (9.6b) for $\hat{K}_2$ in Equation (9.5) for community 2 and then substitute the resulting equation into Equation (9.5) for community 1, solving out $\hat{K}_1$. The result is

$$\hat{p}_k = -\frac{\left(\dfrac{\rho_{k2}}{\eta_2} + \dfrac{\rho_{l2}}{\sigma_2}\right)\alpha_K\tau_1 + \left(\dfrac{\rho_{k1}}{\eta_1} + \dfrac{\rho_{l1}}{\sigma_1}\right)\tau_2}{\left(\dfrac{\rho_{k2}}{\eta_2} + \dfrac{\rho_{l2}}{\sigma_2}\right)\alpha_K + \left(\dfrac{\rho_{k1}}{\eta_1} + \dfrac{\rho_{l1}}{\sigma_1}\right)}. \tag{9.7a}$$

If the communities have identical constant returns to scale technologies, identical tastes [$h(\cdot)$ functions], identical population to land ratios, and start from identical tax positions (either no taxes or $t_1 = t_2$), then we can argue that the communities start from identical equilibria *in terms of equal housing and land prices* (not size). Then and only then (in the absence of a Cobb-Douglas world), we can argue that $\rho_{k2} = \rho_{k1}, \rho_{l1} = \rho_{l2}, \sigma_1 = \sigma_2$, and $\eta_1 = \eta_2$. In that simple case

$$\hat{p}_k = -\left(\frac{K_1}{K}\tau_1 + \frac{K_2}{K}\tau_2\right) = -\tau_1 - \frac{K_2}{K}(\tau_2 - \tau_1). \qquad (9.7b)$$

In Equation (9.7b) the national return on capital *falls* by the weighted sum of community tax rates, or by the rate in community 1 plus [minus] the weighted excess [deficit] of τ_2 over τ_1. That is, if $\tau_2 > \tau_1$, p_k falls by more than τ_1 and less than τ_2.

What happens in low-versus high-tax communities? Suppose community 1 is the low-tax community. The p_k falls by more than τ_1. Substituting (9.7b) back into (9.5) to solve for $\hat{K}_i$, we find

$$\hat{K}_1 = \left(\frac{\tau_2 - \tau_1}{\dfrac{\rho_l}{\sigma} + \dfrac{\rho_k}{\eta}}\right)\frac{K_2}{K}, \qquad \hat{K}_2 = -\frac{K_1}{K_2}\hat{K}_1.$$

Thus $\hat{K}_1 > 0$ and $\hat{K}_2 < 0$ when $\tau_2 > \tau_1$; and capital moves from the high to low tax community. From (9.1c) we know that

$$\hat{p}_i = -\frac{\rho_k}{\eta}\hat{K}_i.$$

Thus $\hat{p}_1 < 0$ while $\hat{p}_2 > 0$. Consumer housing prices fall in the low-tax community. Thus not only are all taxes paid for in the low-tax community but also consumers gain through reduced housing prices. The results for the high-tax community are the opposite—the price of capital does not fall by the full amount of their tax rate and consequently their housing prices rise. These are the basic notions contained in Mieszkowski (1972), Courant (1977), and Hobson (1982).

What about how land prices change? Substituting for $\hat{p}_k$ from (9.7b) back into (9.5) we solve for $\hat{K}_i$. Then substituting back into (9.1c) we solve for $\hat{p}_i$ and $\hat{p}_i$. Finally substituting into (9.3c) for $\hat{p}_k$ and $\hat{p}_i$ we find

$$\hat{p}_{l1} = -\tau_1 + \frac{K_2}{K}\frac{\rho_k}{\rho_l}[1 - (\eta\rho_l/\sigma + \rho_k)^{-1}(\tau_2 - \tau_1),$$

$$\hat{p}_{l2} = -\tau_2 - \frac{K_1}{K}\frac{\rho_k}{\rho_l}[1 - (\eta\rho_l/\sigma + \rho_k)^{-1}](\tau_2 - \tau_1).$$

In each community land prices decline by their tax rates plus an adjustment for tax rate differentials. Providing $(\eta\rho_l/\sigma + \rho_k) > 1$ (e.g., $\eta \to 1$ and $\sigma < 1$), the percentage decline in land prices is less [greater] than the tax rate increase in the low- [high-] tax community.

We also note that with immobile residents the introduction of public goods transformed from manna (i.e., public good production does not employ tax-exempt capital and land) leaves the analysis basically unchanged, even if consumers highly value the public services. In fact, providing the level of public services do not appear in the $h(\cdot)$ function, no new equations are needed to analyze property tax incidence, and the results are identical to what we derived above.

National Markets: Mobile Local Residents

With mobile local residents we have two equations additional to (9.6) defining national equilibrium. First, the national population must be divided between regions 1 and 2; and, second, utility levels must be equalized across regions. Thus

$$N_1 + N_2 = \bar{N}, \qquad (9.8a)$$

$$\hat{N}_2 = -\alpha_N\hat{N}_1, \qquad \alpha_N \equiv N_1/N_2, \qquad (9.8b)$$

$$V(y, \mathring{p}_1) = V(y, \mathring{p}_2), \qquad (9.9a)$$

$$\varepsilon_1\hat{\mathring{p}}_1 = \varepsilon_2\hat{\mathring{p}}_2, \qquad \varepsilon_i \equiv \frac{\partial V}{\partial \mathring{p}_i}\frac{\mathring{p}_i}{V}, \qquad (9.9b)$$

where $V(\cdot)$ is the indirect utility function.

Now to solve the model we combine equations (9.1c) and (9.5) for both communities with (9.6b), (9.8b), and (9.9b) to get Equation (9.7b), assuming both communities have the same constant returns to scale technologies, same preferences, and same initial taxes. (Note, now given labor is mobile, the fact that they start with the same land/population ratios is a result not assumption.) Thus the analysis of the impact of τ_1 and τ_2 on the national returns to capital is unchanged.

However, the analysis of what happens to communities internally changes. From (9.9b) we know $\hat{\mathring{p}}_1 = \hat{\mathring{p}}_2$. But equating (9.1c) for both communities given (9.6b) and (9.8b) implies $N_1 = \rho_k K_1$, which in turn implies $\hat{\mathring{p}}_1 = \hat{\mathring{p}}_2 = 0$. Thus utility levels and gross of tax housing prices are unaffected by the fact that communities impose differential taxes. Intercommunity differentials in local relative to national average tax rates are all reflected by differential changes in land prices. Since $\hat{\mathring{p}}_1 = \hat{\mathring{p}}_2 = 0$, then p declines by more in the high-tax community (i.e., it declines by the tax rate).This is reflected in land prices where

$$p_{l1} = -\tau_1 + \frac{\rho_k}{\rho_l}\frac{K_2}{K}(\tau_2 - \tau_1)$$

$$p_{l2} = -\tau_2 - \frac{\rho_k}{\rho_l}\frac{K_1}{K}(\tau_2 - \tau_1)$$

so that land rents in the high-tax community fall relative to those in the low-tax community.

Again, the introduction of public goods into the model does not affect the analysis of what happens to p_k in response to τ_1 and τ_2, *assuming* we *start* with identical equilibria in the two communities, although it complicates the analysis of internal changes. To solve for the change in p_k starting from identical communities, we simply equate the $\hat{p}_k$'s in communities 1 and 2 from Equation (9.5), solve for $\hat{N}_1$, and substitute back into one of the (9.5)'s to get Equation (9.7b).

In summary, the national return on capital falls by the same proportion whether residents are immobile or not, or whether the revenue is spent on public goods or not. The proportion by which the returns on capital fall lies between the tax rates in the high- and low-income communities. Except in examining the precise changes in land rents, the distinctions between mobility versus immobility and public goods versus no public goods do not matter in examining the national incidence of the property tax. These distinctions only matter in examining tax incidence at the margin—who pays for tax increases in a situation where only one community raises its tax rate.

While these results have been derived in a one-good world, they carry forward in qualitative terms to a multigood world. One primary simplification has been to ignore the impacts on wages of property taxes. In a multigood world, some of the local deviations in property taxes from the national average can be reflected in wages, as well as land rents (see Henderson, 1977, Chapter 2; Brueckner, 1981b; and Wilson 1982).

1.2   The Perspective of One Community

We now turn to the analysis of one community that raises its tax rate, while all other communities hold their's fixed. We now assume there are many communities so that each individually has no affect on national capital market prices. This analysis will tell us two things. First, it will tell what the burden is in one community at the margin if it raises its taxes. For example, if a low-tax community raises its rate slightly, while *in total* its tax rate may remain below the initial national decrease in capital prices relative to a nationwide no-tax world, at the margin its current tax increase may be paid for locally. Second, it will tell us what effective *marginal* cost of public goods a community may rationally perceive in public decision making. Again, we start with immobile residents.

Immobile Residents

Given that only one community out of many adjusts its tax rate, the price of capital to it is fixed so that $\hat{p}_k = 0$. Thus solving (9.5) for $\hat{K}_1$ and then (9.1c) we get

$$\hat{p} = \frac{1}{1 + \dfrac{\rho_l \eta}{\rho_k \sigma}} \tau < \tau.$$

Similarly solving (9.3b) we get

$$\hat{p}_l = -\frac{1}{\rho_l + \dfrac{\rho_k \sigma}{\eta}} \tau < 0.$$

Thus residents partially pay for increased taxes through higher housing prices; but prices rise by less than τ. The remainder is paid by lowered land costs and returns to landowners. These results demonstrate the basic conclusions of Mieszkowski (1972) in this context. The introduction of public goods does not change this analysis at all [providing $h(\cdot)$ does not contain public goods as an argument]. However, local residents in choosing g might perceive that their posttax cost of housing will rise less than a tax rate increase and that public-good costs to them are implicitly subsidized by lowered returns to landowners. This idea and how it might influence public-good provision will be discussed in Chapter 10.

Mobile Residents

If residents are perfectly mobile and only one community raises tax rates, then utility levels in that community must remain unchanged from the national level. From Equation (9.9a) this implies $\hat{p} = 0$ or $\hat{p} = -\tau$. This in turn implies from (9.3b) that

$$\hat{p}_l = -\tau/\rho_l.$$

Thus tax increases (which bring no benefits) are fully capitalized into lower land values. The mechanism for this is that population leaves the community, thereby reducing the local demand for the fixed land supply. These effects can be shown by noting that if $\hat{p}_l < 0$, then $\hat{K} < 0$ in (9.4) and thus $\hat{N} < 0$ from (9.1c).

This analysis changes completely if public goods are spent on valued public services, since the increased taxes may bring forth greater benefits than costs and result in in-migration. With public goods, Equation (9.9a) is revised so $V = V(y, \dot{p}, g)$, where g is the per person level of public services. We now have two new equations involved in describing partial equilibrium for the one community that raises tax rates. First, the supply of people to it is infinitely elastic at the going utility level in national labor markets, or

$$V(y, \dot{p}, g) - \bar{V} = 0, \tag{9.10a}$$

$$-(p + \tau) + \frac{g}{\dot{p}h} m\hat{g} = 0, \qquad m \equiv (\partial V/\partial g)/(\partial V/\partial y), \tag{9.10b}$$

where in differentiating (9.10a) we have utilized Roy's identity $[h = -(\partial V/\partial \dot{p})/(\partial V/\partial y)]$, substituted in (9.2b), and defined m as the marginal evaluation of public services. Second, the community has a balanced public budget constraint. Assuming identical residents and that publicly provided local services are what Samuelson termed "private" goods at the margin of consumption, we write the constraint as

$$N(tph) = cgN \tag{9.11a}$$

$$(1 - \eta)\hat{p} + \left(\frac{1 + t}{t} - \eta\right)\tau = \hat{g}, \tag{9.11b}$$

where c is the cost of a unit of public services. Note $dt/t = [(1 + t)/t]\tau$. Substituting (9.11a) into (9.10b) for $g/(\dot{p}h)$, we rewrite (9.10b) as

$$-(\hat{p} + \tau) + \left(\frac{t}{1 + t}\right)\frac{m}{c}\hat{g} = 0. \tag{9.10c}$$

To solve for the impacts of raising taxes to finance more public services, we combine (9.10c) and (9.11b) to solve out for $\hat{g}$. The result is

$$\hat{p} = -\frac{1 - \dfrac{m}{c}\left(1 - \dfrac{t}{1 + t}\eta\right)}{1 - \dfrac{m}{c}\dfrac{t}{1 + t}(1 - \eta)}\tau. \tag{9.12}$$

How do we evaluate (9.12)? Suppose voters set g to maximize indirect utility $V(y, \dot{p}, g)$ subject to the public budget constraint that $g = tph/c$. Substituting for g into $V(\cdot)$ and maximizing with respect to t, we get

$$\frac{\partial V}{\partial t} = \frac{\partial V}{\partial \hat{p}} p + V_g \left(\frac{ph}{c} + \frac{tp}{c} \frac{\partial h}{\partial \hat{p}} p \right) = 0,$$

where we have assumed that voters perceive no impacts of t on p but recognize the impacts of $\hat{p}$ changes on $h(\cdot)$. Dividing by $\partial V/\partial y$, invoking Roy's identity, and canceling out ph, we get after rearrangement an optimality condition that

$$m = c \left(1 - \frac{t}{1+t} \eta \right)^{-1}. \tag{9.13}$$

If $\partial V/\partial t > 0$ so tax rates are too low, then $m > c[1 - \eta t/(1+t)]^{-1}$; while, if $\partial V/\partial t < 0$ so tax rates are too high, then $m < c[1 - \eta t/(1+t)]^{-1}$.

We can now evaluate (9.12). If we are raising tax rates infinitesimally in the neighborhood of the "optimal" level of g in (9.13), then $\hat{p} = 0$ [from the numerator of (9.12)] and hence $\hat{\hat{p}} = \tau$ (also indicating that voters' perceptions that $\hat{p} = 0$ are correct). Thus in the neighborhood of optimal public-good level, this lowers potential utility levels. Then $\hat{p} < 0$, $\hat{\hat{p}} < \tau$, $\hat{p}_l < 0$, and $\hat{K} < 0$. housing prices. In this case no capitalization occurs [$\hat{p}_l = 0$ given $\hat{p} = 0$ and hence $\hat{K} = 0$ in (9.4)], and population increases where $\hat{N} = \eta\tau$ in (9.1c), as housing consumption falls in response to the increase in $\hat{p}$.

Suppose we are not starting from the optimal level of g. If g is underprovided ($\partial V/\partial t > 0$), then $\hat{p} > 0$ in (9.12) and hence $\hat{\hat{p}} > \tau$. This implies $\hat{p}_l > 0$ in (9.3b), and hence from (9.4), $\hat{K} > 0$. Hence from (9.1c) $\hat{N} > \tau\eta$. Thus raising public goods up toward the optimal level increases potential utility in the community, attracting new residents, which drives up land prices, so that the potential gain in utility is eliminated by capitalization into higher land and housing prices. However, if g is already overprovided and we then raise its level, this lowers potential utility levels. Then $\hat{p} < 0$, $\hat{\hat{p}} < \tau$, $\hat{p}_l < 0$, and $\hat{K} < 0$. Whether population increases or decreases depends on the parameters of the model and how far from the optimum we are $[\hat{N} = \hat{p}(\eta + \sigma\rho_k/\rho_l) + \eta\tau]$. Note that as long as $\hat{\hat{p}} > 0$, and thus housing and land demand are falling, there is more room for people in the community. In essence, raising g above an already too-high level makes landowners worse off, but allows for the possibility that community population can increase at the same utility level.

In summary, from a global perspective, property taxes are primarily paid for by capital owners and landowners; but if property taxes are spent on valued public services in a world where residents are mobile, then at the margin, residents bear the burden of property taxes. Thus if a community develops a higher than average demand for public services and raises its tax rate to finance those services, its residents will pay for the marginal increases in public services.

1.3   Variations in the Property Tax Rate within Cities and Capitalization

The final consideration involves the burden of variations in property tax rates *within* a metropolitan area. Since wages and capital rentals within the urban area are everywhere the same, internal variations in tax rates must be borne by housing consumers or landowners through variations in housing and land prices. We examine two reasons why effective tax rates may vary internally in a metropolitan area and the effect of these variations on housing and land prices.

Assessment Practices

The first reason tax rates may vary within an urban area is institutional in nature. Although the official property tax rate may be the same, the effective rate may vary because the assessed value of housing relative to the market value may vary. For example, as general housing values inflate over time, assessment practices may be such that the assessed value of housing is unevenly updated. In that case, houses whose assessed values have declined the most relative to their market values are lightly taxed compared to other houses. This would appear to be an inequitable situation that should be changed.

For the initial owners, who may be either occupants or rentiers, it is true that those whose homes have an assessed value that falls the most relative to market values benefit from being lightly taxed. Moreover, these lighter taxes mean that buyers would be willing to pay a premium to purchase these houses relative to more heavily taxed houses. This premium arises because market prices will adjust so that the gross price of equal-quality houses will be equalized across the metropolitan area, where this price is the purchase price plus the present value of future expected tax liabilities. Any lighter tax burden that is expected to persist is fully capitalized into a higher purchase price of a house. Therefore, initial owners benefit from the light taxes in each period they occupy the house and then a capital gain when they sell the house equal to the future discounted value of the lighter taxation.

However, because people who purchase these homes from initial owners pay the same gross price for housing as those who purchase relatively heavily taxed homes, any unexpected movement to change the situation and update and equalize assessment practices will only *create* (not eradicate) inequalities among newer owners. If assessments are changed to reflect current market prices, those people who paid high net-of-tax housing prices because of previously low taxes will suffer higher taxes and then a capital loss when they sell; those with previously high taxes will benefit from lower taxes and then a capital gain when they sell. In this case equity rests on maintaining the status quo or meeting expectations. Of course, regular announced reassessment is equitable since it is expected and fully reflected in housing prices.

Differing Fiscal Jurisdictions in a Metropolitan Area and Capitalization

The second reason why property tax rates may vary within a metropolitan area is that the area may be divided into different fiscal jurisdictions with differing tax rates. These differing rates may affect housing and land rents within and between communities. This affect on rents has implications discussed in Chapter 10 for the efficiency of land use, as well as for assessing the burden of property taxes. I illustrate this problem with a simple example taken from Hamilton (1976).

Suppose there are two types of consumers in a metropolitan area, high-housing consumers (h people) and low-housing consumers (l people). There are three communities: homogeneous high-housing, homogeneous low-housing, and mixed-housing communities (h, l, m communities). Because of zoning or developers' strategies in the provision of housing, h people consume the same level of housing h_h in the h and m communities and similarly for l people who consume h_l housing in the l and m communities. Due to institutional factors or because h and l people have the same demand for public services, the level of public services is the same in each community. These two assumptions allow us to isolate the pure effect of property tax differences on housing prices, without having to consider the effect of housing or public good consumption differences.

What differences in housing and land prices will arise in the metropolitan area? Comparing the h and m communities, in the m community the average tax base, or average housing consumption, is lower, due to the presence of l people, and to finance the same level of services requires a higher tax rate. High-income people are perfectly mobile between the two communities and hence must have the same level of utility. Given that they consume the same level of public services and housing in the two communities, in order for them to have equal utility, their expenditures on all other goods must be equalized between the communities. Given the same incomes and expenditures on all other goods, the gross expenditures on housing must be the same, or $p_h^m h_h (1 + t^m) = p^h h_h (1 + t^h)$ where p_h^m is the unit price of h housing in the m community, p^h is the price in the h community, and t^m and t^h are the corresponding tax rates. Therefore

$$p_h^m = p^h \frac{1 + t^h}{1 + t^m}.$$

Given $t^h < t^m$, $p_h^m < p^h$ by the amount needed to exactly compensate h people in the m community for their higher taxes. To express this in asset prices, as opposed to rental prices, one simply adds up the current and future discounted rental prices. Comparing the m and l communities, l people in the m community benefit from the presence of h people, relative to l people in the l community. Using the same type of reasoning as above, we can show

$$p_l^m = p^l \frac{1 + t^l}{1 + t^m}$$

where p^l, p_l^m, and t^l are, respectively, the prices of low-level housing in the l and m communities, and t^l is the tax rate in the l community. Since $t^l > t^m$, $p_l^m > p^l$. These price differences between the same-quality housing in different communities maintain a stable equilibrium with respect to residential movements. They reflect the fact that, through capitalization, housing prices adjust with tax rates to maintain the same gross price of housing for equal-quality housing, and thus fiscal differences are fully capitalized into housing prices.

While this makes sense, these equations only describe *relative* price differences between the same type of housing in different communities. We need to determine absolute prices as well, which brings out several problems in the analysis. To determine absolute prices, we first assume that the price of housing in the homogeneous communities is the same, or $p^l = p^h$; and it equals the opportunity cost of housing in its alternative use such as agriculture. Developers must be paid this price before they give their land to residential use in the l or h communities. If $p^l = p^h$, this implies from the above equations that

$$p_l^m > p^l = p^h > p_h^m.$$

If housing is malleable and lot size can be redesigned in the long run, this implies that some type of zoning will be needed to maintain this solution and stop the conversion in the m community of high-level housing into low-level housing. If there are competitive developers in the m community, not only will the owners of high-housing land be receiving a price below opportunity cost, but they will profit by switching their land to low-housing use, until prices are equalized in all uses. Given the derivation of the housing price equations (and even allowing housing consumption to vary between similar people in different communities), this equalization can only occur when the m community becomes homogeneous in one or the other of the land uses. This suggests that, without a type of perfect zoning that can fix housing consumption levels, these types of capitalization solutions cannot be maintained in the long run since the basis for capitalization cannot be maintained.

However, Hamilton (1976) pointed out that with respect to the actions of developers, the solution is stable without zoning if there is only *one* developer in the m community or if transfer payments among developers are feasible. This occurs because it can be shown that the average price of housing in the m community remains the opportunity cost of housing, which equals p^l and p^h.[1] However, even if the developer could be happy with the solution, it still may not be stable with respect to the actions of renters. Renters have an incentive to recontract, where h people in the m community would benefit by renting out portions of their low-priced housing to l people. Therefore, even if there is just one developer, zoning may still be needed to prevent renters from converting one type of land use to another.

2. FISCAL FEDERALISM

The federal government intervenes in the affairs of local governments by transferring tax money to regions and cities. In this section I examine the economic reasons behind such transfers. In Section 3, I examine the impact on local decision making of certain types of transfers.

In the literature there is an extensive discussion of equity and efficiency reasons for transferring money among regions, and by implication among cities (see Oates, 1972, for a review of the literature and issues). One set of grounds for the efficiency of transfers in a situation where labor is perfectly mobile is considered in the analysis of interregional externalities in Chapter 12. Another consideration deals with a situation where labor is assumed to be imperfectly mobile between regions, and real wages and employment rates are lower in some regions than others. National policies may be designed to encourage employment in depressed areas, on the equity grounds of redistributing income and resources to depressed areas. Given the high mobility of labor across regions and a variety of studies indicating that real wages are virtually equalized for similar-skilled people across regions, these policies no longer seem so relevant. Thus in this section I focus on three other sets of issues that may justify inter- or intraregional transfers initiated by a federal or state government. These are income redistribution, tax burden redistribution, and the fiscal fragmentation of metropolitan areas.

---

[1] The proof of this is simple but tedious; we outline one way of proving the proposition. We make use of expressions for each community, stating that taxes collected equal public service expenditures. Into the taxes equal dollar expenditures expression for the m community we substitute for p^m and p^m from the equations in the text. Into the result we substitute for t and t^h from the taxes equal expenditures expression for the homogeneous communities. If we simplify the resulting expression, substitute in for expenditures from the original taxes equal expenditures expression for the m community, and rearrange terms, the resulting expression states that the average price paid in the m community equals the opportunity cost of housing.

2.1 Income Redistribution

Income redistribution is the transfer of income to individuals who have low earning capacities. In our discussion, individual equity is considered a public good. In the past in the United States, income transfers to individuals were basically a local public service. A primary question is whether income redistribution should remain a local good or whether some type of federal intervention is needed to provide efficient levels of this good. There are definite reasons for maintaining it as a local, as opposed to a national, service. Local provision allows for the expression of local preferences and the determination of redistribution levels that local voters want in their region. Federalization of income redistribution imposes the same level of transfers and consumption of charity on all regions regardless of their preferences.

However, local redistribution presents certain externality problems because of population mobility. First, if a region raises its level of transfers, it may attract poor people from other regions. This raises the cost of giving to one's indigenous poor above the basic cost. This problem of attracting the unwanted poor of other regions should lead regions to underprovide redistribution services to their own poor (although stiff eligibility requirements can remove much of this problem). It is also possible that some regions will deliberately keep redistribution services low in an attempt to induce their poor to emigrate to other regions. Second, because regions have different compositions of rich and poor, the cost of a given level of redistribution per person, or the cost of giving, varies among regions. By moving to a richer region, a wealthy person can consume a given level of giving more cheaply. Moreover, poor regions do not have the tax capacity to finance adequate redistribution programs. This problem of varying capacities of regions to make redistribution payments can suggest that some type of federal intervention in the process is needed.

If federal intervention could provide some base level of redistribution, removing gross regional inequalities, it would remove most of the incentive for the rich and poor to move around to better their transfer position. Room could be left for expression of local tastes, by allowing regions to add to this base level on their own without penalty. This partial federalization would also be efficient to the extent that people in a locality have preferences defined not just over their own poor, but over the poor in all regions.

2.2 Tax Burden Redistribution

Money is sometimes transferred to regions to bring about a redistribution of the tax burden of financing expenditures within regions. Suppose the local tax system is regressive whereas the federal tax system is progressive. By raising federal taxes and redistributing the money to localities, dependence on local taxes is reduced and local taxes can thus be lowered (see Section 3); in this way a regressive tax system is replaced by a progressive one. These federal transfers redistribute the tax burden of financing local expenditures from lower- toward higher-income people. Of course, this result only occurs if the local tax system is less progressive than the federal tax system. In America, where local taxes are primarily property taxes, given the discussion in Section 1, it is unclear which tax system is more progressive, especially in the upper-income ranges. Therefore, reducing local dependence on property taxes may or may not redistribute the tax burden away from lower-income groups.

However, an even more basic problem is that localities may use combinations of tax systems (income, property, sales, etc.) which in aggregate are more or less progressive than the federal tax system because local voters want a tax system which is respectively either more or less progressive. There is no reason to assume the degree of progressivity imposed federally is either optimal nationally (and no rigorous general criterion to determine optimality) or optimal for the voters in each locality.

2.3 Externalities from Metropolitan Fiscal Fragmentation

There has been tremendous suburban population growth in recent decades combined with a leveling off of or even a decline in core city population in metropolitan areas. In the United States this suburbanization has involved fiscal fragmentation of metropolitan areas, where there may be 50 or more local jurisdictions in a large metropolitan area. The people who have suburbanized have tended to be higher-income people, whereas lower-income people have tended to remain behind in the core cities.

One explanation of the greater propensity of higher-income people to suburbanize is that, as cities grow, over time higher-income people move out simply to take advantage of the cheaper land prices at the edge of the metropolitan area. This idea was discussed in Chapter 1. Federal tax loopholes connected with home ownership and the desire of higher-income people for newer homes are also reasons suggested for this phenomenon. However, the suburbanization process seems to be more complex than is suggested by these reasons, particularly given that suburbanization of *high*-income people has occurred only in American cities and has, for example, not occurred to anywhere near the same extent in Canadian or European cities. American suburbanization seems to be linked with a process of fiscal separation, where higher-income people form fiscally independent communities, rather than remaining part of the core city.

The fiscal reasons for suburbanization are based on the following notions. If there are public goods in a core city financed through a property tax, higher-income people are fiscally disadvantaged for two reasons. First, the level of public goods as determined by majority vote is usually less than that desired by high-income people. Second, higher-income people have a higher tax base, or value of housing, and they pay proportionately more in taxes than lower-income people. They can avoid this disadvantage by moving beyond the legal fiscal boundary of the core city and forming a homogeneous suburb that is fiscally independent of the core city.

A restraint on the suburbanization process is the increase in commuting costs, given that the suburb must form beyond the core city's fiscal boundary. Another restraint is the reduction in the short run of the relative price of core city to new suburban housing as the demand for the core city housing stock falls with the exodus of people. If we have a core city with no suburbs, there are three things that will start suburbanization. Probably all of these have been important in American suburbanization. One is growth in the public sector, increasing the fiscal benefits of moving. Another change is reduction in commuting costs, reducing the costs of suburbanization. This reduction may occur because of technological change in the transportation sector or because of investment in highways. It could also occur because of decentralization of production activity in the city away from the CBD into the suburbs. The third change is simply city growth, reducing the gap (if any) between the legal fiscal and effective residential edges of the core city or the increment in commuting costs resulting from moving beyond the fiscal boundary to a suburb.

In Chapter 10 I argue that, when suburbanization involves stratification of the population into homogeneous communities, there are certain desirable efficiency properties of this stratification. These properties pertain to the efficient provision of public services, where through stratification people reveal their preferences for public services. In homogeneous suburbs all people get to consume their most preferred level of public services rather than some nonoptimal level, given the social marginal costs of providing public services. However, suburbanization has also presented some other efficiency and equity problems involving the disruption of public services in core cities. We now look at some of these problems and try to determine to what extent they can be solved through federal government intervention. The first problem is an equity one; the second an efficiency one.

As suburbanization in a metropolitan area occurs, the loss of higher-income people from the core city means a reduction in not just the total but also the average tax base in the core city. This decline in the average tax base in the core city may result in lower per person public expenditures in the core city and a loss in welfare for lower-income people. However, whether public expenditures for lower-income people actually fall when higher-income people leave depends not just on the change in tax base, but also on the distribution of public expenditures among the population that existed before higher-income people left. This distribution may have heavily favored higher-income people, in which case the loss of higher-income people may result in no losses in net fiscal benefits for lower-income people.

A second problem with suburbanization is that after high-income people leave the core city they may continue to use the public facilities of the core city, such as roads, police protection, art galleries, and libraries, when commuting to work or recreation in the core city. In general, they may not pay for the cost of these services. If this is so, this represents the traditional spillover, or externality, situation where public service benefits of a government extend beyond its fiscal boundary. For example, if public services are provided by the core city such that marginal costs equal internal marginal benefits, this means that social marginal benefits, including the spillovers, exceed marginal costs of providing core city services. In this situation if the recipients of the spillovers can be taxed and the money used to subsidize provision of the goods that spill over, everyone could in theory be made better off. Recipients of spillovers would be taxed according to their marginal benefits from spillovers, and this money would be used to subsidize public service provision at the margin so that, in effect, social marginal benefits are equated with marginal costs. Whether the suburbanites in fact benefit from this program depends on whether they have to pay taxes on intramarginal units of public services that are already provided and they have been consuming for free, or whether they only pay taxes to subsidize the increases in services. The subsidization could be effected by using federal taxes raised in greater proportion from the middle- and upper-income suburbs to subsidize provision of those public services in core cities whose benefits spill over into suburbs. Connally (1970) and Pauly (1970) presented analytical examples of tax-subsidy programs that would lead to optimal provision of services under varying assumptions about whether the public services are pure public goods, pure private goods, or congested goods. Note that there is a presumption that suburbs on their own will not bribe, or subsidize, the core city to increase public services. The problem is that there are many suburbs that will collectively benefit from such an increase. Hence the usual free-rider and organizational problems of suburbs getting together to make joint decisions will stop any individual suburb from voting to adequately subsidize core city services.

It is not clear how important the spillover problem is. Bradford and Oates (1974) presented a strong case for the view that suburbanites contribute more to the core city fiscally than they take out. Some of the core city services consumed by suburbanites are paid for by user fees. Second, when shopping in the core city, suburbanites contribute to the local treasury by paying any local excise taxes; and when working in the core city, they contribute through any local wage taxes. Moreover, usually the core city has a higher proportion (relative to the population) of the metropolitan area's industrial and commercial base. Hence, the core city benefits from property taxes on productive capital not found in suburbs. Alternatively viewed, by suburbanites commuting to work in the core city and thus contributing to the core city labor force needed to maintain and attract the industrial base of the core city, these suburbanites confer a fiscal benefit on the core city in terms of a greater industrial base. On the other hand, these suburbanites also avoid environmental disamenities connected with industries locating in or near their residential areas.

3. THE IMPACT OF FEDERAL GRANTS ON LOCAL JURISDICTIONS

If transfers are made among regions or cities for any of the reasons suggested in the preceding sections, one important question to investigate is the effect of these transfers on the internal allocation of resources. In this section I examine the effect of transfers made to local governments on the provision of local public services and the well-being of different local residents. Much of what I state is contained in the literature by Bradford and Oates (1971) and Fisher (1979), and there is a very good elaboration of the basic issues in Mieszkowski and Oakland (1979).

3.1 The Partial Equilibrium Approach

The first approach to the intergovernmental grants problem is a partial equilibrium one. By this is meant that the grants that local governments receive are free in the sense that the size of their grant does not affect their federal taxes. This assumption is consistent with a situation where the program only results in grants to a few communities out of the many in the nation, so that the national tax increase used to finance the grant is tiny and has a negligible impact on the taxes of the benefiting communities. Other communities effectively pay for the benefits going to the few recipients.

Given that the grants are free to a particular community, the basic analysis has focused on the types of grants that are made and their impact on local government spending. I note three general types of grants.

1. *Lump-sum grants*. The federal government transfers a lump sum to be spent on local public goods. In general, we shall assume there are no restrictions on the way these grants may be used. In theory, the federal

government may impose limits on the cutback in local expenditures or restrictions on the type of services that the money may be used to finance; but in practice these restrictions are not binding either because they are not enforced or because the restrictions are only restrictions on accounting while the actual transfers are fungible (i.e., by cutting back your own expenditures on a program you can effectively transfer money to other programs). As suggested in Section 2, the purpose of such grants may be to help fiscally disadvantaged communities or to replace local government taxes that may be raised from regressive types of taxes with federal taxes.

2. *Open-ended matching grants.* The federal government agrees to subsidize local expenditures on certain categories of public expenditures by paying a fixed fraction of each dollar of local expenditures. This type of grant has the feature that, given the federal rate of subsidization, local rather than national decisions on the level of local expenditures actually determine the total amount of federal expenditures on grants. Such grants might be designed to encourage local expenditures on public services whose benefits spill over into other communities. Alternatively, they might be used to encourage the provision of services the federal government feels local governments should be providing that they are not providing, at least in the quantity deemed fit by the federal government.

3. *Closed-ended matching grants.* These are the same as the second type of grant except that the federal government restricts the total amount of dollars it will pay out in subsidies.

Before outlining the impact of these types of grants, we must make assumptions about political decision making in a community. We assume the level of community public services is determined by majority vote in a political system where voters have perfect information. The equilibrium level of services chosen will be that which is demanded by the median voter. Under the median voter hypothesis, if we rank community members according to their desired level of services, the median voter is the median person in the ranking.[2] The median voter determines the level of public services since that is the only stable electoral outcome. If public services are higher [lower] than that demanded by the median voter, a majority including the median voter will vote to decrease [increase] public services. The political system may be either a two-party system with each party competing for the center of the road or a referendum system where people vote and revote on the level of public services until voting no longer changes the level chosen. If individuals have identical preferences and if tax shares are a monotonic function of income, the median

---

[2] As assumption of single-peaked preferences for public services is needed here; but that simply is equivalent to assuming that utility functions are monotonic and strictly quasi-concave.

voter is the median-income person (Barr and Davis, 1966). Of course, if all residents are identical, each person is effectively the median voter and gets what he wants.

The Impact of Intergovernment Grants

First, I investigate equilibrium in a community prior to federal transfers. Residents consume a publicly provided good g, housing h, and all other goods x. The good is financed by a property tax t applied to housing values R such that $R \equiv ph$, where p is the price of housing. Total taxes raised, $t\sum_i R_i$, equal total public good costs cgN, where c is the price of public services g, and N is the community population supplied. Therefore

$$t = cg/\bar{R}, \tag{9.14}$$

where $\bar{R}$ is the average housing value in the community. The level of public goods is chosen by the median voter. The ith voter pays tR_i in taxes, and in choosing g, the voter is concerned with the tax price of g, which is $\partial(tR_i)/\partial g$. Substituting for t from (9.14) we see that $tR^i = cg(R_i/\bar{R})$. Ignoring any impacts of changes in t on housing demand (i.e., assuming $R^i/\bar{R}$ is invariant to tax changes), the tax price facing the voter, Υ_i, is

$$\Upsilon_i = c\frac{R_i}{\bar{R}}. \tag{9.15}$$

Note that the voter's tax price is the cost of a unit of public services multiplied by his housing consumption relative to the community average. Within the community, tax prices will vary, so that from (9.15) high housing consumers have higher tax prices. In a homogeneous community, $\Upsilon = c$. The median voter who controls the political process chooses g based on $\Upsilon_m = cR_m/\bar{R}$ relative to other prices and income.

This is illustrated in Figure 9.1. In Figure 9.1, on one axis I have lumped h and x together as a composite commodity z (whose relative prices do not change and which are separable from g in the utility function); and I draw in indifference curves between g and all other goods (priced at 1). The slope of the budget line for the median voter is $-\Upsilon_m$, and he chooses point a and consumption levels z_a for himself and g_a for everyone in the community.

What is the impact of a matching grant program? The federal government offers to pay $s\%$ of all public-goods costs in the local community, so that the local community's public budget becomes $\sum_i tR_i = cgN(1 - s)$, in which case the tax price to the median voter becomes

$$\Upsilon_m = c\frac{R_m}{\bar{R}}(1 - s).$$

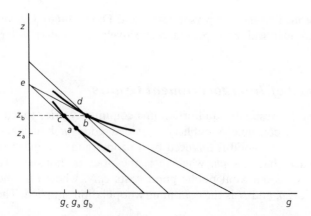

FIGURE 9.1   The partial equilibrium impact of grants on the median voter.

The lower price induces the median voter to raise the community consumption of g, assuming g is a normal good. In Figure 9.1 the budget line rotates anticlockwise; the new budget line represents the resources over which the median voter has command in choosing between z and g. We go to a new point, such as b, where z_b may lie above or below z_a. At point b in Figure 9.1, $z_b > z_a$. The new level of g consumed in the community is g_b. The federal government pays for $g_b - g_c$ units of public services (which takes us back to the budget line for the median voter's own personal resources). Given we chose arbitrarily to make $z_b > z_a$, at point b in Figure 9.1, $g_c < g_a$, or the amount the median voter (and every other resident) personally spends on g declines relative to the no-subsidy level.

In summary, in Figure 9.1 the community's response to the subsidy is to lower its tax rate t, lower its own commitment to the public sector, and raise its consumption of both public and private goods. In drawing Figure 9.1 and specifying Equation (9.15a), I have assumed there is no "flypaper effect" or "money illusion." The median voter perceives the full subsidy rate in making voting decisions and has complete control over the local public budget (albeit, assuming a constitutionally given tax system).

What is the impact of a lump-sum grant, and how does it compare with a matching grant? A lump-sum grant of D to the community changes the public budget so that $D + t \sum R_i = cgN$. Thus, the ith voter's taxes change to

$$tR_i = cgR_i/\bar{R} - \bar{D}R_i/\bar{R}, \qquad (9.16)$$

where $\bar{D} \equiv D/N$, the per resident amount of the grant. In absolute terms, the ith voter perceives that he is receiving a grant equal to $\bar{D}R_i/\bar{R}$ to divide in whatever way wanted between z and g. Tax prices Υ_i equal $\partial(tR_i)/\partial g$ and are unchanged from (9.14). In essence the lump-sum grant is equivalent to an income transfer shifting out the budget line in Figure 9.1. The higher one's housing consumption, the larger the absolute grant from (9.16) one gets.

How does a lump-sum grant compare with a matching grant for the median voter? Suppose the amount of the lump-sum grant is such that it equals $c(g_b - g_a)N$ in Figure 9.1, the grant given under the matching program. Thus $\bar{D}(R_m/\bar{R}) = c(g_b - g_a)$, or the amount going to the median voter shifts out his budget line in 9.1, so that it just passes through point b, with slope $c(R_m/\bar{R})$. For an equal transfer grant, the median voter ends up on a higher indifference curve at a point such as d in Figure 9.1. The point should be obvious. In the absence of other considerations, it is better to make lump-sum grants, rather than grants through mechanisms that distort prices. Only if we want to distort choices, as, for example, when local public service benefits spill over into other communities, should matching grants be used.

We can also examine the effects of closed-ended matching grants in this framework. Starting from point e on the vertical axis, the slope of the budget line would initially be $-\Upsilon_m = -[c(R_m/\bar{R})](1 - s)$ as with the open-ended grant. However, as we move down the new budget line, there will be a kink in the line when the level of potential federal government transfers, which equals the horizontal distance between the new and the pretransfer budget lines, reaches the maximum allowed. After the kink, the slope of the new budget will be $-c(R_m/\bar{R})$. Whether the median voter will view this program as a subsidy or income-type grant depends on which segment of the budget line the voter's highest indifference curve will be tangent to.

Finally, we note that, while under any of these grants the median voter obviously gains, in a mixed community it is not necessarily the case that everyone else gains, even though everyone's budget line shifts out. The problem is that everyone is subject to the median voter's preferences, and this voter's response to the grant could make some people worse off. The point is easy to illustrate. We do so, assuming a lump-sum grant program. In Figure 9.2 we draw in the original budget lines for a low-income person and the median voter. Initially the median voter is at point a and the low-income person at point b. Note the slopes of the two budget lines differ given $\Upsilon_M > \Upsilon_L$ for the low-income person. A lump-sum grant shifts out the budget lines to the dashed lines for each consumer. The median voter now chooses a higher level of public services at point c forcing the low-income person to point e, and a lower indifference curve. This can occur because the low-income person is "over-consuming" to begin with. This phenomenon can also be illustrated with a matching grant.

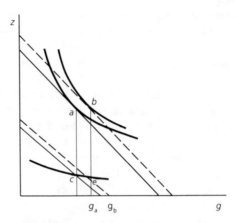

FIGURE 9.2   Impact on low-income person.

3.2   A General Equilibrium Approach

In contrast to the partial equilibrium approach in Figure 9.1, the general equilibrium approach assumes that all localities receive grants and that these grants are directly financed out of federal taxes. Therefore, an average increase of $1 in grants in all regions means an average increase in taxes of $1 in all regions. Grants cannot change the total of resources available to the aggregate of local communities. However, they can redistribute money among regions, increasing the incomes of those regions where federal grants exceed taxes raised to pay for the grant program. Similarly, the grants can redistribute money locally, given that the cost of the program to an individual is proportional to his federal tax share and, as we saw in Equation (9.16), the benefit of the program in terms of an effective increase in income is proportional to the individual's local tax share. Then, for example, if the federal tax system is progressive and the local tax system is regressive, a grant program will tend to shift out the budget line of low-income people relative to high-income people.

In this general equilibrium context, I wish to make three basic points, illustrated with simple examples. The first point involves lump-sum grants. Given a national program such as revenue sharing, money will be redistributed by some type of formula. Typically formulas redistribute money on a population basis with either an equal per capita grant nationwide or a per capita grant that increases with the inverse of per capita income.

My first point is that whichever of these two types of formula is used, as long as the program is financed by a proportional, progressive, or by sufficiently mild, regressive federal income tax, the overall impact will generally be to redistribute income from high- to low-income regions. Consider a country composed of a homogeneous high-income region and a homogeneous low-income region. A program is instituted to impose proportional federal taxes to finance a nationwide equal per capita grant program to local governments. Revenue raised is $t(N_L y_L + N_H y_H)$, where t is the tax rate and N_L, N_H, y_L, and y_H are, respectively, the populations of the low- and high-income regions and their per person incomes. The grant per capita to each locality is $t(N_L y_L + N_H y_H)/N$, where N is national population. Then local resources after the income tax and the grant program available to persons in the low-income versus high-income regions are

$$\text{low income: } y_L(1 - t) + t\frac{N_L y_L + N_H y_H}{N} = y_L + \frac{N_H}{N} t(y_H - y_L) > y_L,$$

$$\text{high income: } y_H(1 - t) + t\frac{N_L y_L + N_H y_H}{N} = y_H - \frac{N_L}{N} t(y_H - y_L) < y_H.$$

Thus income to be spent locally rises [falls] in the low- [high-] income community. If the federal tax is progressive or if the per capita grant increases with the inverse of per capita income, the amount of the transfer will only be increased.

The second point deals with open-ended matching grant programs. A problem with these programs is that, in order for the nationwide program budget to balance, the government must have perfect knowledge of consumer voting preferences. Consider an economy of identical people, where initial equilibrium for one person in one community is illustrated in Figure 9.3 at

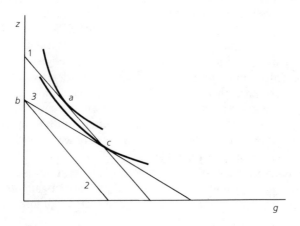

FIGURE 9.3   General equilibrium impacts.

point a. The government imposes a federal income tax shifting back everyone's budget line to 2 and then announces a matching grant program to redistribute the money. (A per capita grant program would take us back to the original budget line.) The matching grant program rotates the budget line counterclockwise from point b, as illustrated by budget line 3. For the program budget to balance, equilibrium must be back on the original budget line (each person's resources) as at point c. However, for that point to be an equilibrium, people's indifference curves must be tangent to the new rotated budget line exactly at that point c. The problem, of course, is that for any arbitrary matching rate and rotation from point b, the tangency point of an indifference curve to the rotated budget line will generally be either exterior or interior to budget line 1, in which case the program will run, respectively, a deficit or a surplus. The problem for the federal government is to pick the generally unique matching rate that will get us to point c, which requires a knowledge of the shape of the consumer indifference curve—that is, precisely how consumers will respond to the matching program in terms of local public expenditures. Note in our world of identical individuals everyone is worse off at point c after the program, than before at point a.

The final point concerns national redistributive formulas that give grants according to local tax effort. Suppose there is a positive relationship between local tax effort and grant money received. This relationship provides an incentive for localities to increase their taxes so as to increase the size of their grants. To demonstrate this, Fisher (1979) developed a model with two regions competing for a fixed pot of transfers. The level of transfers is determined by relative local tax effort, where relative (to the other area) increases in local taxes lead to increased public expenditures, constrained by the fact that there is a fixed sum of federal money to be split among the regions. Under the Cournot behavioral assumption that each region takes as given the other region's tax effort, the two regions will raise their local expenditures to compete for the pot. Suppose the two regions are of identical size and income. *Before* federal intervention, they are providing an *optimal* level of public services. After federal intervention, by competing for federally raised money in an attempt to increase their transfers, they increase public services. Since nothing else has changed in the economy—there are the same resources, there is the same total regional and national income after transfers, and the regions always achieve identical equilibria—they are made worse off because local expenditures rise above the optimal level.

Essentially in this case competing for the federal pot is a mirage. The two identical regions by competing for a fixed pot cannot gain anything from the competition; yet if one region does not compete it will lose out.

10

Provision of Local Public Services and the Tiebout Model

In this chapter I analyze a model of local public service provision based on the Tiebout (1956) model and then go on to discuss alternative and more complex versions of the model. In the Tiebout model, people in an economy stratify into different communities that are each relatively homogeneous in terms of residents' demands for local public services. Given the focus of this book, the central concern is with analyzing the jurisdictional fragmentation of a metropolitan area, or, in essence, suburbanization. This focus on community formation within a metropolitan area is also consistent with the Tiebout assumption that incomes are exogenous to the process (e.g., determined in the CBD irregardless of residential arrangement).

My presentation is based on Ellickson's (1971) refinement of the Tiebout model and subsequent work utilizing that framework by Hamilton (1975, 1976), McGuire (1974), and others. The distinctive feature of the framework is that, implicitly or explicitly, there is in the long run a mechanism by which communities can form, grow, shrink, or disappear. This feature is consistent with the situation in the United States where the growth rate of new communities approaches the urban population growth rate, and annexations or detachments of land in existing communities are commonplace. Beyond this feature the various works using this framework differ in their treatment of land, the financing of local public services, the role of developers and local governments, the role of scale economies, the use of zoning, the depiction of consumer types, the existence of capitalization, etc. I follow Ellickson and explicitly have land in the model, use a property tax to finance public services which introduces a tax distortion into the model, and assume a local political process that determines public services. Beyond that, I try to present the most important issues concerning the Tiebout model.

In the second part of the chapter I briefly consider versions of the Tiebout model where there is in the long run no opportunity for formation of new communities or changes in the size of existing communities and point out problems with such models. In the third part of the chapter I move from the long-run static models common in the literature and characterized in the first two parts of the chapter to a dynamic context where communities are growing over time. In this context, I analyze conflicts among initial residents, later residents, developers, and excluded residents. I also outline the process of the intertemporal determination of land prices in suburbs.

Before turning to the analytical sections, I briefly give an overview of the basic thrust of Tiebout type models. A basic problem in all public service models is how to attain Pareto-efficient solutions, whereby tastes are revealed in the political process and people's demands individually and in aggregate are fulfilled. In the strictest form of the Tiebout model, people stratify into communities within which everyone has identical, fulfilled demands. By the process of jurisdictional fragmentation, under appropriate conditions, tastes are revealed and local public services are in essence converted into having the characteristics of pure private goods that in the absence of externalities are provided efficiently. This is the famous "voting with their feet" result. The literature focuses on how this solution occurs, what its features are, and what inhibits the attainment of efficient outcomes.

1. THE BASIC MODEL WITH ENDOGENOUS COMMUNITIES

In the first part of this section, we assume consumers in a metropolitan area or region are divided into discrete groupings, each containing identical-income people, starting from the lowest income level y_1 and going to the highest level y_n. These incomes are exogenous to the problem. People choose to live in communities for the purpose of jointly consuming public services, where the demand for public services varies with income. The number of people in each income group is potentially large enough to support a separate community. Tastes can also vary across people, providing again that each cell containing people with identical demands is sufficiently large to support a separate community (see below).

Throughout this section we assume the number and size of communities is endogenous and that they form on land of uniform quality and amenities, which can be available in either fixed or elastic supply. For example, these could be suburbs forming on the outer fringe of a metropolitan area equidistant from the CBD. In any case, land will be allocated within and across communities so that its prices (and marginal products) are equalized throughout the economy, just as in any regular market for a uniform commodity.

Beyond these central features, the basic endogenous community model can support and in turn be supported by various characterizations of the role of developers, the collective behavior of residents, and the behavior and nature of governments. For example, within a community (but not across communities), the land may be owned by one developer or a group of developers who act collectively. Alternatively, land owners within a community may behave atomistically. Residents or groups of potential residents may act collectively in a political sense, or there may be no political activity. If governments exist, they may be a passive reflection of the collective wishes of their residents, or they may be economic agents on their own with their own set of objectives. One of the tasks of this section is to show how these differing assumptions interact and what alternative sets of assumption will support the basic solutions.

Before turning to the elements of a solution and the various types of solutions and their problems, I present the basic structure of consumer behavior and characteristics of public services.

1.1 Consumer Behavior and the Nature of Local Public Services

Consumer Side

Consumers in the area maximize identical utility functions defined over housing h, public services g, and all other goods x, subject to a budget constraint. Income, denoted by y, equals $x + (1 + t)ph$, where p is the rent on housing, for housing competitively produced with inputs of land and capital and a constant-returns-to-scale technology. The effective property tax rate t (the multiple of the tax and assessment rates) is defined for rental as opposed to asset prices. We define the gross or total price of housing as $\hat{p} = p(1 + t)$. It is $\hat{p}$ that the consumer views as the opportunity cost of housing, as opposed to p, which is the pretax cost of housing. Given that the consumer views $\hat{p}$ rather than p as the price of housing, the choice of housing relative to other goods may be distorted (see Chapter 9).

Maximizing the utility function with respect to market goods and rearranging terms, we find the usual marginal rate of substitution equals the private marginal cost condition for housing, or

$$\frac{\partial V'/\partial h}{\partial V'/\partial x} = \dot{p}. \tag{10.1}$$

From the first-order conditions we can also specify demand equations for market goods, which when substituted back into the direct utility function yield the indirect utility function

$$V = V(y, \dot{p}, g). \tag{10.2}$$

The function $V(\cdot)$ is increasing in income and public services and decreasing in g. Note in the derivation of Equation (10.2) that it is assumed the consumer can choose any level of h at the going $\dot{p}$. This implies that we are assuming there is no zoning of housing services per se and no problems of indivisibility.

We want to determine which communities consumers will choose to live in so as to maximize utility, given the $\dot{p}$ and g combinations offered across potential communities. The problem is somewhat similar to allocating consumers to their optimal locations in Chapter 1. We first examine how much consumers are willing to pay to live in different potential communities offering different levels of g. Inverting Equation (10.2) we get a bid rent function where

$$\dot{p}^0 = p(V, y, g). \tag{10.3}$$

The amount consumers are willing to pay for housing in a particular community is $\dot{p}^0$, given their income y and the level of g offered them. To find the properties of this function, we differentiate to get

$$\frac{d\dot{p}}{dg} = \frac{\partial V/\partial g}{-\partial V/\partial \dot{p}} > 0.$$

Recalling Roy's identity, where $\partial V/\partial \dot{p} = -h(\partial V/\partial y)$, we can substitute in for $\partial V/\partial \dot{p}$. Defining m to be the marginal evaluation of a unit of g, or $(\partial V/\partial g)/(\partial V/\partial y)$, we can then rewrite the expression above as

$$d\dot{p}/dg = h^{-1}m. \tag{10.4}$$

Equation (10.4) is the slope of a bid rent function showing the tradeoff between $\dot{p}^0$ and g for utility held constant. In Figure 10.1 I present a set of indifference or bid rent curves I_1 whose positive slope at each point is given by Equation (10.4). As indifference or bid rent curves shift down, utility *increases*. Figure 10.1 also shows a convex opportunity locus S, which is derived later. Bid rent curves are assumed to be more concave than the opportunity locus to ensure a well-behaved equilibrium.

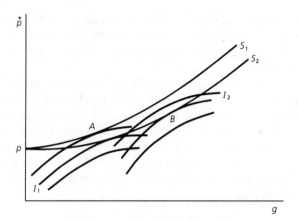

FIGURE 10.1   Bid functions for suburbs.

Before turning to the supply side, we need to determine the effect on these bid rent curves of income differences. Differentiating (10.4) with respect to income, we get

$$\frac{\partial(d\dot{p}/dg)}{\partial y} = h^{-1}my^{-1}(\eta_{m,y} - \eta_{h,y}) \gtrless 0, \tag{10.5}$$

where $\eta_{h,y} = y(\partial h/\partial y)h^{-1}$ and $\eta_{m,y} = (\partial m/\partial y)ym^{-1}$. If the income elasticity of the marginal evaluation of public services is positive and if it is greater than the income elasticity of demand for housing, then the slopes of the bid rent curves increase with income. (See a similar discussion in the context of leisure evaluation in Chapter 1.) To narrow our discussion, we shall assume this is the case, and note that basic results are unchanged if (10.5) is negative. Accordingly, in Figure 10.1, we show a second set of bid rent curves I_2 for a higher-income person, where these bid rent curves are steeper at the point of overlap than those for lower-income people.

Supply

In any suburb that forms, all residents consume the same quality and quantity of public services g. Throughout most of the discussion, we assume that the community can produce or purchase units of g at constant unit cost. Publicness in the consumption of g arises because the cost of providing a unit of g to *all* residents is $c(N)$, where N is community population and $dc/dN \geq 0$. Total community cost of providing g to all residents is $gc(N)$. If g is a pure public good, $dc/dN = 0$. If g is a mixed or congested good, $dc/dN > 0$, with the special case $dc/dN = c/N$ where g is a pure private good. The usual presumption is that dc/dN is small for low levels of N but increases as a community grows, reflecting perhaps increasing administrative costs, difficulties with supplying services to a spatially diffused population, or some forms of congestion.

We start by assuming that public services are in each community provided by a local government, where perfectly informed voters choose the government that maximizes their utility (see later). We shall generally assume that the cost of services must equal tax revenues raised. That is, any local government must balance its budget either because of constitutional controls or because of voter control. Total taxes are tpH, where H is the sum of the N individuals' housing consumption in the community. Equating costs and revenues, we have that

$$t = gcp^{-1}H^{-1}. \tag{10.6}$$

Substituting this into the expression for the gross price of housing where $\dot{p} = p(1 + t)$, we then have a supply relationship between $\dot{p}$ and g, or

$$\dot{p} = p + H^{-1}gc(N). \tag{10.7}$$

As we shall see below, in equilibrium, p must be the same across communities. Then for a given population, or a fixed $c(N)$, $\dot{p}$ is generally an increasing function of g. Under a common specification, voters and local governments naively ignore at the margin the impact of increases in g and $\dot{p}$ on H and N. In that case

$$d\dot{p}/dg = c(N)H^{-1} > 0. \tag{10.8}$$

Later we shall consider alternative behavioral assumptions. Note with the naive version, it is still the case that $d^2p/dg^2 > 0$; or as we actually increase g and hence t, $\dot{p}$ must rise at an increasing rate because the tax base H is declining due to the normal price effect on demand as $\dot{p}$ rises.

Whatever we assume about voter perceptions, for any N, given the intercept p and a slope defined by (10.8) or something similar, we have a supply relationship between g and $\dot{p}$. How does this relationship vary with N? To answer this question we must examine the question of optimal community size. In doing this we assume communities are homogeneous, since that will generally be the case in the solutions we consider. Optimal community size for any g is that which minimizes gross housing costs $\dot{p}$. Therefore, at an optimal N for any g chosen by any voting condition, from Equation (10.7)

$$\frac{\partial \dot{p}}{\partial N} = gcH^{-1}N^{-1} \left| -\frac{N}{H}\frac{\partial H}{\partial N} + \frac{dc}{dN}\frac{N}{c} \right| = 0. \tag{10.9}$$

Since within each community residents all have the same income, average housing consumption H/N will equal consumption of a new resident, or marginal consumption $\partial H/\partial N$. Then $N/H(\partial H/\partial N) = 1$; and from (10.9) optimal community size occurs when $(dc/dN)N/c = 1$ or the marginal cost of providing a unit of g equals the average cost (i.e., average costs are minimized). If $(dc/dN)N/c = 1$ is uniquely satisfied, that implies all homogeneous communities have the same optimal size regardless of income level and amount of g. (This only holds because unit costs are specified to be a function of N and not g. If they are a function of g, optimal suburb size is the same for each level of g but will vary with g.) For simplicity we assume $(dc/dN)N/c = 1$ (or there are constant costs in providing g to the population) over a wide population range, beyond some initial critical population level. Therefore, for homogeneous communities, optimal size for much of our analysis is effectively any N beyond some critical level.

In Figure 10.1 for a community population beyond the critical level, we show a supply relationship whose slope is given by (10.8) or a corresponding equation (see later). [Note that the slope at any point is then invariant with respect to N, since $c(N)$ and H change in the same proportion as N changes holding $\dot{p}$ and g constant.] Everyone in this suburb has the same income level. What happens to the supply curve if community income level changes? Differentiating (10.7) with respect to y holding g constant and assuming H is a normal good, we find

$$\partial \dot{p}/\partial y = -gcH^{-2}(\partial H/\partial y) < 0. \tag{10.10}$$

Because as income rises the average tax base in the community rises, the tax rate and $\dot{p}$ needed to finance any g decline. Therefore in Figure 10.1 the supply curve is depicted as rotating down as income rises.

1.2 The Basic Stratification Solution

I first present a general characterization of equilibrium in this type of model and then analyze equilibrium in detail. In the model, individual developers or groups of developers offer separate communities to potential constituencies of residents, perhaps specifying possible g and $\dot{p}$ levels in the community. The situation is such that there are enough developers so that the intercommunity process of community formation is competitive. Moreover, there is flexibility so that individual developers' holdings of land can be split across communities as well as grouped and regrouped to allow for perfectly divisible and endogenous community land areas and numbers of communities. In summary, the market for land is similar to the market for any commodity of uniform quality.

On the public service side, while developers may make suggestions to facilitate the process of community formation, the actual level of g in any community is determined by majority vote; and under a median-voter hypothesis, g will equal the level demanded by the median voter. In these simple political models, the median-voter solution can represent the dominant outcome of potentially repeatable referendums or the outcome of a two-party competitive political process. Since in a homogeneous community all voters are identical, ultimately each voter will get his most desired level of services, given prices and income. This voting process occurs simultaneously with community formation.

In essence, in solving for equilibrium in terms of a tatonnement process, one could conceive of two markets—a housing market where people bid for housing, and a "market" where people vote for public services. Voting takes the form both of people voting "with their feet" by moving across communities and of people voting through the ballot box within each community for the public service level that maximizes their utility. As we shall see momentarily, one of these voting processes is in fact redundant. However, for the moment, equilibrium in the metropolitan area is achieved when communities are designed such that all markets across all communities clear simultaneously. In the resulting solutions, land developers are renting land within and across communities to the highest bidders, consumers are living in the community that has the best p and g combination for them, and within each community the g, t combination is chosen by the median voter. An equilibrium solution is one where no new community can be designed and sustained that offers a more attractive feasible fiscal and housing package to any group than they currently experience. Let us now turn to the details of this depiction of equilibrium and the markets involved. We distinguish between equilibrium within and across communities.

Intracommunity Equilibrium

Within any community, what determines the equilibrium level of g and t, assuming for now that in fact communities will end up being homogeneous? The voters in a community seek to maximize $V(\dot{p}, g, y)$ where $\dot{p} = p + H^{-1}gc(N)$. If voters are naive and do not perceive the impact on, say, H of changes in g and t and hence $\dot{p}$, then $\partial V(p + H^{-1}gc(N), g, y)/\partial g = 0$ implies a maximization condition

$$Nm = c(N). \tag{10.11}$$

This is the tangency condition in Figure 10.1 for a point such as A or B for, respectively, low- and high-income communities, for the slope of the relevant bid rent curve in (10.4) and the slope of the relevant supply in (10.8). At this tangency point, in each community consumers are on their lowest indifference curve in g, $\dot{p}$ space possible given the supply relationship they perceive.

Equation (10.11) is also the Samuelson condition for the consumption of public services, where the sum of the marginal rates of substitution in consumption equal the marginal cost of provision. In a homogeneous community under our behavioral assumption, this level of services will be unanimously confirmed by majority vote.

If voters are more sophisticated as in Epple, Filimon, and Romer (1983), they will recognize the impact of changes in g and $t(\dot{p})$ upon their own h and hence total H in a community of identical individuals. In that case, differentiating Equation (10.7) yields

$$\frac{d\dot{p}}{dg} = \frac{H^{-1}c(1 - \gamma)}{1 - \eta\tau},$$ (10.8a)

where $\eta = -(\partial h/\partial\dot{p})(\dot{p}/h)$ is the price elasticity of housing demand, $\gamma = (\partial h/\partial g)/(g/h) \gtrless 0$ indicates the degree of substitutability ($\gamma < 0$) or complementarity ($\gamma > 0$) between g and h, and $\tau = t/(1 + t)$ represents the degree of taxation. Then as recognized by Epple and Zelenitz (1981) the optimality condition for g is that

$$Nm = \frac{c(1 - \gamma)}{1 - \eta\tau}.$$ (10.11a)

Provision of g based on Equation (10.11a) is more efficient than provision based on Equation (10.11), because it accounts for the tax distortion present in housing consumption. With the tax distortion, housing is "underconsumed." A second-best solution for g consumption in the spirit of Chapter 7 is to also underconsume it. In Equation (10.11a) the opportunity cost of g is raised from c to $c/(1 - \eta\tau)$ (ignoring γ), where the rise is an increasing function of η (the sensitivity of housing to price distortions) and τ (the extent of the property tax distortion). This increase in opportunity cost is tempered [enhanced] if h and g are complements [substitutes].

One could also argue that sophisticated voters would account for the impact of g on migration to and from the community. However, if g is optimally provided so $\partial V/\partial g = 0$, infinitesimal changes in g from the optimal level have no impact on utility offered by the community and hence on migration. Thus in equilibrium we do not have to account for this potential effect.

Equilibrium in the land and housing markets in a community requires that all residents be housed at a uniform unit price and that all land and housing supplied be consumed. However, since the community can costlessly contract or expand at a constant unit price of land and hence housing, what we are really interested in is the intercommunity land market.

Intercommunity Equilibrium

What conditions characterize equilibrium across communities? First, in an equilibrium solution, communities will be of optimal size, since if any community does not satisfy Equation (10.9), a land developer will set up an optimal-sized community and attract the residents of the inefficient-sized community by offering them a higher utility level. In particular, there will be at least as many communities as types of residents (i.e., income groups). However, any income group can be split into the largest integer number of communities possible where each community is at least as large as the efficient threshold level in Equation (10.9). In the range between having one community per income group and this largest integer number, the actual number of communities is indeterminate. Determinacy may be achieved by having a U-shaped $c(N)$ curve, where equilibrium size is the size that minimizes $c(N)$. However, such determinancy presents lumpiness problems in dividing a fixed-sized income group into a precise integer number of communities of the optimal size.

The second characteristic of equilibrium solutions in this context is that there is perfect stratification so all communities are internally homogeneous. In Figure 10.1 a nonstratification solution is unstable since low-income people would be worse off in a higher-income community and vice versa. For example, in the high-income community a low-income person would be on a low-income indifference curve passing through point B, which is higher than the indifference curve going through point A. Thus nonstratification is not an equilibrium and would result in an exodus of high- or low-income people, or both. In a mixed community, the preferences for public services of only one group (the majority) of people will be satisfied, and the minority will want to leave. In Section 1.4, I consider a situation where Figure 10.1 does not pertain and stratification may not be sustainable without additional assumptions.

A third characteristic of intercommunity equilibrium is that the net-of-tax housing price across communities must be the same, reflecting the spatially invariant price of capital and the assumption that land is of uniform quality. If this price p is higher in one community than in others, that means the price of land will also be higher. Developers in low land-return communities can then compete successfully for the residents of the high-priced community. If land is available in infinitely elastic supply, then p is determined by the fixed opportunity costs of land and capital. If metropolitan land supply is fixed, then housing and land prices are determined such that within and across communities the demand for housing and land equals the supply, given in equilibrium a uniform land price across communities. If land is available in noninfinitely elastic supply, the price of land is determined by the intersection of the aggregate demand curve for land (summed across communities) with the supply curve.

What roles do developers play in this process? As in any simple long-run model, their role is to act to rule out potentially inefficient solutions, by potentially earning profits from converting potentially bad solutions to good ones. In our model they can simply be atomistic land owners who act to equalize the price of land within and across communities. Community formation can then be a process of people milling around and forming potential clubs or communities of people until there is a division of consumers into communities and corresponding internal political equilibria that are sustainable. By sustainable we mean no other feasible division (see below) can dominate this one for any group. We have argued such a division must involve optimal-sized, homogeneous communities. Developers can play a role in this process of milling around and grouping and regrouping by suggesting solutions—by designing communities. In this simple world, however, it is not critical that they do this. By the same token, if they do design and own communities, there need not be an internal political process, as we shall now see.

1.3 Alternative Specifications of Developer and Political Behavior

No Political Behavior

Suppose communities are, in essence, for-profit clubs owned by a single landowner or group of landowners who act collectively. These club owners, or developers, collect land rents and taxes and finance public services. Within a community the developer seeks to maximize

$$N[(p_l - \bar{p}_l)l + tph - cg], \tag{10.12}$$

where l is lot size, N is the number of residents, $\bar{p}_l$ is the fixed (as perceived by the developer) opportunity cost of land, and p_l is the price the developer charges for land in the community. The developer can also provide the housing, in which case per person profits would be $ph - \bar{p}_l l - p_k k + tph - cg$, reflecting capital costs $p_k k$. Our formulation allows contractors or residents to provide housing (apart from land); but the two formulations yield identical results.

Equation (10.12) is maximized subject to the constraint that the developer provide residents with utility at least as great as they receive elsewhere, $\bar{V}$, and subject to the definition of land rents $p_l l = ph - p_k k$ and the constraint that housing supplied $[h(k, l)]$ equals housing demanded $[h(y, \dot{p}, g)]$ per person. We maximize (10.12) subject to $V(y, \dot{p}, g) - \bar{V} = 0$,

$p_l l - (ph - p_k k) = 0$, and $h(k, l) - h^D(y, \dot{p}, g) = 0$, for housing supply equals demand. Maximizing with respect to p_1, l, g, and t, we get Equation (10.11a) plus a balanced fiscal budget where $tph = cg$. This solution is repeated and plays a critical role in Section 3. Thus in attempting to maximize profits, the developers who are competitive across communities will replicate an efficient political outcome.

In Figure 10.1, in essence people are shopping for $\dot{p}$, g combinations, surveying the offerings of potential clubs. They will pick from the clubs that offer them the $\dot{p}$, g combination at the tangency of their indifference curves with the supply curve of the relevant optimal-sized community. By voting with their feet, they eliminate the need for internal local political processes, and they also rule out inefficient developers. If a developer offers inefficient (or "exploitative") public service provision, his customers will simply go elsewhere. In a long-run model, local political processes and developer ownership of communities are alternative assumptions to realize the same result. Only in a dynamic context as developed in Section 3 of this chapter do the assumptions start to complement each other.

However, it should be recognized that the two approaches involve different information requirements. With political processes and sufficient milling around in a costless tatonnement process, equilibrium is achieved where all anyone needs to know is their own preferences. Without political behavior, the developer must know the preferences of residences, or the shapes of their utility functions to carry out his maximization problem.

Hamilton's Perfect Zoning

If developers own all the land within a community and control public service provision, in theory they have the power to achieve Pareto-efficient solutions where the property tax distortion is eliminated. In maximizing profits in Equation (10.12), this simply involves the developers also choosing h such that, in contrast to Equation (10.1), $V_h/V_g = p$. The developers then offer residents all or nothing housing and g determined by Equation (10.11) for a fixed sum of $hp(1 + t)$. While such a solution is theoretically feasible in a long-run model characterized by perfect information, in a dynamic context with durable housing (Chapter 4) residents who own rather than rent could let their houses deteriorate until $V_h/V_y = \dot{p}$.

When this type of solution was first proposed by Hamilton (1975), he suggested that zoning could be used to attain and maintain the optimal h levels. In fact, even without developer activity, residents could vote for zoning laws that imposed optimal h levels on themselves. Further, zoning laws in a dynamic context could prevent homeowners from free-riding and over time from reducing h from a level where $V_h/V_y = p$ to one where $V_h/V_y = \dot{p}$.

Unfortunately, as we saw in Chapter 5, zoning of h consumption levels is not an available policy instrument, which is why we dub it "perfect" zoning. The impact of available zoning instruments does not allow first-best solutions.

Governments as Agents

We have assumed that the local political process is a perfect vehicle for reflecting the wishes of voters. Of course, governments may not passively reflect the wishes of their voters but may have their own objectives (Downs, 1956). Due to problems of imperfect information and free-rider problems in responsible voting, residents may imperfectly control their governments. This problem is beyond our scope, but we can ask whether governments have the latitude in general to exploit residents or developers. In a long-run solution with perfect information, "bad politics" is not possible. If a government does not satisfy Equation (10.11) or (10.11a) and balance the public budget, even if residents cannot vote the government out of office they can vote with their feet and move to a community with a better government. Second, the government cannot exploit the developers. If a government in a community attempts to lower the return to land below its equilibrium level, the developers will simply put their land in competing uses.

1.4   Stability and Efficiency of Stratification

In Figure 10.1 the configuration of indifference curves and equilibrium points was carefully depicted so as to ensure that stratification of the population into homogeneous communities was "naturally" stable. In Figure 10.2 we consider an alternative configuration where indifference and supply curves are drawn such that, if a lower-income person moved into the higher-

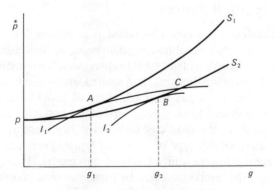

FIGURE 10.2   Stability of stratification.

income community, he would be better off. For example, in Figure 10.2, in homogeneous type 1 communities people consume at point A. However, any type 1 person would be better off (on a lower indifference curve) if he moved to a type 2 community and consumed at point B. Although the level of public services g_2 is not the person's desired one, the low tax cost to the type 1 person makes the move beneficial. Note that adding just one low–tax-base person to the high-income community will have a negligible impact on S_2. Thus stratification can only be maintained if the higher-income community can exclude lower-income people. Assuming that direct or discriminatory exclusionary laws are illegal, exclusion can still be effected in several ways noted below.

Before turning to these we note that exclusion is efficient or mixing is inefficient (assuming scale effects in public services have been exhausted). Here mixing involves an attempt by lower-income people to exploit the high tax base and low tax rate of higher-income communities. However, even if we forced a mixed tax base (through fiscal transfers among communities) on higher- and lower-income people, so that all people have the same tax base, everyone would still be better off being fiscally separated. If still fiscally separated, the two groups each get to consume their desired and differing levels of public services. If forced into the same community, either some compromise level of services too high for one group and too low for the other would be provided or the politically dominant (numerically) group would force the other (through majority voting) to consume at its level.

An alternative proposition is that forcing communities to mix in order to redistribute income from high- to low-income people through the fiscal system is inefficient. It would be better to explicitly redistribute income through a direct income tax and supplement policy, and to allow consumers to stratify for the purpose of consuming public services.

Explicit or Implicit Zoning

Theoretically, the community could pass zoning laws requiring all residents to consume the level of housing demanded by higher-income people. Then lower-income people will not want to enter the suburb because, first, they are forced to consume more housing than desired, and second, their tax base is raised such that they must pay their full share of providing g_2. This latter consideration is sufficient to exclude lower-income residents since they only want to consume g_2 at less than cost (otherwise they want g_1). Although in Chapter 5 we ruled out this type of zoning of housing services, we saw there that effective zoning lowers utility levels of purchasers. Thus, for example, zoning lot sizes at the levels consumed by higher-income people, distorts the input selection of lower-income people. For lower-income people the resulting inefficiencies from zoning raise the effective cost of housing. In Figure 10.2 the supply relationship facing lower-income people entering the type 2 community then rotates up. Beyond some minimum lot size and upward rotation in the supply relationship, lower-income people will no longer want to enter the community. If the necessary minimum lot size for exclusion is less than or equal to that desired by higher-income people, the supply relationships facing them will be unchanged.

Other Exclusionary Methods

Since the use of any type of zoning to exclude lower-income people has been questioned in the courts in the United States in recent years, it is useful to consider other exclusionary tactics that higher-income residents could employ. First, they could "oversupply" public services, raising the tax rate beyond what low-income people are willing to pay. Such a situation is illustrated by point C in Figure 10.2.

Second, they could "bribe" lower-income people not to move into the community by subsidizing from their own budget the provision of public services in lower-income communities. This would raise the supply curve in the higher-income community and lower it in the lower-income community, making the lower-income community a more attractive place to live and the higher-income community a less attractive place to live. At some level of subsidization a lower-income person would not want to enter. This subsidization is in effect a mixing of the tax bases of the high- and low-income communities. However, the subsidization solution maintains stratification and allows higher-income people to retain political control of their community and both groups to consume their desired level of services. Thus subsidization dominates a solution where low-income people enter, and the higher-income suburb becomes a mixed suburb.

1.5 Capitalization

There is no capitalization in this stratification model for two reasons. First, there is perfect stratification so there is no basis for identical consumers comparing an inferior situation in one location with a superior situation in another. Second, land is of uniform quality, and community sizes and numbers are endogenous. Thus, for example, in Figure 10.2, even the threat of mixing is not sufficient to drive up the price of land and housing in the higher-income community so as to make potential low-income residents indifferent between being in a type 1 community and being in a high-income community (with the S_2 origin (p) shifted up so that, at the new A point, the new S_2 intersects I_1). This raising of land prices above the equilibrium price would induce developers to offer alternative communities to high-income people with lower housing prices.

As noted earlier, this equilibrium constraint on land prices rules out the existence of inefficient communities and exploitive governments, where inefficiencies and exploitation might be capitalized into lower land values. For this reason, parts of the literature proclaim (correctly under our current assumptions) that there can be no *long-run* capitalization, reflecting differing fiscal situations.

Hamilton (1976) did design an ingenious situation where mixing of population and capitalization is both efficient and stable. The key is *identical demands* for public services on the part of high- and low-income people. Without this restriction the solution collapses. Although the situation is implausible, I briefly outline his solution to illustrate the capitalization concepts involved. This solution in a different context is examined in Chapter 9, when discussing capitalization. Hamilton considered an example of a situation with two types of consumers: those with high housing demand and those with low housing demand (h and *l* people), who had identical demands for public services. He assumed the existence of three types of communities: homogeneous high housing, homogeneous low housing, and mixed housing (h, *l*, and m communities). He showed that if housing consumption of h and *l* people in the m communities is zoned to be that level demanded by h and *l* people in the h and *l* communities, the solution with a mixed community could be stable with respect to both the actions of developers and residents. Housing prices adjust to reflect capitalization of the fiscal benefits and disadvantages for, respectively, *l* and h people living in the m community. However, in the m community the rise in the revenues from all *l* housing exactly cancels out the revenues from all h housing relative to their homogeneous counterparts, so that the developer is indifferent as to stratification or mixing. This solution was detailed in Chapter 9.

1.6   Land of Nonuniform Quality

Providing community sizes remain endogenously determined, introducing land of varying quality introduces no qualitative problems. To see this, consider the monocentric model of a city in Chapter 1 where land quality varies by access to the CBD. Assume for the moment that our public services are provided and priced just like one of the private goods (e.g., the z good) in that chapter. This would be consistent with a situation where the threshold level of scale effects in Equation (10.9) is so minimal that each ring or even portion of a ring of residents equidistant from the CBD can be its own homogeneous community in which h, g demands and combinations are the same.

Then equilibrium is as in Chapter 1. Comparing different communities in different (but neighboring) rings across which residents are identical, land prices differ representing capitalization of the benefits of differential access. If each ring represents different income levels, then the benefits of differential access are imperfectly capitalized as in Figure 1.1 in Chapter 1. The equilibrium land area occupied by all communities and hence the lowest-quality level of land occupied (land at the city edge) are also determined as in Chapter 1.

Complexities arise when land within a community is of differential quality. Even if residents are homogeneous, they will then generally have different public-service demands. If g, t must be uniform within the community, given housing prices will vary with land quality (access), tax payments and desired h, g combinations will also vary. This problem of variable demand within a community is examined next in Section 1.7. However, these considerations do not challenge the conclusions we have reached so far.

1.7 Nonstratification Models

So far we have stuck to the Tiebout presumption of stratification. While this is a useful benchmark model, in general, the presumption that there are at least enough consumers of each type to fully exploit scale economies in local public-service provision may be very unrealistic. Thus we examine a generalization of the Tiebout model that exists in the literature but remains in incomplete form. The most straightforward version assumes there exists a continuum of consumers who are uniformly distributed over a given interval by income (Epple, Filimon, and Romer, (1983).

Suppose momentarily that two communities form from this continuum. What would be some of the characteristics of such a solution, apart from our long-run equilibrium condition that the price of land and pretax housing be equalized across communities? A basic part of the solution is depicted in Figure 10.3. In Figure 10.3 the continuum of consumers is split in two; all people with income lower than the person with indifference curve I_b are in community 1, and all people with higher incomes are in community 2. In each community the level of g is determined by the median voter—which in this case of identical tastes and differing incomes is the median-income person in each community in equilibrium. The median voters' preferences are represented by I_m^1 and I_m^2 in communities and 1 and 2, respectively, and equilibria are at points A and C. In each community all those with higher [lower] incomes want more [less] g at the current $\dot{p}$, given the rotation of indifference curves as income changes from Equation (10.5). Note in depicting equilibrium for each g we have assumed S_2 lies below S_1 given per person housing in S_2 is larger and hence the tax rate for any g is lower. However, this ignores any difference in scale effects discussed below.

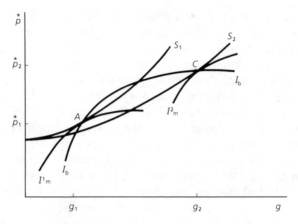

FIGURE 10.3   Heterogeneous communities.

The person with indifference curve I_b is the "border" person who is indifferent between communities. Note for such a person to have equal utility across communities, $\mathring{p}_2 > \mathring{p}_1$ if $\mathring{g}_2 > \mathring{g}_1$. In equilibrium no one has an incentive to switch communities since all people with incomes higher [lower] than the I_b person prefer community 2 [1]. Thus in summary there is political equilibrium in each community and equilibrium in land markets and in community allocation across communities.

Endogenous Numbers of Communities and Stability

The critical question that has not been analyzed in the literature is whether such an equilibrium can be sustained. The key ingredient involved is scale economies. If only two communities form and that solution can be sustained, it implies that scale effects are sufficiently strong that a third community could not form; the loss of scale in any one community from splitting the population three ways rather than two ways exceeds the gain from having a narrower distribution of demands. For example, if a third community tried to form from the upper tail of income beyond the median-income person in the second community represented in Figure 10.3 at point C, it might fail because the supply curve relevant to its voters would lie substantially above S_2. Note if in fact a third community could be sustained, in general some people would lose in moving from two to three communities. For example, the median voter at C under two communities would probably end up in a smaller community (higher supply curve) where he was no longer the dominant voter. This raises an issue of global stability, which in this case refers to shifting coalitions. If three communities formed from two, the losing parties might try to realign residents into new coalitions to shift back to two communities.

There is also a question of local stability raised by Epple, Filimon, and Romer (1983). In Figure 10.3, if a tiny interval of people around the border person shifts from one community to the other, will the utility of the new border person be higher in the gaining community than in the losing? If so, further flows will follow. Once again scale plays a critical role. While the gaining community becomes more heterogeneous, its scale is enhanced reducing the costs of public services. However, even without scale effects, local stability is a problem. The border people moving into, say, the high-income community move the median voter in that community down the income scale closer to them in preferences, which can improve their welfare relative to what they could attain in the losing community.

These types of issues have yet to be resolved in the literature.

2. THE MODEL WITH FIXED COMMUNITIES

Suppose rather than the numbers and sizes of communities being flexible and endogenous that they are fixed. This characterization has arisen in the literature (e.g., Epple and Zelenitz, (1981). I argue that such a characterization presents problems because without further assumptions it removes the ability of the land market to adjust to equalize land prices across communities and renders equilibrium indeterminate.

Within each community, political equilibrium is still characterized by Equation (10.11) or (10.11a). Second, land and housing market equilibria within communities still function regularly to allocate goods at a uniform price within each community. The problem concerns land markets across communities. What forces are there to equalize land prices across communities, so that in aggregate land supply equals demand at an equilibrium price $\tilde{p}_l$, or

$$\sum_{i=1}^{n} N_i l_i(\tilde{p}_l) = \sum_{i=1}^{n} \bar{L}_i, \qquad (10.13)$$

where n is the fixed number of communities, $\bar{L}_i$ the fixed land area in community i, N_i the number of residents in i, and $l_i(\tilde{p})$ the per resident demand for land in i.

Without a mechanism to equalize land prices across communities, any number of solutions are possible. For example, suppose there are only two types of communities, rich and poor. In comparing the sets of rich and poor communities, there will be a wide range of allocations of the fixed numbers of communities between rich and poor and resulting divergent land prices between rich and poor communities consistent with stable stratification. As discussed earlier, stability of stratification can mean that given g^R, $\hat{p}^R$ in a rich community, poor people will not want to enter. For any g^R, there will be a range of $\hat{p}^R$ and corresponding p^R intercepts to the supply curve in Figure 10.2 where poor people will not want to enter. However, even if poor people want to enter, stratification can be maintained by zoning (or the developer simply refusing to sell to poor people).

Second, without a land reallocation mechansim, within either set of rich or poor communities, any one community can provide services *inefficiently* [i.e., not governed by Equation (10.11) or (10.11a)] and still keep some residents. The inefficiencies will be capitalized into lower land prices so utility levels are maintained while landowners simply lose out. In summary, without a land market mechanism for allocating community land uses, the long-run equilibrium solution is in some sense arbitrary—a function of the history of what communities were first occupied by the rich versus the poor, or the efficient versus the inefficient. But there is no history in single-period, long-run models; that requires a different type of model presented in Section 3.

The simplest way to restore determinant outcomes is to give land developers an active role in the model. Let us assume land within each community is owned by either a single developer or development company or consortium but that there are sufficient communities and companies to maintain competition across communities. That assumption is sufficient to restore unique solutions and equalized land prices across communities. Suppose the land company in one community is earning either more or less rents by having land in one particular use versus another. Then either other land companies will convert their communities to this particular use or the community will switch uses, until land prices are equalized across communities and competing uses such that Equation (10.13) is satisfied. For example, in the two-income group the allocation of the fixed number of communities between the rich and the poor is now determinant. Land companies will adjust the land use of their communities until the allocation of rich and poor communities is such that within and across communities, the derived demand for land in housing equals supply at equalized land prices. As another example, what happens if there are inefficient local governments? In theory, the land companies can boot out inefficient resident voters and switch community land use to efficient voters.

The notion of a world where landowners can act collectively in communities to boot out their entire populations may seem extreme. In a long-run solution the more realistic instantaneous adjustment process lies in allowing community boundaries and numbers to be flexible as in Section 1 so that in essence the market for land becomes like any other market, with communities able to annex and detach land at the going market price. One suspects that people who assume fixed boundaries and numbers of communities are trying to introduce dynamic elements into the process, where adjustment to long-run solutions are constrained by nonmalleability of the housing stock and the resulting difficulties in adjusting community land uses. While it is important to consider the impact of durability of community housing and population composition, that should be done explicitly in a dynamic context. We turn to that next.

3. THE TIEBOUT MODEL IN A DYNAMIC SETTING

We now place the Tiebout model in a dynamic setting where durable land and capital are nonmalleable (or malleable only for a considerable threshold expense) and residents have horizons extending beyond a single period. For example, consider a two-period world and look at one community. Period 1 initial residents move into the community where they plan to stay for the second period in the same house (either moving is costly or there is some particular advantage to not moving as we shall see later). Housing consumption chosen in period 1 by initial residents is also their consumption in period 2. In period 2, there may be new additional entrants and further development of the community. In period 2, the community will have a history—a stock of durable houses, perhaps a charter, and a set of laws and zoning regulations. More important for our analysis, in period 1 the actions of economic agents will be affected by their expectations as to future public policies. As one example, the purchase decisions of initial residents in terms of their willingness to pay for housing in this community and their choice of housing consumption levels will be critically affected by their expectations about what will happen in period 2 in terms of future public-services levels and future community tax bases and rates.

In this situation Henderson (1980) showed that it is not optimal for the developer to simply undertake period-to-period policies that maximize profits from period to period, taking as given the past decisions of residents. Rather it is optimal to maximize the present value of profits, taking into account the impact of expected future policies on residents' choices today. Achieving that solution requires the developer to *contractually fix the future policy actions of himself and the residents* at the time of development. Once into the future, as we shall see, it is individually advantageous at that time for either party to try to break the contract and in essence try to expropriate each other's profits or land values. The potential for these types of activities must be eliminated to achieve optimality. This situation meets Kydland and Prescott's (1977) classic illustration of a time-inconsistency problem, where consistent solutions are not optimal and optimality can require the imposition of rules in period 1 to remove discretion in policy making in period 2. In our context, the public policy instruments of concern are future public-service levels, tax rates, zoning laws governing housing consumption (and hence tax bases), and the right to actually develop (e.g., the free issuance versus denial of building permits). Although this problem can be cast in time-inconsistency terms, there is also an emphasis on imposing rules in period 1 to avoid conflicts once into period 2 between developers, resident-voters, and governments over the choice of public policy instruments.

In this section, I analyze the intracommunity institutional arrangements in a dynamic setting that are required to achieve optimal outcomes and how these arrangements differ according to whether there is politics or not. I show that, under the correct institutional arrangements, plans formulated in dynamic models are consistent with the central features of the long-run equilibrium solutions derived in Section 1. I also analyze intercommunity equilibrium.

3.1 Intracommunity Equilibrium

To introduce dynamic considerations, I utilize a simple two-period model. I look at a community that forms in period 1 and retains all its residents in their original houses through period 2. In period 2 there may or may not be community growth through new residents entering. I explicitly deal with the no-growth situation, but reference at critical points the growth situation, which is the setting in Henderson (1980). My expositional strategy is to present optimal solutions and what is required to achieve them. How the breakdown into inferior solutions can occur is analyzed, but the various inferior solutions are not all catalogued. Nor will there be an analysis of the considerations of cheating and developer reputation that arise in a multiperiod model where there is on-going community growth.

In period 1, initial residents face a fluid situation, where they may choose whatever community and housing consumption levels they want, looking across communities forming in a competitive process (see Section 3.2). We consider a community where N_1 people join, each maximizing an intertemporal utility function $V(x(1), x(2), g(1), g(2), h)$, where $x(j)$ is consumption of all other goods in period j and $g(j)$ is per person consumption of public goods in period j. Housing consumption chosen in period 1 is h, and it cannot be changed in period 2, so that we capture nonmalleability and durability. Residents have a wealth constraint $W = x(1) + x(2)D + h(p + t(1) + Dt(2))$, where D is a discount factor, p is the purchase price of a house, and $t(j)$ is the effective property tax price combining assessed prices and tax rates. Efficient outcomes will require that residents must either purchase a house or, equivalently in a two-period model, pay a fixed two-period rent set in period 1. If the price is not all contracted in period 1, landlords could raise period 2 rents according to what the costs of moving are and according to what alternatives then exist for these initial residents. Under our assumptions, residents receive indirect utility

$$V(W, p + t(1) + t(2)D, g(1), g(2)).$$ (10.14)

We start with a solution where developers set up communities as clubs and there is no political process. This is the model in Section 1.3. In setting up a community to maximize the present value of profits from land sales, we assume the developer perceives that residents can achieve $\bar{V}$ in utility elsewhere and that land is available at a fixed opportunity cost $\bar{p}_l$. Thus, the present value of profits are

$$\pi = [p_l(1) - \bar{p}_l(1 + D)]lN_1 + [t(1) + t(2)D]N_1 h(\cdot) - cN_1[g(1) + g(2)D],$$ (10.15)

where $p_l(1)$ is the sales price of land held for two periods [at a two-period opportunity cost of $\bar{p}_l(1 + D)$] and l is lot size set by the developers. The developer maximizes (10.15) subject to $\bar{V} - V(\cdot) = 0$, housing production equals consumption $(H - N_1 h^D(\cdot) = 0)$, and the definition of land rents $[p_l(1)lN_1 = pH - p_k K]$. As in Section 1.3, who actually builds the housing is immaterial. Besides balanced public budgets, we get

$$pH_l = \bar{p}_l(1 + D),$$ (10.16)

$$m(1) = \frac{c}{1 - \tau\eta}; \qquad D^{-1}m(2) = \frac{c}{1 - \tau\eta}.$$ (10.17)

Equations (10.17) correspond to Equation (10.11a), where now $m(j) \equiv [\partial V/\partial g(j)]/[\partial V/\partial W_1]$ and $\tau \equiv [t(1) + Dt(2)]/[p + t(1) + Dt(2)]$. However, for simplicity we have ignored γ, the potential for h, g substitutability or complementarity. Equation (10.16) states that land is employed according to its opportunity cost. In selling land, the developer makes an offer to each resident of l units of land for $p_l(1)l$ in revenue (reflected in housing purchase costs), choosing l according to $\bar{p}_l$, not $p_l(1)$. Of course, $\bar{p}_l(1 + D)$ may generally equal $p_l(1)$, as we note later.

Without politics, the developer is responsible in period 2 for providing $g(2)$ at the level indicated by Equation (10.17) with a balanced budget, since the consumption level and prices residents paid for housing in period 1, presumed efficient levels of $g(2)$ and a balanced budget. The problem is that in the absence of contractual constraints the developer has no reason to get $g(2)$ to satisfy Equation (10.17). If there is no growth, in fact the developer could set taxes to run a budget surplus, within the confines of not overtaxing to the extent that the community becomes deserted, and the developer would then pocket the surplus. Or with new entrants, even with a balanced budget constraint, the developer's concern in setting public-good levels would be to consider only the preferences of new residents so as to maximize the revenue that can be extracted from them. Thus if residents *purchase* their land in period 1 and the developer does not enact the expected $g(2)$, $t(2)$ combination, the original residents will lose either if they remain in the community or if they sell since they will absorb a capital loss and incur moving costs. Community residents recognize this problem and will only choose optimal consumption patterns if there is an institutional arrangement that will ensure that the optimal $g(2)$, $t(2)$ combination is realized.

Such an institutional arrangement is a binding contract signed by the developers and initial residents, guaranteeing the $g(2)$ and $t(2)$ implicit in Equation (10.17) and a balanced budget, much like the homeowner association contracts in the United States in new towns (Reichman, 1976). This removes any possibility of discretionary action on the part of the developer in period 2. If there will be additional entrants in period 2, their housing consumption levels must also be contractually fixed in period 1. Otherwise in period 2, initial residents would try to zone them above efficient levels to increase the tax base while developers might try to set them below efficient levels (Henderson, 1980), or sell to much lower-income (and tax base) people. Note in that situation, contracts must protect both parties, removing not just the discretionary powers of the developer but also the discretionary powers of initial residents in terms of setting future zoning laws and of freely granting future development rights (i.e., building permits). Otherwise in the future the residents will expropriate the developer's profits by zoning very large housing consumptions or charging for building permits. These binding contracts do have the disadvantage in a situation with uncertainty of having to preset $g(2)$ before the state of nature is known in period 2. If we assume it is not feasible to write contracts specifying alternative public service levels for each possible state of nature in period 2, and it is only possible to specify one service level, then that level is only efficient on average (i.e., in an expected utility sense, not ex post once we know the state of nature).

What happens if we reintroduce a political process? If the community experiences no growth in period 2, our problems are solved. We start with developers in period 1 setting up a community in a competitive environment. They may suggest a level of $g(1)$ and the corresponding $t(1)$ that are then ratified by the voter-residents after they purchase their land. The main role of the developer is to offer homogeneous communities in a Tiebout framework. In period 2 the same group of homogeneous residents votes for the $g(2)$, $t(2)$ combination satisfying Equation (10.17). With no growth, if voters control the political process fully, discretionary policy making is no problem. Of course, the cost of any inefficiency in public service provision in period 2 is borne directly by residents as direct losses if they remain in the community or as capital losses on housing values if they sell out.

What happens if the community grows in period 2? Then good politics is not enough. There are two problems if initial residents control the political process in period 2 (Henderson, 1980). First, with new entrants, $g(2)$ should be provided according to a type of Samuelson condition, whereas initial residents would generally vote to satisfy only their own preferences. Note we expect new residents to be fundamentally different from initial residents, if only because they have different histories or are at different life-cycle stages. Second, initial residents in period 2 would vote in zoning laws forcing up the housing consumption of new residents above the efficient level so as to increase the tax base of new residents and lower community tax rates (White, 1975). In essence both activities reduce the profits from sales received by developers in period 2 and in essence are a way for inital residents to indirectly usurp the period 2 profits of developers. If the potential for these activities is not eliminated, the choices of all agents will be affected in period 1, and we will move away from an optimal solution.

If the land company continues to be the developer in period 2, optimality can only be achieved if again $g(2)$ and zoning and development laws governing the future are fixed in period 1 and in essence there is no period 2 political process. However, if the land company is not the developer in period 2, under certain conditions things can work out even with period 2 political process. For example, if initial residents buy out the developer in period 1 and share the profits from land sales to new residents in period 2, then their profit-maximization problem becomes what used to be that of the developer, and they will satisfy the relevant efficiency conditions. An alternative is for competitive developers rather than a single development company to own the land in period 2 and for the community to hold the development rights. Then, with competition, in order to develop their individual plots the developers will have to pay the community for the right to develop, transferring to them at the limit all profits from land sales. This is not a far-fetched solution.

In many situations, one developer sets up a community and makes the initial sales. Later development is done piecemeal by individual developers proposing small developments and being granted development rights (rezoning, building permits, etc.) in return for supplying the community with certain public services (e.g., infrastructure) at developer expense. In either case the principle invoked is simple. As long as initial residents are the only recipients in period 2 of development profits (so that there is only one set of identical objective functions involved in decision making), they have an incentive to satisfy optimality conditions. However, if they can only indirectly usurp development profits, then they will vote for inefficient public service levels and zoning laws in period 2.

3.2   Intercommunity Equilibrium

Intercommunity equilibrium as represented by the solution planned for communities forming in period 1 is again similar to that in Section 1, assuming competitive formation of communities. With competitive community formation, in a situation where communities do not grow and hence by implication any new period 2 people are housed in new communities, the depiction of intercommunity equilibrium is simple. In equilibrium, $\bar{V}$ for initial residents should be such that the price developers charge residents, $p_l(1)$ equals the two-period opportunity cost of land $\bar{p}_l(1 + D)$, so that, in Equation (10.19), $\pi = 0$. This corresponds to the single-period solution in Section 1. The number of communities that forms as in the endogenous community situation in Section 1 is either indeterminate or determined by dividing the population into optimal-sized communities based on a U-shaped c function. In summary, period 1 planned solutions are consistent with long-run equilibrium in land markets. Moreover, any new communities that form in period 2 with new residents follow the model in Section 1.

If initial communities grow in period 2, the depiction of intercommunity equilibrium is similar but can require some adjustments. In competitive equilibrium, as before with endogenous community formation, the present value of developer profits will be zero, and land prices will in a critical sense be equalized to opportunity costs across communities. However, there is no reason to expect period 1 and 2 entrants to a community to pay the same prices for housing and land.

In particular, period 2 entrants, given the durable communities that formed in period 1, may face a restricted set of communities each offering different alternatives and may conceivably be willing to pay a considerable premium to live in the community that offers them the best public service package. In that case, future entrants may generate profits above the opportunity costs of the developer. However, with perfectly competitive community formation is period 1, where the present value of profits approaches zero, this implies that initial residents buy at prices below opportunity cost. That is, so as to get access to future profits by being the developer upon whose land this community forms, developers compete away and transfer future profits to initial residents via lowered land prices. Thus, overall in the community, there is a time averaging of land prices to opportunity costs, but intertemporally there are distinct patterns of prices diverging from opportunity cost.

In some situations, this phenomenon can lead to intriguing patterns of land prices across communities. We consider a polar example of this. Suppose there are n types of consumers in period 1 who stratify into n different communities where, for example, $W^1 < W^2 < \cdots < W^n$ and $g^1(j) <$

$g^2(j) < \cdots < g^n(j)$. Scale considerations are such that in period 2 there are not a sufficient number of entrants to support any new communities. However, in period 2 there are still n corresponding sets of entrants, where entrants with y^k incomes will generally end up in the W^k, g^k community. Suppose as the literature commonly assumes that, for y^k people, their best feasible alternative (where they will not be excluded because they have a relatively high tax base) is the $k - 1$ community. Given prices in the $k - 1$ community, our y^k people should be willing to pay a premium to live in the k community where there is a more attractive public service package for them. Hence, in equilibrium, developers can charge prices such that $p_l^{k-1}(2) < p_l^k(2)$.

Imposing this pattern across communities $p_l^1(2) < p_l^2(2) < \cdots < p_l^n(2)$, or there is a pyramiding of prices as wealth rises across communities. The price of land $p_l^1(2)$ is anchored to be no less than $\bar{p}_l$; otherwise the developer in that community would not sell for residential use to the potential entrants in period 2. Thus prices in all other communities must exceed opportunity cost.

The pyramiding of prices above opportunity costs in period 2 reflects the capitalization of fiscal differentials between pairs of communities—that is, the fiscal differential capitalized into land (and housing prices) for k people of moving from the $k - 1$ to the k community (but not from the $k - 2$ to the k community since the $k - 1, k - 2$ gap reflects the differential for $k - 1$ people). It arises despite perfect stratification *within* any period. However, given competitive community formation in period 1 where this pyramiding of prices is anticipated by rational agents, if the present value of profits are zero in each community, that implies a reverse pyramiding of period 1 prices where $p_l^1(1) > p_l^2(1) > \cdots > p_l^n(1)$. In this polar case, tomorrow's high-priced (exclusive?) communities are today's bargains.

11

The System of Cities in an Economy

In Chapters 1 and 2, I examined equilibrium in a single city, where that city faces fixed terms of trade, a fixed rental rate on capital, and an exogenous supply curve of labor. The fundamental question left unanswered by this analysis is how equilibrium in the total economy is determined; or how the terms of trade, capital rental rates, and cost of labor facing an individual city are set in national markets. How does any city fit into the system of cities in an economy? How and why are factors allocated to any city from national factor markets; or how do cities compete with each other for factors? Why are some cities large and others small? Why do some grow and others decline?

In this chapter I examine the system of cities in an economy. First, a general equilibrium model of a static system of cities is described where all resources are ubiquitous and cities in the economy are situated on a flat featureless plain where there is no agriculture. I assume that the economy endowments of capital and labor are fixed and capital and labor are perfectly mobile among cities. This specification allows us to isolate fundamental problems in the evolution of a system of cities, even before complications such as growth and natural resources are considered. Then I consider the effect on a system of cities of growth and international trade.

In the chapter the long-run equilibrium numbers and sizes of cities are solved for, with the analysis focusing on how market solutions evolve. To illustrate the arguments, specific solutions, questions of stability and uniqueness, and conflicts between capital owners and laborers and between local and national governments, I use a specific functional form model. The specific functional form model developed here is simpler than the one used in Chapters 1 and 2 but it allows for solutions to problems that would otherwise remain somewhat intractable.[1] Moreover, for the problems addressed in this chapter I can use this simpler model of the internal structure of cities to illustrate propositions about a system of cities without loss of generality. Although I retain spatial dimensions in the simpler model, it is also possible to use a spaceless model, as in Henderson (1974c, 1982a, 1982b).

First, the solution for a single type of city or a system of identical cities is presented. Then an economy with multiple types of cities is examined.

1. ONE TYPE OF CITY

Before presenting the model used to solve for a system of cities, we need to examine the economic agents in the model and the nature of their behavior, so as to determine what elements must be incorporated into a model of cities.

The Economic Agents in the System

In the model there are two basic groups of people, laborers and capital owners, whose decisions help determine city size. Laborers choose a city to live in from among the existing and potential cities of the economy, and thus through their location decisions they help determine city sizes. In picking a city in which to live, laborers examine the income, commuting costs, and housing prices associated with different cities and pick the city that offers them the highest utility level. We generally assume that laborers are identical in skills, tastes, and factor ownerships. In stable-market solutions, these identical laborers must achieve equal utility, or else bidding for spatial locations within a city and population movements between cities will continue until a set of prices and locations is determined that yields equal utilities.

Capital owners choose how much to invest in different cities, and thus through their investment decisions they help determine city capital stocks and influence city populations. Capital owners need not live in the cities where their capital is employed; therefore, in making investment decisions, they are not concerned with living conditions, such as rents and commuting costs, in

---

[1] The intractability comes when trying to compare equilibrium with optimal solutions in this chapter and the next. To do that, we have to remove all sources of inefficiency in the model. In particular, we must allow the CBD boundary u_0 to vary so that Equation (2.4) is satisfied and the city must pay out (rather than retain) agricultural land rents (this is the basic algebraic problem).

those cities. In making investment decisions, capital owners are concerned only with maximizing the return on capital. Since capital is perfectly mobile, in equilibrium we expect the rental return on capital to be everywhere equal.

We initially assume that capital owners do not work in cities as laborers and hence that they do not need to live in cities at all. They live either in the countryside or on the edges of cities where in both cases they rent land at the opportunity cost (usually zero) in agriculture and incur no commuting costs. In the model we are not concerned with their location decisions since they neither affect city sizes nor are affected by city sizes. Later we shall consider a situation where capital owners work as laborers in cities, commuting and paying urban costs of living; and then we shall be concerned with their location decisions.

There are three other groups of people in the model who are less visible[2] but whose role is important in determining what city sizes evolve, given the location decisions of laborers and investment decisions of capital owners. First, there are entrepreneurs (who could be capital owners), who implicitly manage production activity and ensure that factors are efficiently employed within firms. Second, there may be city governments seeking to be elected. By competing to be elected and remain in office, governments attempt to enact policies concerning city size that maximize the perceived welfare of city residents. Although the behavior of this group of people is interesting, in this chapter its actions are not as critical as they are in Chapter 2.

The third group of people are developers (who could also be city governments), who set up cities and manage land bank companies. In each city, land is owned collectively by all city residents through shares in a land bank company that efficiently manages that city's land. Each resident owns an equal share in the company. The land bank company pays out dividends, which normally equal average per capita land rents paid out less some negligible (invisible) return paid to the developer. This full distribution of land rents through dividends offered is ensured in a model with identical cities by competition among developers of existing and potential cities for residents, where dividends offered are one element in attracting residents to cities. However, if one city is in some way more efficient than other cities, this full distribution may not occur, at least initially; and the income of the developer may go up temporarily. The temporary increase in income to developers from

---

[2] The term less visible is used because in long-run equilibrium solutions payments to these groups of people are not usually explicitly considered. This can be defended on two grounds. Total payments to these groups and the size of these groups are negligible *relative* to the total population in the economy. Second, these groups may subsist on short-run profits made on innovations relative to other firms and cities. Their static equilibrium long-run return is zero.

setting up or designing more efficient cities is critical to arguments later in the chapter because it provides an incentive for developers to design efficient cities.

1.1   A Simplified Model of a City

The location decisions of laborers and investment decisions of capital owners depend on the market opportunities they face, in terms of utility levels and capital rentals. Therefore, to solve for city sizes, which are in part determined by these decisions, I develop a model of a city to show how capital rentals and utility levels vary in the economy as city size varies.

In the simplified model of a city I make the following new assumptions relative to the model in Chapters 1 and 2. The CBD becomes a point, or all urban land is residential, and land is not used in commercial production. The degree of scale economies ε is fixed for the discussion that follows. In the residential sector, housing services are produced solely with land; capital is not used in housing production. Lots are of fixed equal size throughout the city. Commuting costs are now specified to be all out of pocket, directly affecting the budget constraint. The time and leisure aspects of travel are not explicitly considered. Finally, it is assumed that rents at the city edge, or agricultural rents, are zero.

Residential Sector

Consumers maximize utility, or $V = x^a z^b l^c$, where lot size l is fixed equal to one, subject to a budget constraint $y - p_l(u) - tu - p_x x - p_z z = 0$; where y is income, $p_l(u)$ is the rent per fixed lot size; and t is the cost of commuting (there are back) a unit distance. Maximizing utility with respect to x and z, we have $aV/x = \lambda p_x$ and $bV/z = \lambda p_z$. Combining to get $bp_x x = ap_z z$ and substituting in the budget constraint for first x and then z, we have demand equations $x = a/(a + b)[y - p_l(u) - tu]p_x^{-1}$ and $z = b/(a + b)[y - p_l(u) - tu]p_z^{-1}$. Substituting these into the utility function, we get the indirect utility function

$$V = A(y - p_l(u) - tu)^{a+b}, \qquad (11.1)$$

where

$$A = p_x^{-a} p_z^{-b}[a/(a + b)]^a [b/(a + b)]^b.$$

Spatial equilibrium for identical consumers requires that $\partial V/\partial u = 0$. From equation (11.1), this means that $\partial p_l(u)/\partial u = -t$ or increased transport costs with increased commuting distance are offset by reduced rents. Integrating the equation $\partial p_l(u)/\partial u = -t$, we get $p_l(u) = C_0 - tu$. To evaluate the constant of integration we note by assumption that $p_l(u_1) = 0$ or $p_l(u_1) = 0 = C_0 - tu_1$. Therefore, the rent gradient is

$$p_l(u) = t(u_1 - u). \tag{11.2}$$

Total land rents in the city are

$$\int_0^{u_1} (2\pi u)p_l(u)\, du = \int_0^{u_1} (2\pi u)t(u_1 - u)\, du = \tfrac{1}{3}t\pi u_1^3.$$

If these rents are divided up equally among residents, then per person rental income is $\tfrac{1}{3}t\pi u_1^3/N$. However, given that lot size is fixed at one where N is city population,

$$N = \pi u_1^2. \tag{11.3}$$

Therefore per person rental income may be written as (where $u_1 = N^{1/2}\pi^{-1/2}$)

$$\text{per person rental income} = \tfrac{1}{3}tN^{1/2}\pi^{-1/2}. \tag{11.4}$$

We can now define the equilibrium utility level for a representative person in the city. We take the person at the city edge. This person's income is wages, p_n, plus per person rental income of $\tfrac{1}{3}tN^{1/2}\pi^{-1/2}$. Land rents $p_l(u_1)$ are zero and commuting costs are tu_1, where $tu_1 = tN^{1/2}\pi^{-1/2}$ from Equation (11.3). Substituting these relationships into the indirect utility function in Equation (11.1), we have

$$V(u_1) = A(p_n - \tfrac{2}{3}tN^{1/2}\pi^{-1/2})^{a+b}. \tag{11.5}$$

To determine wages in this equation we turn to the production sector of the economy. Analysis of the production sector also indicates how capital rentals vary with city size.

The Commercial Sector

The firm production function is $x = N^\varepsilon n^\alpha k^{1-\alpha}$ where n and k are, respectively, firm employment of labor and capital; N is city population; and N^ε is the scale economy shift factor. Given that all firms are identical in technology, total city production may be written as $X = N^\varepsilon N^\alpha K^{1-\alpha}$, where N is city labor force and K is city capital stock. Note for simplicity we assume city labor force equals city population, or the labor-force participation parameter is normalized to one. The first-order conditions for firm profit maximization state that $p_n = p_x \alpha N^\varepsilon n^{\alpha-1} k^{1-\alpha}$ and $p_k = p_x(1 - \alpha)N^\varepsilon n^\alpha k^{-\alpha}$ Normalizing so that $p_x = 1$, at the city level we have

$$p_n = \alpha(K/N)^{1-\alpha}N^\varepsilon, \tag{11.6}$$

$$p_k = (1 - \alpha)(K/N)^{-\alpha}N^\varepsilon. \tag{11.7}$$

Aggregate Relationships in the City

Equation (11.7) describes p_k as a function of the K/N ratio and city population. For a given K/N, because of scale economies, p_k increases continuouly as N rises. This relationship is pictured in Figure 11.1 by what is termed a capital rental, or p_k, path. From Equation (11.7), if K/N rises [falls], at each N the capital rental path shifts down [up], a normal factor ratio effect. Note that if land is reintroduced as a factor of production, for reasons discussed in Chapter 2, the p_k path could eventually turn down as city size increases. Commercial land rents may escalate so quickly that to maintain a competitive output price, payments offered to all other factors must decline.

Equation (11.6) shows how wages vary with city size. As is the case for capital rentals, wages increase continuously as city size increases for a given K/N ratio. The wage path shifts up [down] at each point if the K/N ratio increases [declines]. We substitute Equation (11.6) back into the indirect utility function to get

$$V = A[\alpha(K/N)^{1-\alpha}N^{\varepsilon} - \tfrac{2}{3}tN^{1/2}\pi^{-1/2}]^{a+b}. \tag{11.8}$$

We limit parametric values to ensure that the expression in the brackets in Equation (11.8) is positive [or $\alpha(K/N)^{1-\alpha}N^{\varepsilon} > \tfrac{2}{3}tN^{1/2}\pi^{-1/2}$].

Before turning to solutions to city sizes, we must determine how V varies with city size. Differentiating Equation (11.8) with respect to N while holding K/N constant yields

$$\frac{dV}{V} = (a + b)A^{1/(a+b)}V^{-1/(a+b)}[\alpha\varepsilon(K/N)^{1-\alpha}N^{\varepsilon} - \left(\frac{t}{3}\right)N^{1/2}\pi^{-1/2}]\frac{dN}{N}. \tag{11.9}$$

This is a potentially unwieldy relationship to work with since for different parametric values $dV/V \gtrless 0$ over some or all ranges of city sizes. To limit the number of solutions that we must consider, we assume that parametric values

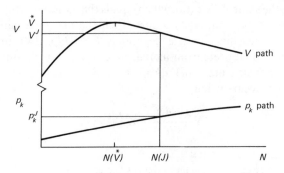

FIGURE 11.1 Factor reward paths.

are such that as N increases from zero, dV/V is initially positive, then zero, then negative. [Since we have assumed that $\alpha(K/N)^{1-\alpha}N^{\varepsilon} > \frac{2}{3}tN^{1/2}\pi^{-1/2}$, for dV/V ever to have a negative value, ε must be less than $\frac{1}{2}$]. This relationship between V and N is graphed in Figure 11.1 by what is termed a utility path. If K/N increases [declines], this path shifts up [down] at all points due to the beneficial factor ratio effect on wages. The utility path in Figure 11.1 has a unique maximum when $dV = 0$; or, rearranging Equation (11.9), at the maximum V city population is

$$N(\overset{*}{V}) = [3\alpha\varepsilon\pi^{1/2}t^{-1}(K/N)^{1-\alpha}]^{1/(1/2-\varepsilon)}. \tag{11.10}$$

For parametric values of $K/N = 1$, $\alpha = \frac{3}{4}$, $\varepsilon = \frac{1}{4}$, $t = \frac{1}{10}$, $N(\overset{*}{V}) = 9{,}880$.

Having derived and defined utility and capital rental paths as pictured in Figure 11.1, we can now solve for city sizes.[3]

1.2   The Solution to City Sizes

To solve for city size we make use of the factor reward paths in Figure 11.1. In Figure 11.1 for city sizes smaller than the one that maximizes utility, which is $N(\overset{*}{V})$, both groups of people in the model experience increases in real factor income as city sizes increase. Thus city sizes smaller than $N(\overset{*}{V})$ are not equilibrium ones, since up to at least $N(\overset{*}{V})$ any city larger than current cities will always be able to attract factors from the smaller cities because it can pay them more. However, beyond $N(\overset{*}{V})$, whereas capital owners benefit from further increases in city sizes, laborers are made worse off. It is in this range beyond $N(\overset{*}{V})$ that equilibrium city sizes occur.

With one type of city in the economy, there is a unique stable equilibrium city size, such as depicted by $N(J)$ in Figure 11.1. We first define the properties of $N(J)$ and then demonstrate the uniqueness and stability of the solution.

Two conditions define $N(J)$. First, all cities are identical, which means all cities have the same K/N ratio, which equals the national ratio, and all cities are of equal size. Second, $N(J)$ occurs when the marginal gains to capital owners from increasing city size beyond $N(\overset{*}{V})$, $K(dp_k/dN)$, just equal the marginal losses to laborers from increasing city size, which are $N(dV/dN)$ in utility units or which are $N(dV/dN)/(\partial V/\partial y)$ in monetary units. Therefore market city size occurs when

$$N\frac{dV/dN}{\partial V/\partial y} + K\frac{dp_k}{dN} = 0. \tag{11.11}$$

---

[3] Similar paths can be derived using the model in Chapter 2. In differentiating equations of the model and solving, we now hold K/N, rather than p_k, fixed.

Substituting in Equation (11.9) for dV/dN, from Equation (11.1) for $\partial V/\partial y$, and from Equation (11.9) for dp_k/dN, and rearranging terms, we find

$$N(J) = (3\varepsilon\pi^{1/2}t^{-1})^{1/(1/2-\varepsilon)}(K/N)^{(1-\alpha)/(1/2-\varepsilon)}. \qquad (11.12)$$

Note that $N(J)$ is a strictly monotonic function of the K/N ratio (given $\varepsilon < \frac{1}{2}$, $a < 1$).

Before (after) $N(J)$, the gains to capital owners exceed (are less than) the losses to laborers. This is critical since it implies that, at any other city size, total factor returns could be increased by moving city size to $N(J)$. For the illustrative parametric values used earlier, where $K/N = 1$, $\alpha = \frac{3}{4}$, $\varepsilon = \frac{1}{4}$, and $t = \frac{1}{10}$, $N(J)$ is 31,200.

In stating that $N(J)$ is the solution we must assume that the economy is very large and there are many cities of size $N(J)$. This assumption must be made because there is a divisibility or lumpiness problem here, which can be illustrated as follows. Suppose there is currently economy population for two and a half cities of size $N(J)$. In Section 1.4, I argue that the market solution will be to have two cities form with the remaining half city split evenly among the two cities, so they are each one and a quarter times $N(J)$. However, as the number of cities increases, any remainder is split among more and more cities, and the part of the remainder going to any one city becomes very small. Then all cities may approach size $N(J)$. In this section we assume the economy is sufficiently large so that this condition is met and there are no problems with lumpiness. Once we have solved for city size $N(J)$, we divide $N(J)$ into the total economy population to ge the total number of cities in the economy.

Realizing $N(J)$ as a normal competitive equilibrium solution may depend on the behavior and nature of land developers. We assume land developers are competitive, each attempting to set up new cities by attracting investment and population and forming new land bank companies. We also assume for now that land developers are fully knowledgeable, the meaning and implication of which will become apparent later. Given these assumptions, we show that the $N(J)$ solution is the only globally sustainable solution. The proof is in two stages. First, we show that *if* cities satisfy Equation (11.11) and are sizes $N(J)$, they must be *identical*, or have both the same size $N(J)$ and the same K/N, in order for utility levels and capital rentals to be equalized across cities. We then show that stable city sizes must satisfy Equation (11.11) or be sizes $N(J)$. We combine the latter stage of the proof with a heuristic description of the movement from a nonequilibrium solution to an equilibrium solution.

Suppose cities satisfy Equation (11.11) or are of sizes $N(J)$. The question is whether cities in equilibrium could be nonidentical and have different K/N and hence different $N(J)$ but still pay the same factor rewards.

The negative answer may be seen as follows. Substituting from Equation (11.12) for $N(J)$ into Equations (11.7) and (11.8), we find

$$V = C_1(K/N)^{1/2(1-\alpha)(a+b)/(1/2-\varepsilon)}, \qquad p_k = C_2(K/N)^{(\varepsilon-\alpha/2)/(1/2-\varepsilon)}.$$

Therefore, for city sizes $N(J)$, V is a strictly monotonic function of the K/N ratio (given $\varepsilon < \frac{1}{2}$). Hence any two cities satisfying Equation (11.11), such that utility levels are equalized between the cities, must have the same K/N ratio and hence, from Equation (11.12), the same size or $N(J)$. The same statements apply to the p_k function (unless $\varepsilon = \alpha/2$). Therefore, if Equation (11.11) is satisfied, cities must be identical.

It remains to show that cities must satisfy Equation (11.11) and be sizes $N(J)$. Suppose cities are not size $N(J)$ but are some larger size, such as $N(A)$ in Figure 11.2. We start the analysis assuming cities are identical at $N(A)$ with a K/N equal to the national ratio. This is done only for expositional simplicity in describing the process by which we move to equilibrium solutions; we shall show that any city with any K/N must satisfy Equation (11.11). In the solution at $N(A)$, developers have dissipated profits through competition for factors, so that land rents are fully distributed. At $N(A)$, capital rentals are higher and utility levels lower than at $N(J)$. Suppose a land developer sets up one city of size $N(J)$ where producers borrow at the prevailing high capital rental rate. In this new city producers temporarily operate at a lower K/N ratio than in the rest of the economy, so that they can pay competitive capital rentals given reduced scale efficiencies in production. The effect of the temporarily lower K/N ratio is to shift the p_k path up in this one city and the V path down relative to other cities.

In this new city the land developer will be able to ensure that utility levels are competitive and, unlike developers in other cities, the developer will

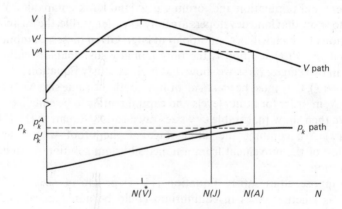

FIGURE 11.2   Solutions to city sizes.

be able to retain some land rental income as profits. This occurs for two reasons. Given the definition of $N(J)$ in Equation (11.11), if the city were to operate with the national K/N ratio [which pertains in cities of size $N(A)$], the sum of factor rewards would be maximized at $N(J)$. At any other size the sum of factor rewards would be less. *Therefore, for the same K/N a city of size $N(J)$ will be able to pay factor rewards at $N(A)$ and have a surplus left over.* [This in itself is sufficient to show that any city with any K/N must satisfy Equation (11.11), or else an entrepreneur could set up another city (with the same K/N) satisfying Equation (11.11) and could both hire away the factors in the first city and make a profit.] The fact that, when moving from $N(A)$ to $N(J)$, producers operate temporarily with a lower K/N only enhances this surplus, since the losing factor, capital, is used relatively less than the gaining factor, labor. (Alternatively viewed, producers operate at the temporarily efficient K/N ratio given the current opportunity cost of capital.)

The developer who manages the land bank company simply takes this surplus out by retaining some land rental income. The developer pays out sufficient dividends to ensure that, including wages, laborers are getting the same or higher utility levels than in the rest of the economy. The magnitude of this surplus may be illustrated using the example where $K/N = 1$, $\alpha = \frac{3}{4}$, $\varepsilon = \frac{1}{4}$, $a = b = \frac{1}{2}$, and $t = \frac{1}{10}$. If $N(A) = 40,000$, then from Equations (11.7) and (11.8) initially $p_k = 3.535$ and $V = 1.542$. Suppose an entrepreneur sets up a city of size $N(J) = 31,200$ and borrows at the prevailing rate $p_k = 3.535$. For this rate, from Equation (11.7), K/N in this one city will be 0.92. For $K/N = 0.92$ and $N = 31,200$, the city could offer utility levels from Equation (11.8) of $V = 1.558$. If the entrepreneur skims off the surplus, his temporary profits are $31,200(1.558 - 1.542)$ utils, which are converted to monetary units by dividing by $\partial V/\partial y = \frac{1}{2}$. This equals \$1,070. [If the city operated with the same K/N as nationally, profits would be less (\$845) since capital would be used inefficiently relative to the current price.]

This profit earned by the developer will induce other entrepreneurs to set up cities of smaller sizes, such as $N(J)$.[4] In the national factor markets, given the lower K/N initially associated with a smaller city size and factor prices at $N(A)$, this will reduce [increase] the aggregate demand for capital [labor]. This in turn will bid up utility levels and lower capital rentals relative to those at $N(A)$. In the process the entrepreneur will be forced to pay out more land rental income in order to attract residents. City sizes and factor prices will

---

[4] We have implicitly assumed for expositional purposes that entrepreneurs can limit city sizes to $N(J)$. This is not essential. The setting up of any new city of size less than $N(A)$ will cause all cities to fall in size (as they lose population to the new city). As long as it is profitable to set up a city of size even slightly less than $N(A)$, an entrepreneur will set up a new city. Entrepreneurs will keep setting up new additional cities until all cities are forced to size $N(J)$.

adjust and new cities will continue to spring up, attracting residents and investment as long as old cities are of inefficient sizes, or until Equation (11.11) is satisfied and land developers' profits are dissipated through competition for laborers to form cities. A similar argument can be used to show that cities smaller than $N(J)$ are also not sustainable. In short, with identical cities, any city size other than $N(J)$ is globally not sustainable.[5]

A problem with the foregoing discussion is that it is not clear that we should be ascribing to entrepreneurs the actions depicted. For new cities to spring up if other cities are of inefficient size, we have assumed that there are entrepreneurs in the economy who have sufficient information on the properties of efficient cities and are willing to gamble that they can design a city that is of more efficient size than existing sizes. Suppose that no one knows about the properties of efficient cities nor is there any certain way of investing explicitly to discover this information. Therefore, there would be no basis for entrepreneurs to set up new, more efficient-sized cities. Then, to achieve efficient city sizes it would be necessary to allow over time random entry or random attempts to set up cities. An entrepreneur, essentially by accident, sets up a city of more efficient size and hence attracts residents to that city. In doing so, the entrepreneur makes a temporary profit. Other entrepreneurs will observe this profit and adjust their city sizes accordingly. That is, over time, people will "learn" what more efficient city sizes are. This argument essentially proposes that any inefficient solution is not sustainable in the long run, since any random entrant would lead to the disintegration of an inefficient market solution. A competitive equilibrium solution at $N(J)$ may require agents called developers but they need not be especially knowledgeable.

There are a number of additional points that can be made about the solution. First, it is consistent with the partial equilibrium model in Chapter 2. In a partial equilibrium model, city sizes may be determined by city governments seeking to restrict city size so as to maximize utility levels, given the prevailing return on capital (or by developers seeking to maximize profits). This behavior yields city sizes of $N(J)$. The proof of this is as follows.

In a partial equilibrium model, $\bar{p}_k$ is exogenous to the city and the city can only influence local utility levels. If $\bar{p}_k$ is exogenous, from Equation (11.7) we may solve for K/N as a function of $\bar{p}_k$ and N. Substituting for K/N into Equation (11.6) for wages, we find that $p_n = \alpha(1 - \alpha)^{(1-\alpha)/\alpha} \bar{p}_k^{(\alpha-1)/\alpha} N^{\varepsilon/\alpha}$.

---

[5] The question of sustainability may be illustrated as follows. Suppose that with all cities at $N(A)$, an entrepreneur sets up one city that is *slightly* smaller. If the entrepreneur makes a profit, other entrepreneurs will set up (slightly) smaller cities and the $N(A)$ solution will not be sustainable. In general, non-sustainability in the present context means that any movement (not just large movements) toward $N(J)$ from current city sizes yields profits for developers. This is true if the monetized sum of factor rewards declines strictly monotonically as we move away from $N(J)$.

Therefore, from Equation (11.5) indirect utility may now be written as

$$V = A[\alpha(1 - \alpha)^{(1-\alpha)/\alpha}\bar{p}_k^{(\alpha-1)/\alpha}N^{\varepsilon/\alpha} - \tfrac{2}{3}tN^{1/2}\pi^{-1/2}]^{a+b}.$$

From the point of view of the city government, efficient city size occurs when $\partial V/\partial N = 0$ for p_k fixed, or when

$$\alpha(1 - \alpha)^{(1-\alpha)\alpha}\bar{p}_k^{(\alpha-1)/\alpha}(\varepsilon/\alpha)N^{\varepsilon/\alpha-1/2} = \tfrac{1}{3}t\pi^{-1/2}. \qquad (11.13)$$

However, in equilibrium in national factor markets, where utility levels and capital rentals must be equalized across cities, cities must be identical.[6] This means from Equation (11.7) $p_k = (1 - \alpha)(\overline{K/N})^{-\alpha}N^\varepsilon$ where $\overline{K/N}$ is the national K/N ratio. Substituting this expression for p_k into the optimality condition yields a city size defined by the expression for $N(J)$ in Equation (11.12). Hence, the partial equilibrium and general equilibrium approaches are consistent.

Note, the diagrammatic analyses of partial and general equilibrium solutions differ. In the general equilibrium diagrams such as Figures 11.1 and 11.2, the K/N ratio is held fixed as we move out the V and p_k paths and achieve a city size of $N(J)$, past the maximum point of the V path. In the corresponding partial equilibrium diagram, p_k is held fixed (while K/N varies) and efficient city size occurs at the maximum of the new V path (for K/N varying). That maximum point of course is $N(J)$.

Another point is that in the present context with only one type of city, I show in the next chapter that $N(J)$ is the Pareto-efficient city size when incomes are determined on the basis of factor ownership and private marginal products. Since $N(J)$ is the point where total real factor rewards are maximized, or where the marginal gains to capital owners from increasing city size just equal the marginal losses to laborers, this is intuitively appealing. However, as we shall discover later, for multiple types of cities, market solutions may not always be efficient, due to scale externality problems.

These last points about the general equilibrium solution being consistent with the partial equilibrium solution and Pareto efficiency are simply illustrations of the usual competitive equilibrium results. They illustrate the normal ideas of the discipline of the market-place and the workings of atomistic competition where we are discussing cities instead of firms. The firm/city faces fixed output and input (capital) prices set at the industry/national level. For a firm/city to survive, it maximizes profits/utility levels, competes for its market share of sales/residents, and through competition

---

[6] This can be shown as follows. In any city $p_k = (1 - \alpha)(K/N)^{-\alpha}N^\varepsilon$. We substitute this into the equation for V and differentiate both the p_k and this V equation, allowing N and K/N to vary. Both N and K/N must vary such that $dV = dp_k = 0$, so factor rewards remain equalized. Given that, it is possible to show there is no nonzero variation in N and K/N that is consistent with Equation (11.13) being satisfied. Therefore cities must be identical.

achieves efficient size. This behavior results in a Pareto-efficient set of input and output prices and welfare levels. The existence of land developers seeking to maximize profits ensures that scale economy benefits of increasing city size versus commuting cost increases are traded off implicitly or explicitly to achieve optimal city size.

Political Problems

The city size $N(J)$ is not what either capital owners or laborers would want to impose on all cities in the economy. If these groups knew the shape of the paths in Figure 11.2 and income was distributed according to marginal productivity, they would favor national legislation to alter sizes of all cities. Laborers would favor policies that tend to reduce equilibrium city size below $N(J)$. Capital owners would promote national policies that tend to increase equilibrium city size. However, it is not clear that either group could ever have an idea of what these paths look like, nor could they organize to promote their legislation over the opposing legislation of the other group. If both groups behave somewhat atomistically, they generally perceive that both the borrowing rate and the utility level are fixed in national markets by market forces; they will perceive that they are individually maximizing their own welfare at city size $N(J)$. However, to the extent that capital owners could collude, they would work to promote national policies encouraging the growth of individual city sizes.

1.3   Capital Owners as Laborers

So far, we have assumed that capital owners are a separate group of people who do not commute to the city center and who live at city edges or in the countryside. Hence their travel costs and housing expenditures are independent of city size and exogenous to the problem. Suppose instead that capital owners also work as laborers, commute to the city center, and incur urban costs of living. How does this affect our analysis? We assume capital ownership is equally divided among all laborers in the economy. Capital rentals are now spent in cities. However, capital owners, given perfect mobility of capital, do not need to invest in the city where they live. They can invest in any city in the economy.

City sizes are now determined by the location decisions of capital owner–laborers and the investment decisions of these people. In investing, people seek to maximize the nominal return on capital. In locating they seek to maximize utility, given commuting and housing costs and income. The utility level of the capital owner–laborers is determined as follows.

In addition to land rental income, per person income now equals $p_n +$ $p_k(K/N)$ where K/N is the national capital-to-labor ratio and hence the per person ownership of capital. From the marginal productivity conditions of the firm, $p_n + p_k(K/N) = \alpha N^\varepsilon (K/N)^{1-\alpha} + (1 - \alpha)N^\varepsilon (K/N)^{1-\alpha}$ if cities have the same K/N ratio as the national ratio. Therefore from Equation (11.5) the utility of a representative person is

$$V = A[N^\varepsilon (K/N)^{1-\alpha} - \tfrac{2}{3}t\,N^{1/2}\pi^{-1/2}]^{a+b}. \tag{11.14}$$

In Figure 11.3 we plot V as a function of N under parametric restrictions that yield the curve pictured. We also plot the p_k path.

Equilibrium city size now occurs at $N(\dot{V})$ when the utility path is maximized. If we maximize V in Equation (11.14) with respect to N, $N(\dot{V})$ is given by the expression for $N(J)$ in Equation (11.12). This implies that market city size is the same in this model whether capital rentals are spent in cities by laborers or they go to capital owners. This result only occurs because lot size is fixed. In models where lot size is endogenous, city size is smaller if capital rentals are spent in cities. If income per person goes up in cities, more housing and land will be demanded. More land demanded implies for the same population an increase in the spatial area of the city and hence in commuting costs. That is, for any given city size and scale economies, the marginal and total commuting costs rise if capital rentals are spent in cities. Hence city sizes should be smaller.

To show that $N(\dot{V})$ is the equilibrium city size we could repeat the stability arguments given earlier and show that developers maximize profits by moving city size to $N(\dot{V})$. If one city size increases beyond $N(\dot{V})$ in Figure 11.3, even though it can pay higher capital rentals to its own or other residents, the utility level it can offer residents declines, so that no one would want to live in that city. That is, at $N(\dot{V})$ only, real factor income from all sources is maximized. We can also show that $N(\dot{V})$ is consistent with partial equilibrium

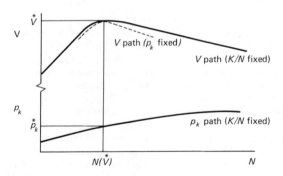

FIGURE 11.3 Capital owners as laborers.

city size determination. The argument is as follows. City governments seek to maximize V in Equation (11.4) where they view the borrowing rate on capital and capital income of city residents $(p_k K/N)$ as fixed. Maximizing the perceived utility of city residents and setting $\partial V/\partial N = 0$ yields Equation (11.13). Incorporating the constraint of a cleared national capital market by substituting $p_k = (1 - \alpha)N^\varepsilon(K/N)^{-\alpha}$ into Equation (11.13), as we did earlier, we find that partial equilibrium city size turns out to be $N(\dot{V})$.

Note that because the capital rental path rises beyond $N(\dot{V})$, it is possible that laborers in their role as capital owners will lobby with the federal government for larger city sizes to raise their capital income. If cities other than the one in which an individual capital owner lives increase in size and the owner rents capital in these cities, the owner's income rises and he is better off. Each capital owner thus has an incentive to increase other people's city sizes. If capital owners collectively succeed in increasing city size, then all capital owners/laborers will be worse off.

1.4   City Size with Lumpiness

In the preceding sections we ignored the lumpiness problem by assuming that there was a sufficiently large number of cities to make the problem negligible. When lumpiness exists, cities in general will not be size $N(J)$. To limit the possible solutions, we are going to impose restrictions on city sizes through stability requirements. Throughout this section it is assumed that capital owners are a separate group of people who do not work as laborers.

In general, it is possible to show that when there are two or more cities, no city size can be less than that size where the utility path has a maximum. That is, all city sizes must lie at $N(V)$ or beyond. Smaller city sizes are generally unstable.[7] This restriction is imposed on solutions below.

---

[7] We assume that the shape of utility and capital rental paths are as in Figure 11.4. Suppose there are two cities of size $N(m)$. A random movement of a few units of capital and labor (say, maintaining the existing K/N ratio in each city) from one city to another would raise [lower] V and p_k in the gaining [losing] city. This would induce further factors movements between cities and hence the original solution is unstable. Alternatively, suppose a city were of size $N(m)$ and other cities of size $N(n)$ where the corresponding differences in utility and capital rental paths ensure equalization of both utility and capital rentals between cities. Then $V(m)$ shifts down and $p_k(m)$ shifts up relative to $V(n)$ and $p_k(n)$ through the m city having a lower K/N ratio relative to other cities. A random movement of a unit of capital and labor to the $N(m)$ city would raise utility and capital rents there relative to other cities and would result in further movements of factor to that city. Size $N(m)$ is unstable. The only possible exception is if there are only a few cities, one of size $N(m)$ and perhaps only one of size $N(n)$. Then when there is a random factor movement to the smaller city, there is an appreciable effect on factor rewards in the larger city(s). With many cities this effect is dissipated among so many cities as to be negligible.

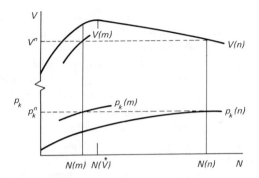

FIGURE 11.4   Utility and capital rental paths.

We heuristically demonstrate lumpiness solutions as follows. Suppose the economy is growing with a fixed K/N ratio. There is currently only one city in the economy, with utility and capital rental paths as pictured in Figure 11.5. As this city grows past size $N(J)$, at some point a second city will form when the losses to laborers from there being only one city just equal or start to exceed the gains to capital owners or when

$$N\frac{\Delta V/\Delta N}{\partial V/\partial y} + K\frac{\Delta p_K}{\Delta N} \geq 0, \tag{11.15}$$

where Δ indicates a discrete change. Alternatively stated, the sum of the monetary value of utility levels and capital rentals is increased by two cities forming. Such a point could be at $2N(m)$, where the city splits into two cities,

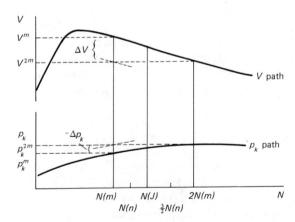

FIGURE 11.5   City size with lumpiness: a fixed K/N ratio.

each of size $N(m)$ [providing $N(m) \geq N(\overset{*}{V})$ for stability]. As these two cities grow, when they each reach some point, such as $(3/2)N(n)$, a third city forms and all cities are size $N(n)$. As the economy grows, city size oscillates around $N(J)$ until at the limit the number of cities approaches infinity and city size approaches and remains at $N(J)$ with further growth (when a new city forms, each existing city's loss or contribution of factors becomes negligible). This is the no-lumpiness case discussed extensively earlier.

Achievement of these city sizes follows from the behavior and nature of land developers. Once Equation (11.15) is satisfied, a developer can always attract residents and investment to a new city since the total monetary value of utility plus capital rental levels has risen. For example, when there is just one city larger than size $2N(m)$, in a potential new city of size $N(m)$ an entrepreneur can match utility and capital rental levels in the initial city with some profit left over. By paying current market factor rewards the entrepreneur will temporarily operate with a lower K/N ratio than nationally (hence the dashed shifts in the V and p_k paths). This will result in a reduced national demand for capital relative to labor and downward pressure in the existing city (whose K/N ratio is also being forced up) on capital rentals relative to utility levels. The result is that, as the new city forms and the old city shrinks and we approach the new equilibrium city sizes $N(m)$, capital rentals [utility levels] will fall [rise] by discrete amounts, as pictured in Figure 11.5.

There are potential problems in achieving this solution. First, to set up a new city of size $N(m)$ requires starting or at least planning to start the city at this size, not anything smaller, or else the city will not be able to pay competitive factor rewards, given Equation (11.15). For this to happen, the entrepreneur must recognize the problem as it is pictured in Figure 11.5, understanding what factor reward payments can be paid out at different city sizes. That is a major information requirement for an entrepreneur, where he must know the *nature* and *extent* of scale economies and commuting costs at different city sizes and their impact on both utility levels and capital rentals. Second, if cities can limit entry, once the initial city reaches size $N(J)$, it will exclude all new people, forcing a second city of small inefficient size to form. Our stability requirements rule this out, but given effective means of restricting city size, it presents alternative possibilities for solutions.

2. EXTENSIONS

In this section I outline various extensions of the basic model analyzed in the literature (Hochman, 1977; Henderson and Ioannides, 1981; Henderson, 1982a, 1982b). Here I focus on a description and the intuition of the results from the literature, since a technical presentation would take several chapters.

2.1 Multiple Types of Cities

So far, we have discussed city size when there is only one type of city. Our results generalize directly to a situation in which there are two or more types of cities. Each type of city specializes in the production of a different traded good or bundle of goods. Specialization occurs if there are no production benefits or positive externalities from locating two different industries in the same place. If they are located together, because workers in both industries are living and commuting in the same city, this raises the spatial area of the city and average commuting costs for a given degree of scale economy exploitation in any one industry. Separating the industries into different cities allows for greater scale economy exploitation in each industry relative to a given level of commuting costs and city spatial area. This characterization of scale economies is consistent with empirical evidence (Henderson, 1985a). However, the extent of specialization is limited by the costs of trade between different types of cities and production interrelations between industries. Industries that use each other's inputs, a common labor force, or a common public good or intermediate input, such as a transportion system, will tend to locate together.

Characterizing equilibrium in the economy when there are several types of cities is straightforward if there are large numbers of cities of each type. The size and number of each type of city depend on the degree of scale economies in the production of that city's traded good, on the demand for the city's output as determined in national and/or international markets, and on the factor intensity of that good relative to the factor endowments of the economy.

More specifically, equilibrium city size is determined in a market setting, where each city seeks to maximize the utility of its residents for a fixed perceived rental price of capital. This solution satisfies the global criterion that in equilibrium for *any* city

$$N \frac{\Delta V / \Delta N}{\partial V / \partial y} + K \frac{\Delta p_K}{\Delta N} = 0,$$

where N and K are *national* endowments and the changes in V and p_K while being viewed in the one city also occur nationally (given equilibrium requires equalized factor rewards nationally).

Comparing different types of cities, each type will generally have a different efficient size. City types specializing in traded goods with a greater degree of scale economies will be larger, because they will achieve a larger size before the marginal scale economy benefits of increases in city size will be overtaken by the marginal increases in costs of living. Larger types of cities will occupy a greater spatial area and hence will have higher average commuting costs and rent gradients. For consumers to have equal utility between larger and smaller types of cities, this requires labor income to rise monotonically with city size, so as to compensate for the higher costs of living. Note while one might casually infer that larger cities are more "efficient" because on the production side wages and value added per worker are higher, the inference is incorrect once the costs of housing people in larger cities are accounted for.

What determines the numbers of each type of city and how are utility levels and capital rentals are both equalized across cities of very different sizes and types? Given efficient sizes for each type of city, the numbers of each type are determined by the *relative demand* for its traded good product and the economy's size. Note that from a national perspective there are constant returns to scale, given cities are all at efficient sizes. Doubling national factor endowments would double the number of cities of each type leaving all prices unchanged—that is, the economy would simply replicate itself. Equalization of factor rewards across types of cities occurs through capital-to-labor ratios and traded good prices for each type of city adjusting, consistent with national full employment and the right number of cities of each type needed to produce the equilibrium proportions of traded goods demanded in national output markets.

Note this direct link between national output patterns and the numbers of each type of city is the underlying determinant of the size distribution of cities, given a particular city size is associated with each type of city. If the relative demand for one type of city's product increases, the numbers of that type of city will increase relative to other types of cities. If that type of city is a very large one, then the numbers of large cities relative to small cities in the economy will increase. Thus any type of empirical size distribution relationship such as the rank size rule[8] only reflects the outcome of underlying forces determining national output composition and hence city type and size composition.

Given this perspective, one can assess the impacts on the spatial allocation of resources and the size distribution from national policies that superficially may appear to have no spatial content (Henderson, 1982a). For example, policies that subsidize the provision of one type of product nationally relative to other products will increase the relative output of that product nationally. This implies the number of cities producing that type of product will expand and that will change the size distribution of cities

---

[8] The rule-of-thumb version of the rank size rule is as follows. Rank all cities in the economy so the largest is ranked 1 and the *n*th largest, *n*. If rank is multiplied by city population for each city, the rule is that the multiple is the same number (equals the population of the largest city) for all cities in the economy. See Beckmann (1958).

according to whether that type of city is relatively large or small. Examples of policies that alter the national composition of output include trade restriction policies such as tariffs and quotas, capital subsidies particular to certain types of industries, and research and development subsidies particular to certain types of industries.

An example of another type of policy with unintended spatial impacts is effective minimum wage laws. Suppose the minimum wage is set at the current level in some visible industry, such that it lies between prevailing wages in the largest versus the smallest cities. For example, suppose it is set at the wage in iron and steel industries in medium-sized cites. For large cities the minimum wage law imposes no constaints, while cities smaller than steel cities must all raise their wages to the level prevailing in these medium-sized cities. To achieve equilibrium in national labor markets with equalized utility levels, costs of living in these smaller cities are going to have to rise to dissipate the wage premium now received by workers in smaller cities. This increase in costs of living happens by smaller cities growing into medium-sized cities. The results in a strict setting would be the elimination of smaller cities with the products from these types of cities being produced in inefficiently larger cities and a decline in the numbers of the types of cities producing these products.

2.2 Trade and Growth

Because there are constant returns to scale at the national level, extending the model to incorporate basic international trade and economic growth theorems is straightforward. In terms of economic growth, consider an economy whose population is growing at the rate n. Assume there is no technological change. In the steady state the net national capital stock also grows at the rate n to maintain constant factor rewards. Since all inputs and outputs expand at the rate n, the numbers of each type of city (with invariant efficient sizes) also grow at the rate n. In summary, the economy simply replicates itself at the rate n.

Technological change can dramatically alter these results. For example, suppose there is continuous technological improvement lowering commuting costs in cities. This means efficient city sizes of all types are continuously increasing, because the city sizes at which marginal scale benefits equal marginal living cost increases are continuously expanding. This increase in efficient city sizes in itself is a force reducing the numbers of cities required to house a given national population. Combining technological change and population growth, the numbers of cities of each type may rise or fall depending on whether the technological-change force that reduces the number of cities needed is outweighted or not by the population-growth force that increases the number of cities needed to house an expanding population.

In terms of international trade theorems, the results for the two factor–two traded good model apply directly. In a system of cities context, it means we have two types of cities, with national constant returns to scale, although locally there are economies of scale, nontraded goods, and spatial dimensions. For our two types of cities, assume one produces x and the other z and that x is the relatively capital intensive good.

Then we compare two economies in a many-economy world that face fixed terms of trade (or fixed relative prices of z and x), have identical technologies, and have consumers with identical tastes. The economy with the higher national capital-to-labor ratio will have relatively more x type relative to z type cities (Rybczynski theorem). In fact, if the two economies have identical populations, the economy with the greater capital stock will have absolutely more x type cities and absolutely less z type cities. Moreover, given these economies face the same terms of trade, despite any differences in sizes and relative compositions of output and types of cities, they will pay the same absolute factor rewards. Note, however, the assumptions for the factor price equalization theorem to hold in this case are very strict. Not only must economies have identical traded good technologies, but tastes for housing and commuting technologies must be the same so that cities of each type are identical across economies. The final trade theorem of interest is the Stolper–Samuelson theorem, which states that as the price of, say, x rises relative to z, the return to the factor used intensively in producing x, which is capital here, will rise relative to the return to the other factor. Thus a tariff protecting the x industry will raise the return on capital relative to utility levels, as well as causing an expansion of the x industry and x type cities.

12

The Efficient Allocation of Resources in a System of Cities

In this chapter, I examine the Pareto-efficient allocation of resources among and within cities in an economy, as solved for by an omniscient social planner. I then interpret the planner's solutions in a market economy and determine whether market solutions, such as presented in the previous chapter, correspond to the planner's solutions. Given the nature of the questions asked in this chapter, we can revert to the general functional form model used in Chapter 1 and derive results for a general monocentric model of a city.

In specifying the model we continue to assume that urban agglomeration occurs because of external economies of scale in production. Given the specification of these scale externalities, when people migrate, they affect the level of scale efficiencies and the productivity of other factors in the cities they leave and enter. In making their location decisions they do not account for these external effects; and, therefore, under certain conditions they may make socially inefficient location decisions.

We also consider the possibility of agglomeration occurring because of scale economies in consumption. For example, people may agglomerate in cities for the purpose of exploiting the publicness of pure public goods. By definition, the addition of another person in the city does not affect other people's consumption benefits from a given level of government expenditures on pure public goods. However, an additional person does reduce everyone else's tax cost, since there is now an additional person to share in taxes. For example, if the cost of a unit of public goods is $1 and tax shares are equal, the per person tax price of a unit of public goods is $1/N$, where N is city population. As population grows, the per person unit tax price declines, a benefit to all residents from adding population. This phenomenon is sometimes called a fiscal externality, since people do not account for the positive or negative effect they have on other people's tax costs in the cities they enter or leave. This may lead to situations where people's location decisions may not always be socially optimal.

The arguments in this chapter define important relationships, particularly those between land rents and the degree of scale economies that must hold when cities are Pareto-efficient in size. Second, in comparing market city sizes with Pareto-efficient city sizes, the analysis provides an efficiency basis for federal intervention into the affairs of cities or local governments. The arguments in this chapter for efficient federal intervention are based on the work of Flatters, Henderson, and Mieszkowski (1974), who developed their results in a regional Ricardian model rather than an urban model. Mirrlees (1972) has also worked on a similar problem. It is important to note that intervention on efficiency grounds should be distinguished from intervention based on equity considerations in a model with imperfect mobility of labor, where the federal government may want to transfer income from richer to poorer cities and regions. This type of intervention was discussed in Chapter 9.

To obtain criteria for the efficient allocation of resources in an economy, the usual welfare maximization problem facing a social planner is to maximize the utility of a representative individual subject to production and resource constraints, holding the utility level of all other individuals constant. We place an additional constraint on the social planner, which is designed to make planning solutions directly comparable to market solutions. People with the same utility functions and opportunity sets must have equal utility levels. This constraint ensures that planning solutions are consistent with stable-market solutions where, with nondiscriminatory government intervention,[1] identical perfectly mobile people must achieve identical utility levels, given their respective spatial locations in a city or economy (see Chapters I and 11).

In maximizing utilities, the planner is concerned with the welfare of two basic groups of people in the model: laborers and capital owners. For most of

---

[1] Government intervention does not discriminate in outcomes among individuals in a group, although it may discriminate within certain limits among groups of individuals (e.g., progressive taxation). If factor supplies and effort are fixed, then most planning solutions can be realized in a market economy through taxation alone, *given* the equal utility constraint.

this chapter we assume that laborers are identical in skills, tastes, and factor ownership, so that they all achieve the same utility level. Given two differing groups of people, by definition, a planner's Pareto-efficient solution is one that either maximizes the utility of laborers while holding the welfare of capital owners fixed or maximizes the welfare of capital owners while holding the utility of laborers fixed.

In the planning solution, the utility of laborers is a function of their consumption of produced goods and urban amenities such as commuting time and hence leisure. On the other hand, capital owners need not live in the cities where their capital is employed. We assume capital owners live either in the countryside outside cities or on the edges of cities, where in both cases they rent land at the price (usually zero) of agricultural land and incur no commuting costs. Therefore the amenity consumption of capital owners is exogenous to the problem. For the planner the only variable affecting the welfare of capital owners is their consumption of market goods. Therefore the planner's problem is to maximize the utility of laborers either for a fixed total consumption of capital owners or, equivalently, for a fixed real return per unit of capital (given a fixed capital stock).

I first present a solution for the situation where there is only one type of city in the economy and there are sufficient cities of that type so we may effectively ignore the lumpiness problem mentioned in Chapter 11. In this situation the size that is individually efficient for one city will be efficient for all cities, given that all cities will be identical. I then turn to the more interesting case in which there are multiple types of cities and some lumpiness in the solutions.

1. ONE TYPE OF CITY

With only one type of city and no lumpiness problems, the planner's allocation problem is simple. Given that cities have identical production and consumption technology, they will all attain the same size and have the same characteristics. In particular, their capital-to-labor ratio K/N will equal the national ratio. Therefore, the only question is what is the optimal size of any representative city and hence of every city. The planner's problem can be formulated as follows.

As in Chapter 1 a consumer at distance u from the city center consumes the city's produced good $x(u)$, its import good $z(u)$, housing $h(u)$, and leisure $e(u) = T - tu$, where t is unit distance commuting time. The utility function of a resident at location u is $V = V(x(u), z(u), h(u), e(u))$. City population is N, and u_0 and u_1 are CBD and city radii. Therefore, for any city, the planner seeks to maximize the utility V^0 of a representative individual subject to constraints, or to

$$\max J = V^0(x(u), z(u), h(u), e(u)) \tag{12.1}$$

$$+ \int_{u_0}^{u_1} \lambda_1(u)[V(x(u), z(u), h(u), e(u)) - V^0] \, du \tag{12.1.1}$$

$$+ \lambda_2\left(N - \int_{u_0}^{u_1} N(u) \, du\right) \tag{12.1.2}$$

$$+ \lambda_3\left(N - \int_0^{u_0} n(u) \, du\right) \tag{12.1.3}$$

$$+ \lambda_4\left(K - \int_{u_0}^{u_1} k(u)N(u) \, du - \int_0^{u_0} k(u) \, du\right) \tag{12.1.4}$$

$$+ \int_{u_0}^{u_1} \lambda_5(u)[2\pi u - l(u)N(u)] \, du \tag{12.1.5}$$

$$+ \int_0^{u_0} \lambda_6(u)[2\pi u - l(u)] \, du \tag{12.1.6}$$

$$+ \int_{u_0}^{u_1} \lambda_7(u)[T - e(u) - tu] \, du \tag{12.1.7}$$

$$+ \int_{u_0}^{u_1} \lambda_8(u)[h(l(u), k(u)) - h(u)] \, du \tag{12.1.8}$$

$$+ \lambda_9(\bar{C} - K/N) \tag{12.1.9}$$

$$+ \lambda_{10}\left[\int_0^{u_0} G(N)x(n(u), k(u), l(u))(1 - t_x u) \, du - \int_{u_0}^{u_1} x(u)N(u) \, du\right.$$

$$\left. - \int_{u_0}^{u_1} p_z z(u)N(u) \, du - p_k K\right]. \tag{12.1.10}$$

The λ_i and $\lambda_i(u)$ are multipliers. Constraint (12.1.1) is the equal utility constraint for laborers who are the city residents. Where $N(u)$ and $n(u)$ are, respectively, population and employment at location u, constraints (12.1.2) and (12.1.3) state that city population equals the sum of all people living in the city and city population equals labor employment, or labor is fully employed in the city. Constraint (12.1.4) is a full employment of capital constraint where the sum of capital used in residential construction plus the sum of business capital equals the city's stock of capital. Constraints (12.1.5) and (12.1.6) state that land supplied ($2\pi u$) equals land used for residential or commercial purposes at each distance from the city center. Leisure and housing production at each distance are defined in (12.1.7) and (12.1.8). Constraint (12.1.9) requires that all cities face a fixed capital-to-labor ratio equal to the national ratio, or that there be full employment in the economy.

The final constraint is a production–consumption, or balance-of-trade, constraint, faced by the planner at the national and hence local level. The first term in (12.1.10) from Equation (1.26) is total production in the city available (after paying transport costs) for distribution at the retailing–transport node at the city center. Where $x(u)$ is per person consumption at u, the second term is total city consumption of x, or per person consumption summed over all people and locations. The third term is the cost to the planner in units of x of importing z from other economies (or other cities, later in the chapter). The final term is the city's production of x allocated to capital owners. This is the number of units of capital multiplied by the fixed return p_k in units of x allocated by the planner to capital owners per unit of their capital stock. Note that it is assumed the city pays nothing for the land it is located on, or agricultural land rents are zero.

Problem (12.1.0) and the constraints (12.1.1)–(12.1.10) define the welfare maximization problem. If we maximize the Lagrangian with respect to the different variables, we get a set of first-order conditions that mostly relate to the resource allocation within the city. They are the standard ones, namely, that the marginal products of mobile factors should be equalized in all uses within the city, that marginal rates of substitution in consumption should equal ratios of marginal costs or the marginal rates of transformation, and that the marginal products of land at the border of competing uses such as the CBD should be equalized. Since these conditions are standard, we do not present them specifically in the text.[2] Moreover, since we have already introduced externalities into the internal structure of the city in Chapter 3, market solutions discussed here will be consistent with efficient internal

---

[2] Relevant first-order conditions are

$$\partial J/\partial K = \lambda_4 - \lambda_9/N - \lambda_{10}p_k = 0,$$

$$\partial J/\partial n(u) = -\lambda_3 + \lambda_{10}G(\partial x/\partial n)(1 - t_x u) = 0,$$

$$\partial J/\partial N(u) = -\lambda_2 - \lambda_4 k(u) - \lambda_5 l(u) - \lambda_{10}x(u) - \lambda_{10}p_z z(u) = 0,$$

$$\partial J/\partial k(u) = -\lambda_4 N(u) + \lambda_8(\partial h/\partial k) = -\lambda_4 + \lambda_{10}G(N)(\partial x/\partial k)(1 - t_x u) = 0,$$

$$\partial J/\partial l(u) = -\lambda_5 N(u) + \lambda_8(\partial h/\partial l) = -\lambda_6 + \lambda_{10}G(\partial x/\partial l)(1 - t_x u) = 0,$$

$$\partial J/\partial x(u) = \lambda_1(u)(\partial V/\partial x) - \lambda_{10}N(u) = 0,$$

$$\partial J/\partial h(u) = \lambda_1(u)(\partial V/\partial h) - \lambda_8 = 0,$$

$$\partial J/\partial z(u) = \lambda_1(u)(\partial V/\partial z) - \lambda_{10}p_z N(u) = 0.$$

resource allocation within the city. They are the standard ones, namely, allocation of resources among cities.

To solve for Pareto-efficient city size, we maximize the Lagrangian in (12.1.0) with respect to N to get a first-order condition

$$\frac{\partial x}{\partial N} = \lambda_2 + \lambda_3 + \lambda_9 \left(\frac{K}{N^2}\right) + \lambda_{10} \int_0^{u_0} \left(\frac{dG}{dN}\right) x(u)(1 - t_x u) \, du = 0. \quad (12.2)$$

To solve for λ_9 we maximize J with respect to K and then $k(u)$ and perform appropriate substitutions. To solve for λ_3 we maximize J with respect to $n(u)$. Finally, to solve for λ_2 we first maximize J with respect to $N(u)$ and then $k(u)$, $l(u)$, $h(u)$, and $x(u)$ to perform further necessary substitutions. All these first-order conditions used in substitution are listed in footnote 2. The result is

$$\frac{\partial V/\partial h}{\partial V/\partial x} h(u) + p_z z(u) + x(u)$$

$$= G(N)\frac{\partial x}{\partial n}(1 - t_x u) + \frac{\varepsilon X}{N} + \frac{K}{N}\left[G\frac{\partial x}{\partial k}(1 - t_x u) - p_k\right]. \quad (12.3)$$

In writing Equation (12.3) it is assumed that housing is produced with a linear homogeneous production function, so that $h = k(\partial h/\partial k) + l(\partial h/\partial l)$. The term ε is defined to be $(dG/dN)(N/G)$, which is the elasticity of scale effects with respect to the labor force. The term X is total net city output of x, and it equals

$$\int_0^{u_0} G(N)x(u)(1 - t_x u) \, du.$$

The left-hand side of Equation (12.3) is the social costs to the economy of adding an additional resident to the city. This is the value of the additional consumption of x, z, and h (in units of x) that a new resident takes from the total available, such that all residents have equal utility. Note that amenities or commuting costs borne by this resident are not a direct cost to the social planner, although any differential amenity or leisure loss borne by the resident must be compensated with produced goods to maintain equal utility with other residents.

The right-hand side of (12.3) is the social benefit to the planner of adding an additional resident to the city. The first term is the private marginal product of n. The second is the scale externality or the effect of an additional member of the labor force on efficiency as measured by increased output of all firms. Therefore, the first two terms are the social marginal product (SMP) of labor to city x. The third term is the net benefit to the city that results from employing the additional capital that comes along with the additional resident so as to maintain the fixed capital-to-labor ratio in the economy. (The net benefit [loss] to laborers from additional capital is proportional to the difference between the additional contribution to production of a unit of capital $[G(N)(\partial x/\partial k)(1 - t_x u)]$ and unit payment for capital (p_k). This difference is multiplied by the additional quantity of capital matching the new resident, or K/N, to get the full net benefit from this additional capital.)

Equation (12.3) states that optimum city size occurs when the marginal social benefits to city residents of increasing city size equal the social marginal costs (SMC) given fixed consumption of capital owners.[3] The question is whether this condition is satisfied in a market economy. To find that out, we must first interpret Equation (12.3) in a market context.

1.1 The Market Interpretation of One Pareto-Efficient Solution

The Pareto-efficient solution we examine in a market context is the one for a competitive economy where factors are paid the value of their marginal product by profit-maximizing firms, and land rental income in a city is divided up equally among laborers by a city land bank company. In that case, since capital is paid the value of its marginal product, $p_k = G(N)(\partial x/\partial k)(1 - t_x u)$; and the capital effect term equals zero in Equation (12.3).

In a market economy, as suggested earlier, given consumer and producer optimization behavior and perfect competition, the first-order conditions in footnote 2 with respect to consumption of x, z, and h and employment of k, n, and l will be met. Of relevance here are the marginal rate of substitution and marginal productivity conditions, which state that $(\partial V/\partial h)/(\partial V/\partial x) = p(u)$, where $p(u)$ is the unit price of housing in terms of x and that the wage rate $p_n = G(N)(\partial x/\partial n)(1 - t_x u)$. Substituting these conditions into Equation (12.3), we get

$$p(u) + p_z z(u) + x(u) = p_n + \varepsilon X/N. \tag{12.4}$$

The left-hand side of (12.4) is the expenditures of a resident. This equals the resident's income in a market economy where income is composed of wages

---

[3] Note that if there is more than one type of labor in the economy, this condition becomes more complicated. Cities still remain identical, and thus the ratios of the first type of labor to both capital and the second type of labor must remain fixed. If we add the necessary consumption, production, resource, and spatial constraints for this second type of laborer, and maximize J with respect to the first type of labor, Equation (12.3) has a new term on its right-hand side. This term adds on the difference between the SMP of a second type of laborer and the consumption of that person, multiplied by the increase in type-two labor as type-one labor increases. Essentially, to the benefits of having an additional type-one laborer, we add the net costs–benefits of the matching increase in type-two labor.

plus a land rental share that equals average land rental income. Therefore, Equation (12.4) reduces to

$$\text{land rent share} = \varepsilon X/N. \tag{12.5}$$

This equation defines a general relationship that must hold in a market economy, when any individual city is of efficient size. This condition has a simple intuitive explanation.

The benefit of an additional resident to other residents in the city is the increase in production available to them caused by increased production efficiency, or $\varepsilon X/N$. The cost to initial residents in the city is the additional land rent share (or share in old production not paid out in wages and capital costs) that must now be allocated to the new resident. Optimal city size occurs when the increases in new production to residents, $\varepsilon X/N$, equal the losses in old production, or an additional land rent share. Since per person land rents in a market economy start at a nominal level and then rise with city size (see Chapters 1 and 2) and marginal scale economies are positive and perhaps declining, initial net marginal benefits of additional residents are positive. These net marginal benefits then may start to decline as land rents rise and marginal scale economies decline. Optimal city size is reached when net marginal benefits decline to zero.[4]

1.2   Are Market Solutions Pareto-Efficient?

Under the assumption of only one type of city, Equation (12.5) is generally satisfied in market solutions, indicating that market solutions are Pareto-efficient. For example, in the model in Chapter 11, which is a special case of the current model, average rental income from Equation (11.4) is $\frac{1}{3}t\, N^{1/2}\pi^{-1/2}$. From the production function $\varepsilon X/N = \varepsilon(K/N)^{1-\alpha}N^{\varepsilon}$. Equating these terms to obtain the optimal city size criterion in Equation (12.5) yields the result that for a Pareto-efficient city,

$$N = (3\varepsilon\pi^{1/2}t^{-1})^{1/(1/2-\varepsilon)}(K/N)^{(1-\alpha)/(1/2-\varepsilon)}.$$

From Equation (11.12), this is identical to the condition defining $N(J)$, the market city size in Chapter 11.

This equivalency makes sense for two reasons. First, the statement of the planner's problem, which is to maximize laborers' utility for a given return to capital, is consistent with the way in which market solutions were defined in

---

[4] Of course, there is no certainty that Equation (12.5) is satisfied at a unique city size or even that it is satisfied at all. Given different assumptions about how marginal scale economies change with city size, optimal city size could be infinite or infinitesimal or there could be a number of local optima where Equation (12.5) is satisfied.

Chapters 2 and 11. In a partial equilibrium model, city governments limit city size so as to maximize laborers' utility given a fixed borrowing rate on capital.[5] In a general equilibrium model, equilibrium city size occurs when the sum of total capital rental income and monetized utility levels is maximized. This sum can only be maximized when, while holding one element constant, the other is maximized. Accordingly, under the current assumptions, the market determination of city size and the planning solution are simply different ways of stating and approaching the same maximization problem.

The equivalency also makes sense from an externality perspective. Laborers in a market economy move to equalize the private marginal benefits of moving among cities. From a social perspective, they should incorporate into their calculus any external effects from their location decisions and move to equalize the social marginal benefits of moving among cities. However, if all cities are identical, the magnitude of these external effects will be equal between all cities; and when laborers move to equalize private marginal benefits they will incidentally equalize social marginal benefits. Therefore, the fact that laborers do not account for migration externalities does not adversely affect the allocation of resources in this simple situation.

1.3 Public Goods

So far we have assumed that external economies of scale are the basis for agglomeration. Suppose we assume instead that the basis is the existence of local pure public goods.

The planner's problem in solving for optimal city size is easily revised to incorporate public goods. We assume the city is still monocentric and people still commute to work in the CBD. The level of public services g enters each utility function and the cost of public goods in units of x enters the

---

[5] Equation (12.5) and the condition for efficient partial equilibrium city size are simply different ways of defining equivalent changes in real income. In a partial equilibrium model, we examine the changing utility level of a representative person at the expanding city edge, with an infinitesimal change in city population. We can show that the utility change in monetary terms equals the individual's change in income minus the value of increased leisure losses as the city edge shifts out. To maintain spatial equilibrium all peoples' rent payments throughout the city must increase by an amount equal to the value of the additional lost leisure of the representative individual. So, the monetized utility change of this person equals his income change minus the increase in per person rent payments in the city. The representative person's income change equals the per person increase in production due to increased scale economies minus the per person reduction in share of initial land rents (due to additional sharers) plus the increase in per person land rental income (due to the general increase in land rents). This last term cancels out with the representative person's value of increased lost leisure in the monetized utility change calculation. If we multiply the resulting utility change expression by N and set it equal to zero, the result is Equation (12.5).

consumption–production constraint (12.1.10). We assume that the cost of g in units of x is one. Resolving the maximization problem assuming there are no longer (marginal) economies of scale yields two important results. First, there is the Samuelson condition on public good consumption, or

$$\int_{u_0}^{u_1} N(u) \frac{\partial V/\partial g}{\partial V/\partial x(u)} \, du = 1.$$

Second, the new condition on optimal population is[6]

$$\frac{\partial V/\partial h}{\partial V/\partial x} h(u) + p_z z(u) + x(u) = \frac{\partial x}{\partial n}(1 - t_x u). \tag{12.6}$$

The marginal benefit of adding a new resident is that person's marginal product. The marginal cost of adding a new resident is the additional consumption of goods that must be allocated to that person such that he has equal utility with other residents, given prevailing commuting costs and the level of public goods.

In market variables the consumption of private goods equals income less taxes paid for the public good. Income equals land rent shares plus wages, which equal the marginal product of labor. Substituting these into (12.6) yields

$$\text{land rent share} = \text{per person taxes.} \tag{12.7}$$

In market terms, to other residents the marginal cost of an additional resident is the land rent share the new resident gets. The marginal benefit is the tax share that person incurs, reducing everyone else's taxes. City size is optimal when these are equalized.

As explained in Flatters, Henderson, and Mieszkowski (1974), another implication of Equation (12.7) is that total taxes and hence total expenditures on public goods should equal total land rents in the city. (This result does not depend on the way land rents are distributed.) This could be realized by taxing away all land rental income and using that revenue and only that revenue to provide public services. This is an equivalent policy to Henry George's proposal in 1879 of a single tax levied on land rental income to tax away all surplus land rent (above frontier rents, which are zero here) (see George, 1938). In some sense the foregoing analysis is a modern vindication of Henry George, although the intent and logic behind the proposals are somewhat different.

Similar to the scale externality situation, we expect Equations (12.6) and (12.7) to be satisfied in a market economy given the competitive behavior of land developers in setting up cities. The Samuelson condition will be satisfied within cities, given competitive city governments seeking to be (re)elected by providing public services efficiently.

---

[6] This assumes capital is paid its marginal product.

2. MULTIPLE TYPES OF CITIES

Suppose instead of there being just one type of city there are multiple types of cities, each type specializing in the production of a different traded good. Moreover, suppose that although there are a large number of cities in the economy, there is not a sufficient number of any one type to assume away lumpiness problems. Given these assumptions, I illustrate the planner's problem using an example with only two types of cities, each specializing in the production of a different good. The second type of city specializes in the production of z (see Chapter 11 on specialization arguments). I also show that the results generalize to situations with many types of cities.

The maximization problem in (12.1) can be adjusted fairly easily to account for two types of cities. Added on to the constraints of (12.1.0) are a second set of employment and spatial characteristics [constraints (12.1.2)– (12.1.8)] for the type z city, a constraint equalizing utility levels between types of cities, full employment constraints for the economy [replacing (12.1.9)], and a production–consumption constraint for the z good.[7]

---

[7] Where m and q are the numbers of the x- and z-type cities, $\bar{K}$ and $\bar{N}$ are economy endowments, γ_i are the multipliers for the z city, and z superscripts refer to variables for type z cities, the new maximization problem is to

$$
\max J = V^0(x(u), h(u), z(u), e(u)) + \int_{u_0}^{u_1} \lambda_1(u)(V^0 - V(x(u), z(u), h(u), e(u)))\, du
$$

$$
+ \int_{u_0^z}^{u_1^z} \gamma_1(u)[V^0 - V(x(u), z(u), h(u), e(u))]\, du + \lambda_2\left[N - \int_{u_0}^{u_1} N(u)\, du\right]
$$

$$
+ \gamma_2\left[N^z - \int_{u_0^z}^{u_1^z} N(u)\, du\right] + \lambda_3\left[N - \int_0^{u_0} n(u)\, du\right] + \gamma_3\left[N^z - \int_0^{u_0^z} n(u)\, du\right]
$$

$$
+ \lambda_4\left[K - \int_{u_0}^{u_1} k(u)N(u)\, du - \int_0^{u_0} k(u)\, du\right] + \gamma_4\left[K^z - \int_{u_0^z}^{u_1^z} k(u)N(u)\, du\right.
$$

$$
\left. - \int_0^{u_0^z} k(u)\, du\right] + \int_{u_0}^{u_1} \lambda_5(u)[2\pi u - l(u)N(u)]\, du + \int_{u_0^z}^{u_1^z} \gamma_5(u)[2\pi u - l(u)N(u)]\, du
$$

$$
+ \int_0^{u_0} \lambda_6(u)[2\pi u - l(u)]\, du + \int_0^{u_0^z} \gamma_6(u)[2\pi u - l(u)]\, du
$$

$$
+ \int_{u_0}^{u_1} \lambda_7(u)[h(u) - h(l(u), k(u))]\, du + \int_{u_0^z}^{u_1^z} \gamma_7(u)[h(u) - h(l(u), k(u))]\, du
$$

$$
+ \lambda_8(\bar{N} - mN - qN^z) + \gamma_8(\bar{K} - mK - qK^z)
$$

$$
+ \lambda_9\left[m\int_0^{u_0} G(N)x(1 - t_x u)\, du - m_u\int_{u_0}^{u_1} x(u)N(u)\, du - q\int_{u_1^z}^{u_1^z} x(u)N(u)\, du - p_k mK\right]
$$

$$
+ \gamma_9\left[q\int_0^{u_0^z} F(N)z(1 - t_z u)\, du - m\int_{u_0}^{u_1} z(u)N(u)\, du - q\int_{u_0^z}^{u_1^z} z(u)N(u)\, du - p_k^z qK^z\right].
$$

If we maximize the new Lagrangian with respect to N and N^z and combine the conditions to solve for a condition describing the optimal allocation between x- z-type cities, the result after substitution of various other first-order conditions is

$$
G(N)\frac{\partial x}{\partial n}(1 - t_x u) + \frac{\varepsilon X}{N} - \left[\frac{\partial V/\partial h}{\partial V/\partial x}h(u) + x(u) + \frac{\partial V/\partial z}{\partial V/\partial x}z(u)\right]
$$
$$
= \frac{\gamma_9}{\lambda_9}\left\{F(N)\frac{\partial x}{\partial n}(1 - t_z u) + \frac{\varepsilon_z Z}{N} - \left[\frac{\partial V/\partial h}{\partial V/\partial z}h(u) + z(u) + \frac{\partial V/\partial x}{\partial V/\partial z}x(u)\right]\right\},
$$

$$\tag{12.8}$$

where ε and ε_z are the scale effect elasticities with respect to population or, for example, $\varepsilon = dG(N)/dN[N/G(N)]$. Total outputs per city of x and z available for consumption at the retailing–transport node of each city are represented by X and Z.

In the first line, the first two terms represent the social marginal benefits in units of x of increasing population to city x, which from above equal the SMP of labor to city x. The last three terms in parentheses are the SMC to the city or the value (in x units) of the additional consumption of x, z, and h of a new resident such that all residents have equal utility.

The second part of Equation (12.8) is the corresponding expression for city z. In the brackets everything is defined in z units, but $\gamma_9/\lambda_9 = (\partial V/\partial z)/(\partial V/\partial x)$ converts the second line to x units. The first two terms are the SMP of labor to city z (SMP$_z$) and the last three are the SMC$_z$.

We may thus rewrite (12.8) more informally as

$$
\text{SMP} - \text{SMC} = \text{SMP}_z - \text{SMC}_z. \tag{12.8a}
$$

If there are more than two types of cities, (12.8a) reads $\text{SMP} - \text{SMC} = \text{SMP}_z - \text{SMC}_z = \text{SMP}_i - \text{SMC}_i$ for all i. Equation (12.8a) states that the gap between the SMP and SMC of labor should be equalized in all cities. If, for example, $\text{SMP} - \text{SMC} > \text{SMP}_z - \text{SMC}_z$, city x is underpopulated. Since the gap between per person productivity and consumption is greater in city x, we could move a person from city z to city x with utility levels unchanged and have a residual of goods left over.

The basic concern is under what conditions Equation (12.8) will be satisfied in a free-market economy. The problem in attaining efficient city sizes given more than one type of city is due to the existence of different degrees of external economies of scale between cities. If economies of scale differ between cities, the external effect of labor migration decisions will differ among cities. Laborers will move to equalize the private marginal benefits of moving among cities; but given different marginal scale effects, the social marginal benefits will not equalized. Given the way in which land rents are distributed in the model, there is also a problem of land rent shares varying among cities. Under alternative distribution schemes, such as rents going to a group of rentiers, the land rent share problem disappears but the scale economy problem does not.

To determine which cities are under- or overpopulated in a market economy, as in Section 1, we interpret Equation (12.8) in a market economy where factors are paid the value of their marginal product. The SMP of labor in city x equals $p_n + \varepsilon(X/N)$. Given that price ratios equal marginal rates of substitution in a competitive economy, SMC of labor equals expenditures on market goods, which equals net income. Net income is wages plus the share in land rental income. Therefore, Equation (12.8) becomes[8]

$$\varepsilon(X/N) - \text{land rental income share in city } x$$

$$= \varepsilon_z(Z/N) - \text{land rental income share in city } z. \qquad (12.9)$$

To see when Equations (12.9) and (12.8) are likely to be satisfied without federal government intervention, we examine several possible situations in city x relative to city z. In any equilibrium, utility levels will be equalized between cities. If we define an indirect utility function for the person at the edge in each type of city, then in equilibrium

$$V = V(y^x, p_x, p_z, p(u_1), T - tu_1^x) = V(y^z, p_x, p_z, p(u_1), T - tu_1^z),$$

where y^i and u_1^i are, respectively, the income and radius of city type i, and it is assumed that land rents at the two city edges are equal. Thus commuting distance and income are the two variable arguments in the utility function. Suppose x cities are larger due to greater *total* or *intramarginal* scale economies and thus x cities pay greater wages and greater land rental income (average rents paid and hence rental income rises with city size, as in Chapter 2). However, relative to the smaller z cities with lower income, people in x cities are no better off because they have less leisure. An equilibrium holds.

Given this, because land rental income in x cities is greater than in z cities, if *marginal* scale effects are lower in x cities than in z, then from Equation (12.9) x cities must be *overpopulated*. If marginal scale effects are greater in x cities than in z cities in this case, then either city may be overpopulated. If x [z] cities are overpopulated, some form of federal intervention is necessary to tax people living in x [z] cities and subsidize people living in z [x] cities to encourage population movements from x [z] to z [x] cities until Equation (12.8) is satisfied. [The taxes would now be a part of Equation (12.9) since they are now part of income. A tax-subsidy solution rather than just a subsidy

---

[8] Note that if land rental income is paid out to rentiers, then Equation (12.9) would read $\varepsilon(X/N) = \varepsilon_z(Z/N)$. Efficiency would only occur in the market solutions if marginal scale effects were equal, although this could have a disagreeable effect on income distribution.

solution or just a tax solution is suggested, since it should be possible to design a solution where total taxes equal total subsidies or the program is self-financing.]

Note that these statements and the general approach to the problem of population allocation in this chapter reject a partial equilibrium approach to the problem of determining whether cities are optimal in size. Under a partial equilibrium approach, viewing one city on its own when the social marginal benefit of labor exceeds the private marginal benefit of labor, it might seem desirable to subsidize immigration to that city. From a general equilibrium perspective, however, this is incorrect. Subsidizing labor to migrate to one city would draw population away from other cities where the social marginal benefit of labor also exceeds the private marginal benefit. If these external effects are the same among cities, no subsidization is required.

In the foregoing discussion, the existence of external economies of scale is the basis for inefficiencies in population allocation among cities. One can introduce a variety of other externalities connected with population size, such as congestion on roads (see Mirrlees, 1972) or congestion in the provision of public services (see Flatters, Henderson, and Mieszkowski, 1974). These considerations result in other terms being added to Eqution (12.8). For example, for congestion, two new terms would enter, describing the increased travel costs for commuters in cities x and z from adding additional residents who then increase congestion levels. As always, the question whether a particular city is over- or underpopulated depends on the magnitude of its positive and negative externalities *relative* to other cities.

This analysis of externalities is concerned with optimal population allocation at the margin among cities. There is, however, another problem that is more global in nature. Cities individually would be best off satisfying Equations (12.3)–(12.5) where the marginal benefits and costs of an additional resident are *equal*. However, the economy is usually best off when there is a *gap* between marginal benefits and costs that is equal between all cities. This is the problem mentioned in Chapter 11 that, with lumpiness, free-market equilibrium will result in cities that are not the most efficient size individually. This provides a basis for city governments to try to restrict their city sizes to the individually efficient level by excluding some residents, who would then be forced into very small, inefficient cities.

However, if there are sufficient cities of both types, the lumpiness problem becomes negligible, and both the global and marginal problems of allocating labor between cities will be solved. As the number of each type of city becomes very large, the gap between the SMP and SMC of population for each type of city in Equation (12.8) approaches zero. At the limit both gaps are zero, so both Equations (12.8) smf (12.3) are satisfied. That is, with no lumpiness, all cities approach their individual efficient sizes, and there is no longer a problem of population allocation at the margin. This is intuitively appealing.

When the number of cities becomes very large and they approach their most efficient size, we approach a constant-returns-to-scale world. That is, doubling the economy's endowments would double the numbers of each type of city, leaving city size unchanged, and would double production, without affecting utility levels or capital rentals. In this de facto constant-returns-to-scale world at the economy-wide level, the problem of misallocation of resources from external economies of scale vanishes.

2.1 Public Goods

If we reintroduce pure public goods as the basis for agglomeration, there is also a problem of population allocation if cities are of different sizes. Assume cities are of unequal size and x-type cities are larger because of greater *intra*marginal scale economies. However, we assume for simplicity that marginal scale economies ε and ε_z are currently zero. Maximizing the relevant Lagrangian (with public goods entering utility functions and production–consumption constraints) yields the population allocation condition that

$$\frac{\partial x}{\partial n}(1 - t_x u) - \left[\frac{\partial V/\partial h}{\partial V/\partial x}h(u) + \frac{\partial V/\partial z}{\partial V/\partial x}z(u) + x(u)\right]$$

$$= \frac{\partial V/\partial z}{\partial V/\partial x}\frac{\partial z}{\partial n}(1 - t_z u) - \left[\frac{\partial V/\partial h}{\partial V/\partial x}h(u) + \frac{\partial V/\partial z}{\partial V/\partial x}z(u) + x(u)\right]. \qquad (12.10)$$

Interpreting Equation (12.10) in a market economy, we see that the expressions in square brackets are expenditures on market goods. These expenditures equal income less taxes. Income comes from wages and land rent shares. Given these relationships, in a market context Equation (12.10) becomes

land rent share in x − per person taxes in x

= land rent share in z − per person taxes in z. \qquad (12.11)

This condition is unlikely to be satisfied in a market economy. If city x is larger than city z by assumption, land rent shares in city x are larger than in city z. The relative magnitude of per person taxes can be shown to depend on the compensated price elasticity of demand for public goods, given the dependence on the unit tax price of people's demand for public goods (Flatters, Henderson, and Mieszkowski, 1974). The per person unit tax price of public goods in units of x is $1/N$, where N is city population and the cost of a unit of public goods in terms of x is one. Since N is larger in the x city, the tax price of public goods is lower in the x city; but utility levels are equal. If the compensated elasticity of demand equals one, expenditures on public goods, and hence per person taxes, will always be equalized among regions, regardless of differences in unit tax prices. (We use the compensated elasticity since, in comparing cities and tax prices, utility is held constant.) If the elasticity is greater [less] than one, expenditures will be greater in the low [high] tax price city or in the larger [smaller] city. Given that the x city is larger and has a larger land rent share, Equation (12.11) can only be satisfied if tax shares are larger in city x. This could only occur if the compensated elasticity were greater than one; but for optimality it would have to be the precise magnitude such that tax costs satisfy Equation (12.11), given land rents. Otherwise, federal intervention in the form of income taxation and subsidization will be needed to encourage optimal population movements.

For public goods, we can see from Equation (12.11) that this problem of misallocation of resources can also be solved by distributing land rents and tax shares on a national basis, so that everyone in the economy pays the same taxes and gets the same land rent shares. The idea is that tax or land rent *shares* do not in themselves affect or represent production or consumption capabilities in the economy. Therefore if we equalize these shares nationally so that no one has an incentive to move to pay less taxes or to get more land rents, then the population will make correct location decisions, based on national marginal productivity and public good exploitation conditions. Note, however, this implies the national government must supply local public goods and satisfy the local Samuelson condition. In a voting model utilized to determine public services in a market economy, it is not clear that local preferences will be revealed to the national government so that they may satisfy the Samuelson condition or that the national government will be politically bound to provide local public goods efficiently.

3. CONCLUSIONS

In this chapter I showed that in general there is a problem of population allocation among cities. Given an economy with multiple types of cities and a few cities of each type, if there are external economies of scale in production or pure public goods in consumption, federal government intervention will be needed to ensure an efficient allocation of resources among regions. Such intervention will involve the subsidization of labor incomes in underpopulated cities and taxation of income in overpopulated cities.

References

Aaron, H. J. (1975), *Who Pays the Property Tax?* Washington: Brookings Institute.

Agnew, C. E. (1976), "Dynamic Modeling and Control of Congestion-Prone Systems," *Operations Research* **24**, 400–419.

Agnew, C. E. (1977), "The Theory of Congestion Tolls," *Journal of Regional Science* **17**, 381–393.

Alonso, W. (1964), *Location and Land Use.* Cambridge: Harvard Univ. Press.

Anas, A. (1978), "Dynamics of Urban Residential Growth," *Journal of Urban Economics* **5**, 66–87.

Arnott, R. J. (1980), "A Simple Urban Growth Model With Durable Housing," *Regional Science and Urban Economics* **10**, 53–76.

Bailey, M. J. (1957), "Note on the Economics of Residential Zoning and Urban Renewal," *Land Economics* **35**, 288–292.

Barr, J., and O. Davis (1966), "An Elementary Political and Economic Theory of the Expenditures of Local Governments," *Southern Economic Journal* **33**, 149–165.

Baumol, W. J., and D. F. Bradford (1970), "Optimal Departures from Marginal Cost Pricing," *American Economic Review* **60**, 265–283.

Baumol, W. J., and W. E. Oates (1975), *The Theory of Environmental Policy.* Englewood Cliffs: Prentice-Hall.

Beckmann, M. J. (1958), "City Hierarchies and Distribution of City Size," *Economic Development and Cultural Change* **VI**, 243–248.

Beckmann, M. J. (1974), "Spatial Equilibrium in the Housing Market," *Journal of Urban Economics* **1**, 99–107.

Bradford, D. F., and W. E. Oates (1971), "Towards a Predictive Theory of Intergovernmental Grants," *American Economic Review* **61**, 440–448.

Bradford, D. F., and W. E. Oates (1974), "Suburban Exploitation of Central Cities," in

Redistribution Through Public Choice (H. M. Hochman and G. Peterson, eds.), pp. 43–94. New York: Columbia Univ. Press.

Brown, J. and H. Rosen (1982), "On the Estimation of Structural Hedonic Price Models," *Econometrica* **50**, 765–768.

Brueckner, J. K. (1981a), "A Dynamic Model of Housing Production," *Journal of Urban Economics* **10**, 1–14.

Brueckner, J. K. (1981b), "Labor Mobility and the Incidence of the Residential Property Tax," *Journal of Urban Economics* **10**, 173–182.

Chipman, J. S. (1970), "External Economies of Scale and Competitive Equilibrium," *Quarterly Journal of Economics* **84**, 347–385.

Connally, M. (1970), "Public Goods, Externalities, and International Relations," *Journal of Political Economy* **78**, 279–290.

Courant, P. (1977), "A General Equilibrium Model of Heterogeneous Local Property Taxes," *Journal of Public Economics* **8**, 313–327.

Courant, P. and J. Yinger (1977), "On Models of Racial Prejudice and Urban Residential Structure," *Journal of Urban Economics* **4**, 272–291.

Courant, P. (1978), "Racial Prejudice in a Search Model of the Urban Housing Market," *Journal of Urban Economics* **5**, 329–345.

Davis, O. A., and A. B. Winston (1964), "The Economics of Complex Systems: The Case of Municipal Zoning," *Kyklos* **17**, 419–445.

Diamond, D. (1976), "Income and Residential Choice," unpublished Ph.D. thesis, Univ. of Chicago.

Diewert, M. E. (1974), "Applications in Duality Theory," in *Frontiers of Quantitative Economics* (D. A. Kendrick and M. D. Intriligator, eds.), Vol. 2, pp. 106–171, Amsterdam: North-Holland.

Dixit, A. (1973), "The Optimum Factory Town," *Bell Journal of Economics and Management Science* **4**, 637–654.

Ellickson, B. (1971), "Jurisdictional Fragmentation and Residential Choice," *American Economic Review* **61**, 334–339.

Ellickson, B. (1983), "Indivisibility, Housing Markets, and Public Goods," in *Research in Urban Economics* 3 (J. V. Henderson, ed.), pp. 91–116, Greenwich: JAI Press.

Epple, D., and A. Zelenitz (1981), "The Implications of Competition among Jurisdictions: Does Tiebout Need Politics?" *Journal of Political Economy* **89**, 1197–1217.

Epple, D., R. Filimon, and T. Romer (1983), "Housing Voting and Moving: Equilibrium in a Model of Local Public Goods with Multiple Jurisdiction," in *Research in Urban Economics* 3 (J. V. Henderson, ed.), pp. 59–90, Greenwich: JAI Press.

Filipiak, J. (1981), "Unloading of Congestion in Deterministic Queueing Networks," *Optional Control Applications and Methods* **2**, 35–45.

Fisher, R. (1979), "A Theoretical View of Revenue Sharing Grants," *National Tax Journal* (June).

Flatters, F., J. V. Henderson, and P. M. Mieszkowski (1974), "Public Goods, Efficiency, and Regional Fiscal Equalization," *Journal of Public Economics* **3**, 99–112.

Fujita, M. (1982), "Spatial Patterns of Residential Development," *Journal of Urban Economics* **12**, 22–52.

George, H. (1938), *Progress and Poverty*. New York: Modern Library.

Grieson, R. E., and J. R. White (1981), "The Effects of Zoning on Market Structure and Land Markets," *Journal of Urban Economics* **10**, 271–285.

Greenberg, M. A., and D. W. Wright (1974), "Staggered Hours Demonstration: Final Evaluation Report," Ontario Ministry of Transportation and Communications, mimeograph.

Guttman, J. (1975), "Predicting the Effect of Variable Working Hours on Peak Period Congestion," Univ. of Chicago, mimeograph.

Hamilton, B. W. (1975), "Zoning and Property Taxation in a System of Local Governments," *Urban Studies* **12**, 205–211.

Hamilton, B. W. (1976), "Capitalization of Intrajurisdictional Differences in Local Tax Prices," *American Economic Review* **66**, 743–753.

Harberger, A. C. (1974), *Taxation and Welfare*. Boston: Little Brown.

Hardman, A. (1983), "Effects of Rent Controls on an LDC Housing Market," paper prepared for Lincoln Land Institute conference on rent control, November 9–10, 1983.

Hartwick, J. M. (1971), "Consumer Choice When the Environment is a Variable: The Case of Residential Site Selection," Discussion Paper No. 50, Queen's Univ., Canada.

Henderson, J. V. (1974a), "Optimum City Size and the External Diseconomy Question," *Journal of Political Economy* **82**, 373–388.

Henderson, J. V. (1974b), "Road Congestion: A Reconsideration of Pricing Theory," *Journal of Urban Economics* **1**, 346–365.

Henderson, J. V. (1974c), "The Sizes and Types of Cities," *American Economic Review* **64**, 640–656.

Henderson, J. V. (1977a), *Economic Theory and the Cities*, 1st ed. New York: Academic Press.

Henderson, J. V. (1977b), "Externalities in a Spatial Context: The Case of Air Pollution," *Journal of Public Economics* **7**, 89–110.

Henderson, J. V. (1980), "Community Development: The Effects of Growth and Uncertainty," *American Economic Review* **70**, 894–910.

Henderson, J. V. (1981), "The Economics of Staggered Work Hours," *Journal of Urban Economics* **9**, 349–364

Henderson, J. V. (1982a), "The Impact of Government Policies on Urban Concentration," *Journal of Urban Economics* **12**, 280–303.

Henderson, J. V. (1982b), "Systems of Cities in Closed and Open Economies," *Regional Science and Urban Economics* **12**, 280–303.

Henderson, J. V. (1985a), "Efficiency of Resource Usage and City Size," *Journal of Urban Economics*, forthcoming.

Henderson, J. V. (1985b), "Property Tax Incidence with a Public Sector," *Journal of Political Economy*, August.

Henderson, J. V. (1985c), "The Impact of Zoning Policies Which Regulate Housing Quality," *Journal of Urban Economics*, forthcoming.

Henderson, J. V., and Y. M. Ioannides (1981), "Aspects of Growth in a System of Cities," *Journal of Urban Economics* **10**, 117–139.

Henderson, J. V., and Y. M. Ioannides (1983), "A Model of Housing Tenure Choice," *American Economic Review* **73**, 98–113.

Hobson, P. (1982), "The Determinants of Property Tax Incidence," Queen's University, mimeograph.

Hochman, O. (1977), "A Two-Factor, Three-Sector Model of an Economy with Cities: A Contribution to Urban Economics and International Trade Theories," University of Chicago, mimeograph.

Inman, R. P. (1978), "A Generalized Congestion Function for Highway Travel," *Journal of Urban Economics* **5**, 21–34.

Johnson, M. B. (1964), "On the Economics of Road Congestion," *Econometrica* **32**, 137–150.

Kydland, F. E., and E. C. Prescott (1977), "Rules Rather Than Discretion: The Inconsistency of Optimal Plans," *Journal of Political Economy* **85**, 473–492.

Loury, G. C. (1978), "The Minimum Border Length Hypothesis Does Not Explain the Shape of Black Ghettos," *Journal of Urban Economics* **5**, 147–153.

McGuire, M. (1974), "Group Segregation and Optimal Jurisdictions," *Journal of Political Economy* **82**, 112–132.

Mas-Colell, A. (1977), "Indivisible Commodities and General Equilibrium Theory," *Journal of Economic Theory* **16**, 443–456.

Meade, J. E. (1952), "External Economies and Diseconomies in a Competitive Situation," *Economic Journal* **62**, 54–67.

Meyer, J. R., J. F. Kain, and M. Wohl (1965), *The Urban Transportation Problem.* Cambridge: Harvard Univ. Press.

Mieszkowski, P. M. (1972), "The Property Tax: An Excise or a Profits Tax," *Journal of Public Economics* **1**, 73–96.

Mieszkowski, P., and W. H. Oakland, eds. (1979), *Fiscal Federalism and Grants-in-Aid*, COUPE Vol. 1, Urban Institute.

Mills, E. S. (1967), "An Aggregative Model of Resource Allocation in a Metropolitan Area," *American Economic Review* **57**, 197–210.

Mills, E. S. (1972) *Studies in the Structure of the Urban Economy* Baltimore: Johns Hopkins Press.

Mills, E. S., and D. M. de Ferranti (1971), "Market Choices and Optimum City Size," *American Economic Review* **61**, 340–345.

Mills, D. E. (1983), "The Timing of Urban Residential Land Development," in *Research in Urban Economics* 3 (J. V. Henderson, ed.), pp. 37–58. Greenwich: JAI Press.

Mirrlees, J. A. (1972), "The Optimum Town," *Swedish Journal of Economics* **74**, 114–135.

Mohring, H. (1970), "The Peak Load Problem," *American Economic Review* **60**, 693–705.

Montesano, A. (1972), "A Statement of Beckmann's Model on the Distribution of Urban Rent and Density," *Journal of Economic Theory* **4**, 329–354.

Murray, M. P. (1983), "Mythical Demands and Mythical Supplies for Proper Estimation of Rosen's Hedonic Price Model," *Journal of Urban Economics* **14**, 327–337.

Muth, R. (1969), *Cities and Housing.* Chicago: Univ. of Chicago Press.

Oates, W. E. (1972), *Fiscal Federalism.* New York: Harcourt.

O'Malley, B. W. (1974), "Work Schedule Changes to Reduce Peak Transportation Demand," Port Authority of New York and New Jersey, mimeograph.

Oron, Y., D. Pines, and E. Sheshinski (1973), "Optimum vs. Equilibrium Land Use Patterns and Congestion Tolls," *Bell Journal of Economics and Management* **4**, 619–636.

de Palma, A., M. Ben-Akiva, and M. Cyna (1983), "Dynamical Model of Peak Period Congestion," *Transportation Research B*, forthcoming.

Pauly, M. V. (1970), "Optimality, Public Goods and Local Governments: A General Theoretical Analysis," *Journal of Political Economy* **78**, 572–585.

Pratt, J., D. Wise, D. Wise, and R. Zeckhauser (1979), "Price Differences in Almost Competitive Markets," *Quarterly Journal of Economics.*

Reichman, U. (1976), "Residential Private Governments," *University of Chicago Law Review* **43**, 253–306.

Rose-Ackerman, S. (1975), "Racism and Urban Structure," *Journal of Urban Economics* **2**, 85–103.

Rosen, S. (1974), "Hedonic Prices and Implicit Markets," *Journal of Political Economy* **82**, 34–53.

Rothenberg, J. (1967), *Economic Evaluation of Urban Renewal.* Washington, D.C.: Brookings Institute.

Rothschild, M. (1973), "Models of Market Organization with Imperfect Information," *Journal of Political Economy* **81**, 1283–1308.

Schall, L. D. (1976), "Urban Renewal Policy and Economic Efficiency," *American Economic Review* **66**, 612–628.

Schelling, T. C. (1969), "Models of Segregation," *American Economic Review* **59**, 488–493.

Schelling, T. C. (1971), "Dynamic Models of Segregation," *Journal of Mathematical Sociology* **1**, 143–186.

Shelton, J. P. (1968), "The Cost of Renting *vs.* Owning a House," *Land Economics* **44**, 59–72.

Siegan, B. (1970), "Non-Zoning in Houston," *Journal of Law and Economics.*

Skelley, C. (1985), "Essays on Rent Control," Brown University, unpublished Ph.D dissertation.

Smith, B. A. (1981), "A Study of Racial Discrimination in the Housing Market," in *Research in Urban Economics* 1 (J. V. Henderson, ed.), pp. 131–200, Greenwich: JAI Press.

Solow, R. M., and W. S. Vickrey (1971), "Land Use in a Long Narrow City," *Journal of Economic Theory* 3, 430–477.

Spence, M. (1974), *Market Signalling: Informational Transfer in Hiring and Related Processes*, Cambridge, Mass.: Harvard Univ. Press.

Stahl, K. (1980), "Externalities and Housing Unit Maintenance," University of California at Berkeley, mimeograph.

Stull, W. J. (1974), "Land Use and Zoning in an Urban Economy," *American Economic Review* 64, 337–347.

Sweeney, J. (1974a), "A Commodity Hierarchy Model of the Rental Housing Market," *Journal of Urban Economics* 1, 288–323.

Sweeney, J. (1974b), "Housing Unit Maintenance and the Mode of Tenure," *Journal of Economic Theory* 8, 111–138.

Tiebout, C. (1956), "A Pure Theory of Local Public Expenditure," *Journal of Political Economy* 64, 416–424.

Tietenberg, J. H. (1974), "Comment," *American Economic Review* 64, 462–466.

Tolley, G. S. (1974), "The Welfare Economics of City Bigness," *Journal of Urban Economics* 1, 324–345.

van Lierop, J. (1982), "House Price Structure and Market Equilibrium," *Journal of Urban Economics* 11, 272–289.

Vickrey, W. S. (1965), "Pricing as a Tool in Coordination of Local Transportation," in *Transportation Economics*, Washington, D.C.: Natl. Bureau of Economic Research.

Wheaton, W. C. (1979), "Monocentric Models of Urban Land Use: Contributions and Criticisms," in *Current Issues in Urban Economics* (P. Mieszkowski and M. Straszheim, eds.), pp. 107–129. Baltimore, Md.: Johns Hopkins Press.

Wheaton, W. C. (1982), "Urban Residential Growth under Perfect Foresight," *Journal of Urban Economics* 12, 1–21.

Wheaton, W. C. (1983), "Theories of Urban Growth and Metropolitan Spatial Development," in *Research in Urban Economics* 3, (J. V. Henderson, ed.), pp. 3–36, Greenwich: JAI Press.

White, M. J. (1975), "Fiscal Zoning in Fragmented Metropolitan Areas," in *Fiscal Zoning and Land Use* (E. S. Mills and W. E. Oates, eds.), pp. 175–202. Lexington Mass.: D. C. Heath and Company.

Wilson, J. D. (1982), "Local Property Taxes and Public Services in an Economy with Perfectly Mobile Labor," Columbia University, mimeograph.

Wilson, J. D. (1983), "Optimal Road Capacity in the Presence of Unpriced Congestion," *Journal of Urban Economics* 13, 337–357.

Wilson, J. Q. (1966), *Urban Renewal*. Cambridge, Mass.: MIT Press.

Yinger, J. (1976), "Racial Prejudice and Racial Residential Segregation in an Urban Model," *Journal of Urban Economics* 3, 370–382.

Yinger, J. (1981), "A Search Model of Real Estate Broker Behavior," *American Economic Review* 71, 591–605.

Index

269

DATE DUE

DEC 1 5 1987	JUN 2 1 1990
JAN 1 6 1990	NOV 0 9 1990
MAY 2 5 1990	
OCT 2 3 1990	DEC 0 6 1990
DEC 0 3 1990	
APR 2 2 1998	
BRODART, INC.	Cat. No. 23-221